Security Planning

Susan Lincke

Security Planning

An Applied Approach

Susan Lincke
University of Wisconsin-Parkside
Kenosha, WI, USA

Please note that additional material for this book can be downloaded from http://extras.springer.com

ISBN 978-3-319-36560-2 ISBN 978-3-319-16027-6 (eBook)
DOI 10.1007/978-3-319-16027-6

Springer Cham Heidelberg New York Dordrecht London

Softcover reprint of the hardcover 1st edition 2015

Printed on acid-free paper

Springer International Publishing AG Switzerland is part of Springer Science+Business Media (www.springer.com)

Preface: How to Use This Book

This book is useful in security planning. The best design will eventually involve both business and IT/security people. This text was written for people who are not computer experts, including business managers or owners with no previous IT background—or overworked IT people (or students) who are looking for a shortcut in understanding and designing security. The text has examples to help you understand each required step within the workbook.

The associated Security Workbook has been designed to guide security neophytes through the security planning process. You may edit this Microsoft Word version of the Security Workbook for your own organization's use. This tool is available from your text download site or the book's web site at http://extras.springer.com.

This book can be used out of order, although it is recommended that you read the first section to understand security threats, before proceeding to later chapters. Also, Chap. 5 on Business Continuity and Chap. 7 on Information Security are very important before proceeding to Chap. 8 on Network Security and later. While you may execute the chapters out of order, each chapter is important in making your organization attack-resistant.

Advanced sections within each chapter are optional reading and not absolutely necessary to develop initial security plans. They offer a broader knowledge base to understand the security environment and address relevant background topics that every security professional should know.

It is important to recognize that even large well-funded organizations with full-time professional security staff cannot fully secure their networks and computers. The best they can do is to make the organization a very difficult target. The problem with security is that the attacker needs to find one hole, while the defender needs to close all holes—an impossibility. However, with this text you are well on your way to making your organization attack-resistant.

This book guides security planning for a simple-to-medium level security installation. After your design is done, you must implement your plan! While you can do much security planning without IT/security expertise, eventually IT experts are needed to implement the technical aspects of your plan. It will be useful at that time to discuss your security design with your IT specialists, be they in-house or external.

For organizations requiring a high level of security, such as banks and military, this text is a start but is insufficient by itself. This book is a stepping stone also for organizations that must adhere to a high level of security regulation and standards. Chapter 3 on Security Regulation introduces many of the American information security regulations that organizations may need to address as well as the PCI DSS standard. Chapter 3 defines which chapters you should pay attention to for each type of regulation—but the book does not describe all requirements of each regulation. The best implementation can start with this book, but also address each item of each regulation or standard your organization must adhere to.

The author and publisher do not warrant or guarantee that the techniques contained in these works will meet your requirements. The author is not liable for any inaccuracy, error, or omission, regardless of cause, in the work or for any damages resulting therefrom. Under no circumstances shall the author be liable for any indirect, incidental, special, punitive, consequential, or similar damages that result from the use of, or inability to use, these works.

To the Security Instructor

Many materials are available with this text for your teaching use. Instructor/Student materials are included on the companion web site, at http://extras.springer.com. Extra materials include the following:

1. *Lecture PowerPoints*: PowerPoint lectures include end-of-lecture questions for discussion in class. These questions are patterned after ISACA's CISA and CISM questions.
2. *Health First Case Study, Security Workbook, and Solution*: A case study involving security planning for a hypothetical Health First doctor's office is available for classroom use. Each chapter on security design in this text has at least one associated case study to choose from, within the Health First Case Study. This case study includes discussion by the Health First employees, discussing the business scenario. The Security Workbook guides students through the security process. A Solution is available on the companion web site for instructors. If you choose to do the case study, it is helpful to understand/present the applicable Health Insurance Portability and Accountability Act (HIPAA) regulation before starting the case study (for schools in the United States).
3. *Health First Requirements Document Case Study*: The Secure Software chapter will enthuse students who intend to be software or web developers. The Health First Case Study includes cases where students add security to a professional Requirements Document. The security-poor Requirements Document is available for download.

4. *Instructor Guide*: There is guide to how to use this case study in your classroom. You may also use the Security Workbook as a service learning exercise with small businesses, who often welcome the free help, if you choose.

Addressing Educational Criteria

This text addresses sections of the *National Security Agency (NSA) Center of Academic Excellence (CAE)* 2014 plan, including five Mandatory and 15 Optional Knowledge Units. While the NSA does not certify any texts, this text was written to meet these requirements, as outlined on the companion web site. The Mandatory Knowledge Units include Cyber Defense, Network Defense, Fundamental Security Design Principles, IA Fundamentals, and Policy, Legal, Ethics and Compliance. Optional Knowledge Units include Cybersecurity Planning and Management, Data Administration, Digital Forensics (less exercise), Fraud Prevention and Management, IA Architecture, IA Compliance, IA Standards, Network Security Administration, Overview of Cyber Operations, Secure Programming Practices, Security Program Management, Security Risk Analysis, Software Assurance, and Vulnerability Analysis. More details are at the instructor web site.

The text also meets most *ACM* Information Assurance and Security "Core" requirements for Computer Science, including Foundational Concepts, Principles of Secure Design, Defensive Programming, Threats and Attacks, and Network Security. Addressed electives include Security Policy, Secure S/W Engineering, and most of Web Security and Digital Forensics at the familiarity level. The mapping of requirements to chapters is outlined on the companion web site.

Finally, the base of this text is derived from ISACA's Certified Information Systems Auditor® (CISA) and Certified Information Security Manager® (CISM) study guides related to security. Other parts of these guides are generally covered by other courses, such as project management, networking, and software engineering. Students may pass these exams with additional study, particularly using ISACA's CISA or CISM question disks.

Acknowledgments and Disclaimers

Many thanks go to people who used or reviewed the materials, or assisted in the development of the case study. They include Stephen Hawk, David Green, Heather Miles, Joseph Baum, Mary Comstock, Craig Baker, Todd Burri, Tim Dorr, Tim Knautz, Brian Genz, LeRoy Foster, Misty Lowery, Natasha Ravnikar, and the University of Wisconsin-Parkside for funding my sabbatical. Thanks also to the National Science Foundation, who funded the development of the workbook and case study (though this work does not necessarily represent their views). Finally, thanks to the organizations and people who worked with my students and me in service-learning projects and who must remain anonymous.

The case of Einstein University represented in this text is purely fictional and does not represent the security plan of any actual university.

Kenosha, WI, USA Susan Lincke

Contents

Part I
The Problem of Security

This part informs why security is an issue that must be addressed. It delves into current problem areas that certain industries may specifically need to address, related to hackers and malware (Chap. 1), internal and external fraud (Chap. 2), and regulation for American-based companies (Chap. 3). Understanding inherent threats well will help in later parts to define your organization's specific security needs.

Chapter 1
Security Awareness: Brave New World

> The confidence that people have in security is inversely proportional to how much they know about it. (Roger Johnston [1])

Computer security is a challenge. If you are an attacker, you only need to find one hole…but if you are a defender, you need to close all holes. Since it is impossible to close all holes, you can only hope to close most holes, layer your defenses (like you layer clothes when going out in the freezing cold), and hope that the intruder will find an easier target elsewhere.

How do you close most holes? The first step is to educate yourself about security and ways crackers attack. The next step is to ensure that all your employees understand their roles in guarding security. This chapter is about educating yourself about malware and computer attackers, and what you can do to defend your office, your mobile devices, and your home computers.

1.1 With Security, Every Person Counts

Imagine you open 20-some emails daily. Today you receive one with a promising video. You click to download it. Most emails are innocuous, but this one contains hidden malware. While you enjoy your video, the video is also secretly executing a worm and turning your computer into a zombie. You are now, unknowingly, infected (but the video was cool!)

Opening email is like playing the game of Russian Roulette—eventually you lose. Whether you open an email attachment, follow a link to an infected web site, or insert an infected CD or electronic drive into your computer, you are taking risks. But why would someone want to attack your computer?

If you are very lucky, the *cracker* or *hacker* (i.e., sophisticated computer user, here used negatively) is just trying to have fun. Some malware, or malicious software, may simply send a message to your screen. If it is a *Denial of Service* (DoS) attack, the attacker will interrupt your computer service by causing your computer

S. Lincke, *Security Planning*, DOI 10.1007/978-3-319-16027-6_1

to lockup periodically, clearing your hard drive (e.g., Shamoon), or running a program that heavily uses system resources, making your computer sluggish. If it is a *worm*, it may automatically email itself to your friends or try in other ways to connect to neighboring computers within your network. If it is a *virus*, it will attach itself to a useful program and will execute with that program—and possibly install itself as a start up program to ensure it is automatically executed when your computer powers up.

If you are unlucky, the cracker has criminal intent. The attacker may make himself known, for example, by encrypting your disk and demanding payment to unencrypt it. This *ransomware*, (e.g., CryptoLocker), can corrupt backups before demanding payment [2]. One Massachusetts police force paid $750 to decrypt their disk [3].

Alternatively, the intruder program may hide, waiting to steal information from you, such as your credit card number, password, or confidential information. In this case, she may install a *keystroke logger* which records the keys you enter. Then, as you enter your credit card information, these keystrokes are secretly sent over your internet connection to the criminal. Soon you see unusual charges on your credit card statement or maybe your financial account(s) are wiped clean. American credit card numbers are generally sold for $10, while European credit card numbers are sold for $50 a piece [4]. In bulk, credit card numbers go for as low as $1 a piece [5]. Prices are low due to successful criminal rings, such as Gonzalez's, who cracked and exposed over 170 million credit card numbers [6].

The video-carries-malware is one type of Trojan horse. Similar to the Greek story during the Trojan war, when the Achaean army hid inside a large wooden Trojan horse given as a gift to the city of Troy, a computer *Trojan horse* is a real program that is advertised to do one thing (e.g., display a video clip), while it secretly also does something malicious. The Zeus Trojan has turned millions of computers into Zeus bots (zbots) [7], mostly in the U.S. and often via Facebook [8]. It became 'popular' in 2007 and it still consistently ranks in the top 5 malware problems [9]. Zeus stays dormant on a compromised computer until the victim logs into a bank site. Then, it steals the victim's passwords and empties the victim's accounts [8]. It also can impersonate a bank's website in order to collect private information, such as social security numbers and/or bank account numbers, to sell on the black market.

The malware may install a *backdoor*, which is a program that enables the attacker to gain entry to your computer without a password. A *rootkit*, when installed, hides all tracks of the attacker, including modifying computer logs and causing the operating system utilities to not display programs that the attacker executes. Many proprietary secrets have recently appeared within Chinese companies, who then compete with the original companies for their business—without the expense of product development.

Alternatively, a criminal may want to use your computer to store exploit or spam software, or host illegal movies or pornography. Why should they buy computers when they can 'own' yours for free? The malware may turn your computer into a *zombie* or *bot* (short for robot). First they insert a backdoor to freely access your computer, then install a rootkit to hide their tracks, and finally insert control software into your computer. The control program enables them to house hidden files (e.g., illegal movies or pornography) on your computer, or to launch attacks against other computers. A criminal organization may create an army of these bots, called a *botnet.* They then sell time on the botnet at an average price of $100 per 1,000 infected computers [9]. Remember the law of supply and demand? If supply is high, the price becomes low… and today the supply of bots is high.

The kinds of exploits that botnets may perform include massive spamming, Distributed Denial of Service attacks, password cracking, and hiding other illegal attacks. In each of these exploits, hundreds or thousands of computers (or bots) are commanded to attack. *Spamming* generates the massive impersonal emails we receive daily. *Distributed Denial of Service (DDOS)* includes attacking an organization by, for example, jamming their web site with bogus web requests—and then extorting money to stop the exploit [10]. *Password cracking* programs automatically guess passwords, until a successful login occurs. Alternatively, a file containing password hashes can be copied from an infiltrated computer and a large set of bots can analyze the passwords at their leisure. All of this can happen to your computer(s), and you don't even know it!

Criminals or crackers can launch attacks using email and web scams. *Phishing* is the use of an email scam, where the email serves as a hook and you are the fish! An email from 'your' bank can request immediate action, or ask you to help in transferring money from a foreign country. The email can be well-written to fool even the best of us—or poorly written to attract only the most gullible of us. *Spear phishing* is when a particular person is targeted for a special scam email, using knowledge of their interests, friends, and lifestyle. *Pharming* is a web scam, where a scam webpage can resemble a real webpage. Often a phishing email may include a link to pharmed webpage. Click on the link and you may become infected—or may unknowingly give them your account information! However, it is not only pharming sites that are infected with malware. Google reports that it flags some 10,000 sites daily for infections and warns web masters and users during Google searches [11].

Why doesn't law enforcement stop this? It is very difficult. The Internet crosses borders without passport control and jurisdiction is an issue. During the last century, if someone wanted to rob a bank, they would physically have to go to the bank with a gun. Today, unsophisticated computer crackers can rob a bank in the United States without leaving their living room in Africa or Asia. They can purchase or rent a malware toolkit containing a keystroke logger and use it to obtain credit card numbers [12]. In addition, a criminal may live in Russia, 'own' a botnet control computer in Yugoslavia, and 'own' bots all over the world. Thus, if a government tracks an exploit to a bot, they will likely need to involve multiple governments and agencies in tracking the attack to the original criminal. Many governments have higher priority problems than Internet crime occurring in other countries. In fact, criminal organizations may be normally operating businesses. Intelligent criminals can and do hide their tracks internationally, making a traceback to the original source very difficult. As a measure of defense, the FBI now stations cyber-security experts at embassies in various parts of the world to negotiate with local law enforcement [10].

Spyware includes keystroke loggers, but also software which monitors your website accesses to sell your interests to data warehouses, or uses your camera and/or microphone to record your actions. It is estimated that spyware/keyloggers are included in 75 % of all malware [2]. *Adware* may show pop-ups of specific ads, or prevent you from accessing specific web sites, including certain search engines.

These are the common types of exploits that every computer user should be aware of. If law enforcement cannot help protect you much, then you must protect yourself and your organization. The next section discusses what every user should do to protect themselves. More advanced security measures will be discussed in later sections of this text.

1.2 Protecting Yourself

Obviously, the best way to protect yourself is to never be vulnerable: never connect to the Internet, or any other network, turn off your wireless network connection, and never load files from external sources. Do all this and your computer is still vulnerable to physical access. If you are not willing to live the life of an Internet hermit, then you have chosen to take non-negligible risks. You can only minimize risks, not eliminate them.

It is most important to set up your computer properly to combat malware. Procure *antivirus software* and ensure that security options—including a firewall—are turned on. Antivirus software matches signatures (or snippets) from viruses and worms against the files in your computer. A good antivirus software will observe your software as it executes to determine, if the file you plan to download has a virus or if your firewall is turned off. Some antivirus software also monitors your transmissions and the specific *port* numbers (or application IDs) you are sending and receiving from. An example of a port is web HTML, email SMTP, or secure file transfer protocol SFTP. This port use information is aggregated over thousands of computers. When a new pattern of usage emerges, such as computers suddenly using an unusual port number, then this emerging application is observed for malware activity. Antivirus software is an important investment in all of your computers—laptop, smart phone, tablet—because malware is likely wherever you read email, open webpages, and download applications.

A second step in combatting malware is to ensure that the operating system, applications, and antivirus software are *updated* regularly. Modern day programs are large and complex, and often have bugs (or defects). Crackers and criminals often take advantage of these bugs, issuing attacks specifically against them. These bugs are periodically found and fixed by the manufacturer, by *patching* software.

One such example of a software bug (and proof that all operating systems are targeted) was the Mac Fakeflash virus. This virus infected one half million Macs by downloading itself through a hole in Java software without any user action or notification. Apple promptly published a fix. Users who downloaded patches immediately were the safest against this (and other) threats [13].

A third step in setting up your system against malware is to ensure your *firewall* is enabled. Firewalls vary in capability, but a firewall for a personal computer generally ensures that your computer filters incoming transmissions by application type. For example, firewalls generally allow outgoing transmissions from your computer, and replies to that transmission using the same port. Your firewall should discard strange incoming requests on unused ports. A personal computer firewall (by itself) will not filter malware transmissions within allowed incoming packets.

A fourth must-do is to use excellent passwords. Any cracker knows that your login is probably your email name, and can use automated password-guessing software to quickly guess your password. A *Dictionary Attack* uses software that iterates through a password dictionary of common names and words to guess your password. A *social engineer* will try your favorite people, pets, teams, hobbies and more as potential passwords. If neither of these short-cut methods work, then the cracker may try a *brute force attack*. With this exploit, all possible combinations of passwords starting with: a, aa, ab, ac, and so on will be attempted until yours is found. If we assume the attacker has access to a botnet, then the job of guessing passwords is divided among many computers. If your password is eight characters long and you use the alphabet, numbers, and punctuation in your password, it may take 2 h or less to break into your account. In the CITIZENFOUR documentary, Snowden estimates that it takes the NSA 2 days to guess a ten-character password. Longer passwords are better. At a rate of 2.6×10^{18} guesses per month, a password of 12 alphabetical characters can take up to 96 years, or up to 500 years if you also include numbers in your password. Thus, it is important to use long passwords and avoid any common words or names in your password.

To give you a good idea of how to create a secure password, see Fig. 1.1. An alternative mechanism is to use the first letters of a phrase in a song, quote,

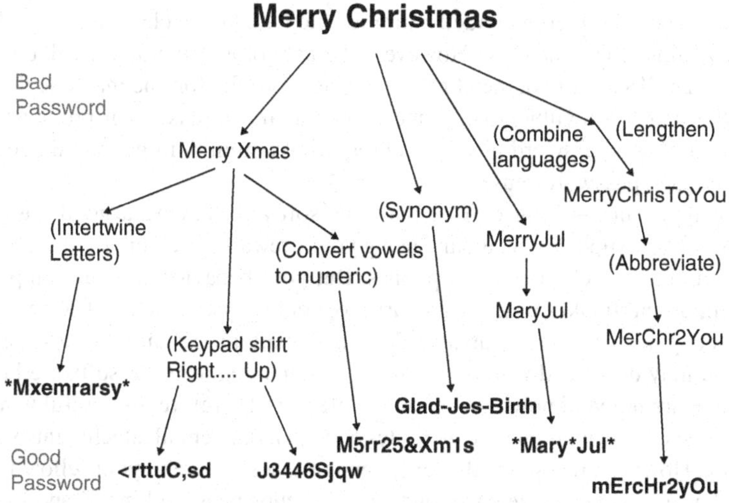

Fig. 1.1 Methods to create a good password

Table 1.1 A comparison of password requirements

	PCI DSS vers. 3 [14]	CIS Microsoft Windows 8 [15]
Minimum password length	Seven characters	Fourteen characters
Account lockout threshold	Six invalid attempts	Five invalid attempts
Account lockout duration (with clear lockout counter)	30 min	15 min
Screen saver time-out	15 min	15 min
Maximum password age	90 days	60 days
Minimum password age	Not specified	1 day
Password history retention	4	24
Password complexity requirements	Numeric and alphabetic	3 of 4: uppercase alpha, lowercase alpha, numeric, punctuation

poem or prayer. For example, the song: "Take me out to the ball game, Take me out with the crowd" turns into the password Tmo2tbgTmowtc. One advantage of this technique is that when you need to change passwords, you can simply go to the next phrase in the text: Bmsp&c1dci1ngb. Finally, never divulge your password or write it down and never retain default passwords.

Table 1.1 shows requirements as recommended by the Payment Card Industry (PCI) [14] and Center for Internet Security (CIS) [15]. PCI's low seven-character password minimum is only secure when combined with the other password requirements: changing passwords frequently and auto lockouts. Password dictionary and brute force attacks issue password guesses as fast as the network can carry; locking out a login after five to six invalid attempts for at least 15–30 min slows these attacks. However, if a cracker hacks an administrator account, they may copy the password file and make password guesses at extremely fast rates on their own machines. The CIS recommended minimum length of 14 characters is a better defense against these attacks. However, if passwords are not reused on other machines (as CIS requires), then breaking a password file for one machine does not make other machines vulnerable. Since users may try to reuse their previous passwords, retaining a password history and requiring a minimum password age helps to counter such password reuse.

These four steps—using current antivirus software, having a good password, ensuring software updates occur, and using your firewall—are important setup steps for all computers, including smart phones. But your behavior on your computer is just as important. It takes time for antivirus, operating system, and software companies to recognize and defend against daily new exploits. Even with these precautions, you may download *zero-day attacks*, which are attacks for software bugs or worms that are not yet known and without defenses. Therefore, be careful to access or download only from reputable web sites and open only email attachments you are expecting. However, recognize that even reputable websites and your fellow friends and employees may be infected; web and email infection rates are 1 in 566 and 1 in 196, respectively [16].

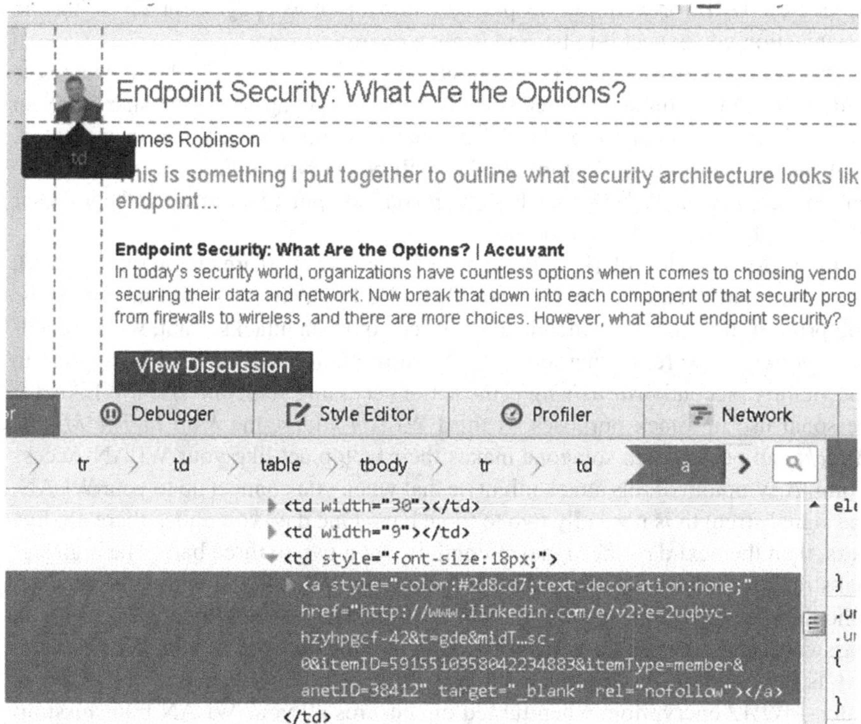

Fig. 1.2 Looking at links within an email

One way to protect yourself with email is to determine where a link is going before you click on it. With a Firefox browser, for example, you may point the cursor over a link, right click, select Inspect Element, and observe a web link URL, as shown in Fig. 1.2 in white text. The email URL starts with www.linkedin.com, a relatively safe organization; I felt confident following the link. Most browsers have this capability via some means.

Smart phones are also prime targets for malware, caused in part by the popularity of downloaded apps [16]. Popular mobiles are particularly targeted, such as Android models. Approximately 32 % of mobile malware steals information [12]. It is safer to buy software from a trustable source, such as the Google Play store or Amazon's Android application store [17]. These stores periodically scan for malware, and remove the bad apps that they find. Avoid third-party sites. Also, use reputable mobile antivirus software.

Another defensive precaution is to be wary of divulging secrets, such as your financial, health, business or personal identity information, on your computer and the Internet. It is a smart idea, for example, to not use a debit card on the Internet. Make charges using only one credit card on the Internet, manually pay that card monthly, and double-check the charges! If you do divulge secrets on a webpage, be sure the URL (or web link) displayed at the top of webpage is precisely for the organization you expect it to be, and is not a pharming scam!

Any secrets you divulge on the Internet should be *encrypted*, which means it is undecipherable without a secret key. Encrypted webpages always start with an '*https*:' in the URL, instead of 'http'. The final 's' stands for secure, as in encrypted. This means that your credit card number will be encrypted during transmission—but do recognize that a keystroke logger on your computer would see and copy your number before the encryption occurs.

Encryption is particularly important for a wireless local area network (WLAN), which are particularly prone to attack. WLANs broadcast to everyone within the footprint of the network, which leads to three common attacks. First, with specialized *sniffer* software, unencrypted WLAN information can be read by anyone in the vicinity. Second, *war driving* is the act of accessing someone else's WLAN for personal use or attack purposes. A third WLAN attack, the *Man In The Middle Attack*, can occur when someone makes their laptop act like your WLAN Access Point. A symptom of this attack might be that when you connect up to your WLAN, the signal strength is normally two to three bars. One day, you notice there are five bars, then the next day, the signal strength is again two to three bars. The high signal strength day you communicated not with your WLAN, but with your attacker, who then forwarded the packets to your WLAN. The attacker obtained your login, password, and now has the capability to log into the network as you. WLAN security is important to protect against these attacks. Certain versions of WLANs are safer—*WPA2* encryption, when turned on, ensures all your WLAN transmissions are encrypted.

If you observe strange behavior in your computer, then it is a good idea to re-scan with your antivirus software. You may want a second opinion, and run a second set of malware detection software and spyware detection software (e.g., Spybot Search and Destroy or Windows Defender). Unfortunately, not all malware is detected by every version of antivirus software.

When you detect malware, it is a good idea to have the computer *rebuilt*, even if the antivirus cleared the malware. This includes reloading the operating system, all applications, and your data. This may be particularly important if the attacker installed a backdoor and made manual changes that your automated antivirus software cannot possibly find. As all information may have been compromised, you should change all passwords on the affected system, as well as all passwords on any system you may have logged onto from the infected computer. Lurking spyware may have recorded credentials for all these systems.

This chapter focuses on basic security awareness. Each person in your organization should be minimally aware of this level of security literacy, regardless of their position. This is particularly important when people use their home computers or smart phones to do business work, or communicate with business computers. Most people find this information useful, not only for their business computers, but also home computers—and will thank you for informing them.

Convincing employees to be careful is important but may not be sufficient. Businesses should consider blocking social media websites; prevent the installation of applications on business computers; and evaluate endpoint security products, which have additional security features compared to a simpler, signature-based antivirus software [12].

1.3 Criminal Attacks to an Organization

If you are a business manager, a computer programmer, or otherwise employed in an IT/Security field, you should be aware of how an organization can be attacked, beyond user security awareness. Threats may arise from disgruntled employees or contracts, political enemies, financially-motivated criminals and spies or spying governments. We review each of these in turn.

A *logic bomb* is a program where the author has inserted code to potentially do something malicious at a triggered time. An example might be that a software program may fail if the company fails to pay a maintenance fee or a programmer is fired and is attempting to retaliate.

Spying and disruption are the goals of some governments and hacker groups. Anonymous is a unorganized *hacktivist* organization which supports some political causes (e.g., Mexican miner rights, Wikileak support) in bad ways (e.g., DDOS attacks, defacing or taking down websites). For example, Operation Payback involved a massive DDOS attack on Visa, MasterCard, Motion Pictures of America, and the Recording Industry of America for 5 months starting September 2010 [18]. Credit cards were attacked after they suspended payment for WikiLeaks. In addition, some Anonymous members have been arrested for common credit card theft [19].

Company websites are prone to attack from *cyber-crime*. In July, 2013, five foreign hackers stole and sold 160 million credit card numbers from a number of companies, including J.C. Penney, 7-Eleven, JetBlue, Heartland Payment Systems (a credit/debit processing company), Citibank, PNC Bank, Nasdaq, supermarket Hannaford, and the French retailer Carrefour. The technique used by these criminals was an *SQL Injection Attack*, where a criminal alters database commands by manipulating forms at websites, in order to extract or change information in the database. Heartland disclosed that it lost $200 million with the credit card losses [4].

Web cracking is lucrative, attracting organized crime who often live outside the countries they are attacking. Crime rings tend to have specialized skills, where each person has a specific role: the skilled person who breaks into sites, the person who extracts credit card information, and the person who sells the data [4]. When caught internationally, they can be extradited to the country where the crime was committed. One well-known crime ring includes the Russian Business Network, which specializes in malware, identity theft, and child pornography [8].

The antidote to web cracking is skilled *penetration testing* (or pen testing). Criminals do this with your web site, and you must too to find all security holes before they do. Also, if your organization develops any software or firmware, it is important to have programmers who are skilled in software security, develop or review all code.

The *Surveillance State* is where a government monitors Internet traffic and data. The U.S. National Security Agency (NSA) and/or Federal Bureau of Investigation (FBI) have intimidated a number of organizations, including Verizon, Google, Yahoo, Microsoft and Facebook, but unfortunately gag orders prevent companies from speaking out [20]. Snowden's releases have uncovered that nearly 200 million records were sent to NSA from Yahoo and Google for December, 2012, including email metadata (headers) and content [21]. The NSA has requested or manipulated companies to water down encryption algorithms; install backdoors in software products; as well as provide communication data [22]. The British intelligence agency, GCHQ, has legally installed malware that turned on computer microphones and cameras without an owners' consent [23].

One story that has emerged is the story of Lavabit, a company which provided secure email services [24]. Lavabit had been asked to place taps on a few accounts and had complied. However in the spring 2013, the FBI asked Ladar Levison, Lavabit's founder, for a tap for Snowden. They asked for passwords for all his clients, the organization's private key (which decrypts all encryptions sent by the company), and computer code. Levison attempted to negotiate to provide Snowden's information daily, but the FBI wanted the information in real time (minute by minute). Levison provided a paper copy of the company's private key using a difficult-to-convert font, and was fined $5,000 per day by a court until he provided it electronically. After 2 days, Levison provided the key electronically and closed his company down. That day, he wrote on his website: "I would strongly recommend against anyone trusting their private data to a company with physical ties to the United States." [25]

Unfortunately, this government spying and intrusion is making buyers wary of products from any countries involved in information warfare or surveillance state actions, due to disintegrated trust [26]. Snowden argues, in documentary CITIZENFOUR, that freedom of speech requires the right to privacy, and that dictatorships rely on surveillance for their control. In response to Snowden leaks, American President Obama promised to name a new senior official to implement new privacy measures, to protect the American people, ordinary foreign people, and foreign leaders when a "compelling national security purpose" is not evident [27].

China is also known to be a surveillance state, in addition to Russia, Korea and Great Britain. *Theft of intellectual property* is a case where a company puts money into designing a product, but soon finds it must compete with a Chinese company, who stole the design. This stealing occurs through obtaining access to a network and *exfiltrating* (or copying) proprietary information—from servers, user terminals, but even from printers! [28] The Aspen Institute estimates that 373,000 jobs and $16 billion in profit are lost annually due to proprietary espionage [28]. This serious problem has been repeatedly discussed at the presidential level, between U.S. and Chinese leaders. China's cybertheft, directed by units of the People's Liberation Army, targets designs of many commercial products and military aircraft. After former CIA system administrator Edward Snowden's published American government secrets to Wikileaks, the Chinese argue that the American government itself hacked into Chinese government, military, research, educational and business organizations [29]. However, the U.S. government insists that it does not steal proprietary secrets to give to U.S. companies for economic reasons.

The New York Times has published its experience with a Chinese intrusion, which is an example of a lengthy targeted attack, called an *Advanced Persistent Threat*. It is mentioned here, because of the depth of information provided by their story [30]. Hackers most likely gained initial entrance through spear phishing, set up backdoors into users' machines, and then installed 45 pieces of custom malware, the majority of which was not recognized by antivirus software. Hackers also stole passwords for every Times employee and proceeded to hack into the personal computers of 53 employees. Security experts indicate that the Chinese were interested in learning about informants for reports relating to China's prime minister, Wen Jiabo. Fortunately, they left other stories and customer data alone. Hacker teams started their attacks at 8 AM Beijing time, and hacked continuously, sometimes until midnight. Attacks were launched through American universities, which have labs filled with computers. After 4 months of attacks, the New York Times finally managed to eliminate the Chinese threat, through the assistance of the Mandiant Security Company. Other publicized stories of Chinese attacks include stolen information about Chinese dissidents and Tibetan activists. The Wall Street Journal and Washington Post have also reported being hacked [10].

Governments fear that the next wars will involve computer attacks to infrastructure, such as power, water, financial systems, military systems, etc., as part of *information warfare*. *Cyberweapons* are extremely cheap compared to the military variety, and can cause as much or more damage. Thus, protecting utilities and other critical infrastructure is a high priority. The first publicized use of cyberweapons was the 2010 Stuxnet worm, reputedly developed by the U.S. and Israel. Stuxnet took out nearly 1,000 Iranian centrifuges, or nearly one fifth of those in service within Iranian nuclear power plants [31]. Iran replied by attacking American banks and foreign oil companies [30].

The escalating cyberwar is creating a black market in *zero-day* (new) attacks. Hackers used to give away their knowledge of software defects to software companies like Microsoft and Apple. Now, governments are paying more than the $150,000 top price that Microsoft is willing to pay for these bugs [32]. This lucrative market for bugs has resulted in new hacking firms who openly publicize their wares. Known governments purchasing these defects include Israel, Britain, India, Russia, Brazil, North Korea, several Middle Eastern countries, and the United States.

Other countries apparently involved in cyber-warfare include China and Russia [33]. Russia's apparent preferred method of cyber-warfare is DDOS, which was used against Estonian government, financial institutions and newspapers in 2007, and Georgian government websites and Internet infrastructure in 2008. It is believed that China used infected, command-and-control email against embassies, foreign ministries, and Tibetan exile centers in 2009. The Canadian government was infected with a spyware virus in 2011 that was traced back to China.

Crackers can threaten anything computerized, including your car and home. Security researchers have shown that car brakes and steering could be remotely controlled [34]. Seven hundred home security cameras were hacked, and peoples' private lives were put on display on webpages [35]. If a company does not protect its software products, by taking security very seriously, it can find its products hacked and its problems publicized in the news. The organization can then expect a very expensive visit from the Federal Trade Commission (FTC). The FTC may specify a 20-year-security compliance audit program (as it did for TRENDnet [35]) and may launch megafines when laws are violated. You will read more about this in Chap. 3 on Security Regulation.

If you are an organization that has vital proprietary information or trade secrets, accepts credit cards, manages money, owns computers, creates products with software in them, and/or plays a vital role in your community, security is an issue for you. Criminals know small businesses are easier to break into. Symantec reports that small businesses are the attack target 31 % of the time [12], often because smaller subsidiaries, storefronts, or partners are more easily cracked into than larger, partner organizations [36]. Table 1.2 reveals that different exploits can be classified as part of cyber-security history. Unfortunately, older threat types do not disappear as new threats emerge.

Hopefully this chapter has been informative and made you think of potential threats to your organization. The Security Workbook, available at http://extras.springer.com, enables you to document these threats as part of the Workbook's

Table 1.2 History and categories of internet crime

Threat type	Year: Example threats
Experimentation	1984: Fred Cohen publishes "Computer Viruses: Theory and Experiments" [37]
Vandalism	1988: Jerusalem Virus deletes all executable files on the system, on Friday the 13th [7]
	1991: Michelangelo Virus reformats hard drives on March 6, Michelangelo's birthday
Hactivism	2010: Anonymous' Operation Payback hits credit card and communication companies with DDOS after payment cards refuse to accept payment for Wiki-Leaks
Cyber-crime	2007: Zeus Trojan becomes 'popular'; turns computers into zbots and spyware steals payment card numbers
	2008, 2009: Gonzales re-arrested for sniffing WLANs and implanting spyware, affecting 171 million credit cards [38]
	2013: In July 160 million credit card numbers are stolen via SQL Injection Attack. In Dec., 40 million credit card numbers and 70 million customer information are stolen through Target stores. California indicates 167 data breaches are reported this year [39]
Information warfare	2007, 2008: Russia launches DDOS attack against Estonia, then Georgia news, gov't, banks [33]
	2010: Stuxnet worm disables 1,000 of Iran's nuclear centrifuges
Surveillance state	2012: State affiliated actors mainly tied to China quietly attack U.S./foreign businesses to steal intellectual property secrets, summing to 19 % of all forensically analyzed breaches [2]
	2013: Lavabit closes secure email service rather than divulge corporate private key to NSA without customers' knowledge

Chap. 2. Writing them there will help with future chapters. The questions to consider include:

a) Select the threats which are a concern in your industry: Experimentation/ Vandalism, Hacktivism, Cyber-crime, Information Warfare, Intellectual Property Theft, Surveillance State. List your threats in priority order and describe a scenario and the potential damage for each threat.
b) List the exploits (or attacks) that are most likely to occur in your workplace. For each exploit, describe what the impact might be for your workplace.

Fraud is also associated with identity theft, credit card fraud, and misuse of organizational funds. That is the topic of our next chapter. While this section informs about security threats, later sections consider how to mitigate these threats. The three basic pillars of security include Confidentiality, Integrity, and Availability. *Confidentiality* ensures that information/equipment is made available only to the people who should have access to it. *Integrity* ensures that information/equipment is accurate, and modified only by authorized persons. *Availability* ensures that information/equipment is available to qualified persons at the time they need it.

1.4 Questions

1. *Vocabulary*. Match each meaning with the correct word.

Worm	Ransomware	Penetration test	Distributed denial of service
Virus	Spear phishing	Cyber-crime	Zero-day attack
Spyware	Firewall	Trojan horse	Man in the middle attack
Adware	Patching	Denial of service	Surveillance state
Backdoor	Spamming	Dictionary attack	Advanced persistent threat
Rootkit	Phishing	Keystroke logger	Cyber-weapon
Botnet	Pharming	Social engineer	Information warfare
Sniffer	War driving	Exfiltrate	Password cracking
WPA2	Hacktivist	Logic bomb	Brute force attack

a) Malware that modifies the operating system to hide the actions of an attacker.
b) A safer transmission protocol for Wireless Local Area Networks.
c) Proprietary information is secretly transferred to an outside destination.
d) The login-password authentication process is attacked using a large set of commonly defined words or names.
e) An attack motivated by financial self-interest resulting in fraud or theft.
f) Software which monitors what you type in order to learn secrets, such as payment card information or passwords.
g) An attacker with political motives.
h) An email scam mailed to masses of people, looking for gullible victims.
i) Software requests and implements updates to fix security problems.
j) An attack that intentionally uses up a computer's resources.

k) An infected set of computers that can be commanded to host illegal files or launch attacks.
l) A hacker attacks a selected target using multiple sophisticated techniques.
m) One country attacks another through IT attacks, potentially harming important utilities, government, financial and news institutions.
n) A hacker uses wireless local area networks without permission or authorization.
o) A useful program that fails to advertise its malicious function.
p) A type of malware that inserts itself into useful code.

2. *Threat Analysis*. Consider an industry you currently work in or would like to work in. Industries can include: retail, banking/finance, government, health services, not-for-profit, and corporations. Review the threats described in this chapter.

   a) Select the general threats that are likely to be a concern in your selected industry from the following list: Experimentation/Vandalism, Hacktivism, Cyber-crime, Information Warfare, Intellectual Property theft, Surveillance State. List these threats in priority order and describe a likely fictional (or actual) scenario and the potential damage, for the top 4 threats.
   b) List 8 exploits (or computer attacks) that are most likely to occur in your selected industry. For each exploit, describe a sample scenario of how it might occur and an impact scenario for your workplace. Complete the following table, which provides one example for a school-based threat.

Exploit type	Attack scenario	Likely impact on organization
Example: Botnet	Students access websites and unknowingly download spyware and botnet software	School computer labs are turned into a big botnet machine, resulting in massive transmissions to/from the school

3. *Search the News*. Use your online library or newspaper to look up actual examples of malware or other hacking attacks that have been in the news or in an industry magazine. Based on the news articles, select five attacks of your choice and write one summary paragraph on each. Provide one or more references for each paragraph. Follow the same reference format as used in the Reference section of this text. An example reference might look like:

   [1] Popper N, Sengupta S (2013) U.S. Says Ring Stole 160 Million Credit Card Numbers. New York Times. 25 July 2013.

   Helpful hint: To find news articles, go to your university library website, and find a 'database' associated with business or computers, that includes news stories. Once you have found an appropriate database, enter the exploit type as a search term, and if possible, select 'full text' as an option to get the full news articles.
4. *Security Training*. You have been hired as a security trainer or technical writer. Provide a one-page informational description on one attack type, describing the threat and one or more prevention techniques to avoid this threat. Find additional information to include in your write-up to make the article interesting, informative and useful.

References

1. Johnston R (2011) Security maxims. http://www.ne.anl.gov/capabilities/vat. Accessed 20 Mar 2011
2. Verizon (2013) Verizon 2013 data breach investigations report http://www.verizonenterprise.com/DBIR/2013. Accessed 20 Oct 2013
3. Griffith C (2013) Pay up or your data dies: CryptoLocker ransomware hits Australia. The Australian, 5 December 2013
4. Popper N, Sengupta S (2013) U.S. says ring stole 160 million credit card numbers. New York Times, 25 July 2013
5. Pereira J, Levitz J, Singer-Vine J (2008) U.S. indicts 11 in global credit card scheme. Wall Street Journal, 6 August 2008
6. Reuters (2009) Man accused of stealing stores' data pleads guilty. New York Times, 29 August 2009
7. Smith R (2013) Elementary information security. Jones & Bartlett Learning, p 102
8. Perlroth N (2013) Malware that drains your bank account thriving on Facebook. New York Times, 3 June 2013
9. Hoffman KE (2013) Botnets 3.0. SC Magazine, pp 30–31. http://www.scmagazine.com. Accessed July 2013
10. Brelsford E (2013) 2014: a cyber odyssey. In: ISACA Chicago chapter meeting. Rosemont, IL, 13 December 2013
11. Perlroth N (2013) Google adds malware statistics in transparency report. New York Times, 25 June 2013
12. Symantec (2013) Internet security threat report 2013, vol 18. Symantec Corp., 13 April 2013
13. Perlroth N (2012) Widespread virus proves macs are no longer safe from Hackers. New York Times, 6 April 2012
14. PCI Security Standards Council (2013) Requirements and security assessment procedures, v 3.0, November 2013. www.pcisecuritystandards.org
15. Center for Internet Security (2013) CIS Microsoft Windows 8 Benchmark, v 1.0.0. 31 January 2013
16. Symantec (2014) Internet security threat report 2014, vol 19. Symantec Corp., April 2014
17. Biersdorfer JD (2013) Q&A: avoiding mobile malware. New York Times, 8 July 2013
18. Chen BX, Perlroth N (2013) U.S. accuses 13 hackers in web attacks. New York Times, 3 October 2013
19. Perlroth N, Moynihan C (2013) Lulzsec hacker pleads guilty. New York Times, 28 May 2013
20. Perlroth N, Markoff J (2013) NSA may have hit companies at a weak spot. New York Times, 26 November 2013
21. Gellman B, Soltani A (2013) NSA infiltrates links to Yahoo, Google data centers worldwide, Snowden documents say. Washington Post, 30 October 2013
22. Perlroth N, Larson J, Shane S (2013) NSA able to foil basic safeguards of privacy on web. New York Times, 5 September 2013
23. Scott M (2014) British court rules in favor of electronic surveillance. New York Times, 5 December 2014
24. Perlroth N, Shane S (2013) As FBI pursued Snowden, an E-mail service stood firm. New York Times, 2 October 2013
25. Menn J (2013) Encrypted email service thought used by Snowden shuts down. Reuters. http://www.reuters.com/article/2013/08/09/us-usa-security-snowden-email-idUSBRE97800520130809. Accessed 9 Aug 2013
26. Stiennon S (2013) Keynote lunch: how the surveillance state is changing IT security forever. In: SC Congress Chicago, 20 November 2013
27. Crowley S (2014) Obama's speech on N.S.A. phone surveillance (transcript). New York Times, 17 January 2014
28. Gore A (2013) The future: six drivers of global change. Random House Inc, New York, NY, p 75

29. Sanger DE (2013) Differences on cybertheft complicate china talks. New York Times, 10 July 2013
30. Perlroth N (2013) Hackers in China attacked the times for last 4 months. New York Times, 30 January 2013
31. How a secret CyberWar program worked (graphic). New York Times, 1 June 2012
32. Perlroth N, Sanger DE (2013) Nations buying as hackers sell flaws in computer code. New York Times, 13 July 2013
33. Rauscher K (2013) Writing the rules of cyberwar. In: IEEE spectrum, N. American Ed., pp 30–32, December 2013
34. Bilton N (2013) Disruptions: as new targets for hackers, your car and your house. New York Times, 11 August 2013
35. Wyatt E (2013) F.T.C. says Webcam's flaw put users' lives on display. New York Times, 4 September 2013
36. Ferraro P (2013) You are an APT target. SC Magazine, p 16, April 2013
37. Kim D, Solomon MG (2012) Fundamentals of information systems security. Jones & Bartlett Learning, Sudbury, p 360
38. Anon (2010) U.S. department of justice; leader of hacking ring sentenced for massive identity thefts from payment processor and U.S. retail networks. Biotech Business Week, 12 April 2010
39. Perlroth N (2014) Report analyzes extent of data breaches in California. New York Times, 28 October 2014

Chapter 2
Combatting Fraud

> Testifying before Congress not long ago, I explained that I could often get passwords and other pieces of sensitive information from companies by pretending to be someone else and *just asking for it*. (Reformed social engineer, author *The Art of Deception*, Kevin Mitnick p. 3 [1])

While the previous chapter was a must know for all computer users, parts of this chapter are a must know for all employees. Everyone who handles or has access to assets or personal information, such as credit card, medical and financial information, and product or company trade secrets should be on guard for fraud.

One of the largest fraud disasters occurred at Societe Generale, the second largest bank in France. Trader Jerome Kerviel performed unauthorized trades, which the bank fully uncovered on Jan 24, 2008 after discovering it had lost €4.9 billion or $7.14 billion. Kerviel was authorized to trade a few hundred thousand Euros, but his trades totaled €50 billion in exposure. This was well over the entirety of the bank's capital at €36 billion. Kerviel was convicted of abuse of trust, forgery, and hacking, since he forged documents and emails; hid his trades under other employees' accounts; and created fake portfolios and trades to circumvent credit and trade size controls [2].

Fraud can occur in any industry at any level. Fraud has affected nonprofits (e.g., Red Cross, United Way, Nature Conservancy, Smithsonian Institution), universities (e.g., Adelphi University, American University, Princeton University), churches (e.g., National Baptist Convention, St. Vincent Ferrer Parish in Florida, St. Margaret Mary Parish in Chicago), medical (e.g., Blue Cross Blue Shield, HealthSouth, Alleghany Health, Education, and Research Foundation), in addition to corporations [3, 4]. In fact, during the period of the Enron scandal, nonprofit management misused $1.28 billion [4]. These cases mainly involve executives spending organizational funds inappropriately, including lavish personal spending and never repaying 'loans' for hundreds of thousands to millions of dollars. Some crimes also include tax evasion, money laundering, fraud, and/or even extortion. Although these cases mostly involve executives, fraud can be initiated anywhere in the organization. Certainly, fraud is not an area that should be ignored by any sector, and this is one reason for stiff regulation (see Chap. 3).

S. Lincke, *Security Planning*, DOI 10.1007/978-3-319-16027-6_2

The legal requirements for fraud include (1) a loss by the victim or organization, (2) personal gain by the perpetrator, and (3) intentional deception, indicated by a pattern of lying and/or unethical behavior [5]. This third aspect is meant to differentiate between unintentional errors and fraud. Legally, the three key elements of fraud include: Motivation: the perceived need for gain; Opportunity: access to computers, people or assets required to perform the fraud; and Rationalization: a justification that makes the act of fraud acceptable.

This chapter covers both business and IT aspects of fraud. It is important for both business and IT system designers to understand how fraud occurs to prevent it. It is also important for IT personnel to understand the important roles that permissions, or access control, plays in preventing fraud.

2.1 Internal Fraud

Internal or occupational fraud is done by someone who works for the organization. Characteristics of internal fraud include that it costs the organization assets, revenue or opportunity; is concealed by the employee, who receives a direct or indirect benefit; and is a violation of the employee's responsibility to the employer [5]. According to the Association of Certified Fraud Examiners' (ACFE) "2014 Report to the Nations on Occupational Fraud and Abuse" (Copyright 2014), it is estimated that internal fraud costs organizations 5 % of revenue annually, and lasts 18 months on average before discovery [6].

Research has shown that those higher in the organization have access to greater opportunity and assets, and thus are responsible for the most expensive fraud. ACFE reports that the median loss by executives averaged $500,000; managers were at $130,000, and employees at $75,000 [6]. Also, older, college-educated people on average perform more expensive fraud than newer, younger employees. The vast majority of fraudsters (95 %) have no prior fraud conviction.

Categories of internal fraud include asset misappropriation (or stealing), bribery and corruption, and financial statement fraud. *Financial statement fraud* includes violating accounting rules or exaggerating income, through overstating revenue or assets, or understating expenses or liabilities. This may include declaring false sales, valuing obsolete inventory or uncollectable accounts, writing off useful assets as junk, and not recording owed accounts. Financial statement fraud is committed by executives, and ACFE research indicates it is the most expensive type of fraud, with a median loss of $1 million for 2014 [6]. While financial statement fraud has the highest monetary value per incident, it is the least frequent type of fraud: 9 %.

Asset misappropriation is the type of fraud that occurs most commonly, at 85 % of fraud cases [6]. The Association of Certified Fraud Examiners defines asset misappropriation as the "misuse of any company asset for personal gain" and includes theft of cash, inventory, supplies, equipment, checks, and information. ACFE estimates the median loss at $130,000 [6]. The story of Trader Jerome Kerviel is an excellent

Table 2.1 Asset misappropriation definitions

Fraud name	Definition
Check tampering	Forged or altered check for gain
Embezzlement	Abusing a business privilege for personal gain; conversion for personal use
False shipping orders or Missing/defective receiving record	Inventory theft
Ghost employee	Payments are made to a fake employee
Lapping	Theft is covered with someone else's check, which is covered with the next person's check, and so on
Larceny	Theft of funds or assets that company recorded as going to another party
Payroll manipulation	Ghost employees, falsified hours, understated leave/vacation time
Shell company	Payments are made to a fake company, given a believable or similar name as an existing account
Skimming	Taking funds before they are recorded into company records

example of asset misappropriation. Additional types of asset misappropriation are included in Table 2.1 [5, 7].

Fraud involving bribery and corruption occurs in 37 % of all fraud cases and averages $200,000 per instance [6]. Cases often involve multiple types of fraud, as the statistics indicate. Bribery includes kickbacks, collusion and bid-rigging. *Corruption* is defined as an employee influencing business transactions to the employee's unauthorized gain and to the detriment of the employer [8]. Corruption includes: *extortion*: pay me or else; *conflict of interest*: undisclosed biased decisions for gain; *corporate espionage*: selling of company secrets; *false billing*: overcharging for low quality or quantity [5]; and *illegal gratuities*: small payments to gain favor [8].

The industries most vulnerable to fraud include financial industries (16.7 %), and government/public administration and manufacturing (10.2 %) [6]. Departments totaling 77 % of fraud include accounting, operations, sales, upper management, customer service and purchasing. Smaller organizations on average lose larger amounts, mainly due to their fewer controls.

2.1.1 Defenses Against Internal Fraud

Security controls can be preventive, detective or corrective by nature [9]. *Preventive* is preferred, because it prevents fraud from occurring. If fraud cannot be prevented, then it must be found (using a *detective* technique) and corrected (using the *corrective* technique). However, these last two techniques find the fraud after the fact and thus are less preferable. When detective techniques are used, a shorter time interval between threat discovery and handling may limit damage.

Preventive Techniques Prevention is the best defense and should be considered first. The three elements of fraud include Motivation, Opportunity, and Rationalization. Thus, a method of preventing fraud is to ensure that each of these elements is safe [5].

- *Motivation*: Happy, competent employees are less likely to perform fraud. Therefore, if employees are trained to do their jobs competently, have realistic job responsibilities, and are paid well, the organization is removing causes for employee fraud.
- *Rationalization*: If employees are educated as to what is right and wrong, then they can do what is expected of them. When employees are trained in clear policies, and their management consistently exhibits ethical behavior, employees are likely to follow their management's lead.
- *Opportunity*: If employees cannot perform fraud without getting caught, then they are likely to act honorably. Methods of preventing opportunity may be to research each potential employee before hiring them, by checking references and background. A second method is to restrict physical access to assets, and limit computer access to information through access control (or permissions). A third technique is to use checks and balances between employees.

Fraud related to Rationalization can be addressed by management demonstrating ethical values, clear policy documentation and education. The RICE ethical model promotes Respect, Integrity, Communication and Excellence [8]. It was developed in the 1990s and is an example of the kind of values employees would like to see from their organization and participate in. RICE was developed by Enron, and clearly exemplifies how management can say one thing and do another. Another example of unethical management behavior led to employee retribution, when Snowden leaked American government intelligence to Wikileaks and the world [10]. A recent ethics model is the 3Rs: Respect, Responsibility and Results [8]. Respect should be maintained for other people, for company property, and for the law. Responsibility means working cooperatively to meet reasonable job obligations with timely, high-quality work. Results keep an organization in business, but fraud is likely when expectations are unreasonable. The Security Workbook (on companion website) includes a skeleton outline for a Code of Ethics that you can edit for your organization's use.

The best defense against fraud related to Opportunity is the checks and balance technique of *Segregation of Duties*. An example of this is when you go to a movie theater, one person sells you a ticket, while another collects the ticket. Thus, the only way for movie viewer to see a movie for free is if the seller–originator and the ticket taker–distributor are in cahoots. *Collusion* occurs when two or more employees or an employee and a supplier work together to commit fraud. Collusion occurs in about 45 % of fraud cases and result in much larger fraud losses [6].

Figure 2.1 shows the four roles relating to segregation of duties: (1) originator, or the seller; (2) distributor, or the person who provides the product (e.g., ticket taker); (3) verifier, or the person who double checks the transaction; and (4) authorization, or the person who gives permission for the transaction [9]. Authorization can occur before or after the transaction occurred, by a manager who normally

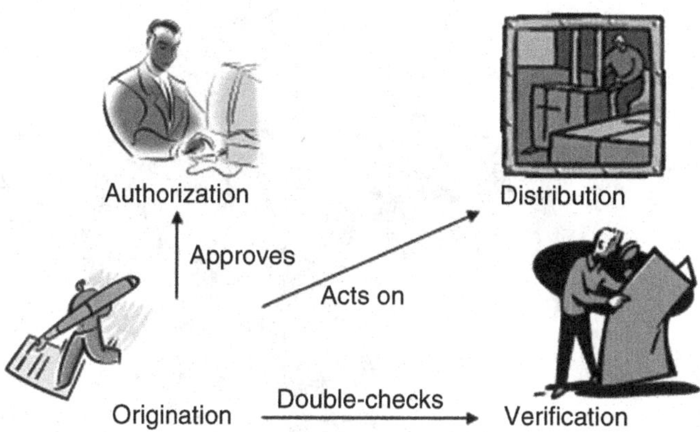

Fig. 2.1 Segregation of duties

reviews and approves transaction data. Verification can occur when a product is tested for quality. Verification is also used in a military setting, for example to access a nuclear device: two authorized workers must enter simultaneously with complimentary identification, both enter their commands separately, leave together, and write separate reports.

Even management should not be trusted with full authority. Delegation of duties is an important control to restrict management privilege, while management authorization and oversight is effective in supervising line employees. If an organization is too small to use segregation of duties, since one person wears many hats, other alternatives may have to suffice. Red flags of fraud can emerge during a fraudster's absence, by using job rotation or mandatory vacations. Note that small businesses tend to suffer greater fraud losses, due to a lack of controls, including segregation of duties.

Preventive techniques are necessary to minimize fraud. While they may stop most employees from committing fraud, they may not inhibit people like Trader Jerome Kerviel of Societe General Bank. Therefore, multiple layered defenses are required, and detective techniques for discovering fraud are highly recommended.

Detective Techniques Assuming fraud can be prevented, it is necessary to detect when fraud occurs, and then try to correct it. Figure 2.2 shows the amount of money typically recovered after a fraud is discovered [6]. ACFE reports that in 58 % of cases, no money or goods were recovered. Only in about 13.6 % of cases is there complete recovery—but this may happen through insurance. With these poor statistics, it makes sense to try to detect fraud as early as possible to minimize loss.

ACFE research has evaluated how fraud is discovered, as shown in Fig. 2.3. The top three techniques of discovery include: tips 42.2 %, management review 16.0 % and internal audit 14.1 % [6]. Notably, fraud losses found by internal controls cost

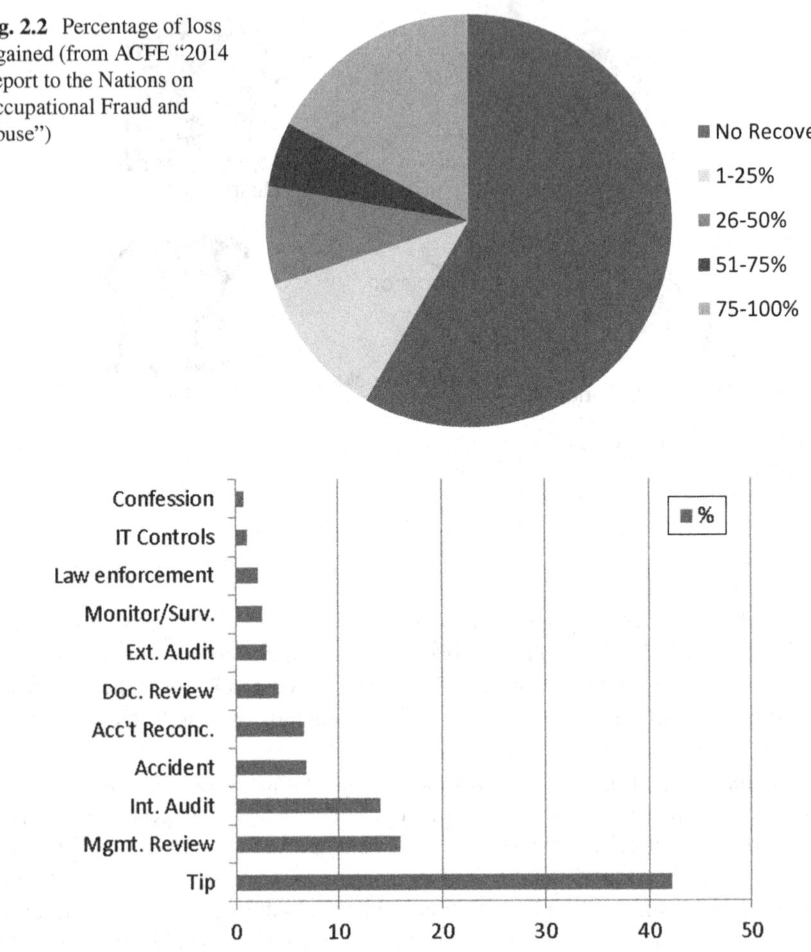

Fig. 2.2 Percentage of loss regained (from ACFE "2014 Report to the Nations on Occupational Fraud and Abuse")

Fig. 2.3 How fraud is detected (from ACFE "2014 Report to the Nations on Occupational Fraud and Abuse")

less than half compared to losses found by external means, such as law enforcement, external audit or by accident. Proactive internal fraud detection techniques also find fraud earlier (9–18 months) compared to being notified by the outside or by accident (20–32 months).

Tips about fraud are provided by employees 49 %, customers 21.6 %, anonymous 14.6 %, and vendors 9.6 % of the time [6]. Thus, a good detective technique to discover fraud is to have a fully publicized mechanism to report fraud, including anonymous reporting. For example, a website monitored by responsible staff would serve well. Educating employees to recognize and report fraud will ensure this highly effective fraud detection technique is viable.

There are some regional differences related to fraud. In North America, 25–30 % of cases involved corruption, while in Asia, Latin America, Europe and Oceana, corruption is the top fraud technique, accounting for 40–51 % of all fraud. For all continents, tip was the most common means of detecting fraud. However, in Asia, Europe and Latin America, internal audit edged out management review for second place in detecting fraud [11].

Audits of the internal and external variety help to establish proper processes to prevent fraud, but not necessarily to find it. If a general audit finds that proper controls are missing, further investigation can look specifically for fraud. Surprise audits may serve as a good detective and preventive mechanism by warning people not to attempt fraud.

When segregation of duties is not possible, detective techniques relating to employee management include job rotation and mandatory vacations [9]. Audit trails record employee actions. They can help determine culpability when fraud is detected, as well as prevent fraud since employees know their actions are monitored. Detective techniques to monitor financial transactions include processing them in a batch, where the processing of each batch of transactions is logged [9]. Reconciliation uses a checksum to ensure transactions are not modified during processing. Any transactions that are rejected go through an exception reporting/verification process.

Corrective Techniques Corrective methods (other than trying to refund money) include refining processes to prevent previously-detected fraud, and punishing fraudsters, by firing and prosecuting them. Punishment is also a preventive technique, since it sends a loud message to others who might attempt fraud. When purchased, fidelity insurance can reimburse an organization that has suffered fraud.

2.1.2 Recognizing Fraud

An example of fraud where segregation of duties was ignored occurred when the Chief Financial Officer had divisional controllers who oversaw various regions [5]. When one controller left, the CFO permanently took over her responsibilities. Checks and balances between the two positions were violated, and the CFO was then able to embezzle from the company. While temporary assumption of some responsibilities may have been acceptable, a permanent loss of checks and balances was problematic. If a report had repeatedly flagged transactions where the originator and authorization roles were performed by the same person, top management should have been reminded to replace the missing staff.

Other accounting techniques that may detect fraud include monitoring for [5, 8]:

- Unusual checks: Out-of-sequence checks, or manually prepared checks from a large company.
- Considerable refunds: Large number of voids or refunds made by a single employee or customer.
- Suspicious vendor payments: Payments sent to nonstandard (unofficial) address or vendors with similar names but different addresses, or unusual changes in vendor activity: new unapproved vendors or sudden high activity.

- Below radar transactions: Managers are able to spend money up until their authorization limit; larger amounts require management approval. An investigative technique is to evaluate all transactions immediately below the personal authorization limit, to investigate high-end expenses. This is also known as breakpoint clustering.

For software implementations, access control can be designed to enforce segregation of duties, and transaction logging can ensure accountability. Methods of enhancing computer software to detect fraud include:

- Validate all input using a valid range or maximum values to detect fraudulent transactions
- Provide reports for unusual situations, such as customer credits, adjustment accounts, inventory spoilage or loss, fixed-asset write-offs
- Calculate and detect anomaly trends, such as unusual amounts or patterns
- Compare vendor addresses and phone numbers with employee data
- Log computer activity, login or password attempts, data access attempts, and accesses from unusual geographical locations.

Internal fraud involving employees often involve red flag behavior, such as an employee living beyond their income (43.8 % of cases), having financial problems (33 %) or unusually close relationships with vendors or customers (21.8 %), and patterns of excessive control (21.1 %) [6]. Financial problems may arise from expensive habits such as gambling, philandering, or drug addiction [5, 12]. Indicators of dishonesty may include cheating in other parts of life, chronic legal problems, a pattern of breaking rules, wheeler–dealer attitude or a criminal background. Employer issues may include dissatisfaction with their job or trying to meet performance requirements. These often manifest as bragging about the damage they could do, using company resources to start a business, and organizing coworkers to start a competing business. Symptoms of fraudsters include social engineering to get additional credentials, not sharing certain information, and refusing to share or swap job responsibilities.

2.2 External Fraud

This section covers various forms of fraud initiated from outside the organization. *Identity theft* occurs when someone assumes another person's credit card number and/or other identification, to obtain money, goods, or services in the other person's name. *Social engineering* is a technique where money, goods, service, information, or access is obtained by assuming one or more fake identities. They are interrelated since identity theft is a subset of social engineering, and social engineering often uses some form of identity theft. This chapter reviews both concepts. All employees should be trained for both areas, but employees who frequently face the public should be trained more extensively.

2.2.1 Identity Theft

The Problem Approximately 12.6 million consumers are victims of identity theft each year, with an average cost to society of $365 each [13]. This affects about 5.26 % of consumers, with higher rates for tablet and smartphone owners. This includes credit card theft and more extensive identity theft, where thieves may open credit accounts, apply for tax refunds, or assume a medical identity. Here are two cases of external identity theft.

Case 1: Wireless Network Theft Albert Gonzalez and his crime ring parked in malls and used computer sniffers to monitor stores' wireless networks. They would record and later sell credit card numbers. As their ring grew more sophisticated, they planted sniffer software on point-of-sale terminals and had the software send every credit card swiped at the store to their database (eliminating the need to sit in a mall parking lot). Eventually they were able to install a sniffer in the TJX payment processing center, enabling them to obtain credit card numbers used at TJ Maxx and Marshalls retailers [14]. In 2008 Gonzalez and his ring of ten others were charged with stealing 41 million credit and debit card numbers from various retailers, including Barnes & Noble, Boston Market, OfficeMax, Sports Authority, TJ Maxx, Dave & Buster's, and other stores. In 2009, he was arrested for stealing an additional 130 million credit card numbers from credit card processor Heartland Payment Systems, 7-Eleven and Hannaford Brothers. Gonzalez was fined $250,000 and sentenced to 20 years in prison, to be followed by 3 years of supervised release [15]. Remarkably, in 2003 Gonzalez had been arrested by the Secret Service, but had been released with supervision when he became an informant! Mr. Yastremskiy, another ring member, was arrested in Turkey and his computer provided many leads and evidence for the case. He was eventually sentenced to 30 years in prison. TJX admitted spending $130 million on legal settlements and other expenses related to the break-in. Problems like this need good solutions; the PCI DSS standard, in Chap. 3 on Regulation, is one such solution.

Case 2: Skimmer Scams A 2010 law enforcement investigation in Salt Lake City found 130 gas stations with skimmers at their gas pumps [16]. A skimmer is a device that fits over or within a credit card reader, and is designed to not be noticeable. When the credit card is used, the payment card number is copied and may be sent via a wireless protocol to thieves waiting in a nearby car or elsewhere. Tiny cameras or keypad overlays record entered PIN numbers. Criminals have developed color-matched skimmers for every ATM machine in use today. To protect yourself and your company, monitor credit card readers at banks and gas stations carefully. Feel the opening of the card slot to see if any part feels loose or poorly connected. Avoid using debit cards at gas stations or cover the PIN digits as you enter them. Report any suspected skimmers.

There are two aspects of common identity theft: obtaining valid credit card numbers, and illegally using credit card numbers (or identity theft). The previous two cases demonstrate how credit card numbers can be massively obtained and then sold on hacker bulletin boards. In addition, point-of-sale (PoS) devices handling payment card information are also heavily targeted [12].

Security solutions include safer technologies and monitoring. PoS devices should be monitored for physical changes. Wireless transmission of payment card information is particularly risky, and must be carefully encrypted by professionals. For security purposes, it is preferable to retain payment card information on disk storage for as short an interval as possible (if at all). Only a restricted number of authorized employees should have physical or computerized access to stored payment card receipts, if data must be retained.

Managing employees is also important. Employees have been solicited to skim payment cards or copy their data for personal gain. Employees handling payment card information should have their background checked. Even temporary employees should be checked and given fewer permissions. Employees should be properly trained to process credit transactions and recognize red flags: payment card numbers shall never be written down in a store, emailed, or stored anywhere outside of normal processing by a PoS terminal. Using state-of-the-art-machines, employees rarely even handle credit cards, since customers can slide their own cards. Payment cards should not be visible to other customers or employees.

Prevention also includes educating employees to detect identity thieves, who use other people's identity illegally. The Federal Trade Commission (FTC) publishes recommendations on how to counter identity theft, as part of the Red Flags Rule [17]. When clients open new accounts, the FTC recommends verifying the identity of the client by checking their picture against a government-issued ID, and matching information (including address) against a credit report, data broker, and/or Social Security Administration Death Master File.

For existing accounts, businesses should confirm the identity of the client using multifactor identification (e.g., card and password/PIN) and validate change-of-address requests. Unusual scenarios may indicate identity theft; some FTC-recommended red flags are listed in Table 2.2 [17]. The FTC recommends personalizing the table for the needs of your organization.

2.2.2 Social Engineering

Truly masterful criminals, such as Frank Abignale (*Catch Me if You Can*) and Kevin Mitnick (*The Art of Deception*) were nearly 100 % successful in their criminal attempts, because they used social engineering often combined with technology, to accomplish their heists. Social engineers con people into doing something they would not ordinarily do for a stranger. Here are some present-day social engineering tricks:

Example 1: Email "Download this free app (or music)! It is so great!" If you follow the link, you must log into your 'social media site', where your login and password are copied. The social engineer then uses your social media credentials to launch their scam or spread spam [18].

Table 2.2 Recommended red flags for identity theft

Red flag category	Example red flag cases
Suspicious documents	Identification or application appears forged or altered Information is inconsistent between ID, what the client tells you and what is in their records Picture or signature differs
Personal identifying information	Information matches other clients: social security number matches another person; other identification matches several clients Information looks suspicious: phone number is to answering service; social security number is on Death Master File; information provided is inconsistent with credit report Incomplete application and client fails to submit additional information Client cannot provide authenticating information beyond what is commonly known (e.g., name, address, phone)
Account activity	A major change in spending or payment habits A change in address, followed by unusual requests: e.g., multiple credit cards Initial use of credit card shows unusual activity: first payment only; purchase of products easily converted to cash: electronics, jewelry Inactive accounts suddenly becoming active Mail is returned undeliverable, while transactions continue
Warnings from a credit agency	Changes to a credit report, inconsistent with client's history Indication of fraud or credit freeze or closed account due to abuse Changes to recent credit transactions: an increase in inquiries or new accounts
Notice from other sources	Law enforcement, a customer, or a victim of identity theft tells you an account has been opened inappropriately or used fraudulently

Example 2: Phone Call "Hi, this is Jake Adams, from <software company>. We have noticed that your computer has malware. I hate to bother you with this problem when you are so busy, but we thought you would want to know and upgrade to our new software. Let me walk you through the fix. Download this software from our link and pay here. <chat, chat, chat> Now run the program.... It should be fixed—you won't have any problems with the new version!"

Example 3: Email "I am a hired gun and someone has hired me. You are my next murder victim. I will ignore the contract on you if you pay ..."

Examples 2 and 3 are listed on the FBI site as scams [19]. Which of the above might fool you? If you would not be fooled by any of them, might a secretary or sales person be fooled? Example two may sometimes originate from your "system administrator". Everyone in the organization should know that system administrators have full rights on a computer—they should never need login or other assistance. FBI advice includes never responding to spam; never purchasing anything through unsolicited email; and using separate public and private-for-friends email addresses [19]. These three cases are very simple social engineering cases.

Alternatively, social engineering scenarios may involve multiple steps [1]. The social engineer first learns insider vocabulary and/or personnel names by scanning web pages, placing fake calls, or garbage dumpster-diving. With insider knowledge, they may then pretend to be a legitimate user (a vice president, system administrator, or from another department). A spear phisher may email an attached 'resume' spoofed to come from 'human resources', or include a link to 'new financial regulations' from a 'financial officer' [18]. A social engineer may telephone, pretending to need or provide help, and may hide their real question among other questions. They may establish a relationship to gain trust for future jobs.

This next more sophisticated social engineering scenario involves multiple phone calls, where each call obtains a piece of information that is used in the next call.

Example 4: Multi-call Social Engineering Example for Medical Scenario John is getting a divorce from Susan. He has a new love, Alice, who he would like to spend more time with. He has considered what to do with his two school-aged children, Jim and Ann. He figures that if Susan retains custody, he will owe a considerable amount in alimony. Frankly, he would like to keep the money. Plus, if he keeps them during the week, Susan can care for them on weekends, leaving his weekend free for golf and quality time with Alice.

However, Susan won't give up the kids easily. Her first love is her children. He has always been too busy—golfing, business, … affairs—for kids. She will want to retain full custody, and she has been a great full-time Mom up until now. So how to fight this?

He has heard from an old friend that she has cancer. If the cancer is serious and he can prove it in court, perhaps she can be judged to be inadequate. If she is on chemotherapy … who will take care of her and the kids? It would be best that he be given main custody (hopefully weekdays).

He decides to ask Alice for help. First he needs to find out which doctor Susan is seeing. Then he needs to get her records. Finally he can talk to his lawyer about the best way of presenting this part of the case. Alice agrees to place the calls to potential doctors.

Call 1: Find Doctor

Date: July 2. 3:05 PM.

Office: This is Dr Anderson's office. How can I help you?

Caller: This is Susan Armstrong. I will be going away to help my Mother soon. I think I have an appointment coming up, and I lost the appointment card. Can you check? The appointment would be for Susan Armstrong.

Office: What is your address and home phone number?

Caller: 262-408-4722. 1245 N Ridge Ave. Kenosha.

Office: Yes, I see you have an appointment next Wednesday at 2:30.

Caller: Good! Well, I think I will leave to visit Mom right after that appointment. Thank you so much, it is now on my calendar. Also – did my PPO pay off my last visits, or do I owe anything extra?

Office: Well we are still awaiting payment for your last appointment at the hospital on June 5th, but the previous visits have all been paid. But they usually take about a month or two to pay.

Caller: Thank you, I will see you next Wednesday at 2:30!

Call 2: Obtain Medical Records

Date: July 8 10:42 AM.
Office: This is Dr Anderson's office. How can I help you?
Caller: This is Susan Armstrong. I will be visiting another specialist for a problem with my leg and foot. She would like to see my prescriptions and my medical history. I would also like a copy for my own records. Can you fax me a copy of my records, and I will be sure to bring the records to the new doctor?
Office: Well, you will have to come in to sign for a copy of your records. Also, doctors usually prefer to have the records sent directly to them.
Caller: I think it is most important that I have the copy, and the doctor said it was ok if I brought my records in. Hmm. I don't have a car available. Can my husband sign for them and pick them up?
Office: No, it needs to be you.
Caller: What if I request a copy in writing, and use our fax machine to send you my signature?
Office: I think that would be acceptable. Our fax number is 262-488-2122. Should we fax the records to the fax number where we get the letter from?
Caller: Yes, that would be extremely helpful. What do I need to include in the letter?
Office: Please include your name, the information you need, the location where the information should be faxed to, and why you are asking for the information. Also include your printed name and signature.
Caller: No problem! Thank you so much for your help.
Office: Any time…

Date July 8, 6:45 PM

Alice: John! We got her medical information! I hooked the laptop up to a phone line at my friend's office, in the conference room, and sent the fax from there. It will be difficult to trace it back to us.
John: And the records say…
Alice: She does have breast cancer.
John: Great! Thanks so much!

The scam was successful! Can you consider how a doctor's office can prevent such a scam?

Defending against Social Engineering Verification procedure might include: (1) verify requester is who they claim to be via proper ID. (2) Verify the requester is currently employed in the claimed position. (3) Verify role is authorized for the request. (4) Record the transaction.

2.2.3 Receipt, Check, and Money Order Scams

New stores must have sophisticated enough systems to guard against these receipt scams, which have been used [20]:

- Get a receipt from the trash and 'return' a product.
- Copy a gift certificate and redeem at multiple locations
- A marked down sale price is reimbursed with a full price receipt. The receipt is copied and collected at multiple locations.
- Fake UPC numbers to pay at a low price then return item at a higher price.

To guard against these scams [20], it is important to retain line-item detail on gift certificates and sales records (receipts) in the company database. Receipts should have security marks on them, such as two-colored ink on special paper or thermochromatic ink. Garbage bins that may receive receipts or other sensitive information should be protected from access and their contents shredded.

Check scams Check crimes may include altered checks, copied checks, and hot checks [20]. To alter a check, typically chemicals are used to erase the payee or amount, then the check is re-printed. For example, an Argentinian modified a ticket-overpayment refund check from Miami, changing a $2 check to $1.45 million—and successfully cashed it [20]. It may be possible to get check information by viewing a check in a checkout line, being paid for yard work or by picking up outgoing mail in a mail box. This allows boxes of checks to be purchased with this information on-line and cashed.

These scams can be avoided by printing checks with printers which stain the check with an ink that cannot be washed out. Normal laser printers are non-impact, where the ink sits on the top of the paper, and can be easily erased. Here are features of good checks [21]:

- Watermark: Subtle design viewable at 45-degree angle toward light and cannot be photo-copied
- Void Pantograph: Faint background pattern on checks: when photo-copied, the background pattern disappears or prints 'VOID'
- Chemical Voids: When check is treated with eradicator chemical, the word VOID appears
- Microprinting: When magnified, the signature or check border is typed words. The resolution is too fine for a photo-copier.
- 3-Dimensional Reflective Holostripe: Metallic stripe contains at least one hologram, similar to credit card.
- Security ink: Reacts to eradication chemicals, distorting the check.
- Thermochromic Ink: Ink reacts to heat and moisture by fading and reappearing

Bad checks tend to be for newly opened accounts: the opening year may be printed on the check, and 90 % of 'insufficient funds' checks are numbered between 101 and 200. Checks are rarely accepted today in stores because of hot checks, resulting in "Insufficient Funds".

Money Orders Money orders are dangerous because they provide information on a checking account. Therefore, it is more secure to have separate incoming and outgoing money order accounts. This prevents someone from asking about a money order account to make a payment, when they actually intend to cash a fake money order using the same account.

2.3 Developing an Action Plan

Hopefully this chapter has provided ideas on types of fraud your organization is prone to and some good defenses to consider. Take advantage of your ideas and write them down in the Security Workbook, Chap. 2. Document your main internal fraud risks and any preliminary notes of how they could be mitigated. Write down your external fraud risks as well as feasible controls to reduce them. Evaluate which aspects of the Red Flag recommendations seemed particularly applicable. Since defining what ethics means for your organization is a good first step, also complete the skeleton Code of Ethics, found within Chap. 3 in the Security Workbook. Chapter 3 on regulation next discusses Sarbanes–Oxley and other laws that effectively protect against fraud. Chapter 10 on personnel security has you design security responsibility and training for your employees.

It is impossible in one chapter to talk about all types of fraud, so this chapter has focused on general information security fraud. The FBI tracks a set of different types of fraud [19]: Antitrust, bankruptcy fraud, corporate fraud, financial institution fraud and failures, health care fraud, insurance fraud, mass marketing fraud, money laundering, mortgage fraud, intellectual property theft, security and commodities fraud, and other white-collar fraud. If your industry is prone to one of these frauds, more information is available at www.fbi.gov/about-us/investigate/what_we_investigate. If you encounter a case of possible fraud, you can report it to the Internet Crime Complaint Center: www.ic3.gov [19].

2.4 Advanced: A Fraud Investigation

Advanced sections are optional reading in this book, and are usually not required to complete a Security Plan. They may provide information for specialized needs or provide background information for those who wish to develop information security as a career.

A forensic audit may investigate for potential fraud when certain financial numbers look suspect. This advanced section considers how a fraud investigation typically occurs [7], and uses an example case as reported by a British fraud examiner, Steve Giles [8]. This U.K. fraud was initially reported as an anonymous tip indicating that a director of a subsidiary was unfairly awarding contracts to certain suppliers, and potentially taking kickbacks. Rumors were circulating—but the

Director was popular and known to meet financial targets, so the fraud was deemed dubious. A covert investigation was initiated.

Step 1: Initial Inquiry The first step in the investigation is to understand what is happening from a financial and/or operational aspect [7]. Do security controls exist and are they always practiced? Does the employee show any of the red flags of fraud? Data mining is the process of analyzing financial transactions to look for suspicious occurrences. Computer Assisted Audit Technique (CAAT) software is a flexible tool that enables searching and analysis, using an audit command language, through a large transaction database [8]. It can identify anomalies, trends and suspicious transactions, such as matched employee and accounts payable contact information.

In our Director case, a covert investigation started by monitoring his phone calls, rummaging through his personal garbage, and analyzing supplier and other financial records and controls. Phone calls could be recorded because organizational policies stated that all employee calls may be monitored. Garbage was photographed and returned. Investigated controls included interviewing staff about segregation of duties practices, reviewing organizational policies related to suppliers, and observing how business was transacted through existing records. In week 3, the Director told his wife in a low voice that "we got 10,000 pounds" from Supplier A. This was corroborated when a personal bank statement with 500,000 pounds from the Caymen Islands was found in his garbage. The board of directors decided to suspend (but not yet fire) the Director and the investigation was to continue with a plan for criminal and civil law suits. They submitted a request to freeze the Caymen Islands bank account, which was successful. They also ordered the Director and employees not to talk to each other, since any discussion could interfere with the investigation. Management requested to be periodically informed of the progress of the investigation.

Step 2: Develop and confirm hypothesis After the pertinent data records are obtained, the auditor analyzes the evidence and hypothesizes on the possible methods of fraud along with who might be involved. The goal is to develop an accurate story of what happened. The analysis may include a timeline of what happened when, pictures of evidence, and/or a diagram showing what evidence relationships: which evidence is associated with certain people and other evidence [7].

In the case of our Director, when the covert investigation became an open investigation, the auditors interviewed staff and suppliers and performed a forensic analysis of accounting records, contracts and correspondence. During interviews, two smaller suppliers indicated their frustration that they could never bid or be considered for larger jobs. The two larger suppliers indicated that they gave rebates for large purchases and that the Director handled all aspects of the supplier relationships personally. While many of the rebates were recorded as income, two million pounds were missing. The auditor, Steve, investigated an accounting report with the Director's handwritten notes on it, which had been salvaged from his garbage. He concluded that someone with initials GG was also being paid in the scheme, when one third was paid back as an overcharge to the smaller suppliers.

Step 3: Collect evidence When it is understood how the fraud occurred, the auditor must collect evidence to be used in a trial. This includes the three requirements of fraud: evidence of organizational loss, personal gain, and deception. The full set of questions that need to be answered include: who decided to make the unethical or illicit changes? Did affected personnel know the correct methods? How far up the management chain did this knowledge go, and could auditors have been complicit? [7]

Computer forensic tools can help by uncovering secret files, decoding encrypted files, and investigating external media and deleted and retained email. Emails can be analyzed from both sender and receiver side, to see if there is a difference in the emails purged. Fraudsters change dates, amounts and/or names of transactions or checks; looking at different sources or versions of documents or transactions can show if and when changes were introduced [7]. For check fraud, an image of a check may be recovered from a computer or printer memory. These tools may also be used during earlier stages of the investigation. 'Discovery' occurs where both plaintiff and defendant provide the main evidence to the opposing side.

In the case of our Director, it was learned from an interview with a supplier that the Director secretly planned to start a competitive business on his own. The Director lied to an employee about having a university degree when he did not. He also rigged the budgets to appear like his organization was coming in below cost. At this point, the Director was fired and a full written report was given to the insurance companies and police. The police never prosecuted, but the fidelity insurance company was happy with the full report and frozen bank account. They reimbursed the company for loss, paying four million pounds and proceeded with the civil case against the Director.

2.5 Questions and Problems

For each of the following questions, be sure to write professionally in essay form.

1. *Vocabulary*. Match each meaning with the correct word.

Collusion	Shell company	Corrective control	Asset misappropriation
Bribery	Larceny	Preventive control	Financial statement fraud
Lapping	Embezzlement	Detective control	Segregation of duties
Skimming	Skimmer	Ghost employee	Red flag rule

   a) Includes origination, distribution, verification and authorization.
   b) A security tool or process that fixes security problems after they occur.
   c) A physical attachment used by criminals to record credit card stripe information.

d) Theft of funds or assets before they are recorded into company records.
e) An employee abuses a business privilege for personal gain.
f) This crime violates business accounting rules.
g) Two or more employees or suppliers work together to defraud an organization.
h) A security tool or process that reduces the opportunity for a security threat to occur.
i) Theft of funds or assets that the organization recorded as going to another party.
j) A device that fits within a credit card reader and copies payment card numbers in a point-of-sale or ATM machine.

2. *Fraud in Your Industry*. Consider one type of fraud in your major or industry specialty (e.g., health, manufacturing, finance, retail, entertainment, education, hotel,…). Describe this one possible fraud, how it could be done, what some red flags would be, and a preventive and detective technique to catch the fraud.
3. *Prioritize Fraud Threats*. Select threats which are a concern in your industry. List your threats in priority order. For each threat, describe a scenario and the potential impact.

   a) Consider insider or employee fraud: financial statement fraud, asset misappropriation and corruption.
   b) Consider external fraud: identity theft, social engineering and receipt/check/money order theft.

4. *Fraud in News*. Find a news article about a case of fraud related to your field. Describe what happened, how the fraud occurred, what it was or will be prosecuted for, and the court's ruling (if available). The news story should be from the last 30 years. Helpful hint: There may be multiple articles about your selected case over time.
5. *Social Engineering*. Write a social engineering case related to your chosen career area. How would you recommend defending against it? Write a procedure, or a numbered, step-by-step description, of how employees should protect against this social engineering scenario.
6. *Security Education*. You have been hired as a security trainer or technical writer. Provide a one-page informational description on one type of fraud, which company employees should be aware of. Write a description of the threat and the action(s) the employees should take to counter this threat. Find additional information via on-line web or library resources to make the article interesting, informative, and useful.
7. *Case Study*. Evaluate the case study in the section: Advanced: A Fraud Investigation. Answer the following questions:

   a) What type of fraud was this?
   b) What evidence was finally available to address the three requirements of fraud?
   c) What controls were violated, as indicated by the story?

2.5.1 *Health First Case Study Problems*

For each case study problem, refer to the Health First Case Study. The Health First Case Study and Security Workbook should be provided by your instructor or can be found at http://extras.springer.com.

Case study	Health first case study	Other resources
Fraud: Combating social engineering	√	Security workbook is optional
Fraud: Combatting social engineering Optional extension: Computerizing the disclosure forms	√	Health first Requirements document HIPAA slides or notes
Developing a code of ethics	√	Security workbook

References

1. Mitnick KD, Simon WL (2002) The art of deception. Wiley, Hoboken, NJ, USA
2. Lim J, Hwa MK (2011) Computer fraud and ethics: the Societe Generale's trading fraud. In: International conference on computer and management (CAMAN) IEEE, pp 1–3
3. Hoggins-Blake R (2009) Dissertation: examining non-profit post-secondary institutions' voluntary compliance with the Sarbanes–Oxley Act. ProQuest Dissertations and Theses, pp 19–51
4. Yallapragada RR, Roe CW, Toma AG (2010) Sarbanes–Oxley Act of 2002 and non-profit organizations. J Bus Econ Res 8(2):89–93
5. Coenen TL (2008) Essentials of corporate fraud. John Wiley & Sons, Inc., Hoboken, NJ, USA, pp 1–200
6. ACFE (2014) Report to the nations on occupational fraud and abuse: 2014 global fraud study. Association of Certified Fraud Examiners (ACFE), http://www.acfe.com
7. Philipp A, Cowen D, Davis C (2010) Hacking exposed computer forensics, 2nd edn. McGraw-Hill, Inc. New York, NY, USA
8. Giles S (2012) Managing fraud risk: a practical guide for directors and managers. John Wiley and Sons, Chichester, West Sussex, England, pp 1–320
9. ISACA (2012) CISA® review manual 2011. ISACA, Arlington Heights, IL
10. Daily report: Snowden trained as hacker while with N.S.A., resume says. New York Times, 5 July 2013
11. ACFE (2012) Report to the nations on occupational fraud and abuse: 2012 global fraud study. Association of Certified Fraud Examiners (ACFE), http://www.acfe.com
12. Verizon (2013) Verizon 2013 data breach investigations report. http://www.verizonenterprise.com/DBIR/2013. Accessed 20 Oct 2013
13. Identity fraud report: data breaches becoming a treasure trove for fraudsters. Javelin strategy & research, Pleasanton, CA, pp 10–12. http://www.javelinstrategy.com. Accessed 1 Feb 2013
14. Stone B (2008) Global trail of an online crime ring. New York Times, 12 August 2008
15. Anon (2010) U.S. department of justice; leader of hacking ring sentenced for massive identity thefts from payment processor and U.S. retail networks. Biotech Business Week, 12 April 2010
16. Vamosi R (2011) Keep your credit cards safe from skimmers. PCWorld, pp 31–32, March 2011
17. Federal Trade Commission (2013) Fighting identity theft with the red flags rule: a how-to guide for business. Federal Trade Commission. http://business.ftc.gov/documents/bus23-fighting-identity-theft-red-flags-rule-how-guide-business. Accessed 25 May 2013

18. Internet security threat report 2014, vol 19. Symantec Corp., April 2014
19. Brelsford E (2014) 2014: a cyber odyssey. In: ISACA Chicago chapter meeting, Rosemont, IL, 13 December 2013
20. Abignale F (2001) The art of the steal. Broadway Books, Broadway, NY
21. Check Fraud Working Group (1999) Check fraud: a guide to avoiding losses. Office of the Controller of the Currency, February 1999. http://www.occ.gov/static/publications/chckfrd/chckfrd.pdf. Accessed 6 July 2014

Chapter 3
Complying with Security Regulation and Standards

> You only exist as a significant Russian cybercriminal if you abide by three rules. You are not allowed to hack anything within the sovereign boundary; if you find anything of interest to the regime you share it; and when called upon for 'patriotic activities,' you do so. In exchange you get 'untouchable status.' (Tom Kellermann, chief cybersecurity officer at Trend Micro [1])

To protect customers, patients, and the general public, a number of laws regulate information security. This chapter includes three sections: (1) U.S. security-oriented laws organizations must adhere to (e.g., HIPAA); (2) security-oriented standards organizations must adhere to (e.g., PCI DSS); and (3) criminal laws that protect organizations (e.g., anti-hacking). Other nations (other than the United States) have their own security regulation. Europe, India and some other nations have regulations requiring adherence to International Security Organization's standards (ISO/IEC 27001-2), or COBIT (See Sarbanes–Oxley regulation) [2] as well as other regulations.

3.1 Security Laws Affecting U.S. Organizations

What security regulation(s) must your organization adhere to? What must you implement as part of that regulation? How important is it to adhere to security regulations? This section briefly addresses these issues and explains implications of non-compliance. In the United States, news agencies have reported that large companies found to violate security regulation have had to pay millions of dollars to government agencies (often to the Federal Trade Commission or FTC). They are often set up with a special program of remediation and monitoring for an extended period of time (e.g., CVS [3], ChoicePoint [3], TJX [3]). These fines and remedial actions are intended to protect individuals from corporations who do not safeguard the security of their customers. Example cases will be described for each regulation. The intention is not to embarrass any particular organization, but rather to illustrate

S. Lincke, *Security Planning*, DOI 10.1007/978-3-319-16027-6_3

Table 3.1 Chapters required for regulation

Chapter notation: R=Required, A=Advisable	State breach	HIPAA	SOX	GLB	Red flag	FISMA	FERPA	PCI DSS
1. Security awareness	A	R	R	R	R	R	A	A
2. Fraud	A	A	R	R	R	R		A
4. Risk		R	R	R	R	R		R
5. Business continuity		R	R	R		R		R
6. Policy		R	R	R	R	R	R	R
7. Information security	R	R	R	R	R	R	R	R
8. Network security	R	R	R	R	A	R	R	R
9. Physical security	R	R	R	R	A	R	A	R
10. Personnel security		R	R	R	R	R		R
11. Incident response	R	R	R	R	R	R	A	R
12. Metrics			R	A	A	R		
13. Audit		R	R	R	A	R		R

the issues. Many organizations will or have reported intrusions. It is hoped that any organization that has paid massive fines is likely to be currently compliant.

This section lays out basic information about each law, including: (1) Example cases showing the need; (2) a definition of who needs to be concerned with the law; and (3) the general requirements of the law. From this description, you may learn which law(s) apply to your organization, and what the laws' basic precepts include. Table 3.1 maps various regulations, and the PCI DSS standard, to chapters in this book. This table will hopefully help you in adhering to applicable laws. Further information on each law is available in the references and on the web, since this general text does not discuss all specific requirements.

3.1.1 State Breach Notification Laws, 2003 and Later

Forty-seven states, the District of Columbia, Guam, Puerto Rico and the Virgin Islands have enacted legislation requiring notification of security breaches involving personal information. The three states currently without notification laws include Alabama, New Mexico and South Dakota [3–4]. Even companies in these three states must adhere to these laws if they sell to customers in many of the other states [3].

The law was first enacted in California in 2003. It was first enforced in 2005 with ChoicePoint, a data broker who sold credit reports and information about consumers. Law enforcement reported that an identity theft ring potentially took personal information for over 160,000 people [3]. The identity theft ring had pretended to be lawful ChoicePoint customers. ChoicePoint paid $10 million in civil fines to the FTC, $5 million to fund a consumer relief program, $500,000 to states impacted by the breach, as well as the cost of sending notification letters to over 160,000 people. The ChoicePoint-FTC settlement included ChoicePoint agreeing to create an information security program and incur yearly independent audits until the year 2026. A second case in 2009 resulted in ChoicePoint reevaluating its security plan and reporting to the FTC on its security efforts every 2 months until 2011.

Applicability This law applies to any organization "… that, for any purpose, handles, collects, disseminates, or otherwise deals with nonpublic personal information." (from the Illinois state breach law [5]) Protected information includes for most states: Social Security number, driver's license number, state identification card number, financial account number or credit or debit card number, "or an account number or credit card number in combination with any required security code, access code, or password that would permit access to an individual's financial account." For some states, including California, Texas, Virginia, Arkansas, and Missouri, private information also includes medical or health insurance information. California law also protects user names and passwords [6]. Private data excludes lawful information available to the public by local, state, or national government.

General requirements While each state breach law may be different, this section provides guidelines describing the general intent of the various breach laws. When a breach of private information is determined, the organization must notify the affected persons in plain English in an expedient and timely manner, at no cost to the person. The disclosure may be delayed by law enforcement for an investigation. The disclosure notification shall inform the victims of the breach, including the (estimated) date and nature of the breach and any steps the data collector has taken or plans to take relating to the breach. The disclosure notification may, in addition, require consumer reporting information, such as the toll-free numbers, address, and website for consumer reporting agencies. It may require a statement indicating that these sources can provide help about fraud or security alerts, or other recommended actions. The data collector may need to cooperate with each victim in matters relating to the breach, short of disclosing confidential information or trade secrets. This notification may be provided in written or electronic form. Special conditions may apply, based on state laws.

An affected victim can include an individual or any type of organization. Government agencies are also subject to this law, and often must also report breaches to a higher state agency. State agencies may be required to securely dispose of information, when it is no longer needed.

In California, New York, and other states, stolen personal information that is encrypted is exempt from disclosure—as long as the encryption key was also not acquired. Texas requires proper information disposal, but it permits encryption: "otherwise modifying the sensitive personal information in the records to make the information unreadable or indecipherable through any means."

Personal information shall be disposed of in a way that renders the personal information unreadable, unusable, and undecipherable. Proper disposal methods for paper documents include redaction, burning, pulverizing, or shredding. Disposal methods for electronic and other media include destroying or erasing the media to "prevent the personal information from being further read or reconstructed".

Penalties may apply if an organization fails to report a breach. Fines may range between $10 and 2,000 per affected person, with a maximum total penalty of $50,000–150,000 per breach situation. New York also requires notification to a state agency. Some states may have additional privacy laws. For example, California includes a health privacy law and consumer report law, as well as separate privacy laws applied to business and government. Texas permits expulsion for students who abuse school computers. To find the privacy laws applicable to a particular state, see the National Conference of State Legislatures (www.ncsl.org/issues-research/telecom/security-breach-notification-laws.aspx) [5].

3.1.2 HIPAA/HITECH Act, 1996, 2009

The Health Insurance Portability & Accountability Act (HIPAA) was passed in 1996. HIPAA initiated a standard for the exchange of electronic health information and regulated the protection of personal health information, within Title II of this comprehensive regulation. This privacy protection is defined in the Privacy Rule, which protects health information whether or not it is computerized; and the Security Rule, which specifically applies to computerized health information. Since the original law lacked sufficient force, the HITECH Act passed in 2009 to strengthen penalties, protect patients who had been harmed, require breach notification, and ensure compliance by both Covered Entities (CE: i.e., health care providers and insurance) and their Business Associates (BA, or contractors) [7].

Background The release of personal health, addiction, or mental health information can result in social isolation, employment discrimination, and a denial of lifesaving insurance coverage. Example abuses include a Midwest banker on the county health board, who matched customer accounts with patient information. He called due all home loans of cancer patients [8]. Eli Lilly and Co. accidentally disclosed over 600 patient email addresses by sending one email, without blind copy, to all registered persons who had requested reminders to take their Prozac prescription [8].

In 2006, CVS pharmacies were caught throwing away unredacted pill bottles, medical instruction sheets, and pharmacy receipts. These contained patient names, addresses, prescriptions names, physician names, health insurance numbers, and credit card numbers. The FTC and Health and Human Services (HHS) each developed separate remediation plans with CVS that included the development of a security plan, security policies, and an employee training program. The remediation plans also required independent audits and HHS monitoring. CVS paid $2.25 million in fines [3].

In 2009, Blue Cross Blue Shield in Tennessee had 57 hard disks stolen, releasing medical information and social security numbers for over one million people. They paid $1.5 million to Office of Civil Rights, incurred a 3-year remediation plan, and spent $17 million in investigation, notification, and protection expenses [9].

Applicability Covered Entities (CE) include health care providers, health plan organizations, and health care clearinghouses. Even organizations which maintain nurses' offices need to be concerned. Business Associates (BA) include organizations who consult for health care organizations [7]. Thus, HIPAA/HITECH applies widely.

General requirements: The Privacy Rule The Privacy Rule ensures that health care providers maintain policies regarding patient privacy, including that health information are not to be used for non-health purposes, such as marketing [7, 8]. Workers shall have minimum access to patient information, sufficient only to do their jobs. Privacy safeguards should be reasonable, including privacy curtains, locked cabinets, paper shredders, and clean desk policies. However, privacy requirements are not to be extreme, such as private, soundproofed rooms. CEs and BAs must track both allowed and unintended disclosures of patient information.

Patients have a right to obtain their own patient information, request corrections, and to know who has accessed their health information. Patients should know how their provider handles privacy, via a Notice of Privacy Practices.

The Security Rule The Security Rule recognizes that Confidentiality, Integrity, and Availability are all important in protecting Electronic Protected Health Information (EPHI) [7, 8]. This regulation is based on risk management, to ensure that security costs correspond with risk. The goal of the regulation is that it is scalable, technology independent, and comprehensive. The regulation outlines technical, administrative, and physical security requirements, while avoiding specifying detailed technologies that are likely to change with time. Each requirement is defined as Required or Addressable, with Addressable options allowing for documented, alternative, effective implementations. Briefly, administrative requirements include risk management, alarm/log monitoring, periodic policy review/audit, and personnel management. Personnel requirements include EPHI access granting procedures, supervision of EPHI access, termination procedures, and sanction policies for HIPAA violations. Physical security requirements include a physical security plan, business continuity plans, documented maintenance records, workstation acceptable use plans, and controls for devices and media (describing proper use, repair, disposal, and backup). Technical controls include individual authentication controls, automatic logoff/lockout, encryption and integrity (message digest) controls, and event/transaction logging.

3.1.3 Sarbanes–Oxley Act (SOX), 2002

During the 1990s and early 2000s, there were a number of corporations who suffered serious and highly publicized accounting fraud [10]. In 2001, Enron was reported to issue statements misleading regulators and the public, and using aggressive accounting techniques in reporting profits. In 2001 and 2002, WorldCom charged expenses as capital expenses, and reported millions in profit, when they should have reported losses. Arthur Andersen LLP, an accounting and audit firm, did not follow General Accepted Accounting Practices, thereby assisting in the misleading financial reports of WorldCom, Enron, Sunbeam, and Waste Management System. This led to the felony conviction of Arthur Andersen in 2002, for obstructing justice [10]. These and other publicized cases resulted in corporate bankruptcies, loss of employee retirements savings in the billions, executive jail time for 15–25 years, and sometimes, restitution fines [3].

As a result of this fraud, the Sarbanes–Oxley act was passed in 2002 to protect stockholders, employees, investors, and other stakeholders. Its general purpose is to address securities fraud, define ethics for reporting finances, increase transparency of financial reporting to stockholders and consumers, ensure disclosure of stock sales to executives, and prohibit loans to top managers.

Applicability This law applies to publicly traded companies who sell stocks on an American stock exchange and must register with the SEC. Therefore, it applies to many international companies, in addition to American companies [3].

Two provisions also apply to not-for-profits. Not-for-profit organizations may consider adherence to additional aspects or the full regulation, in order to gain credibility with donors. Not-for-profits have had their share of major fraud losses, which caused bad publicity. Some states, including New York, California, and New Hampshire, have additional regulation impacting hospitals or nonprofits [11].

General requirements: Requirements for Public, Private, and Nonprofit organizations Two provisions limit organizational interference in ensuring that fraud can be fully disclosed. These provisions, which apply to all organizations, include the Whistleblower provision and a prohibition against destroying certain documents. The Whistleblower provision requires organizations to establish a means to report financial improprieties and complaints, and prevents the organization from punishing employees who report suspected illegal actions to a judicial proceeding. Any person who destroys, tampers with, or conceals documents that could be evidence in a federal investigation or bankruptcy case is liable for up to a 20-year prison term and/or fines [11]. Organizational policies should be written and well-known, and also apply to electronic records, voicemail, and archives [12].

These provisions are part of SOX Section 806 and 301. Other recommended provisions for nonprofit organizations include the full section 301, 302, and 404, which are described below.

Requirements for Publicly-Traded Companies Briefly, the full set of sections of Sarbanes–Oxley includes [10]:

- Section 301: Public companies shall establish an audit committee, which hires a registered accounting firm and establishes policies and procedures for handling complaints concerning finances.
- Section 302: Corporate responsibility for financial reports includes a periodic mandated reporting process, where the signing officer testifies to the accuracy and completeness of the audit report, and is responsible for internal controls. The report in addition lists the auditors, audit committee, and significant deficiencies affecting the business finances.

- Section 401: Enhanced disclosure in periodic reports includes clarity and better defined transactions for financial reporting.
- Section 404: Management assessments of internal controls [13]: Auditors must do an audit beyond the traditional financial audit: they must also audit internal control. Management must provide internal control documentation and perform an assessment of the effectiveness of the organization's internal controls. These controls shall define how significant transactions are processed, how assets are safeguarded, how fraud is controlled, and how end-of-period financial reporting occurs.

Sections 302 and 404 are concerned with reporting the effectiveness of the organization's internal control, and Section 404 impacts information technology and security.

COSO, Committee of Sponsoring Organization of the Treadway Commission, was created to develop standards for Sarbanes–Oxley (SOX) security implementation. COSO defines two areas of control: Process Activity Level and Entity Level controls. Process Activity controls require the documentation of processes and transactions for specific business functional areas, and can be documented as a walkthrough for significant transactions. Entity Level controls include cross-cutting services for many business functional areas, such as IT, personnel, and risk management. COSO then specifies five components: risk assessment, control environment, control activities, information and communication, and monitoring, which then are applied to each of the two areas of Process Activity and Entity Level controls.

COBIT is an application of COSO for IT, and is published by ISACA [14]. COBIT documents Section 404 requirements for information security. To establish Entity Level controls for quality and integrity of financial information (thereby minimizing fraud), the computing environment is best controlled with an implementation of IT best practices. COBIT applies the five COSO components to the IT lifecycle: (1) Evaluate, Direct and Monitor; (2) Align, Plan and Organize; (3) Build, Acquire and Implement; (4) Deliver, Service and Support; and (5) Monitor, Evaluate and Assess. This derives 37 detailed requirements. Key Area Evaluate, Direct and Monitor addresses governance objectives in defining IT's relationship with executive management. Key Area Align, Plan and Organize emphasizes strategic planning, IT-business alignment, and IT-interdepartmental communication. Key Area Build, Acquire and Implement addresses defining requirements, testing configurations, and tracking changes. Key Area Deliver, Service and Support includes managing operations, incidents, problems, continuity, and security. The final Key Area, Monitor, Evaluate and Assess, addresses monitoring of performance, conformance, and internal controls. This comprehensive standard defines a maturity model of six levels (0–5), enabling an organization to ascertain where they are and how they can progress to higher maturity levels. This text and workbook, which addresses information security planning, is only a subset of COBIT.

It is widely recognized that SOX adherence is expensive to implement, but has also resulted in fewer cases of business fraud and accounting scandals [10], and for good reason: CEOs who "recklessly" violate certification of the organization's financial statements faces up to 10–20 years of imprisonment, and $1–5 million, with larger amounts for "willful" violations [11].

3.1.4 Gramm–Leach–Bliley Act (GLB), 1999

This act, also known as the Financial Services Modernization Act, applies to consumer financial transactions. It protects personal financial information, but also allows banks, securities and insurance companies to merge, to allow one-stop-shopping for financial needs [3].

Applicability GLB applies to organizations that significantly engage in financial products or services, including mortgage brokering, credit counseling, property appraisals, tax preparation, credit reporting, and ATM operations with customer knowledge [15].

General Requirements There are three components to this regulation [3]. The *Privacy Rule* requires that financial institutions communicate a Notice of Privacy Practices (NPP) to its customers, at first transaction and annually thereafter. This NPP should describe how the organization protects Nonpublic Personal Information (NPI), which includes name, address, and phone numbers when associated with financial data, social security number, financial account numbers, credit card numbers, date of birth, customer relationship information, and details of financial transactions. However, financial companies may share credit reports and credit applications with third parties, unless a customer specifically 'opts out' of this disclosure type [3].

The *Pretexting Rule* outlaws the use of counterfeit documents and social engineering to obtain customer information. It also requires that organizations include security awareness training for employees. Employees should be trained to recognize and report social engineering attempts.

The *Safeguards Rule* requires financial institutions develop an information security program that describes the administrative, technical, and physical controls used to protect personal financial information [3]. This program must include one or more designated employee(s) to coordinate security, a risk assessment program, control over contractors, periodic review of policies, employee training and other personnel security, physical security, data and network security, intrusion detection, and an incident response program [15].

The major problem with GLB was that it applied only to financial institutions, and not to the myriad of retailers that provide credit. Thus, its scope was too limited.

3.1.5 Identity Theft Red Flags Rule, 2007

A follow-up regulation to GLB, the Identity Theft Red Flags Rule, was passed in 2007 to further minimize identity theft [3].

Applicability The Red Flags Rule applies to any 'creditor', including those who provide credit card accounts, utility accounts, cell phone accounts, and retailers who provide financing. The term 'creditor' is a fairly lengthy definition, which (1) applies to those organizations that provide credit or defer payment or bill customers for products and services, and (2) provides funds for repayment, and/or uses credit reports, and/or provides information to credit reporting agencies about consumer credit.

General Requirements These organizations must provide a written 'Identity Theft Prevention Program', which addresses for their company how Red Flags should be detected and handled by their employees. Agencies regulating this rule established five categories and 26 examples of red flag situations (as outlined in Chap. 2, Fraud). The program should include the list of red flags that apply to the organization, as well as how these red flags shall be detected and handled. Employees shall be trained for Red Flags, and contractual agreements must be specified with service providers. The program shall be reviewed periodically, and approved by the organization's board of directors [3].

The size and complexity of the plan should be commensurate with the organization size. The organization needs to protect 'covered accounts', which includes consumer accounts that involve multiple transactions, or other accounts where the risk of identity theft is 'reasonably foreseeable', such as Internet or telephone accounts, or where there is a history of identity theft [16].

The government may exact civil fines up to $2,500, for violations of the Red Flags Rule [16].

3.1.6 Family Educational Rights and Privacy Act (FERPA), 1974, and Other Child Protection Laws

FERPA protects personally identifiable information (PII) such as name, social security number, and student number [3]. Although not listed as PII, grades are also protected (with some allowances). Students and their guardians at public institutions shall be able to view their records, request corrections to their records, and receive a disclosure notification annually, which tells students of their FERPA rights. Qualifying for these permissions are parents of students younger than 18, students 18 or over, and students attending a school of higher education [17]. Schools may disclose some defined directory information for students, but must enable students to opt out. Information that is not protected by FERPA privacy, includes police records, student majors, grade level, honors and awards, dates of attendance, status (full/part-time), participation in officially sponsored sports or clubs [17]. If a school is found to be in violation of FERPA, e.g., because of repeat offenses, they can lose federal funding.

Other child-related regulations include COPPA and CIPA [3].

3.1.6.1 Children's Online Privacy Protection Act (COPPA), 1998

COPPA protects children's privacy on the Internet, including their name, contact information, images and identifiers, such as social security number, geolocation and IP address [3]. Children may be distinguished from adults by asking for their age or birthdate, or charging a fee via credit card. The law requires parental consent before collecting personal information for children under 13 years. This parental consent may be collected via credit card, toll-free numbers, signed forms, video conference, or a government-issued identification. The website must also widely advertise a Privacy Policy indicating how data is collected, used, disseminated, and how this data can be purged or modified. The FTC has collected $3 million, $800,000 and $250,000 from three organizations violating COPPA.

3.1.6.2 Children's Internet Protection Act (CIPA), 2000

Schools and libraries receiving federal funding must filter web content for children under 17 years [3]. Websites to be filtered include pornography, obscene materials, and materials deemed harmful to minors. Filters can be disabled for adults. An Internet Safety Policy must be available to all users. It shall describe appropriate access and restrictions for minors.

3.1.7 Federal Information Security Management Act (FISMA), 2002

The E-Government Act of 2002 was designed to protect government information for the purpose of economic and national security interests, in the wake of September 11, 2001 terrorist attacks. The E-Government Act's Title III is entitled Federal Information Security Management Act (FISMA). It replaced the less comprehensive Computer Security Act (CSA) of 1987. Both the CSA and FISMA authorized the National Institute for Standards and Technology (NIST) to develop minimum standards. FISMA must be adhered to by federal agencies, their contractors, and other entities whose systems interconnect with U.S. government information systems. FISMA also set in place the US-CERT, which is a national incident response center. This regulation is important, since Federal Chief Information Officer Kundra said in 2010 that government computers are attacked millions of times each day [3].

FISMA adherents must comply with NIST standards, called Federal Information Processing Standards (FIPS). An overview of security requirements is provided in NIST 800-53, *Recommended Security Controls for Federal Information Systems.* This document describes requirements for high, moderate and low impact (or not applicable) information systems. The security category (SC) for each system depends on each information system's highest rating assigned for either confidentiality, integrity, and/or availability. An example category would be [18]:

SC sensor data = {(**confidentiality**, NA), (**integrity**, MODERATE), (**availability**, HIGH)}

The low, moderate and high rating refer to whether the security aspect has a limited, serious or severe/catastrophic impact respectively, on the organization's operations, assets or persons.

The areas that NIST 800-53 addresses include [19]:

(i) Access control: Access to government information is limited to authorized users, processes and devices.
(ii) Awareness and training: All staff are trained to perform security functions as needed to adhere to law and retain secure systems.
(iii) Audit and accountability: System logs are retained to enable investigation into wrongdoing, including tracking individual user actions.
(iv) Certification, accreditation, and security assessments: Organizations are periodically audited and must continuously monitor for the effectiveness of security controls.
(v) Configuration management: Organizations must maintain an inventory and library system for baseline and evolving information (including documentation, software, hardware).
(vi) Contingency planning: Business continuity planning prepares agencies to minimize the impact of availability-related emergency situations.
(vii) Identification and authentication: Access to government computers is provided only to properly authorized users, devices or processes.
(viii) Incident response: Organizations must prepare or plan to appropriately handle security-related incidents, and document and report on these incidents when they occur.
(ix) Maintenance: Information systems shall be properly maintained, and the personnel, tools, techniques and mechanisms, which perform the maintenance, shall be effectively controlled.
(x) Media protection: Paper and computerized data must be securely handled and destroyed.
(xi) Physical and environmental protection: Information systems shall be protected from environmental hazards and physical access by unauthorized persons, and shall be maintained in an environment conducive to proper operation.
(xii) Planning: Organizations shall develop and maintain security plans that describe the security controls, including proper use of computer systems by users.
(xiii) Personnel security: Organizations ensure that personnel and contractors with access to information systems are trustworthy and comply with regulations; that access is revoked when such personnel is terminated; and that sanctions are applied for misuse.
(xiv) Risk assessment: Periodic risk assessment considers risk affecting the agency's mission, functions, image, and reputation, and impacting information assets, operations, and individuals.
(xv) Systems and services acquisition: In-house and outsourced software development shall follow a lifecycle that addresses security, and includes a restricted installation and use of data.
(xvi) System and communications protection: System protection includes methods of software development and system engineering that addresses security;

communications protection includes protecting transmissions at external and key internal boundaries.

(xvii) System and information integrity: Information technology shall protect against malware, monitor alerts, and correct errors in information in a timely manner.

The NIST Federal Information Processing Standards and Special Publications (guidelines) are freely available for access and provide an excellent foundation for any security solution.

3.2 Security Industry Standards

If an organization wants to be in a particular business, some industries require adherence to a standard. Credit card companies require this of organizations accepting payment by credit cards. Emerging standards are expected to apply for defense contracts. Some standards indicate a quality implementation.

Standards have been developed to certify IT and/or security products. The *Common Criteria* (CC) has certified access control devices, biometric devices, databases, smart card systems, key management systems and more [20], and is now the international standard ISO/IEC 15408. CC was developed as an international standard, which includes a number of member countries. Some nations in Europe, for example, use CC to certify devices as privacy-compliant. CC replaces the Rainbow Series (including the Orange Book or Red Book) in American government contracts.

Open Group is another international consortium with mainly industry members. Open Group is vendor and technology-neutral in its aspiration to achieve global interoperability in a secure, reliable and timely manner. It define standards for software architectures, such as enterprise architecture, service oriented architecture, real-time/embedded, UNIX, cloud and trusted technologies. Governments and secure-minded businesses rely on their supply chain vendor standard, entitled Open Group's Trusted Technology Provider standard [21].

3.2.1 Payment Card Industry Data Security Standard (PCI DSS)

Payment Card Industry Data Security Standard (PCI DSS) is an industry standard to establish security for payment card use by merchants and service providers.

Who standard applies to All vendors who accept payment cards associated with Visa, MasterCard, American Express, Discover, and JCB International must adhere to this standard [22]. The initial standard was released in 2004, but refined and clarified in later versions. Version 3.0 is currently applicable as of December 31, 2014.

Table 3.2 PCI DSS requirements

Security areas	General goals	Chapter in text
Build and maintain a secure network	1. Install and maintain a firewall configuration to protect cardholder data	Network security
	2. Do not use vendor-supplied defaults for system passwords and other security parameters	Information security
Protect cardholder data	3. Protect stored data	Physical security, information security
	4. Encrypt transmission of cardholder data across open, public networks	Network security
Maintain a vulnerability management program	5. Use and regularly update anti-virus software or programs	Policy, network security
	6. Develop and maintain secure systems and applications	Secure software (if software development is part of organization)
Implement strong access control measures	7. Restrict access to cardholder data by business need-to-know	Information security
	8. Assign a unique ID to each person with computer access	Information security Security Awareness
	9. Restrict physical access to cardholder data	Physical security
Regularly monitor and test networks	10. Track and monitor all access to network resources and cardholder data	Network security
	11. Regularly test security systems and processes	Audit (internal) and use of external qualified assessors
Maintain an information security policy	12. Maintain a policy that addresses information security for all personnel	Information security, personnel security, risk management, policy, business continuity, incident response

Note that Nevada and Minnesota have state laws requiring compliance with all or parts of PCI DSS [3].

General requirements PCI DSS has twelve general goals, as listed in Table 3.2 [23]. This table maps these requirements to chapters in this book. Each general goal has specific requirements that vary in detail depending on the sophistication of the merchant or service provider. These requirements sometimes require a technological understanding beyond the scope provided by this text, including in areas of network security. However, this book does provide a high-level view, enabling the reader to do basic security design and discuss security technology with a specialist. This preliminary work will assist a Qualified Security Assessor in ensuring that the organization is fully compliant with PCI DSS.

PCI DSS includes 4+ levels of sophistication, which depends on how an organization uses payment cards. For example, Class C organizations transmit payment card information over the Internet but do not store payment card information, while Class D organizations also store payment card information [24]. Hotels are example Class D organizations. The higher risk of storing card information demands a higher level of security: the SAQ C consists of 41 questions, while SAQ D contains 231 questions. Payment card brands may personalize their requirements by deviating from the standard as they so need.

There are three levels of auditors to ensure compliance: an Approved Scanning Vendor (ASV) who is authorized to perform quarterly external vulnerability scans; a Qualified Security Assessor, who can perform annual on-site audits; and an Internal Security Assessor (ISV), who can complete a Merchant's Attestation of Compliance (AOC). Even smaller organizations submit an AOC annually. An audit results in a detailed Report on Compliance (ROC) [23]. The summarized AOC requires that the auditor certify that the merchant is compliant with the 12 PCI DSS requirements, has successfully passed quarterly penetration scans, and uses appropriate payment card equipment [25]. Finally, the AOC is signed by both a qualified QSA and an executive (e.g., merchant) officer, and all documents—scans, ROC, and AOC—are submitted to the acquirer or payment brand [23].

If an organization is found non-compliant, their penalty can include fines, suspension from processing payment card transactions, and bad publicity. Costs may include bank fines, card brand fines, forensic investigation costs, and consumer card replacement costs [26]. Visa may impose a fine per breach incident of $50,000 if the organization was not PCI DSS compliant, and/or $100,000 if Visa is not immediately told of the breach [3]. Breached organizations are fined lesser amounts if they can prove they were fully PCI DSS compliant when the breach occurred. However, companies have reported paying $1–40 million in total fines to recover costs of fraudulent sales.

PCI has two additional standards [22]. The Payment Application Data Security Standard (PA-DSS) ensures that the development of system and application software handling payment cards is secure to an equally high level. PCI's PIN Transaction Security Devices (PTS) is a standard for manufacturers of PIN-handling devices, including point-of-sale machines. In the PCI DSS Attestation of Compliance, merchants are to list their payment card equipment, with versions, which is verified to be PA-DSS compliant.

3.3 Computer Abuse Laws

These laws are meant to protect organizations from attackers. A person can be charged with a misdemeanor or more serious felony crime. Misdemeanor crimes are generally punishable *for* less than 1 year in prison, while felony convictions earn 1 year or more [3]. Both convictions can also result in fines.

The Computer Fraud and Abuse Act (CFAA), 1984 Protects against traditional cracking. The USA Patriot Act of 2001 amended the CFAA by lowering damage thresholds and increasing penalties. The current CFAA protects against trespassing on a Government, financial institution or other 'protected' computer, which is any computer that participates in interstate or foreign commerce or communications [27]. Misdemeanor crimes include negligent damage, trafficking in passwords, and unauthorized access or access in excess of authorization. Felony crimes include

$5,000 damage or a threat to public safety, justice, national security, or physical injury, or if the crime includes fraud, extortion, recklessness or criminal intent [3]. Transmission of malware becomes a felony when it causes $5,000 damage; convictions result in fines and/or 10 years in prison.

Electronic Communication Privacy Act (ECPA), 1986 Disallows eavesdropping of network (felony) and stored data (misdemeanor). The USA PATRIOT Act of 2001 amended ECPA by allowing the government to intercept electronic communications for national security reasons, by requiring a low level of justification [3]. It also enables service providers to request help from law enforcement or government agencies to capture communications of intruders. Finally, it enables service providers to release communications to law enforcement if they suspect crimes or danger to life. Any such freely provided communications, obtained without warrant, may then be used as evidence in court.

Other laws addressing specific areas related to security but outside the scope of this text include [3, 27]:

Child Protection and Obscenity Enforcement Act, 1988 Prohibits known possession of any printed, video, or digital file containing child pornography, which is transported across state lines.

Identity Theft and Assumption Deterrence Act, 1998 Identity theft protects the transfer and use of personally identifiable information. Violations can result in fines and 15–30 years in prison.

Anti-Cybersquatting Consumer Protection Act, 1999 Entities may sue cybersquatters, who acquire a domain name which is a registered trademark or trade name for another organization.

Controlling the Assault of Non-Solicited Pornography and Marketing, 2003 Commercial e-mailers must follow specific requirements, such as using clear subject lines and accurate headers and describing how the recipient can opt out of future emails.

International Traffic in Arms Regulations (ITAR), Export Administration Regulations (EAR) and Regulations from the Office of Foreign Asset Control (OFAC) These laws prohibit export of certain technologies and information overseas, without a license (if export is allowed at all).

Patent Act, 1952; Trademark Act, 1946; Copyright Act, 1976; Digital Millennium Copyright Act, 1998; Economic Espionage Act, 1996, 2012 These all deal with patents, copyright and trademarks.

3.4 Final Considerations

In the United States, Obama issued an Executive Order requesting that the government share with industry its knowledge of cyber-security attacks and prevention [6]. NIST is developing a best practices framework on cyber-security that is voluntary. If your organization adheres to the law and these policies and a data breach occurs, your organization will be relatively safe. Very little cyber-security case law currently exists, but is bound to be developed with time.

Many competing organizations in the same industry do meet to collaborate on security defense. They share known attacks in order to better defend their proprietary information against cyber-crime and state-sponsored spying. While this may be a good idea, it is important to discuss with legal counsel how this can be established and executed while avoiding charges of anti-competitive behavior.

3.5 Advanced: Understanding the Context of Law

Because information security incidents often involve criminals, this book discusses security regulation in a few Advanced sections of the book. In this chapter, understanding the types and jurisdictions of law is useful if you ever consider going to court.

Three sources of law in the United States include [3]:

Criminal Law The prosecution of parties charged with crimes against public order, as specified in the federal and state criminal codes. The evidence must show "beyond a reasonable doubt" that the defendant is guilty. This means that there can be no reasonable doubt in the mind of a reasonable judge or juror, but not that they are 100 % sure.

Civil Law A person, organization or government who has been harmed can ask for redress from the party who inflicted harm. These cases can be based on regulation or common law. Common law follows the general principles and body of traditional or precedent judicial cases that the United States inherited from England. To decide a case, there must be a "preponderance of the evidence", which assumes that it is more probable than not (>50 %) that the wrong action occurred. Some civil cases require a higher "clear and convincing evidence" to convince the court that the wrong action was likely to occur.

Administrative Rules Federal and state governments can delegate responsibility to agencies to create and enforce rules and/or judge cases. There must be a process to ensure fairness. Cases may be reviewed by a federal court. The preponderance of evidence must be at the lowest "not arbitrary or capricious" level, which means that the facts of the case should reasonable correspond to the administrative decision. One such agency making decisions in the security realm is the Federal Trade Commission (FTC). The Federal Trade Commission Act gives the FTC permission to define specific rules for "acts or practices which are unfair or deceptive acts or practices in or affecting commerce" and also sanction violators.

Five different levels of regulation, ordered from highest and most powerful to the less powerful are described below. Lower levels of regulation must conform to all higher levels. They include [3]:

1. *U.S. Constitution:* Defines the structure of the federal government and its relationship with the states. It also includes the bill of rights, outlining personal freedoms.

2. *Federal Laws:* These laws passed by Congress are maintained in the U.S. Code. The constitution allows Congress to regulate commerce between the states, as well as to declare war, print money, and maintain the post office and armed forces.

   Federal District Courts can hear cases relating to the constitution or federal laws, and cases between residents of different states summing to losses over $75,000. The Circuit Court of Appeals and Supreme Courts handle appeals of federal cases. The Supreme Court can also hear cases between different state governments and perform judicial reviews when state or federal laws may violate the Constitution.
3. *State Constitution:* Describes the structure of the state government and relationship between the state and its citizens. It defines an additional set of personal rights on a state-by-state basis.
4. *State Laws:* State governments may pass laws affecting state residents.

   State courts generally include a Trial Court, State Court of Appeal and State Supreme Court. State courts may address cases of state or federal law, but must always apply the hierarchy of laws and consider Supreme Court decisions as precedent. With the long reach of the Internet, crimes may be instigated from outside the state, but can be prosecuted within the state if the crime occurred within state boundaries.
5. *Common Law:* Case tradition provides precedent when regulations do not explicitly address a situation.

   The Internet not only spans states, it also spans nations. This causes additional jurisdiction problems when crimes occur across borders. To counter such crimes and promote cooperation in investigations and prosecution, 53 nations signed a Convention on Cybercrime [3]. This agreement requires members to prohibit certain cyber-crimes and copyright infringement. Forty-two nations, including the U.S., have ratified the treaty.

3.6 Questions and Problems

1. *Vocabulary*. Match each regulation or standard with its applicable area of coverage.

HIPAA	FISMA	Sarbanes–Oxley	State breach notification
FERPA	PCI DSS	Gramm–Leach–Bliley	Identity theft red flags rule

   a) Addresses the privacy and security of health information.
   b) Standard required by payment card companies, to ensure security of payment card information, through audits and network scans.
   c) Addresses privacy of identity information, including social security numbers, financial information, state/driver's license information, and possibly other information.
   d) Secures student information.
   e) Secures information within federal government agencies.

f) Addresses financial statement fraud in corporations.
g) Addresses privacy and security of financial information, including ensuring employees recognize and report social engineering attempts.
h) Organizations reporting or providing credit or credit information must protect customers from social engineering scams.

2. *Evidence Requirements*. Match the type of evidence required with each type of case: administrative, civil, criminal. Then number each evidence level according to the level of certainty required by the jurors to convict, with the most certain as your number 1 selection.

   a) Clear and convincing evidence
   b) Not arbitrary or capricious
   c) Preponderance of the evidence
   d) Beyond a reasonable doubt

3. *Broken Laws Case*. A criminal cyber team sends a phishing email with a white-paper link to a banker at First National Bank. The banker follows the link to the infected web site and unknowingly downloads spyware and a rootkit. The spyware monitors login-password credentials into the company database containing customer information. The criminal team exfiltrates customer financial information, but an Intrusion Prevention System recognizes the data transmission and halts it midway. The security team investigates to find the malware, spending hours with logs, investigating computer work stations, and monitoring transmissions. What laws were broken? What could the criminal team be charged with, if they could be pinned down?
4. *Industry-Specific Regulation and Standards*. For your selected industry/major/specialty, list which regulations and standards your industry definitely and may need to adhere to. Example industries you may select from include: health, manufacturing, finance, retail, entertainment, education, hotel, computer manufacturing, software development, or others. How would this law apply to your industry and why?
5. *Non-IT Aspects of Regulation and Standards*. Consider one of the following American security regulations or standards: HIPAA, Gramm–Leach–Bliley, Sarbanes–Oxley, PCI DSS, or FISMA. What non-IT requirements do they impose that would not be addressed by this text? Some websites provide government- or standards-based information, and thus are authentic sources of information. Consider the sites listed below. If specific links do not work, search the main site using the name of the regulation.

   Note to instructor: Providing some of the documentation within the course's Intranet may be helpful.

   a) HIPAA/HITECH: Chap. 15 of this text or www.hhs.gov (Health and Human Services) and search for HIPAA.
   b) Gramm–Leach–Bliley and Red Flags Rule: Federal Trade Commission: http://www.business.ftc.gov/privacy-and-security

c) Sarbanes–Oxley: www.isaca.org (Organizations for standards/security) Your instructor may provide *'Information Security Student Book: Using COBIT®5 for Information Security'*, available at www.isaca.org. Additional information is at www.sans.org, search for 'COBIT'.
d) PCI DSS: Access information from https://www.pcisecuritystandards.org/security_standards/. Select the PCI DSS link. Register and download 'PCI DSS v3.0'. Skim the Requirements, starting on page 19.
e) FISMA: www.nist.gov (National Institute for Standards and Technology) and search for FISMA. Specific link: http://www.nist.gov/itl/csd/soi/fisma.cfm. Access FIPS Publication 200 first.

References

1. Perlroth N (2014) Online security experts link more breaches to Russian government. New York Times, 28 October 2014
2. Johnson J, Lincke SJ, Imhof R, Lim C (2014) A comparison of international information security regulation. Interdisciplin J Inf Know Manag, Informing Science Institute, 9:89–116
3. Grama JL (2015) Legal issues in information security, 2nd edn. Jones & Bartlett Learning, Burlington, MA, USA, pp. 38–48, 68–270, 350–383
4. Connors TJ (2010) States add more criteria to breach notification laws. Manag Healthc Exec 20(11):10
5. National Conference of State Legislatures (2014) State security breach notification laws. http://www.ncsl.org/issues-research/telecom/security-breach-notification-laws.aspx. Accessed 14 Aug 2013
6. Thompson L (2013) Privacy: the tidal waves of the future. In: ISACA chapter meeting, Rosemont IL, 13 December 2013
7. Kempfert AE, Reed BD (2011) Health care reform in the United States: HITECH act and HIPAA privacy, security, and enforcement issues. FDCC Q, Spring 2011, 61:240–273
8. Dalgleish C (2009) Course: HIPAA compliance. Triton College, River Grove, IL, USA
9. Dowell MA (2012) HIPAA privacy and security HITECH act enforcement actions begin. Employee Benefit Plan Rev, June 2012, 9–11
10. Hoggins-Blake R (2009) Dissertation: examining non-profit post-secondary institutions' voluntary compliance with the Sarbanes–Oxley Act. ProQuest Dissertations and Theses, January 2009, pp 1–51
11. Yallapragada RR, Roe CW, Toma AG (2010) Sarbanes–Oxley Act of 2002 and non-profit organizations. J Bus Econ Res 8(2):89–93
12. Narain LS (2009) Implications of the Sarbanes–Oxley Act for nonprofit organizations. Bus Rev (Camb) 13(2):16–22
13. Ramos MJ (2008) How to comply with Sarbanes–Oxley section 404: assessing the effectiveness of internal control. Wiley, Hoboken, NJ, USA, pp 1–23, 228–229
14. ISACA (2012) COBIT 5: enabling processes. ISACA, Arlington Heights, IL
15. Federal Trade Commission (2006) Financial institutions and customer information: complying with the safeguards rule. http://www.business.ftc.gov/documents/bus54-financial-institutions-and-customer-information-complying-safeguards-rule. Accessed 15 Nov 2013
16. FTC (2013) Fighting identity theft with the red flags rule: a how-to guide for business. Federal trade commission. http://business.ftc.gov/documents/bus23-fighting-identity-theft-red-flags-rule-how-guide-business. Accessed 15 May 2013
17. Carlson CS (2012) Navigate the FERPA nuisance. Quill 100(2):31
18. NIST (2004) Standards for security categorization of federal information and information systems. FIPS Pub 199. National Institute of Standards and Technology, February 2004

19. NIST (2006) Minimum security requirements for federal information and information systems. FIPS Pub. 200. National Institute of Standards and Technology, March 2006
20. Common Criteria (2012) Common criteria for information technology security evaluation: part 1: introduction and general model, vers 3.1, rev 4, September 2012
21. Open Group (2014) The open group. http://opengroup.org. Accessed 26 Dec 2014
22. Payment Card Industry (2013) Payment card industry security standards: PCISSC-OverviewOfStandards.pdf. http://www.pcisecuritystandards.org. Accessed 15 June 2013
23. PCI Security Standards Council (2013) Requirements and security assessment procedures, v 3.0. www.pcisecuritystandards.org. Accessed 15 Nov 2013
24. Payment Card Industry (2013) Getting started with PCI data security standard: PCISSC-GettingStartedwithPCIDSS.pdf. http://www.pcisecuritystandards.org. Accessed 15 June 2013
25. Payment Card Industry (2010) Attestation of compliance for onsite assessments – merchants, ver 2.0, October 2010. http://www.pcisecuritystandards.org
26. Gorge M (2010) PCI DSS for small merchants. SC magazine, October 2010, p 50. www.scmagazineus.com
27. Bragg R, Rohodes-Ousley M, Stasberg K (2004) Network security: the complete reference. McGraw-Hill/Osborne, New York, NY, pp 762–768

Part II
Strategic Security Planning

Strategic planning defines the direction of security based on business needs. This level is normally decided by the highest levels of executive management, because it establishes high level policies and considers long-term decisions. Management input is critical in all security planning exercises, since business management provide the foundational requirements, while technical security staff provide the technological skills.

While this part discusses high-level decisions, the next part on Tactical Security Planning provides the security details. Some people are detail-oriented, and may be more comfortable starting with the next part first. Other people like a big picture view first, before proceeding to details. Our experience in using this material is that certain chapters can be performed in the order that is optimal for your organization or class, as long as you adhere to the warnings provided at the beginning of each chapter and section.

In this strategic planning section, the three chapters can be performed in any order.

- *Chapter* 4 *Managing Risk*: Define the assets and threats to an organization, and perform a cost–benefit analysis for security controls.
- *Chapter* 5 *Addressing Business Impact Analysis and Business Continuity*: Define which information technology functions are critical to your organization, including how long you can survive without IT functionality and with possible loss of data.
- *Chapter* 6 *Governing: Policy, Maturity Models and Planning*: Define the security policies for the organization. Discuss security administration.

Chapter 6 Governing' is a chapter where management decides the high level policies for the organization. For organizations with a lot of security knowledge, Chap. 6 can be defined first. However, organizations that lack security expertise should complete it when they feel very comfortable with security—potentially after completing important chapters in the Tactical Planning section.

Chapter 4
Managing Risk

> Independent groups of hacktivists have been able to break into sites controlled by the FBI, CIA, the U.S. Senate, the Pentagon, the International Monetary Fund, the official website of the Vatican, Interpol, 10 Downing Street in London, the British Ministry of Justice, and NASA (even breaking into the software of the space station while it was orbiting the Earth). (Al Gore, *The Future*, p. 73 [1])

The field of security—and American regulation—realizes that not all organizations need the same level or type of security. Banks need more security than the average small not-for-profit. The idea of risk analysis is to determine where the gold is in your organization, and to design the appropriate security to protect your assets—both informational and physical assets. The three pillars of security are confidentiality, integrity and availability. For risk analysis, we should evaluate for each important asset: must it remain confidential, with integrity, and/or available? Google might be most concerned with availability, while the Social Security Administration might be most concerned with confidentiality and integrity. A pharmacy should be concerned with confidentiality, integrity, and availability. We will consider appropriate controls with these issues in mind.

Security implementations do vary among organizations. External factors affecting the level of security include the industry (e.g., defense) and regulation. Internal factors include culture, organization maturity and history, and risk appetite. *Risk appetite* or *risk tolerance* measures the level or risk aversion that executive management is concerned with. To quickly measure your risk appetite, does your computer run antivirus software? You should, but if not, that might indicate a high risk appetite.

Security is a balancing act between security costs and losses. Security controls can get expensive, since they may include: firewalls, intrusion prevention systems, guards, biometrics, virtual private networks, encrypted storage and transmission, security card readers, policies and procedures, audits and control testing, etc. But costs can also get expensive: hacker attacks, internal fraud, loss of confidentiality, stolen data, loss of reputation, loss of business, penalties, legal liability, theft, and more.

S. Lincke, *Security Planning*, DOI 10.1007/978-3-319-16027-6_4

There are two difficulties in performing risk analysis. The first difficulty is that we do not always know the likelihood of a threat arising. For example, hackers may have infiltrated all of our computer systems, but we have no tool for detecting intruders and are not aware. We think the likelihood of a hacker attack is 0 %, based on past experience, while it is actually 100 %! A second issue is that some costs associated with security attacks, such as reputation, may be intangible and difficult to estimate. These two issues make security risk analysis difficult to perform.

Another difficulty with risk analysis is that its goal is to ensure that the organization does not spend more on security than it would lose if security threats occur. What if your risk analysis helps you to protect your organization, but does not protect your customers or shareholders, who get robbed in the process? Their losses might impact your reputation and may result in lawsuits. For optimistic management with a large risk appetite, this might unduly place customers at risk. From an ethical viewpoint, risk analysis is inherently self-serving, but should protect all involved. We will see a specific example of this in the case to come.

Fortunately, regulation serves to protect customers, shareholders, and the community. The large fines we saw levied in Chap. 3 on regulation also serve to make security costs tangible and measurable. Thus, it makes sense to understand the regulation your organization must adhere to, including all fines and jail time imposed upon no compliance, and factor that in to your risk analysis process. In court cases, judges require that an organization has taken *due care* with risk management: the organization can justify their risk profile and has taken seriously their implementation of security controls.

In Europe, India, and other nations, the law insists on a full security implementation based on security standards, such as ISO 27001.

4.1 Risk Management Overview

Risk management includes all stages of managing risk, as shown in Fig. 4.1.

The first stage, Establish Scope and Boundaries, considers which aspects will be covered as part of your risk management process. Will you consider subsidiaries, national and/or international offices, factory, sales, and/or administration…?

Risk assessment analyzes the risks the organization is likely to face [2]. During the Identification Stage, we define the important assets to secure. During the Risk Analysis Stage, we determine the likelihood and impact of threats occurring, to estimate a cost of each risk. During the Evaluation Stage, we consider security controls to counter or reduce the impact of each risk.

Risk treatment implements controls to reduce risks to acceptable levels. We can eliminate risky behavior, and thus *avoid* risk altogether; implement some controls to reduce the impact or *mitigate* risk; purchase insurance against risk and thus *transfer* financial responsibility of risk; or simply accept or *retain* the risk. *Residual risk* is the risk that remains after our control and avoidance implementations.

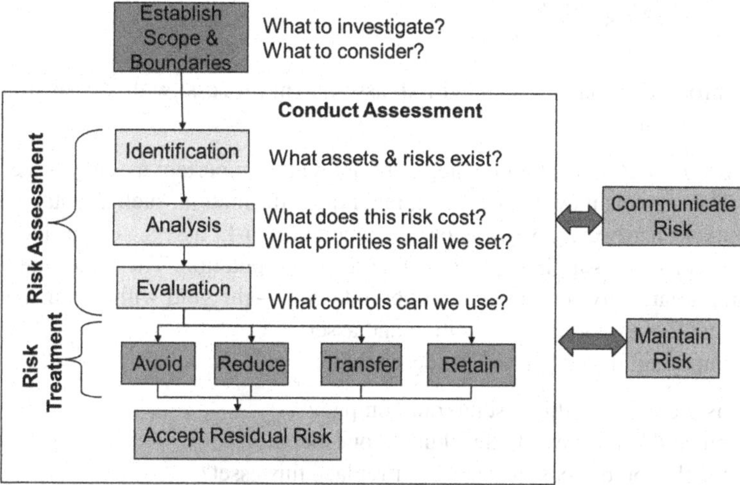

Fig. 4.1 Stages of risk management

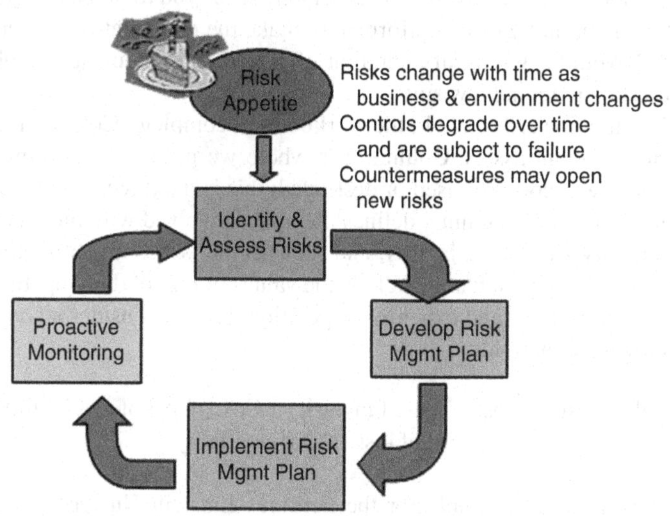

Fig. 4.2 Continuous risk management process (adapted from Exhibit 2.3, CISM® Review Manual 2012 ©2011 ISACA. All rights reserved. Used by permission) [2]

After performing risk analysis and treatment, we monitor risk and communicate our performance to management. Figure 4.2 shows the *security lifecycle*, which is also known as the continuous risk management process [2]. Since risk is about predicting futures (and dealing in uncertainty) then hindsight has perfect vision. As we monitor actual results, and as the business environment changes, we refine our risk understanding, strategy and implementation. With good metrics, we can re-evaluate risk based on updated knowledge.

4.1.1 Assessing Risk

We now proceed through a detailed risk assessment process, with a case study of Einstein University.

Step 1: Identify Risks The first step is to define the important assets you need to protect. These assets may be IT-related, including information, such as databases or documents; or hardware, software, or personnel; or non-IT assets, such as building, equipment, product, supplies, personnel, cash, and reputation. The important thing is to differentiate between the most important assets—the gold within your organization—and less important information and assets.

Four important questions to consider include:

- What is the value of this asset to our company?
- How much does this asset contribute to our income?
- How much would it cost to recover or replace this asset?
- How much might we be liable for, if this asset were compromised?

Each of these questions should be asked relative to confidentiality, integrity and availability. Is the availability of this asset important for you to do business? Would a breach of confidentiality of this information make the organization susceptible to privacy laws? Would a wrongful alteration of information (causing a problem of integrity) lead to a potential law suit?

Table 4.1 is the first risk table in the workbook to complete. Column 1 is where you list your important assets. Column 2 is where we put the direct replacement value if the asset was compromised or destroyed: this is the direct cost for a loss or replacement of an asset. Column 4 defines the issues involved with the asset: confidentiality, integrity and/or availability, and the specific issues involved. Column 3 can then be completed, which may include the values of loss of daily operation, law suit costs, regulatory fines and expenses, reputation, etc. To consider all costs, consider the following equation:

$$\begin{aligned} \text{TangibleCosts} &= \text{Cost of loss of integrity} + \text{Cost of loss of availability} \\ &\quad + \text{Cost of loss of confidentiality} \end{aligned} \tag{4.1}$$

Table 4.1 is a partial example for the fictitious Einstein University, and is an outrageous example of how ethics can lack in the traditional risk management model. The three assets shown are students, instructors, and registration and grades databases. The direct loss value for a student is loss of tuition, and for an instructor is the cost to hire a temporary instructor (although there may be salary savings). Any reader of this book is or has been a student; do you agree you are (or were) only worth this measly amount? A later section in this chapter will address the ethics of risk, including this issue. Until then, further analysis of this case will focus only on the information security aspect, which is the topic of this book.

Table 4.1's Consequential Financial Loss (column 3) is the most complex column to complete. Table 4.2 helps in its understanding, by providing notes and special calculations for any complex consequential financial losses. Both tables are provided in the Security Workbook.

Table 4.1 Identify risk stage

Asset name	$ Value Direct loss: replacement	$ Value Consequential financial loss	Confidentiality, integrity, and availability notes
Student(s) and/ or Instructor(s)	$2,000 per student (tuition) $8,000 per instructor (for replacement)	Lawsuit= $1 Million Investigation costs= $100,000 Reputation= $400,000	(E.g.,) School Shooting: Availability (of persons lives) Issues may arise if we should have removed a potentially harmful student, or did not act fast enough.
Registration Server	$10,000	Breach Not. Law=$520,000 Registration loss per day =$16,000 Forensic help = $100,000	Affects: Confidentiality, Availability. Conf=> Breach Notification Law =>Possible FERPA Violation =>Forensic Help Availability=> Loss of Registrations
Grades Server	$10,000	Lawsuit = $1 million FERPA = $1 million Forensic help = $100,000	Affects: Confidentiality, Integrity. Integrity => Student Lawsuit Confidentiality => FERPA violation Both => Forensic help
Point of Sale Devices	$4,000 per unit	Payment card fines=$1+ million	Affects: Confidentiality, Integrity Affects: registration, cafeteria. Online sales handled by qualified service provider.

Table 4.2 Consequential financial loss calculations

Consequential financial loss	Total loss	Calculations or notes
Lost business for one day (1D)	1D=$16,000	Registration = $0-500,000 per day in income (avg. $16,000)
Breach not. law	$752,000	Breach Not. Law Mailings= $188 x 4000 Students = $752,000
Lawsuit	$1 Million	Student lawsuit may result as a liability.
Forensic Help	$100,000	Professional forensic/security help will be necessary to investigate extent of attack and rid system of hacker
FERPA	$1 Million	Violation of FERPA regulation can lead to loss of government aid, assumes negligence.
Payment card breach	$1-40 M	Visa costs: $50,000 if the organization was not PCI DSS compliant; $100,000 if Visa not immediately told of the breach. Total costs to repay fraud losses reported between $1-40 Million.

Annual security studies provide statistics estimating average security incident costs. Table 4.3 shows an average cost for organizations, as calculated by the Ponemon Institute in 2014 [3]. These numbers range from year to year, but the 2013 statistics are a good average. For example, the average cost per record for a breach

Table 4.3 Statistics from Ponemon Institute's 2014 Cost of Data Breach Study: United States, sponsored by IBM [3]

Category	Breach type	Avg. cost per compromised record
Data breach cost—total	Malicious or criminal attack (44 % of breaches)	$246
	Employee error (31 % of breaches)	$160
	System glitch (25 % of breaches)	$171
	Average	$201
Data breach cost—components	Indirect costs: Internal employee time and abnormal churn of customers	$134
	External expenses: forensic expertise, legal advice, victim identity protection services	$67

Table 4.4 Breach cost by industry, Ponemon Institute's 2014 Cost of Data Breach Study: United States [3]

	Probability of breach (%)	Cost per record	Churn rate
Communications	15.6	219	1.2
Consumer	19.9	196	2.6
Education	21.1	259	2.0
Energy	7.5	237	4.0
Financial	17.1	236	7.1
Health care	19.2	316	5.3
Hospitality	19.5	93	2.9
Industry	9.0	204	3.6
Media	19.7	183	1.9
Pharmaceutical	16.9	209	3.8
Public sector	23.8	172	0.1
Research	11.5	73	0.7
Retail	22.7	125	1.4
Services	19.8	223	4.2
Technology	18.9	181	6.3
Transportation	13.5	286	5.5

over the last 9 years ranged between $138 and 214. A single-calculation estimate of an organization's security liability is the product of the average breach cost per record ($201) times the number of records of protected individual information (PII) the organization processes.

Table 4.4 shows the probability of a data breach for a number of industries, as calculated by Ponemon in 2014. Since these represent a probability of attack, these statistics can be used in risk analysis as a probable likelihood value. Also shown in the table is the average cost in U.S. $ of a breached record by industry, and the churn rate, which is the average percentage of lost customers.

Fig. 4.3 Threats, vulnerabilities, and threat agents

Risk Analysis consists of the next three steps, which include analyzing threats and vulnerabilities; estimating likelihood of exploitation; and computing effective losses.

Step 2: Determine Loss Due to Threats In this step we consider all the probable threats that are likely to occur. These issues will vary, based upon your industry, geographic location, culture and company.

Figure 4.3 helps to explain security vocabulary. A diamond cutter will have diamonds, which are her assets. A *threat* to this industry is theft, but a 'threat' is only a concept; the word 'threat' does not imply that the problematic event has actually occurred. An example of a *vulnerability* might be an unguarded, open door, which increases the possibility of the 'threat' occurring. A *threat agent* in this example is the thief. Risk is the potential danger to assets.

Consider a wide variety of possible threats, threat agents and vulnerabilities. Problems can arise due to any of the following threats [4, 5]:

Physical Threats

- Natural: Flood, fire, cyclones, hail/snow, plagues and earthquakes
- Unintentional: Fire, water, building damage/collapse, loss of utility services and equipment failure
- Intentional: Fire, water, theft and vandalism

Non-physical Threats

- Ethical/Criminal: Fraud, espionage, hacking, identity theft, malicious code, social engineering, vandalism, phishing and denial of service
- External Environmental: industry competition, contract failure, or changes in market, political, regulatory or technology environment

- Internal: management error, IT complexity, poor risk evaluation, organization immaturity, accidental data loss, mistakes, software defects and personnel incompetence.

For the ethical/criminal category (which is the focus of this chapter) possible threat agents include people who perform intentional threats, such as: crackers, criminals, industry spies, insiders (e.g., fraudsters), and terrorists/hacktivists.

Vulnerabilities are the 'open doors' that enable threats to occur. Categories of vulnerabilities include:

- Behavioral: Disgruntled employee, poor security design, improperly configured equipment;
- Misinterpretation: Employee error or incompetence, poor procedural documentation, poor compliance adherence, insufficient staff;
- Poor coding: Incomplete requirements, software defects, inadequate security design;
- Physical vulnerabilities: theft, negligence, extreme weather, no redundancy, violent attack.

Step 3: Estimate Likelihood of Exploitation For each important threat, consider the likelihood (or probability) that the event will occur. Selecting good statistics is a challenge and may come from past experience (yours or others), your best analysis, or (worst case) your best guess. Your experience is a personalized statistic that can be calculated from your metrics and reports. Other's experience may include professional risk assessors (often associated with the insurance industry) and national or international standards or reports, such as that shown in Table 4.4. You may be able to derive reasonable statistics from economic, engineering, or market analysis models, or from experiments. A last resort (but certainly better than no statistic) is your best guess.

Table 4.5 lists recent security statistics, provided by Verizon [6]. These statistics were accumulated from law enforcement, forensic groups, cyber emergency response teams, and service providers worldwide. These statistics evaluate the total set of analyzed attacks, and proportion them out by industry. For example, Accommodation has a rate of 75 % for Point of Sale Intrusion. This means that 75 % of the attacks reported by the Accommodation industry are PoS attacks. Table 4.4 reflects only larger portioned incident types (above 5 %) included in the Verizon report. These statistics can help determine the priority and types of problems that your industry is prone to. These statistics cannot be directly used in risk analysis, since they do not indicate the rate of attack.

While most of the problems are self-explanatory, some need further explanation [6]. Insider Misuse occurs when an employee or trusted party misuses or accesses information or resources beyond their privileges, usually for financial gain, espionage or revenge purposes. The difference between the Payment Card Skimmer and PoS Intrusion attacks is that the first is a physical attack, while the second involves spyware launched via the Internet. The Theft/Loss category includes loss or theft of information assets, with loss occurring 15 times more often as theft.

Table 4.5 Security attacks: excerpts from the Verizon 2014 Data Breach Investigations Report [6]

	40 % or higher	20–39 %	10–19 %	5–10 %
Accommodation	PoS intrusion (75 %)		DoS (10 %)	Insider misuse (8 %)
Administrative	Misc. error (43 %)	Insider misuse (27 %)	Theft/loss (12 %)	Web app attack (8 %)
Construction		Crimeware (33 %)	Insider misuse (13 %) Theft/loss (13 %) Cyber espionage (13 %)	PoS intrusion (7 %) Misc. error (7 %)
Education		Misc. error (20 %)	Web app attack (19 %) Theft/loss (15 %)	Insider misuse (8 %) Crimeware (6 %) DoS (6 %)
Entertainment		DoS (32 %) Web app attack (22 %)	Misc. error (12 %) Insider misuse (10 %)	PoS intrusion (7 %) Theft/loss (7 %)
Finance		Web app attack (27 %) Payment card skimmer (22 %) DoS (26 %)		Insider misuse (7 %) Misc. error (5 %)
Healthcare	Theft/loss (46 %)		Insider misuse (15 %) Misc. error (12 %)	PoS intrusion (9 %)
Information	Web app attack (41 %)	Crimeware (31 %)		DoS (9 %)
Management	DoS (44 %)		Web app attack (11 %) Payment card skimmer (11 %) Cyber espionage (11 %)	Insider misuse (6 %) Theft/loss (6 %) Misc. error (6 %)
Manufacturing		Cyber espionage (30 %) DoS (24 %)	Web app attack (14 %)	Crimeware (9 %) Insider misuse (8 %)
Mining	Cyber-espionage (40 %)	Insider misuse (25 %)	Theft/loss (10 %)	Misc. error (5 %) Crimeware (5 %) Payment card skimmer (5 %) DoS (5 %)

(continued)

Table 4.5 (continued)

	40 % or higher	20–39 %	10–19 %	5–10 %
Professional		DoS (37 %) Cyber espionage (29 %)		Web app attack (9 %) Insider misuse (6 %)
Public		Misc. error (34 %) Insider misuse (24 %) Crimeware (21 %)	Theft/loss (19 %)	
Real estate		Insider misuse (37 %) Misc. error (20 %)	Theft/loss (13 %) Web app attack (10 %)	Crimeware (7 %)
Retail		DoS (33 %) PoS intrusion (31 %)	Web app attack (10 %)	Payment card skimmer (6 %)
Trade		Web app attack (30 %)		Crimeware (9 %) Misc. error (9 %) PoS intrusion (6 %) Insider misuse (6 %) Theft/loss (6 %)
Transportation		Cyber-espionage (24 %)	Insider misuse (16 %) Web app attack (15 %) Crimeware (15 %)	Theft/loss (7 %) Misc error (6 %) Payment card skimmer (5 %)
Utilities		Web app attack (38 %) Crimeware (31 %)	DoS (14 %)	Cyber espionage (7 %)

Miscellaneous Errors include human errors such as sending emails to inappropriate recipients, and publishing, configuration, disposal or programming errors. Crimeware is malware that excludes espionage and PoS theft, which are covered as separate categories.

Recent forensic expertise shows that if an organization is primarily in financial, retail, accommodation or food services, organized crime is the biggest threat [7]. Protected assets include payment cards, financial credentials and bank account information. Instigators from Eastern Europe and North America attack ATM machines, Point-of-Sale machines and servers, databases and endpoint computers. To attack ATMs and PoS machines, they can use physical tampering, via skimmers. For remote access, they may use brute force password guessers to obtain access, then spyware and RAM scrapers to copy card information in computer memory [6].

If an organization is primarily classified as manufacturing, transportation, mining, public or professional services, spying by state-affiliates (87 %) and organized crime (11 %) are the biggest threats [6]. Active state affiliates include China, North Korea, and eastern Europe. Desired assets include password credentials, trade secrets, technical resources (e.g., source code) and classified information. They target mail servers, file servers, directory servers and laptops/desktops. Their favorite attacks include spear phishing, stealing data (passwords, information) and remote control of computers (backdoors, botnet and rootkit).

Step 4: Compute Expected Loss After listing important assets and likely threats, we have a good estimate of the probability these threats will occur. Next we can calculate our estimated annual loss due to risks. There are three common methods to do this: Qualitative, Quantitative and Semi-Quantitative Analysis techniques.

If you have never done risk analysis before, the *Qualitative Analysis* technique is the easiest, fastest and recommended place to start. It is also helpful when you do not know precise threat probabilities or asset costs, such as intangible costs: e.g., what is the cost of loss of reputation following a public announcement of data intrusion? Qualitative Analysis works with intuition and judgment rather than actual cost values. The end result is a list of priority risks to address.

Qualitative Analysis uses the *Vulnerability Assessment Quadrant Map*, shown in Fig. 4.4. The horizontal arrow indicates the impact of the threat on your business, with the far right being 'Threaten Business' and far left being 'Slow Down Business' (see top labels). The middle vertical arrow represents the probability of the event occurring, with the top being '1 week' (or less) and the bottom being '50 years' (see left side labels). This results in four quadrants, with Quadrant 1 in red. When threats lie in Quadrant 1, they have both a high likelihood and a high impact and thus are most serious. The yellow quadrants—Quadrants 2 and 3—either have a high likelihood or high impact, but not both. The threats lying in these quadrants are lower priority than Quadrant 1 threats, but may still be important. Quadrant 4, in green, includes threats that have low probability and low impact, and thus can usually be ignored. The vertical time interval and horizontal business impact labels are not usually shown in Qualitative Analysis, but are provided to help understand magnitude.

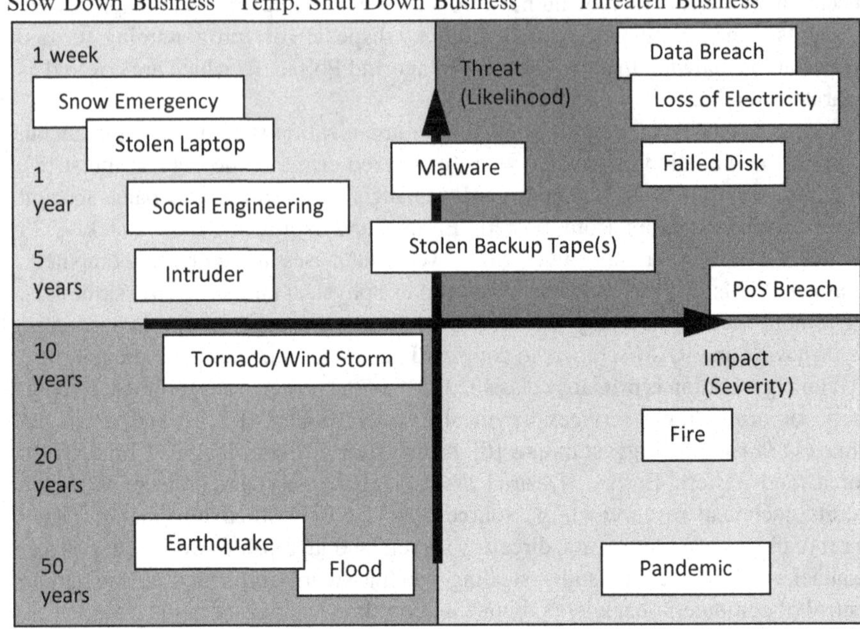

Fig. 4.4 Qualitative risk assessment (color figure online)

Threats are shown in white boxes in Fig. 4.4. The position of the threats should vary by geographic location, industry type, etc. In the Security Workbook, you can alter this diagram by moving threats around to their appropriate quadrants and locations within quadrants, appropriate for your organization.

While Qualitative Analysis is relatively easy, it does not provide an estimated cost of risk expense, nor financial advice on how much to spend on security controls. *Quantitative Analysis* helps with both goals. The first step is to estimate the *Single Loss Expectancy (SLE)*, which is the cost to the organization if a threat occurs once [2]. This expense includes the direct replacement cost plus potentially additional expenses, such as installation. The Annual Rate of Occurrence (ARO) is the probability or likelihood that that a SLE might occur during one year. The *Annual Lost Expectancy (ALE)* is the expected loss per year due to the threat, and is calculated as:

$$\mathrm{ALE} = \mathrm{SLE} * \mathrm{ARO} \tag{4.2}$$

Table 4.6 demonstrates a partial Quantitative Risk Analysis for Einstein University. Row four demonstrates loss of faculty laptops, which have a higher loss rate than the commonly used faculty PCs. If the loss of a laptop costs $1,000, including replacement and installation expense, and the laptops are lost on average every 5 years, then the tangible costs of SLE = $1,000, the ARO = 0.2, and the ALE = $1,000 * 0.2 = $200 per year. If we have ten instructors with laptops, then an

Table 4.6 Partial quantitative risk analysis for university

Asset	Threat	Single loss expectancy (SLE)	Annualized rate of occurrence (ARO)	Annual loss expectancy (ALE)
Registration Server	System or Disk Failure	System failure: $10,000 Registration x 2 days: $32,000	0.2 (5 years)	$8,400
Registration Server	Hacker penetration	Breach Not. Law: $752,000 Forensic help: $100,000 Registration x 2 days: $32,000	0.20 (5 years)	$884,000 x .2 =$176,800
Grades Server	Hacker penetration	Lawsuit: $1 million FERPA: $1 million Forensic help: $100,000 Loss of Reputation = $10,000	0.05 (20 years)	$2110,000 x 0.05 =$105,500
Faculty Laptop	Stolen	$1,000 FERPA = $1 million Loss of Reputation	2 (5 years * 10 instructors) 0.01	$2,000 $10,000
Payment Card Breach	Hacker penetration	$1 Million	0.2 (5 years)	$200,000

accurate direct loss estimate for ARO = 10 * 0.2 = 2, and the ALE would be calculated as ALE = $1,000 * 2 = $2,000 per year. Such losses could also expose grades and Social Security Numbers, leading to a probability of a FERPA investigation and bad press. This could result in additional consequential financial losses, estimated as an SLE = $1 million. This is calculated separately with an estimated ARO = 0.01 or 1 in 100 years, leading to an ALE of $10,000.

For some threats, even a maximum reduction in value will not result in a total loss. For example, a fire may reduce the value of a building from $1 million to $200,000, which is the value of the land itself. In this case, the *exposure factor* is 80 %. The appropriate SLE calculation would be:

$$\text{SLE} = \text{Asset Value}(\text{AV}) \times \text{Exposure Factor}(\text{EF}) \tag{4.3}$$

Challenges with a Quantitative Analysis include [8]:

1. *Unknown statistics.* Determining an appropriate likelihood and (in some cases) impact is difficult. Since crackers do not announce themselves, many organizations do not know if or how many attackers have already broken into their networks. Smaller organizations often lack sufficient security expertise or staff to recognize attackers, or estimate the likelihood of an attack. For accurate statistics, companies often hire risk consultants. Experts can rate the effectiveness of specific security devices, such as specific firewalls, in countering attacks.

2. *Complex Costs*. Risk impacts may be counted two or three times if done improperly. For example, if a hacker breaks into both the registration and grades databases, we are liable only once for FERPA.
3. *Security hides risk*. When implemented well, users get the impression that security is not an issue. How can you estimate the benefits of security, when you are not paying the risks' costs because sufficient security is in place?

A *Semi-Quantitative Risk Analysis* method is a half-way measure between Qualitative Analysis and Quantitative Analysis [9]. While it cannot estimate risks costs, it can rank risks, enabling the prioritization of risks. This technique estimate threats with (for example) five levels of impact and five levels of likelihood, as shown in Fig. 4.5. Each level may be given a meaning [2]. The Impact rating could be defined as follows: Insignificant: No meaningful impact; Minor: Impacts a small part of the business; Major: Impacts company brand; Material: Requires external reporting; and Catastrophic: Failure or downsizing of company. Each impact rating should also have an associated cost range, e.g.: Rare: Very unlikely to occur; Unlikely: Not encountered within last 5 years; Moderate: Occurred in last 5 years; Likely: Occurred in last year; Frequent: Occurs multiple times per year. Risks that fall into the red color ('severe') are most critical, while those falling in the green color ('low') are least serious. A risk priority is calculated by multiplying the Impact and Likelihood ratings, and sorting results for high numbers.

$$\text{Risk Priority} = \text{Impact} * \text{Likelihood} \tag{4.4}$$

Step 5: Treat Risk All risk analysis techniques used in Step 4 provide at least a prioritization of risks, which helps in determining the threats to be addressed. Quantitative Risk Analysis, in addition, provides a financial value that indicates how much to spend on controls. A Corrective Action Plan deals with how the organization

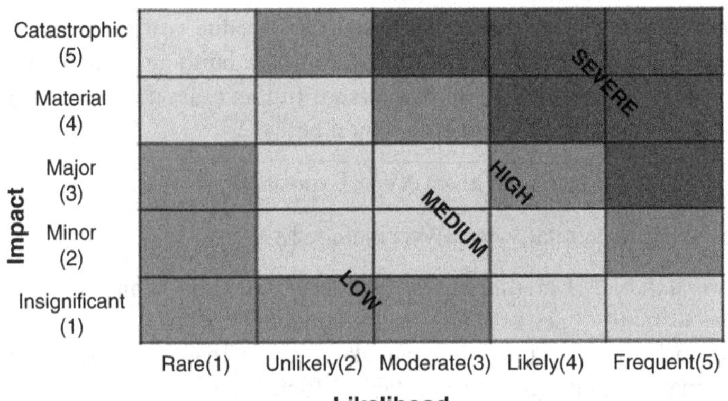

Fig. 4.5 Semi-quantitative risk analysis (adapted from Exhibit 2.12, CISM® Review Manual 2012 ©2011 ISACA. All rights reserved. Used by permission) [2]

will address the risks and prioritize and manage implementation. Each risk should be addressed using one of the following risk treatment types:

Risk Acceptance It is possible to ignore risk, if the risk exposure is negligible. We will handle any arising problem as necessary. E.g.: Snowstorm in Florida.

Risk Avoidance Stop doing risky behavior altogether, such as eliminating the use of Social Security Numbers, and avoiding storage of payment card numbers.

Risk Mitigation Implement control(s) that minimize vulnerability. Two approaches include minimizing likelihood and minimizing impact [2]. Teaching security awareness and using a firewall and antivirus software would minimize likelihood, while developing an Incident Response Plan would minimize the impact of an attack.

Risk Transference Pay someone to assume risk for you, such as purchasing insurance against the threat. This category is recommended for low frequency, high cost risks. While insurance can transfer the financial impact, it cannot transfer legal responsibility (which you retain).

Controls help to mitigate risk. There are many types of controls, and combining or layering controls is most effective. Controls can be preventive, detective or corrective, as mentioned in Chap. 2, although preventive controls are preferable. Additional types of controls include deterrent, compensating, and countermeasure controls [9]. *Deterrent* controls discourage people from deviant behavior. An example would be a policy of firing and/or prosecuting people for security violations or crimes. A *compensating* control is used as a weaker alternative when the recommended control is infeasible. An example might be the logging of critical employee transactions when segregation of duties is not possible. Finally, *countermeasures* are targeted controls, which address specific threats. An example is to use a router in combination with a firewall, to counter high-volume IP packet attacks; the 'border' router (i.e., router at the border to the internet) can discard the obvious attack packets, while the firewall carefully screens the remaining packets.

After a full implementation of controls, some residual risk remains. Figure 4.6 demonstrates that this residual risk should be a fraction of the original risk.

A partial solution for Einstein University is shown in Table 4.7. In this table, the risk and ALE is copied from the previous step in Table 4.6. Controls are considered and priced. If you are new to security, selecting and pricing controls may be difficult. For now consider that specific controls can include technology controls (e.g., firewalls, antivirus software, access control), administrative controls (e.g., security policies, procedures, training), and physical controls (e.g., locks, guards, keycards). Completing this task will be easier after learning about and working with security controls in the other chapters. Security is a system: if you are doing it right, you will be tweaking your work across chapters as you learn more about your business and security.

Recent forensic statistics show that 78 % of all intrusions are rated as 'low difficulty' [7]. In other words, the organizations were an easy attack. Doing a good job of implementing security, including acting on risk management plans and other chapters in this book, should make an organization safe at least from the easy attacks.

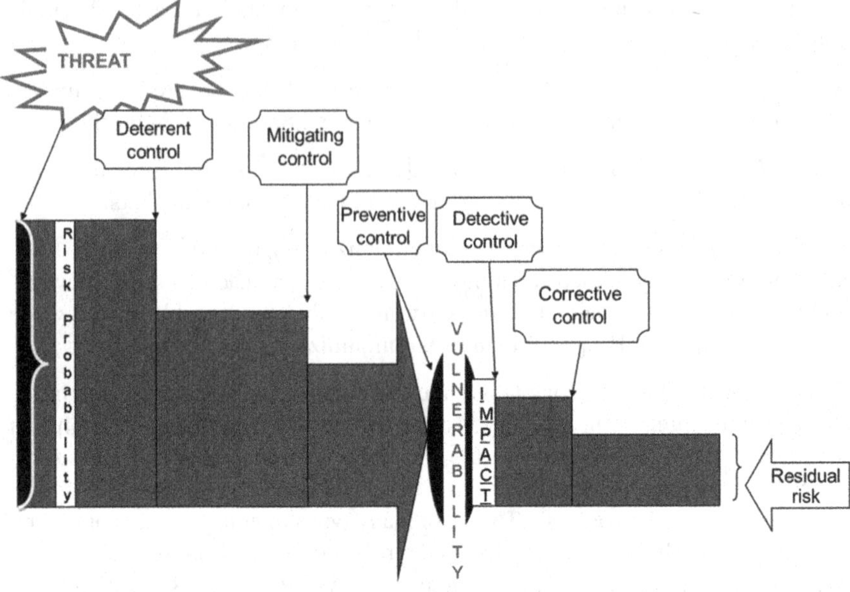

Fig. 4.6 Residual risk after treatment

Table 4.7 Analysis of risks versus controls

Risk	ALE score	Control	Cost of control
Registration Hacker Penetration	$176,800	Unified Threat Mgmt Firewall	$15,000
Payment Card Breach	$200,000	Full adherence to PCI DSS	?
Stolen Faculty Laptop	$2K $10,000 (FERPA)	Encryption	$60
Registration System or Disk Failure	$8,400	RAID (Redundant disks)	$750

Step 6: Monitor (and Communicate) Risk As your business, the industry, and the world changes, your organization's risk profile will also change [9]. You will learn more about the costs and likelihoods of risk as you experience threats. Automated controls may provide better insight, by tracking security threats. Management should monitor their organization's risk profile regularly, including the status of control implementations and compliance audits. Since people tend to avoid discussing risk, the topic must be regularly brought up with appropriate levels of management [4].

Figure 4.7 demonstrates a report that informs management of ongoing issues. It is a color-coded risk scoreboard or dashboard, which uses the stoplight colors: red for serious threats, yellow for lower-priority threats, and green for threat resolution. For each issue the report includes a color indicating the overall status, a brief

Issue	Status	Estimated Cost of Threat
Incident Response	Procedure being defined – incident response	$5,000
Stolen Laptop	In investigation	$2000, legal issues
Cost overruns	Internal audit investigation	$10,000
Security Awareness	Training completed	$500

Fig. 4.7 Sample risk scoreboard (color figure online)

description, and approximate cost. The report is summarized, since senior managers do not need all the technical details. In this table, a flaw in physical security was fixed by training the personnel involved. That issue has been resolved and will not appear in the next report. Some cost overruns are being investigated—these issues are underway. Finally a laptop has been stolen and a new procedure for FERPA incidents is needed. Those are new issues for which remediation is about to begin.

The Risk Assessment process has two main benefits. One benefit is to control costs when disaster strikes—as it inevitably does. Another benefit is in regulatory compliance. In the United States, judges in civil and criminal courts expect organizations to protect themselves and their clients using risk assessment. *Due Diligence* is the responsibility of doing careful risk assessment. *Due Care* is the follow-up responsibility of implementing recommended controls from the risk assessment process. Liability is minimized if reasonable precautions have been taken [9]. However, to achieve due diligence, risk management and policy review should be performed annually.

4.2 The Ethics of Risk

The original purpose of risk management was to ensure that an organization did not jeopardize its existence or security by making very poor decisions. This perspective is a subjective one, to protect the organization itself. In the example of a school shooting (Table 4.1), a student's life may not valued sufficiently highly, since from the school's perspective its loss of income is only from tuition. According to traditional risk assessment techniques in deriving the maximum cost of controls, the school should consider student life equivalent to the cost of loss of tuition.

(This assumes law suits are not likely to occur, unless there is obvious negligence.) While this example is not specifically about information security, it could apply to such cases when someone's identity, health, or privacy is affected.

Three cases involving technology where risk analysis affected human life demonstrated poor decisions due to economic or political reasons [10]. First, the night before the doomed Challenger space shuttle launch, one executive told another: "Take off your engineering hat and put on your management hat." Second, the value of human life is sometimes related to projected income, which unfairly penalizes people in developing nations. In Bhopal, India, where a chemical leak killed nearly 3,000 people, the value of life was estimated so low that its settlement was less than half the Exxon Valdez oil spill's settlement. Third, from a risk perspective, the Three Mile Island nuclear disaster was a 'success' in that no lives were lost; however public acceptance of nuclear technologies eroded due to the ensuing environmental problems and the then-proven threat nuclear energy posed. These three cases show that it is easy to underestimate the cost of others' lives, when your life is not impacted.

Ethical considerations include that human rights are natural or 'God-given' rights, which apply equally to all. W. D. Ross proposed that we have a duty to not harm others physically or psychologically, which means we should avoid harming someone's health, security, intelligence, character or happiness [11]. This view of risk believes that an organization should try to do good to others. While it is not possible to eliminate all risk, considering your customers' or clients' perspectives is a worthy goal. This can occur by including the public in evaluating risk, related to these decisions [10].

In the case of the school shooting, it is first recognized that the school is not responsible for taking the life of the student(s), since the shooter did. However, an ethical school board would attempt to protect students during risk assessment by taking the societal perspective and considering the possibility of losing a number of human lives. Studies on the 'Value of Life' consider that people demand more pay for risky jobs and extrapolate to estimate that a life is worth between $2 and 8 million in 1984 dollars [12]. Using these values as asset losses in Quantitative Analysis is certainly more reasonable than the value of tuition.

4.3 Advanced: Financial Analysis with Business Risk

Three financial analytic techniques may help during quantitative risk analysis. The three techniques include cost-benefit analysis, net present value and internal rate of return. These terms are commonly used by business management and can be used to convince management to expend money for controls.

Cost-Benefit Analysis Implementing security controls has a financial cost, but hopefully would result in a reduction in financial loss. This reduction in expenditures can be described as potential benefits. To simplify a cost-benefit analysis, consider that in Year 0 we purchase the control (–C). In subsequent years, we incur reduced expenses (+Y1 + Y2). These are calculated considering our costs previous to implementing the control, compared to our estimated costs after the control [13]. Thus, a simplified cost-benefit analysis (SCBA) indicates the total cost of a security control over its lifetime, and is calculated as:

$$\text{SCBA} = -\text{C}_0 + \text{Y}_1 + \text{Y}_2 + \text{Y}_3 + \ldots \tag{4.5}$$

If the SCBA results in a positive answer, the organization saves money by spending money for the control. A zero or negative answer results in a break-even or loss, respectively. However, this answer is simplified, since financial analysis assumes that money today is worth more than the same monetary value in the future. Therefore, we need to discount future earnings, in order to determine a financial estimate in today's money (called present value). The *Net Present Value (NPV)* is then calculated by summing each Return for year t, *Rt*, discounted using an interest rate, *i*, often estimated at 10 % [14]. This is shown in Eq. (4.6), where the original cost is specified as a negative R_0 and subsequent reductions in expenses are positive.

$$\text{NPV} = \sum_{t=0}^{N} \frac{R_t}{(1+i)^t} = R_0 + \frac{R_1}{(1+i)^1} + \frac{R_2}{(1+i)^2} + \frac{R_3}{(1+i)^3} + \cdots \tag{4.6}$$

The NPV determines the value to us today of implementing a security control. What if we have a number of potential investments, and we want to determine which is the best investment? An *Internal Rate of Return (IRR)* provides a rate of how much each investment will pay off. The higher the rate, the higher is the payoff. Equation (4.6) is also used to calculate the IRR. However, instead of knowing *i* and calculating NPV, we set NPV to zero and solve for the rate, *i*.

An example might be that encryption software costs $35 per license and we have 100 laptops with confidential data. Our estimated savings in risk for 5 years for this investment is $1,000 per year. Table 4.8 shows the annual calculations, using a discounted interest of 10 %. The NPV sums to $290.78, and the IRR = 13.2 %. The IRR was estimated using the NPV() formula in Excel.

Table 4.8 Calculations of NPV

Year	$ Value	Present value
0	–3,500	–3,500
1	1,000	909.09
2	1,000	826.45
3	1,000	751.31
4	1,000	683.01
5	1,000	620.92
Total	1,500	290.78

4.4 Advanced: Risk for Larger Organizations

Larger organizations may have a more formalized risk process. The NIST risk assessment methodology documents an extended process with documented inputs, outputs and stages as shown in Fig. 4.8.

Previous history can help considerably with generating an accurate likelihood. This can be achieved by using a well-selected set of *metrics* or statistics. Quantifiable metrics should be collected periodically and inexpensively, preferably in an automated way. An example metric might be: how many viruses are the help desk reporting per month? A *baseline* is a measurement of performance at a particular point in time. Using consistently measured data, it is possible to observe changes in the metrics over time, discover trends for future risk analysis, and measure the effectiveness of controls.

Risk management should occur at the strategic organizational level, the business process or project level and the information systems or operational levels [9, 15]. At each level, risk assessment should be consistent with higher levels and related risk assessments. Each level should also consider the details associated with the scope or project at hand, such as a specific software development project [15]. Regardless of level, the scope of the risk project is carefully selected to cohesively focus on, and properly cover, a defined area or product. A Risk Assessment Report is the final output. This report ensures that security controls were tested and pass inspection. The product or area is then *certified* for use.

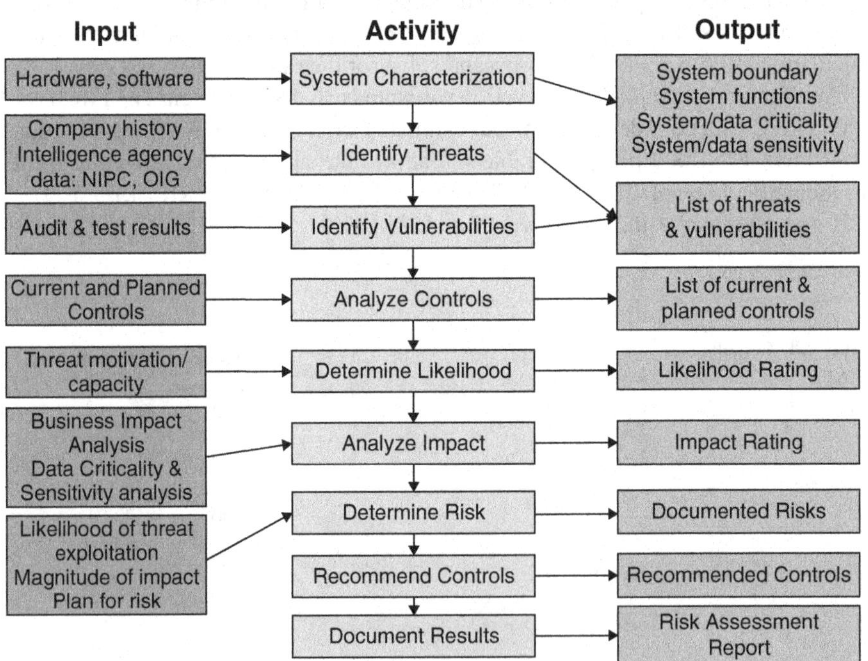

Fig. 4.8 NIST risk assessment methodology (adapted from NIST SP 800-30 [15])

Risk assessment requires business and security people to work together closely. Governance and senior management are responsible for making decisions concerning risk, allocating resources for controls, and evaluating risk assessment results. An Information Security Manager is responsible for coordinating the risk process and developing the risk management plan. The business side is responsible for prioritizing assets and helping to define and implement controls for business processes. Business roles include: Process Owners, who make decisions concerning securing the business process, and Information Owners, who ensure controls are in place to address the three security goals (CIA), including signing off on permissions for access to business data. On the security side, security practitioners design security requirements and implement controls into IT systems, networks, and applications, while Security Trainers develop training materials for security, and educate employees as to security practices. The Chief Information Officer (CIO), as the head IT person, manages IT plans and budgets and works closely with the Information Security Manager. These two roles are preferably separate, since CIOs tend to focus on managing IT processes, whereas the security manager focuses on security—a full-time job at any sizeable institution.

4.5 Questions and Problems

1. *Vocabulary*. Match each meaning with the correct word.

Vulnerability	Risk mitigation	Risk avoidance	Annual loss expectancy
Residual risk	Risk assessment	Risk transfer	Single loss expectancy
Threat	Risk management	Threat agent	Annual rate of occurrence
Qualitative risk analysis			Quantitative risk analysis

   a) A method of eliminating risk by stopping risky behavior.
   b) A method of addressing risk by adding controls to minimize risk exposure.
   c) The financial loss accruing from one risk incident occurring.
   d) The remaining level of risk, after risk controls are implemented.
   e) A risk term addressing the *enabling* of a risk. Example s include: disgruntled employee, insufficient staff, poor documentation.
   f) A risk term addressing a *potential* risk problem. Examples include: severe weather, vandalism, fraud, malware, phishing.
   g) A method of determining risk priority, by using gut feel.
   h) A term denoting the full risk process, including risk planning, determination, treatment and monitoring.

2. *Risk Lifecycle*. Your large organization averages 20-some malware infection reports a month. What might be done in each stage of the Continuous Risk Management Process (shown in Fig. 4.2) to reduce malware infections?
3. *Assets and Threats*. In your selected industry/major/specialty, list what you believe are the top 5 assets and top 5 threats. (If you are in the IT field, instead

select an industry you may choose to work in, e.g., health, manufacturing, finance, retail, entertainment, education, hotel,…)

4. *Qualitative Risk Analysis*. Perform a Qualitative Risk Analysis, using a Vulnerability Assessment Quadrant Map, for your selected industry/major/specialty. Assume this organization is in your home town. Include the most important threats or threat categories listed in Step 2. Hint: Work with a copy of the Vulnerability Assessment Quadrant Map, provided in the Security Workbook.
5. *Quantitative Risk Analysis*. Complete a Quantitative Risk Analysis Table for five major threats in your industry/major/specialty. Find estimates for four asset values and/or likelihoods via searches on the Internet, and document these values, as well as the websites where you found them. Do your best at guessing remaining asset values and likelihoods. Show resulting ALE values.
6. *Selecting Controls*. For five major threats in your industry/major/specialty, discuss whether you would use risk avoidance, mitigation, transference, or acceptance for each, and why. Discuss a possible control for each, and describe whether the control is preventive, detective, or corrective.
7. *Considering Ethics*. In your industry/major/specialty, can you define an area where traditional risk assessment, with its focus on minimizing costs to the owner only, might be unethical? Describe the scenario, and how you might implement a risk strategy that protects all involved.

4.5.1 Health First Case Study Problems

For each case study problem, refer to the Health First Case Study. The Health First Case Study and Security Workbook should be provided by your instructor or can be found at http://extras.springer.com.

Case study	Health first case study	Other resources
Analyzing risk	√	Security workbook

References

1. Gore A (2013) The future: six drivers of global change. Random House Inc, New York, NY, p 73
2. ISACA (2011) CISM® review manual 2012. ISACA, Arlington Heights, IL, pp 75–125
3. 2014 cost of data breach study: United States. May 2014. Ponemon Institute LLC
4. ISACA (2013) CRISC™ review manual 2013. ISACA, Arlington Heights, IL
5. Gibson D (2011) Managing risk in information systems. Jones & Bartlett Learning, LLC, Burlington, MA, pp 392–418
6. Verizon (2014) Verizon 2014 data breach investigations report. http://www.verizonenterprise.com/DBIR/2014. Accessed 30 June 2014

7. Verizon (2013) Verizon 2013 data breach investigations report. http://www.verizonenterprise.com/DBIR/2013. Accessed 20 Oct 2013
8. Pinto CA, Arora A, Hall D, Schmitz E (2006) Challenges to sustainable risk management: case example in information network security. Eng Manag J 18(1):17–23
9. ISACA (2010) CISA review manual 2011. ISACA, Arlington Heights, IL, pp 101–104
10. Herkert JR (1994) Ethical risk assessment: valuing public perceptions. IEEE Technol Soc Mag 13(1):4–10
11. Asiata L-AB (2010) Technology, individual rights and the ethical evaluation of risk. J Inf Commun Ethics Soc 8(4):308–322
12. Kahn S (1986) Economic estimates of the value of life. IEEE Technol Soc Mag 5(2):24–31
13. Gibson D (2011) Managing risk in information systems. Jones & Bartlett Learning, Burlington, MA, pp 101–102
14. Subramanyam KR, Wild JJ (2009) Financial statement analysis, 10th edn. McGraw-Hill Irwin, New York, pp 40–43
15. NIST (2012) NIST special publication 800-30: guide for conducting risk assessments, Rev. 1, National Institute of Standards and Technology, U.S. Dept. of Commerce

Chapter 5
Addressing Business Impact Analysis and Business Continuity

> In most cases, companies don't realize they have been burned until years later, when a foreign competitor puts out their very same product – only they are making it 30 % cheaper. (Scott Aken, former counterintelligence agent and cybersecurity expert [1]).

Consider a pharmacy with a failed centralized computer system. A person needs a critical prescription refilled immediately. His 24-hour pharmacy's computer system is down within the centralized network, which means that other stores in the chain also lack prescription information. Other pharmacies don't have his prescription information, and the doctor's office is closed. This person's choice is visiting a hospital, hoping computer service resumes, or (at best) being miserable all night. This IT failure impacts organization sales and reputation, and may affect human life.

This chapter is about Availability, or the lack of it: what happens to a business when the computer systems fail or cannot operate? *Business Impact Analysis* (BIA) determines how an IT disruption would affect an organization, including the financial, legal, liability, and reputation aspects, and sets business goals to minimize disruption. *Business Continuity* (BC) is about how 'business continues' in the face of IT disruption and selects the controls that should be used to achieve the Availability goals set in the BIA. The *Disaster Recovery Plan* is the detailed IT plan to provide a backup system when normal operation has failed. These topics usually have a direct impact on profitability, since loss of IT often leads to additional expenses and/or loss of business profit.

5.1 Analyzing Business Impact

IT outages will definitely occur. They may occur due to system failures (server, network, or disk failure), external/weather (storms, tornado, earthquake, fire, electric failure), hacker attack (malware, Distributed Denial of Service, penetration), and employee negligence or fraud (incompetence, error, revenge).

S. Lincke, *Security Planning*, DOI 10.1007/978-3-319-16027-6_5

Table 5.1 Event damage classification for disruptive events

Problematic event or incident	Affected business process(es)	Impact classification & effect on finances, legal liability, human life, reputation
Fire	Class rooms, business departments	Crisis. At times: Major Human life
Hacking intrusion	Registration, advising	Major, Legal/liability: FERPA, PCI DSS
Network unavailable	Registration, advising, classes, homework, education	Crisis during school year
Social engineering/fraud	Registration	Major, Legal liability: FERPA, PCI DSS
Server failure (disk/ server)	Registration, advising, classes, homework, education	Major. At times Crisis
Power failure	Classes, All business processes	Crisis during school year Major at other times

The Business Impact Analysis (BIA) is a document that considers the impact of IT failure on the business, how to minimize such failures, and which business processes should be prioritized in the case of limited resources. What adversities could occur? What impact could an IT outage have on the organization financially? Legally? On human life? On reputation? Which business processes are of strategic importance? What is the necessary recovery time period? Key business managers should provide input regarding important business processes, potentially via meetings, interviews, and questionnaires.

The first step in creating a Business Impact Analysis is to define problematic incidents or events that could occur. Disruptive events can be classified by the damage that is incurred. *Event Damage Classifications* may include:

- Negligible: No significant cost or damage
- Minor: A non-negligible event with no material or financial impact on the business
- Major: Impacts one or more departments and may impact outside clients
- Crisis: Has a major material or financial impact on the business

Table 5.1 shows such an impact classification for a university. In further BIA work, Negligible events can be ignored. However, Minor, Major, & Crisis events should be documented and their repairs should be tracked.

When an IT or other disruption occurs, a prepared business implements an *Alternate Mode*, which is the set of business practices where some critical subset of service continues via a backup system (IT or otherwise). Less critical operations may be postponed, performed manually, or languish during this time. Figure 5.1 demonstrates how this occurs. Time proceeds from left to right. The regular service is interrupted by a misfortunate event. No service is provided during the *Interruption Window*, until the Disaster Recovery Plan is implemented to guide the transition to Alternate Mode [2]. Alternate Mode offers a lower level of critical business service,

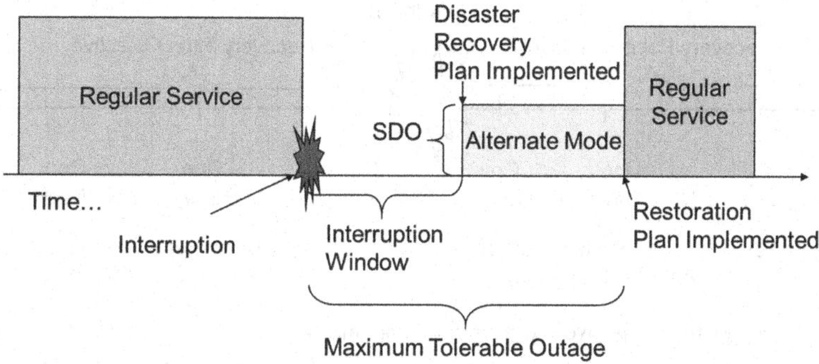

Fig. 5.1 Recovery timeline

Fig. 5.2 Organizational priorities for alternate mode

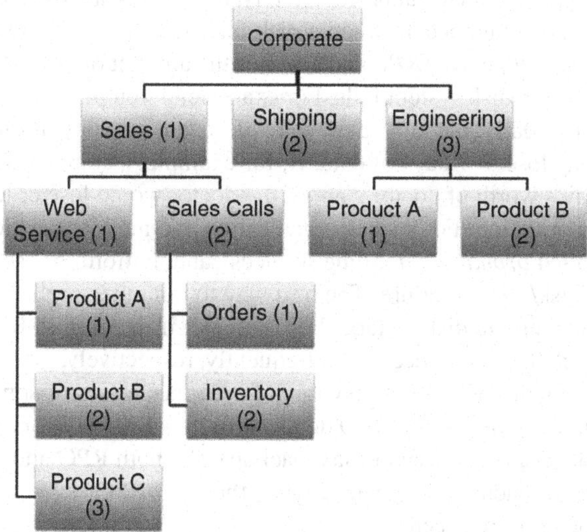

until problems can be resolved. The *Restoration Plan* helps to resolve critical issues and guide IT towards the resumption of regular service.

The *Service Delivery Objective (SDO)* is the selected level of service for Alternate Mode [2]. Business expertise is required to determine the desired level of service during Alternate Mode. Figure 5.2 shows a hypothetical business scenario, where certain aspects of the organization (e.g., certain web sites, service departments, business departments) are ranked at higher priority than other departments. High priority IT processes will resume service in Alternate Mode, whereas lower ranked services' resumption may be postponed. *Maximum Tolerable Outage* is the maximum time the business can endure staying in Alternate Mode.

It is important to define what the maximum interruption window should be for each high priority service. The *Recovery Time Objective (RTO)* is the preferred duration of time between interruption and Alternate Mode implementation for each service.

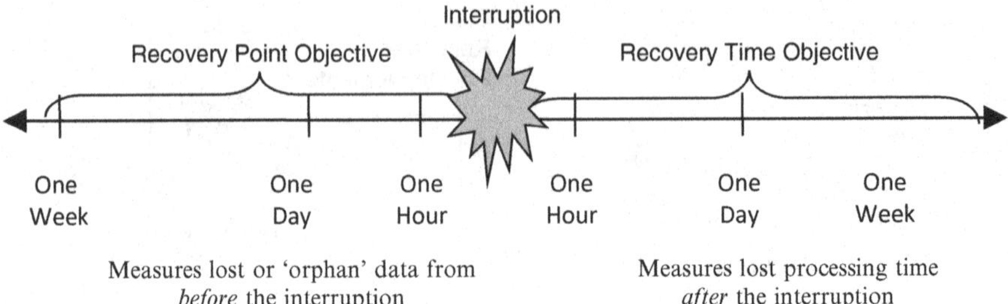

Fig. 5.3 Recovery time objective and recovery point objective

How long can your organization survive this service being down? This decision can depend on financial profit, liability, reputation, and other factors.

Lost data occurs when a disk fails and there is no recent backup. The *Recovery Point Objective (RPO)* determines the amount of data you can afford to lose if your server's disk system fails. For example, if you perform a backup of your main databases daily, the most data you will lose is one day. If you do weekly backups, you may lose 5–7 days of data. If, for example, a computerized doctor's office lost one day's worth of doctor's notes, the doctor would lose critical prescription and health information. For a sales organization, we may lose critical orders. This lost data is called *orphan data*. Some services cannot afford to lose any information following a disk/system failure. The best way to minimize orphan data is frequent backups to an alternate disk or tape. For example, if the desired RPO is 1 day or 1 hour, then backups should occur that frequently, respectively.

Figure 5.3 shows how the RTO defines losses of some amount of service in the future, whereas the RPO defines lost transaction history for some amount of time in the past (i.e., since our last backup). For both RPO and RTO, a smaller loss of data or transactions is incurred when the RTO/RPO statistics are short or low, which is the preferred scenario.

Table 5.2 then shows a partial analysis of RTO and RPO for a university. In this example note that some functions, Registration and Teaching, vary in their criticality during certain days of the year. Also, in some cases having a low RTO is more important than a low RPO, and vice versa.

The RTO decisions can help to categorize data into one of four *Criticality Classes*. We can define an associated preferred RTO for each class. For example, the Vital class's 'short time' may be 1 day or 5 days, depending on organizational needs.

- *Critical:* Cannot be performed manually. Tolerance to interruption is very low.
- *Vital:* Can be performed manually for a short time.
- *Sensitive:* Can be performed manually for a period of time, but may cost more in staff.
- *Nonsensitive:* Can be performed manually for an extended period of time with little additional cost and minimal recovery effort.

Table 5.2 Partial BIA summary for university

Business process	Recovery point objective (h)	Recovery time objective (h)	Critical resources (computer, people, peripherals)	Special notes (unusual treatment at specific times, unusual risk conditions)
Registration	0 hours	4 hours	Registration DB (SOLAR), network Registrar	High priority during Nov–Jan, March–June, August
Personnel	2 hours	48 hours	Personnel DB (PeopleSoft)	Can operate manually for two days with loss of capability
Teaching	1 day	1 hour	D2L, network, faculty files	During school semester: high priority
University Web pages	1 week	1 hour	Web server	Always critical RTO

Information in the Critical and Vital Criticality classes are considered sufficiently important that they should be addressed by the Business Continuity process. We will also use this classification data in the later chapter on Information Security.

5.2 Planning for Business Continuity

Business Continuity is the business plan to offer critical services in the event of a disruption. The *Business Continuity Plan (BCP)* is the detailed business plan that takes the BIA results and describes the solution for how business should continue when a disaster strikes. It should describe: the systems covered, personnel responsibility, the backup plan and site, testing and training, formal procedures, and the location of the Disaster Recovery Plan [3]. The *Disaster Recovery Plan (DRP)* is the detailed IT plan/procedure to guide IS systems recovery to Alternate Mode after an incident occurs.

Different technical solutions can help to achieve different RTO and RPO values, including high-availability solutions, recovery sites, and cloud solutions. This section evaluates these alternatives. An organization should attempt to minimize its losses following an IT failure, by never paying more for recovery than is lost in income due to the failure. Minimal loss is achieved when the price of recovery matches the lost income.

5.2.1 Recovery Sites

This solution does not utilize active redundancy, but instead a backup plan. If a first site fails, a planned second site is configured and brought up. The recovery (RTO) can take hours, days, or weeks. Backup sites can exist within a sizeable

Table 5.3 RPO controls

Business process	RPO (h)	Data file and system/ directory location	Special treatment (backup period, RAID, file retention strategies)
Teaching	1 day	Faculty servers & computers	Faculty servers are backed up daily Recommendation: When faculty uses PCs, faculty should save files on both PC and server Classes are cancelled during extreme weather (for student protection)
Registration	0 hours	Registration DB (Solar), Data Center	RAID provides disk redundancy Server is backed up daily, stored offsite Use mobile site for outages > 3 days
Personnel	2 hours	Personnel DB (PeopleSoft) Data Center	RAID provides disk redundancy Server is backed up daily, stored offsite Use mobile site for outages > 3 days
Web Service	1 week	Data Center	Server is backed up weekly, stored offsite

organization, between cooperating organizations, or with a commercial backup site provider. Here are some options [2]:

Duplicate Information Processing Facility (IPF) Your organization has two sites or subsidiaries. Processing normally occurs locally, but could occur remotely if the local site failed.

Reciprocal Agreement Your organization has an agreement with another organization that enables either of you to use each other's IT facilities, if either IT facilities fail. This option comes with additional issues such as quick access, security, IT compatibility, limited processing resources, priority, and other common issues when attempting to live with strangers. It is recommended to test in advance of a failure, and contractually agree on the access mechanism and maximum duration for such a combined living arrangement.

Commercial backup facilities vary in cost depending on the configuration and access agreement. Options include:

- *Hot Site:* The backup site is fully configured with equipment and networks. Software needs to be reloaded, but can be operational in hours.
- *Warm Site:* The backup site usually has network and disk drives, but may lack sufficient servers for immediate use.
- *Cold Site:* This backup site has electrical wiring and air conditioning, but no IT network or other equipment. It may take weeks to fully configure.

Mobile Site: A trailer can be brought to your site to serve as a hot or warm site. The trailer may be pre-configured with satellite or microwave communication links.

Einstein University uses in-house IT, instead of a cloud service. Table 5.3 on RPO Controls lists the RPO value for each business process (taken from Table 5.2) and describes how the RPO is attained in the Special Treatment column.

Table 5.4 Business continuity summary for critical and vital classes

Criticality class (critical or vital)	Business process	Incident or problematic event(s)	Procedure for handling (name the procedure if extended, describe steps if short)
Vital	Registration	Computer Failure	DB Backup Procedure DB Recovery Procedure—Registration Mobile Site Plan
Critical	Teaching	Computer Failure	DB Backup Procedure DB Recovery Procedure—Teaching Section Mobile Site Plan

High-priority Critical and Vital business processes are further elaborated in Table 5.4, which includes the required procedures and documents to support business continuity. These procedures should be written by technical staff in Section 6 of the Security Workbook.

5.2.2 High-Availability Solutions

High availability solutions use redundancy to minimize failures, enabling an RPO and RTO of seconds or minutes. Here are some example solutions for disk, processing, and network systems [2]:

Redundant Array of Independent Disks (RAID): An array of disks supports redundancy, often via parity. If one disk fails, the remaining disks can deduce the missing information. This relatively inexpensive and popular disk solution is located at one site. If multiple disks fail (e.g., through fire, flood, theft, bad luck) little recovery can be made, except by maintaining off-site backups.

Fault-Tolerant Servers If a primary server fails, a local backup server will resume service. An alternative mode includes:

- *Distributed Processing:* A load is distributed over multiple servers. If one server fails, the remaining server(s) attempt to carry the full load. This model is frequently used for high volume web processing and/or firewalls.

Storage Area Network (SAN) A SAN is a large disk network that can support remote backups, data sharing and data migration between different geographical locations. If one site fails, recovery at a second site is possible.

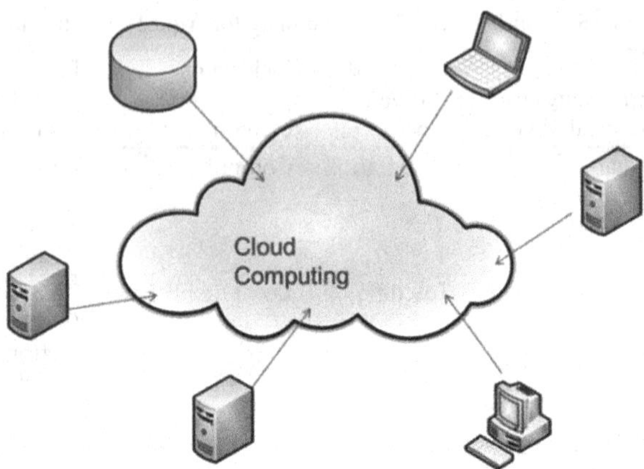

Fig. 5.4 Cloud computing

Network redundancy Redundant networks of the same or different types can survive network equipment or link failures. Networks can detect failures and reconfigure automatically via sophisticated routing protocols such as OSPF or EGRP. Solutions include:

- *Diverse Routing:* One network type (e.g., fiber or radio) supports multiple routes.
- *Alternative Routing:* Two network types, often with different network providers, enable redundancy. This may be implemented over the long-haul (long distance) or last-mile (the local connection between your site and your communications provider).

Big Data databases, such as Hadoop and Mongo, also qualify as high availability systems. This system type is described in an Advanced section of this chapter.

5.2.3 Cloud Services

Cloud computing is a popular technique, even with small businesses. As Fig. 5.4 shows, end user terminals and computers interface with the Internet, and a cloud service provider provides the computing resources. The main advantage of cloud services is resource pooling; customers pay the cloud provider for IT services, and gain broad network access and on-demand, elastic service. These features ensure that you get and pay for the service you actually use, when you want it. Smaller organizations benefit since the cloud can provide IT infrastructure and maintenance at a reasonable cost.

From a Business Continuity perspective, cloud services can be used to house all IT or as a backup (hot site) service. Regardless of how the cloud is used, *service level agreements (SLAs)* define contractual capabilities, such as backup, security,

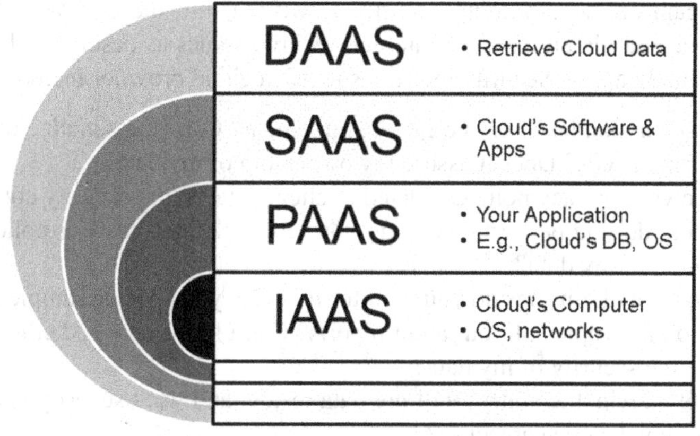

Fig. 5.5 Cloud services

and availability requirements. (SLAs are discussed in Personnel Security.) Some clouds specialize in specific industries, such as health, and adhere to industry security regulations. Without such an agreement, no assumptions about service should be made.

Three different cloud models provide different levels of service. As shown in Fig. 5.5, outer-level services include all the features of inner-level services, plus additional features. They include (from most inclusive to least inclusive) [4]:

- *Software as a Service (SaaS)*: Cloud provider runs own applications on cloud infrastructure.
- *Data as a Service (DaaS):* Cloud provider provides data, normally via a database, for client access.
- *Platform as a Service (PaaS):* Consumer provides application software; cloud provider provides system and software development environment (e.g., web development toolkit).
- *Infrastructure as a Service (laaS):* Cloud provides customers access to processing, storage, networks or other fundamental resources, but customer provides the applications and possibly operating system.

The advantage of cloud (and all three configurations) is that the customer does not need to purchase or manage infrastructure, including equipment, operating system, and often the base level software.

Cloud services can also be categorized by their customer type. *Public clouds* serve any and all customers. *Community clouds* specialize in a particular business, such as medical. These clouds specialize in particular software and security services for that industry. *Private clouds* serve individual customers, and can be owned or leased.

From a security perspective, the cloud offers benefits and concerns. A cloud provider may have security expertise and infrastructure well beyond the capability of a smaller organization—assuming security is written into the contract. Since the cloud is accessed via an insecure Internet, security issues as described throughout this book should apply. Security questions to ask a cloud provider include [4–6]:

- What is your standard Service Level Agreement? Can I personalize this agreement for my needs? Does it assure my ownership of my data?
- What are your privacy policies related to client data? What security controls and monitoring do you perform? How do you report changes in your policies or in the location of my data?
- What types of alarm/logs do you monitor for? Can you provide sample log files?
- Can we obtain copies of your audit reports? Can I hire a certified ethical hacker to assess the security of my data?
- Where (e.g., which country) will my data reside, and what security and privacy laws will my data be subject to?
- What is your policy if law enforcement subpoenas my sensitive information?
- Do you maintain metrics on availability (or downtime), security, use and performance?
- What are your policies for disaster recovery? How do you handle disaster recovery? Are there contractual agreements in place?
- When and how will you report security incidents to us? What information will the reports contain?
- Can I terminate the contract at any time (particularly for security distrust)? How is the contract terminated? How does data export to another cloud provider work, what does this cost, and what are your policies for data destruction?

5.3 Disk Backup and Recovery

Backups are critical regardless of the type of Business Continuity solution used. Employee error, disk failures, and/or malware may corrupt your disks, requiring recovery from backup. Even an on-line, redundant database backup can be corrupted via error or malevolence, requiring recovery from a historical copy. Multiple copies of historical databases should be retained, because it is sometimes necessary to reload a specific previous version in order to retrieve a deleted file or track fraud. In addition, ransomware may corrupt backups (in addition to encrypting disks) to help convince you to pay their ransom [7]. Thus, it is important to not only perform backups, but regularly ensure your backups are functional.

One method of performing backups is the *Grandfather-Father-Son* method, which rotates recent monthly, weekly, and daily backups, respectfully [3]. At the 'son' level, seven backups are retained daily. The backup for the last day of each week graduates to the 'father' level, where five backups are retained for each week in the last month. The last week of each month graduates to the 'grandfather level', where 12 or more monthly backups may be retained. An example of this is shown in Fig. 5.6; however, any father level can be retained in disk or tape form.

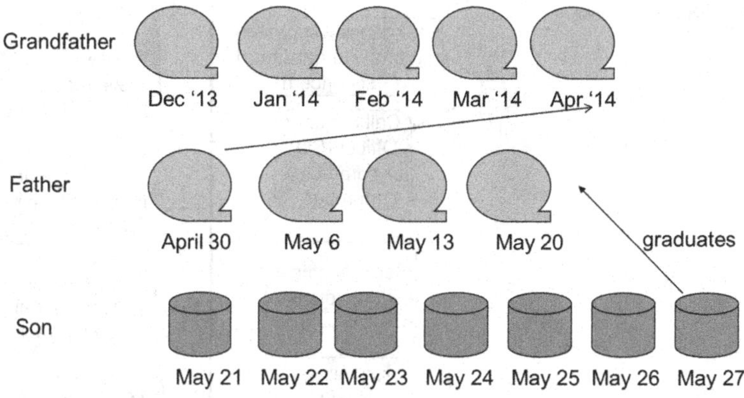

Fig. 5.6 Grandfather–father–son backup rotation

Table 5.5 Types of backup

Daily events	Full	Differential	Incremental
Monday: Full backup	Mon.	Monday	Monday
Tuesday: A changes	Tues.	Saves A	Saves A
Wednesday: B changes	Wed.	Saves A + B	Saves B
Thursday: C changes	Thurs.	Saves A + B + C	Saves C
Friday: Full backup	Fri.	Friday	Friday

Backups may be complete backups of a database, or can be a partial backup, listing only the changes from the last backup. Partial backups may be *differential*, which saves all changes since the last complete backup, or *incremental*, which saves all changes since the last partial backup [3, 8]. Table 5.5 shows an example, where Monday and Friday have full backups, while Tuesday through Thursday have only partial backups. If a reload must occur on Thursday, and differential backup is used, Monday then Wednesday's backups are both reloaded. If incremental backup is used, Monday, Tuesday and Wednesday must all be reloaded. In the Grandfather–Father–Son solution, it is assumed that the Father and Grandfather levels are complete backups.

Backups must be properly labeled and tracked. Labels should include: data set name, volume serial number, date created, offsite storage bin number and possibly accounting period.

Backups should be kept off-site in a library. The library should maintain a detailed inventory of storage media and files. The library site should be sufficiently far away from the main computing center to avoid being affected by any common disaster. The library should be equally secure as the main computing center and to avoid notice should not be labeled. The library should have constant environmental control (humidity-, temperature-controlled, UPS, smoke/water detectors, and fire extinguishers).

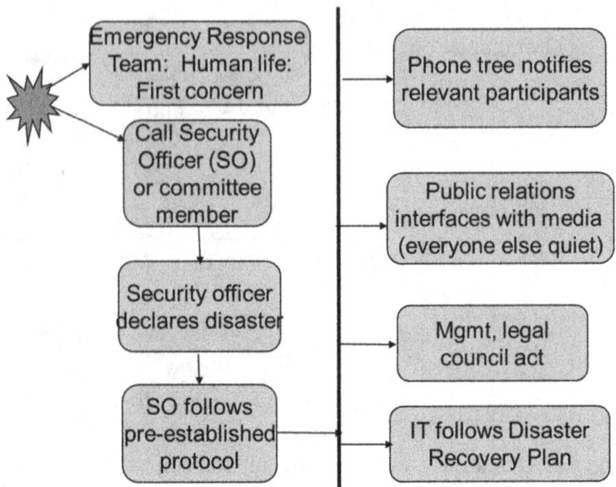

Fig. 5.7 Disaster response

5.4 Preparing for IT Disaster Recovery

Figure 5.7 shows how an organization should respond to a disaster. This *activity diagram* is like a flow chart, where tasks normally occur in order (when you follow the arrows), but the tasks to the right of the thick middle vertical bar happen in parallel. First priority is human life and evacuating people as necessary. When there is a security committee, anyone on that committee can declare a disaster. A pre-established protocol determines what constitutes a disaster and how a security officer should react. The protocol should include using a phone tree to notify participants. IT follows the Disaster Recovery Plan to implement Alternate Mode. The public relations department is responsible for any press release, and legal counsel should advise as to liability, as appropriate. Management should be well-informed to make any critical decisions, including potential resource allocation decisions.

The Disaster Recovery Plan (DRP) should guide this effort for IT. A full Disaster Recovery Plan should include: preincident readiness; a description of how to declare a disaster; evacuation procedures; allocation of responsibilities and contact information; step-by-step procedures for disaster recovery and Alternate Mode operation; and required resources for recovery & continued operations. The DRP should consider details such as: How will the Alternate Mode site be staffed? How will applications, operating systems, databases, networking, and security be brought up and functional? Copies of the DRP must be in hard copy off-site, available where it will be needed.

The contact information should include name, address, and email/phone information for technical assistance: incident response team, software/hardware vendors, insurance, recovery facilities, suppliers, and offsite media. Contact information for general business needs include first responder numbers for fire, police, and emergency health; business recovery including legal, supplies, damage assessment, and salvage; people assistance including training and transportation/relocation (for people and/or equipment).

To ensure a speedy recovery, a crisis should be simulated by testing before a failure or real crisis actually occurs. Testing should start with easy, partial tests, and proceeding up to full, complete tests. A good first test is the *Desk-Based Evaluation/ Paper Test*, where a group steps through a paper procedure and mentally performs each step. The next step is a *Preparedness Test*, where part of the full test is performed. Different aspects should be tested regularly. One example would be a disk failure, which would require a recovery-from-backup implementation. The *Full Operational Test* is a simulation of a full disaster, with a complete implementation of Alternate Mode.

A plan for testing would define when to perform which tests and the objectives of each test. As each test is executed, it should be evaluated for improvements. Both test and DRP procedures can potentially be improved. What went wrong? How can the procedure be completed faster? What needs to be corrected in the procedure? An internal auditor (or other third party) can help by observing and documenting what occurred. This documentation is useful during the analysis process and in external audits.

To summarize this chapter, the BIA-BC process is: Perform a Business Impact Analysis, which prioritizes services to support critical business processes. Define an Alternate Processing Mode to support these Critical and Vital services following a disruptive event. Develop a Business Continuity Plan to support business operations during this recovery period. Develop a Disaster Recovery Plan which guides IT systems recovery into an Alternate Mode. Test the plans to ensure they are functional and will work. Periodically maintain the plans, to ensure that they adapt as the business changes.

5.5 Advanced: Business Continuity for Mature Organizations

Sophisticated organizations that rely heavily on IT should monitor availability metrics, extend documentation, consider purchasing insurance, and prepare with additional testing.

Monitoring availability/reliability rates can determine whether IT is meeting business goals for availability. Businesses advertise their availability as '24/7' for 24 hour a day, 7 days a week. Some strive to be (for example) a 5 9's service, which means the service is up and available 99.999 % of the time. Figure 5.8 demonstrates a reliability metric, which measures the average time a device may successfully run until failure (*Mean Time To Failure—MTTF*), and the average time it takes to fix it (*Mean Time To Repair—MTTR*). *Mean Time Between Failure (MTBF)* is the average of the sum: MTTF+MTTR.

Multiple Business Continuity Plans may be useful for large organizations, as shown in Table 5.6 [3]. The three IT plans are shown in the middle column, and include the Disaster Recovery Plan, IT Contingency Plan, and Cyber Incident Response Plan. The Incident Response chapter describes this third plan at length.

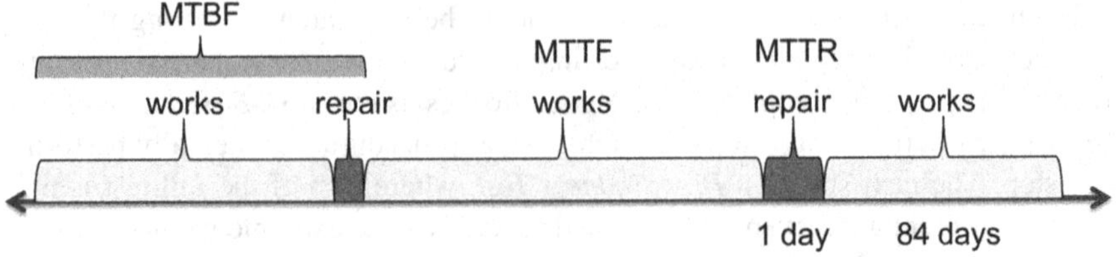

Fig. 5.8 MTBF = MTTF + MTTR

Table 5.6 Plans associated with business continuity

Focus	IT-focused	Business-focused
Event recovery	Disaster recovery plan Procedures to recover at alternate site	Business recovery plan Recover business after a disaster
	IT contingency plan Recovers major application or system	Occupant emergency plan Protect life and assets during physical threat
	Cyber incident response plan Handles malicious cyber incident	Crisis communication plan Provide status reports to public and personnel
Business continuity		Business continuity plan Operate business in alternate mode
		Continuity of operations plan Longer duration outages

Table 5.7 Types of business continuity insurance

Information Processing Facility (IPF) and equipment	Data and media	Employee damage
Business interruption: loss of profit due to IT interruption	Valuable papers & records: covers cash value of lost/ damaged paper & records	Fidelity coverage: loss from dishonest employees
Extra expense: extra cost of operation following IPF damage	Media reconstruction: cost of reproduction of media	Errors and omissions: liability for error resulting in loss to client
IS equipment and facilities: loss of IPF and equipment due to damage	Media transportation: loss of data during transport	

Business plans (right column) include event handling plans to handle aspects of a crisis, and business continuity plans, which describe business operations in a survival (Alternate) mode.

Table 5.7 shows different types of insurance that can help contain major expenses due to a disaster, categorized by protection type: to the Information Processing Facility (IPF), data and media, or employee damage [3].

Testing for larger organizations may include additional types of tests, including [8]:

- *Checklist Review*: Reviews coverage of plan—are all important concerns covered?
- *Structured Walkthrough*: Reviews all aspects of plan, often walking through different scenarios
- *Simulation Test*: Execute plan based upon a specific scenario, without alternate site
- *Parallel Test*: Bring up alternate off-site facility, without bringing down regular site
- *Full-Interruption*: Move processing from regular site to alternate site.

Three test stages are recommended:

1. *Pre-Test*: The test is set up. During Pre-Test, the staff may be prepared and equipment (e.g. for alternate off-site facility) set up.
2. *Test*: The test occurs.
3. *Post-Test*: Consists of analysis, cleanup and improvement. Analysis includes calculating metrics, such as the time required to complete the test, the percent success rate in processing, and the ratio of successful transactions in Alternate versus normal mode. Cleanup involves returning resources and deleting any test data. Improvement incorporates updating the disaster response plans and test plans.

As a result of testing, a *gap analysis* defines where the organization currently performs, compared to the desired level of performance. To achieve the desired level, improvements may require additional equipment or staff involvement, and better training and communication.

Auditors of business continuity should investigate a number of issues [3]. Are documents (BIA/BC/DRP) complete, fully featured, well detailed, accurate, in-line with business goals, and current? Is it clear who is responsible for what in BC/DRP plans, and are they happy, trained, and competent in their jobs? Is the backup site properly maintained and fully functional? Were DRP test plans executed, results analyzed, and corrections made? Is the BCP phone tree current, and do BC/DRP people have copies of required documents off-site? If used, does the hot site have correct copies of software? Internal and external auditors may use these questions to ensure preparedness.

5.6 Advanced: Considering Big Data Distributed File Systems

Reliability can be provided using Big Data databases, which are quick-access distributed databases that can handle large volumes of data: terabyte and petabyte databases. The advantages of the big data databases discussed here include their horizontal scalability, which enable easy expansion by adding commodity servers, and replicated servers, which automatically allocate and store data across multiple servers [9, 10]. However, these databases are noSQL servers; they only support the equivalent of a subset of SQL commands and queries. They do not support SQL joins, for example. Also, while they are great at reliability, they are not known for their confidentiality or integrity security features. Therefore, these aspects must be carefully considered, when necessary. This section considers two popular databases: Hadoop and MongoDB.

Hadoop is a popular database to support Big Data [11]. It is designed for large volumes, quick access, complex data mapping, and reliability through redundancy. Hadoop is an Apache distributed database, which replicates and distributes its data across multiple locations, and reconfigures itself automatically, following a failure. It can be built with standard hardware. Hadoop's two main components are MapReduce and the Hadoop Distributed File System (HDFS), which originated with Google versions. MapReduce handles requests for data operations, which are managed by a Job Tracker across nodes/clusters as <key, value> requests. The HDFS consists of Name Nodes, which track where information resides, and Data Nodes, which actually contain the data. Both Job Trackers and Name Nodes achieve reliability by relaunching requests and redistributing data respectively, following a failure in communication to any node.

Sometimes Hadoop is used as a backend database, with MySQL or HBase used as a front-end interface. MySQL supports SQL queries to handle complex queries, but is slow in a high-volume big data environment. *HBase* is a noSQL server supporting scalability and reliability through redundancy [12]. HBase uses a log-structured merge (LSM) tree to track data, which offers improved performance over Hadoop alone, when a high portion of transactions are inserts and/or random access requests. HBase also offers additional query and analysis capabilities beyond MapReduce, but less than MySQL.

MongoDB is a free document-oriented database that is used by MTV, Forbes, NY Times and Craigslist [9]. The NY Times uses MongoDB to rapidly store and retrieve photos. It orders groups of items into 'collections', which can be retrieved by collection name. These collections can then be sorted and filtered depending on specific field names, such as 'lastname'. Commands to access the database include: insert/save, find, update, remove, and drop, where each is executed as a function call passing record fields' name and value pairs, and can include comparison attributes. MongoDB is faster than traditional databases for larger batches of data, but cannot perform complex data joins.

5.7 Questions

For each of the following questions, be sure to write professionally in typed, essay form.

1. *Vocabulary.* Match each meaning with the correct vocabulary name.

Alternate mode	Disaster recovery plan	Recovery point objective
Sensitivity class	Interruption window	Incident response plan
Criticality class	Business impact analysis	Recovery time objective

a) A level of partial IT service provided as a backup mode, following a major IT failure and emergency recovery.
b) The duration of no service following an IT failure.
c) Following a major IT failure, IT uses this backup plan to resume a partial level of service.
d) The determination of which IT business functions are most critical to the organization.
e) The amount of information that can be lost, following an IT failure; equivalent to lost data since last backup.
f) The permitted amount of time a business function may be nonoperational following an IT failure.
g) A set of categories delineating the criticality of business functions.

2. *Workbook Solution for Specific Industry.* Consider an industry you currently work in or would like to work in. Assume the company is in your geographical region and is NOT a university. You may use the Security Workbook (at http://extras.springer.com), Business Continuity Chapter to complete the tables. For each table, include at least four business processes.

   a) Create an Impact Classification table, similar to Table 5.1.
   b) Create a BIA table, similar to Table 5.2.
   c) Create a RPO Controls table, similar to Table 5.3.
   d) Create a BC Overview table, similar to Table 5.4

3. *Cloud Services.* Look up websites for three different cloud providers.

   a) What security, availability, and backup services do they provide, for what price?
   b) Determine whether each provides SAAS, PAAS or IAAS services.

4. *Procedure Development.* Write a backup/recovery procedure for your computer's data that will enable anyone with your procedure to accomplish the operation. A procedure is a step-by-step description of how to perform an action (similar to the Security Workbook). You may save data to a CD or electronic drive. Answer the following questions in your Backup procedure: How do you initialize the backup? How do you label the backup? What data will you move, where is that data, and how do you move it? What problems might occur and how should they be handled? Also prepare a similar Recovery procedure.

5.7.1 Health First Case Study Problems

For each case study problem, refer to the Health First Case Study. The Health First Case Study and Security Workbook should be provided by your instructor or can be found at http://extras.springer.com.

Case study	Health first case study	Other resources
Addressing business impact analysis and business continuity	√	Security workbook

References

1. Gore A (2013) The future: six drivers of global change. Random House Inc, New York, NY, p 78
2. ISACA (2011) CISM® review manual 2012. ISACA, Arlington Heights, IL, pp 116–121, 227–237
3. ISACA (2010) CISA review manual 2011. ISACA, Arlington Heights, IL, pp 121–132, 295–305
4. Krutz RL (2010) Cloud security: a comprehensive guide to secure cloud computing. Wiley, Hoboken, NJ, p 2, 39–45
5. Behl A, Behl K (2012) Security paradigms for cloud computing. In: Fourth international conference on computational intelligence, communication systems and networks. IEEE Computer Society, Inst. Electrical & Electronics Eng. (IEEE), http://ieeexplore.ieee.org, pp 200–205
6. Cichonski P, Millar T, Grance T, Scarfone K (2012) NIST special publication (SP) 800-61 computer security incident handling guide, Rev. 2. Aug 2012. National Institute of Standards and Technology, pp 261–262
7. Verizon (2013) Verizon 2013 data breach investigations report. http://www.verizonenterprise.com/DBIR/2013. Accessed 20 Oct 2013
8. Harris S (2013) All-in-one CISSP® exam guide, 6th edn. McGraw-Hill Co., New York, NY, pp 885–972
9. Boicea A, Radulescu F, Agapin LI (2012) MongoDB vs Oracle – database comparison. In: Third international conference on emerging intelligent data and web technologies. IEEE, http://ieeexplore.ieee.org, pp 330–335
10. Vora MN (2011) Hadoop–HBase for large-scale data. In: International conference on computer science and network technology (ICCSNT), vol 1. IEEE, http://ieeexplore.ieee.org, pp 601–605
11. Singh K, Kaur R (2014) Hadoop: addressing challenges of big data. In: IEEE international advance computing conference (IACC). IEEE, http://ieeexplore.ieee.org, pp 686–689
12. Ding H, Jin Y, Cui Y, Yang T (2012) Distributed storage of network measurement data on HBase. In: IEEE 2nd international conference on cloud computing and intelligent systems. IEEE, http://ieeexplore.ieee.org, pp 716–720

Chapter 6
Governing: Policy, Maturity Models and Planning

> If we went in with a drone and knocked out a thousand centrifuges, that's an act of war. But if we go in with Stuxnet and knock out a thousand centrifuges, what's that? (Richard Clarke, counterterrorism czar for 3 U.S. presidents. [1])

Executive level management is responsible for strategic business goals (including for IT/security), managing risk, defining policies for the organization, and for staffing security. The previous two chapters addressed risk, including the chapter on Business Impact Analysis. This chapter addresses the remaining executive management responsibilities: strategic planning, policy, maturity models.

Depending on whether you like to work from the top down or bottom up (theory versus details), or whether your interests are mainly technical versus business, this chapter may be completed before or after the Tactical Security Planning chapters, if desired. If you have little knowledge of security technology, and you plan to work with Policy in the Security Workbook, you may find you have better security knowledge after completing the Tactical Planning section.

6.1 Documenting Security: Policies, Standards, Procedures and Guidelines

Security is a large, complex system. To implement effective security requires attention to technology, physical security, and administrative (or people) issues. Working with one security area will impact other areas. For example, aspects of business continuity impact information security, which impacts network and physical security. All areas impact metrics and personnel security. It takes a lot of documentation to plan this sophisticated system, train staff, and provide a knowledge database for staff. Documentation for security includes policies, procedures, standards and guidelines. See Fig. 6.1.

S. Lincke, *Security Planning*, DOI 10.1007/978-3-319-16027-6_6

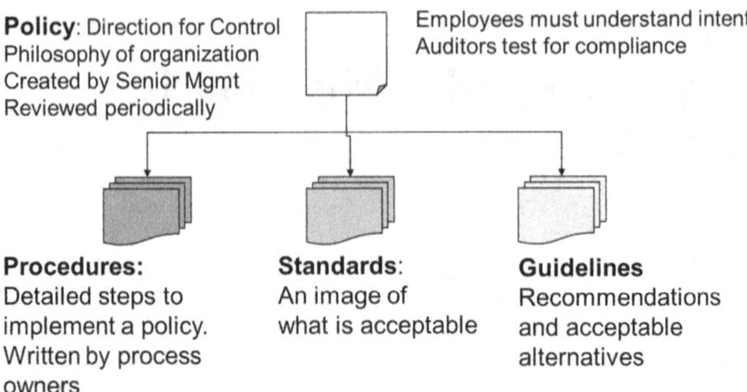

Fig. 6.1 Policies, procedures, standards, and guidelines

Policies are management directives. Policies do not describe how something will be achieved, but does order that something be accomplished. Policies may be high level or detailed. The Security Workbook has a chapter with proposed policies that may be edited for your organization. Examples of high level policies are shown here:

- Risks shall be managed utilizing appropriate controls and countermeasure to achieve acceptable levels at acceptable costs.
- Monitoring and metrics shall be implemented, managed, and maintained to provide ongoing assurance that all security policies are enforced and control objectives are met.

Standards are a detailed implementation of a policy. Standards are mandatory and are often described with the word 'shall'. Examples of standards might include the list of permitted software on a computer; the required length and attributes of a password; and the format of a backup disk label.

Procedures are a description of "how to" complete a task. A procedure often includes numbered steps to take to complete a task. Examples of procedures might include how to perform a disk backup; how to complete a multi-step test for a security audit; or steps to take when a hacker attack is detected. The Security Workbook is a series of procedures, guiding the reader in designing security.

Guidelines are recommendations that should be followed—in some cases, guidelines may not apply. Guidelines are often written with the word 'should'. Examples of guidelines might be how to create a password (e.g., use the first letter for three lines of a song), or which websites you are permitted to access at work. This textbook is a guideline: it tells you how to do things, but it is up to you as to what you actually choose to do.

Some policy documents demonstrate detailed policies, which could also be described as standards. They include:

- *Acceptable Usage Policy*: Describes permissible usage of IT equipment/resources
- *End-User Computing Policy*: Defines usage and parameters of desktop tools

- *Access Control Policies*: Defines how access permission is defined and allocated
- *Data Classification*: Defines data security categories, ownership and accountability

The Acceptable Use and/or End-User Computing Policies are normally signed by employees to indicate that they have read the documents. You will create a Data Classification policy as part of the Data Security chapter. After policy documents are created, they must be officially reviewed/accepted, maintained, disseminated, and tested for compliance.

The security function is toothless and severely handicapped without a good set of management-supported policy documentation.

6.2 Maturing the Organization via Capability Maturity Models and COBIT

Executive management must decide security policies for the organization, but must also understand the maturity level of its IT/security organization. Does the organization understand security? What aspects of security do we do well…and not so well? Are we dependent on key people remaining with the organization for our security implementation? Do we know how much security costs us, and how well we actually perform? These are some of the questions management should know the answers to.

A Capability Maturity Model helps an organization understand where they are performing relative to a standard. There are two well-known Capability Maturity Models related to IT/Security: The COBIT model and the *Systems Security Engineering Capability Maturity Model (SSE-CMM)* model. The SSE-CMM was adopted by the International Standards Organization (ISO) as ISO/IEC Standard 21827. ISO in addition publishes a set of security standards from ISO/IEC 27000 to 27050. These standards address basic security, topical areas (e.g., risk, audit, network security) and industries (e.g., finance, energy utilities).

The COBIT model was developed to help organizations achieve Sarbanes-Oxley compliance (see Fig. 6.2). SSE-CMM and COBIT are similar in nature, and have similar goals for each level. This text briefly describes the COBIT model, but will do so in terms of this text and the Security Workbook. One main difference between COBIT and this text is that this text addresses basic security planning, whereas COBIT® 5 addresses a model of full IT/IS maturity. For full implementation of COBIT, the reference: *COBIT® 5: Enabling Processes* [2] and *COBIT® 5: A Business Framework for the Governance and Management of Enterprise IT* [3], will help guide complete implementation of this comprehensive standard.

An organization might start at *Level 0 Incomplete Process*. Organizations at this level may be doing some or considerable IT/security practices. However, the practices are not fully defined and implemented, nor are they documented. What is done is accomplished by competent individuals.

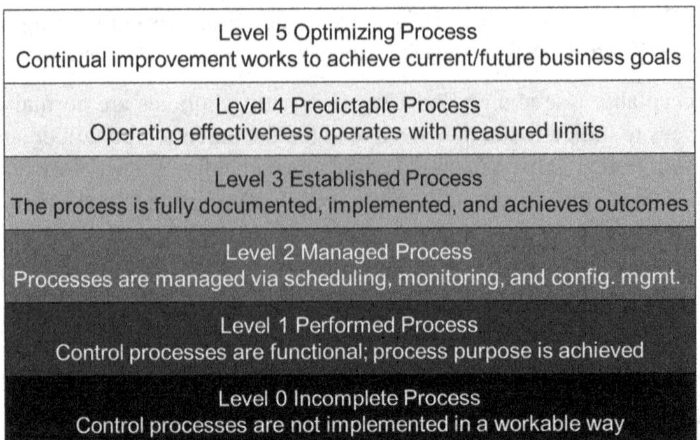

Fig. 6.2 COBIT 5 capability maturity model

Level 1 Performed Process occurs when full functionality of goals is achieved. When this full textbook is read, understood, and implemented, an organization would be at level one, using this text as a standard. However, the text can be implemented without the Security Workbook fully being documented. This would mean that if up-to-speed staff left, the new staff would need to read the textbook and discuss implementation with others.

Level 2 Managed Process means that the organization uses project management and configuration management to manage projects and documents. Plans are documented with schedules: for example, security enhancement and compliance testing (or audit) projects are scheduled and managed. Projects result in work product documents, which are evaluated before acceptance. Work product documents are maintained in a library (also known as configuration management), where previous versions are accessible and controlled. Thus, security documentation is partially developed; if key people leave, some key process knowledge will be lost.

Level 3 Established Process means that security policies, standards, procedures, and guidelines are fully documented and implemented. The organization has not only completed the Security Workbook's Chapter 2 Strategic Security Plans and Chapter 3 Tactical Security Planning, but has also completed Chapter 5 Operational Security Plans. Chapter 5 includes all the technical procedures to implement backup/reload, incident response procedures, etc. This complete documentation is followed by the organization. If key people leave, new people can easily follow the directions of existing organizational documentation.

Level 4 Predictable Process is achieved when we maintain a set of metrics to measure how our security actually performs. Do you know how many hacker attacks you defend against monthly, and how many attacks succeed? When the Metrics chapter of this book is seriously used to understand security compliance and effectiveness, and these security metrics achieve organizational goals, then the organization has achieved Level 4.

Level 5 Optimizing Process sets objectives for security metrics to achieve business goals. For example, fraud may eat 5 % of organizational income, and the organization would like to reduce this number to 2 % or less. Since the organization knows the full level of fraud or security attacks or security costs, and desires to achieve improved performance for business reasons, then new goals are periodically set and projects aim to achieve higher effectiveness.

Achieving higher levels of COBIT is not only complex from the maturity perspective, but also from a breadth perspective. COBIT covers information security (i.e., all of this book) in addition to other topics, such as: manage service agreements, suppliers, quality, change, capacity, software builds, knowledge, operations, budget and costs, etc. COBIT® 5 addresses 37 processes in total. Each process contains a set of Management Practices, which in turn contains a set of Activities. For example, the "Manage Security Services" Process contains seven Management Practices, including "Protect against malware". This Practice in turn contains six Activities including "Communicate malicious software awareness and enforce prevention procedures and responsibilities" [2].

Achieving even COBIT Level 1 is quite an accomplishment. One way to measure progress towards this goal is to create a chart listing the 37 processes, and grading your implementation for each process as N=Not achieved: 0–15 % fulfillment; P=Partially achieved: 15–50 % fulfillment; L=Largely achieved: 50–85 % fulfillment; and F=Fully achieved: 85–100 % fulfillment [3].

There is security documentation for all levels. This book and workbook is a security planning tool, which addresses security from a high level. Maturity models help organizations understand where they rate in managing security. Other documentation helps with technical details of how to implement specific security functions, including: ISO/IEC 270001 and subsequent ISO documents, NIST documents, and security web sites, such as SANS. Security experts, such as Security+, CISSP, CEH and CISA certified professionals can help to configure and test security settings.

6.3 Strategic, Tactical and Operational Planning

IT and information security should fit within the business plans of the organization. *Strategic planning* is decided at the executive level. They consider long-term (3–5 year) planning, which includes organizational goals and regulatory compliance (and for IT: technical advances). The *tactical plan* takes the strategic plan, and defines what needs to be accomplished in the next year to achieve strategic goals. *Operational-level plans* are detailed or technical plans used to implement the tactical plan.

An example of a strategic plan item might be: incorporate the business; market the new Super-Widgit product; or achieve COBIT Level 1. Assuming the third COBIT goal, a tactical plan might define which key areas in COBIT the organization plans to address in the first year, and what might be due each quarter (March, June, September, December). An operational plan would describe the intermediate

Strategic Plan Objective	Time frame
Incorporate the business	5 yrs
Pass an external audit	4 yrs

Tactical Plan: Objective	Time frame
Perform risk analysis	6 mos.
Perform BIA	1 yr
Define policies	1 yr

Operational Plan: Objective	Responsibility	Deliverable	Timeframe
Hire an internal auditor and security professional	VP Finance	New employees hired	Feb 1
Establish security team of business, IT, personnel	VP Finance & Chief Info. Officer (CIO)	Info Sec. Steering Committee has one meeting; people are committed	March 1
Team initiates risk analysis and prepares initial report	CIO & Security Steering Committee	Document: Security Issues	April 1

Fig. 6.3 Strategic, tactical and operational planning

deadlines deliverables and key persons responsible for the tactical goals. By allocating responsibility to specific people, setting dates and naming clear deliverables, progress can be determined and measured. For larger projects, project management may involve many tasks and people. In this case, PERT and GANTT chart tools can be used to organize people (resource allocation), task deliverables and due dates.

An example of such planning for a business considering incorporation is shown in Fig. 6.3. To pass an external audit (at the strategic level) requires performing risk analysis, Business Impact Analysis, and defining policies, which are the tactical goals for the first year. The operational plan starts the detailed task allocation to accomplish the tactical goals. Normally operational goals involve low-level managers, but in this case, the organization is just starting out and upper management must hire the appropriate people.

The development of the best security is a joint responsibility of the information security function and the business function. Business ensures that the security program is in alignment with business objectives. Security helps the business side understand various threats and risks. Business knows which assets to protect, while security knows how to protect them. When things go awry, business sets the priorities, which security implements. Security will lead the efforts and do much of the detailed security work; business helps to define administrative controls, but must also adhere to these controls. Thus, it is critically important that business and security plan security together.

Figure 6.4 lists the steps involved in a security development process. Note that arrows pointing to the data or people show where the data or committee is created. Arrows pointing to the process show where the data or people are used as input to the process.

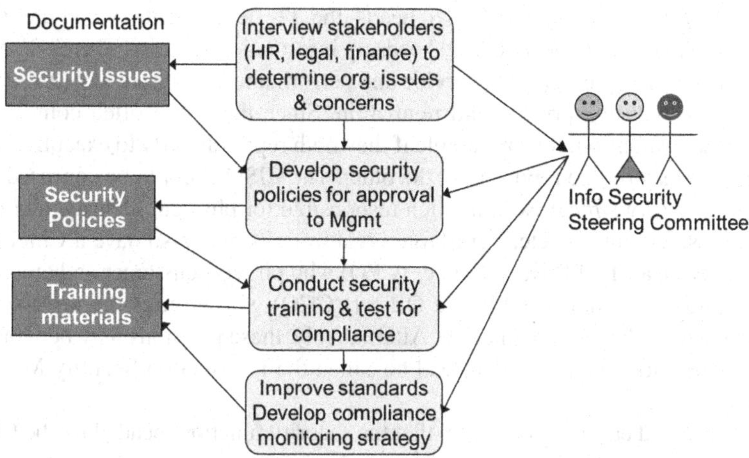

Fig. 6.4 Introducing security to an organization

The best method to introduce security into an organization is to create an Information Security Steering Committee, made up of security and business management. First, an organization chart will identify potential key players that should be befriended. Various stakeholders are interviewed to determine important assets, threats, security issues and security regulation. These issues are combined into a Security Issues document. Many of the key people expressing interest and concern can be invited to become part of the Information Security Steering Committee. This committee can then develop a set of Security Policies from the Security Issues, which are presented to management for review and approval. Once approved, the steering committee uses the Security Policies to develop security training materials and compliance test plans. After cycling through training and testing, the steering committee can perfect training and testing materials.

6.4 Allocating Security Roles and Responsibilities

Larger organizations will have many people involved in the security process. Executive and business management have important part-time roles in security [4–6]. Without their interest, the security organization will have a hard time being effective.

The Board of Directors is responsible for reviewing risk assessment and Business Impact Analysis results, ensuring adherence to regulation, and defining the tone from the top, including penalties for non-compliance of policies.

Executive management's concerns with security include complying with regulation, limiting liability, instituting policy, and controlling risk. They are responsible for instituting a security organization and monitoring its performance through measurements or metrics.

Chief Information Officer (CIO) heads the IT department, while the *Chief Information Security Officer (CISO)* heads up information security. The CIO's main concern is providing computing service and performance, while the CISO's mainly concerns are security, privacy and regulation. Since these two often compete for resources and attention, it is preferable if they both report directly to executive management, instead of one reporting to the other. The CISO is not to be confused with the *Chief Security Officer*, who is often responsible for physical security, including guards, close circuit TV, etc. Very large organizations may also have a Chief Risk Officer (CRO), a Chief Privacy Officer (CPO) who protects customer and employee privacy, and/or a Chief Compliance Officer (CCO) who ensures the organization complies with policy and regulation. Alternatively, these positions may be wrapped into the CISO job, which may instead be called the Information Security Manager position.

As mentioned earlier, it is critical that the security function, headed by the CISO, deals closely with business management to lead the security planning and testing efforts, in addition to authorizing access to IT applications. However, the CISO must have extended relations with all aspects of the business. The CISO must deal with executive management to help plan security strategy, perform risk management, and define policy. The CISO deals with human resources to establish hiring and training standards, define security roles and responsibilities, and handle employee-related security incidents. The CISO deals with the legal department for laws and regulation, and with purchasing concerning security requirements in Requests for Proposals (RFP) and contractual requirements. The CISO works with IT for security monitoring, incident response and equipment inventory. The CISO or security function works with software development to define security requirements, including access control. The CISO or security functions deals with quality control for security requirements/review, change control, and security upgrades/testing.

Other groups are important in that security personnel work closely with them. *Quality Control* tests an end product, to validate that the end product (for example software) is free from defects and meets user expectations. *Quality Assurance* ensures that staff follow defined quality processes during the design or building of a product: e.g., following standards in design, coding, testing, or configuration management. *Compliance* certifies compliance with organizational policies and regulations. For example, compliance could listen to select help desk calls to verify proper authorization occurs when resetting passwords.

The information security department includes other positions, including the Security Architect and Security Administrator [4, 6]. The *Security Architect* is a security engineer, who designs or evaluates security for technology controls: secure network topologies and access control, as well as administrative controls: security policies and standards. They work with compliance, risk management, and audit. Their five main areas of concern include:

- Policy: validate that control systems' rules align with policy and sufficiently restrict access;
- Effectiveness: ensure controls are reliable, automated, and protective without restricting business function;

- Placement: ensure controls safeguard important assets via layers or redundancy;
- Implementation: certify that controls are tested and monitored to ensure continual effectiveness;
- Efficiency: understand the impact to applications and their security when a control fails.

A *Security Administrator* is a system administrator for the security systems. They allocate login/passwords (or authentication/identity management) and permissions (or access control), according to a data owner's decisions. They also configure security, manage patches, test security controls, collect/report security metrics, monitor controls for security violations, and resolve attacks. Other administrative responsibilities may include preparing a security awareness program and reviewing and evaluating security policy.

6.5 Questions

1. ***Vocabulary.*** Match each meaning with the correct word.

Policy	Strategic plan	Operational plan
Guideline	Quality assurance	Quality control
Procedure	Chief security officer	Tactical plan
Standard	Maturity model	Chief information security officer

   a) A measure of the sophistication of the security process in an organization.
   b) An executive level business plan focusing on 3–5 years in the future.
   c) A detailed or technical business plan.
   d) A detailed description of a security rule.
   e) A 'how to' guide to accomplish a task.
   f) A test to ensure a business process occurs in the expected way.
   g) A test to ensure the end product is of sufficient quality.
   h) A management plan that addresses the next year.
   i) A high-level management directive.
   j) A suggested implementation of a security rule.
   k) The highest level business manager in charge of computer security.

2. *Planning COBIT*. Assume that you are a CISO and you have just brought your organization to Level 2 in COBIT's capability maturity model. Your president has announced that achieving level 3 is a strategic priority for the next 5 years. You currently have little security documentation, although your staff has been recently trained. Create a Tactical Plan for the next year, and an Operational Plan for the next quarter to help achieve this goal. (You may review the workbook to determine which aspects might be interesting to implement. Note: There are multiple right answers—the process is important. You may state your assumptions.)
3. *Policy, Standard, Procedure, Guideline*. Review the chapter on risk. What aspects of this text or workbook chapter might be considered a policy, standard, procedure and guideline? If you do not find an example of one of these, write an example.

6.5.1 Health First Case Study Problems

For each case study problem, refer to the Health First Case Study. The Health First Case Study and Security Workbook should be provided by your instructor or can be found at http://extras.springer.com.

Case study	Health first case study	Other resources
Developing a code of ethics	√	Security workbook
IT governance: planning for strategic, tactical, and operational security	√	Security workbook: Appendix B HIPAA slides or notes
Security program development: editing a policy manual for HIPAA	√	Security workbook, HIPAA slides or notes (security rule slides)

Note that the case: *Developing a Code of Ethics* can also be used for the Fraud Chapter

References

1. Rosenbaum R (2012) Cassandra syndrome. Smithsonian 43(1):15
2. ISACA (2012) COBIT® 5: enabling processes. ISACA, Arlington Heights, IL, pp 29–211
3. ISACA (2012) COBIT® 5: a business framework for the governance and management of enterprise IT. ISACA, Arlington Heights, IL, pp 41–45
4. ISACA (2011) CISM® review manual 2012. ISACA, Arlington Heights, IL, pp 116–121, 227–237
5. ISACA (2010) CISA review manual 2011. ISACA, Arlington Heights, IL, pp 121–132, 295–305
6. Harris S (2008) CISSP® all-in-one exam guide. McGraw Hill/Osborne, New York, NY

Part III
Tactical Security Planning

Tactical security planning combines technology and business to a higher degree than strategic security planning, which focuses more on business. This part gets into the nuts and bolts of security.

III.1 Important Tactical Concepts

Unfortunately, security is complex and not entirely predictable. Malware lodged into your home laptop can result in temporary identity theft of your credit card. However, malware lodged into a power utility server may bring down power for many communities, as it did with Stuxnet. This variability in the effect of security occurs because computer networks are a large interconnected system. Network interdependencies are complex and may generate new possibilities, called *emergent properties* [1]. Consider that when hydrogen and oxygen combine to create water, this combination results in vast new possibilities, unusual considering its two ingredients. Similarly when iron and nickel are combined, steel emerges, which is far stronger than either of its parts. Similarly, a combination of attacks may cause more damage than any individual attack launched by itself.

The three basic goals of security to consider throughout this section is CIA: Confidentiality assures that information (and equipment) is accessible only to authorized persons; Integrity assures that information is accurate, modified only by authorized persons in a valid way; and Availability assures that information is accessible to authorized persons when they need to access it. These three goals need to be protected across three domains: during storage (e.g., on disk or removable memory), during transmission, and when data is processed.

Restricting access to all protected assets is one way to guarantee security—but this also prevents organizations and people from doing any functions related to these assets. Thus, there is a balance between security and *usability*. Instead of simply restricting all access, a little extra thought in planning can keep assets safe, while enabling proper usage.

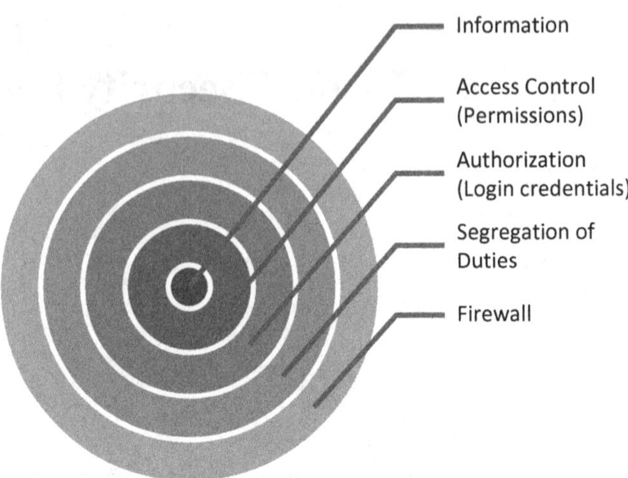

Fig. III.1 Defense in depth

Defense in Depth is a method which requires intruders to counter multiple defenses before successfully achieving their goal. Traditional security, such as a castle-fortress, shows excellent security layering. A *cascading defense* means that as an attacker penetrates a layer, she runs up against other defensive layers. For example, castles were often built on hills or mountains, with trees cut down immediately before the castle walls. Alternatively, there may be a moat. In either case, an attacker cannot get close to the castle without being slowed down and seen. The huge stone castle walls are a second barrier, with armed guard posts to shoot intruders. Thirdly, there is a single entrance, accessible via drawbridge, and protected by guards. Fourth, there may be internal spies inside the castle. Thus, to invade a castle in olden times required beating defense after defense mechanism. The same is sound advice for today's computer networks. Defense in Depth is a concept to consider throughout the book.

A simple defense in depth design for a computer network is shown in Fig. III.1. This onion has many layers of defense mechanisms. Although all layers are useful, some layers can be bypassed: the guards may be bypassed via Internet access; a firewall is bypassed with a valid web application. An attacker may be able to bypass the authorization, access control and segregation of duties layers with valid account credentials; therefore, security awareness training and blocking frivolous social websites and personal email may be critical defenses to add to this design.

This part contains a partial security design for Einstein University (EU). Tables are copied from the Security Workbook: text in typed letters is the skeleton text provided for your editing, whereas printed text shows modifications for the EU case study. While this part helps you to *design* security, it does not *implement* security. At the end of each Workbook design section is a description of the required steps a security administrator/architect will have to take to complete the job.

It is recommended that these chapters are performed in order. Information security provides a foundation for Network Security, which provides a foundation for later chapters. Since security is a system, referencing back and fixing earlier chapters, when working with later chapters, is part of the normal process.

Chapter 7
Designing Information Security

If you store it, they will come (Justine Young Gottshall, Partner, InfoLaw Group [2]).

Previous chapters have emphasized that criminals and spies concentrate on financial account information, trade secrets, and internal organization data. This chapter is all about protecting information assets via the three goals of security, CIA: confidentiality, integrity, and availability. Two additional requirements that may apply include legal and privacy liability. We achieve these goals by classifying information assets and then defining how each class of assets should be protected. That, in a nutshell, is what this chapter is all about.

7.1 Important Concepts and Roles

Important concepts in information security consider retaining and applying CIA to information. The first is minimization related to *Privacy*: personal or private information should only be retained when a true business need exists. Private data is a liability; if you can eliminate information or retain the information for a minimal duration as possible, you limit liability. Some protected personal information is protected by state breach laws, HIPAA, FERPA, GLB, etc., and includes social security numbers, state identification numbers, driver's license numbers, financial account or credit card information, birth date and place, and medical information (including biometric/genetic data). If you retain this information, it is best to eliminate them or retain them for as short a period as possible, unless you have a real business or compliance need.

For many organizations, eliminating credit card information is not on option. In this case, *Need-to-Know* limits the number of people who have access to this information and the type of information to be retained. For example, PCI DSS prohibits retention of payment card PIN information or the card verification code, in any form [3]. To maximize the first CIA goal of Confidentiality, persons should have ability to access data sufficient to perform their primary job role and no more. With payment

S. Lincke, *Security Planning*, DOI 10.1007/978-3-319-16027-6_7

card numbers, PCI DSS requires that these Primary Account Numbers (PAN) are masked before display and any privileges to see these numbers are well-documented as to business need.

It is not only viewing private information that is an issue. The second CIA goal of Integrity ensures that information is correct. To achieve this, only people who should be able to change information are given permissions to do so. *Least Privilege* ensures that persons should have ability to do tasks sufficient to perform their primary job and no more. *Access control* in a computer system enables defining permissions that employees, contractors and/or volunteers should have, and these permissions should allow them to create, view, modify, and delete only the necessary information to do their jobs.

At a higher level, Integrity is best achieved using Segregation of Duties, which ensures that no person can assume two roles: Origination, Authorization, Distribution, and Verification. Employees who have worked at a company for a long time tend to accumulate many permissions. The Data Owners or the personnel office should change permissions for employees as their jobs change, to ensure personnel's permissions are consistent with their current primary job function. A Security Team should design and implement computer applications, processes and systems with segregation of duties in mind.

The third CIA goal, Availability, is concerned that authorized people have access to information when they need it—system failures, slowdowns, and hacker attacks all prevent systems from being available. Availability is addressed in part with Business Continuity, Physical Security, and this chapter. It is helpful, but not absolutely necessary, that readers complete the Business Continuity chapter before continuing.

Business, IT and security all collaborate to protect data, as shown in Fig. 7.1. Important business roles in Information Security include the Data Owner and Process Owner, who may be the same or different people. The *Data Owner* or *Information Owner* is the manager for a business unit who defines which employees get which permissions [4]. As new employees are hired, or jobs change, these permissions should change as per the guidance of the Data Owner.

The *Process Owner* is a manager for a business unit who understands how the business works, and how it should be best protected. They are part of the Information Security Steering Committee, and help to define security documentation and training materials, and enforce policy.

Important technology roles include the Security Architect, who understands security technology and develops security policy, the Data Custodian, and the Security Administrator. The *Security Administrator* is the systems administrator for security systems. The Data Owner defines the permissions and may enter the permissions directly on a computer. If instead the Security Administrator is the person who physically enters permissions, the Data Owner must provide a written, signed copy of the access control orders. Preferably, the Data Owner would hand the signed document to the Security Administrator to ensure that critical permissions could not be faked.

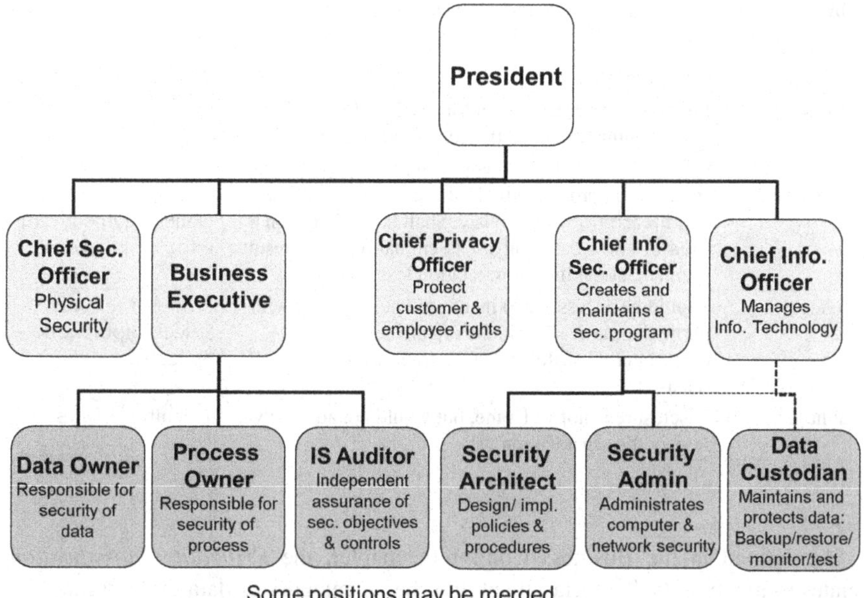

Fig. 7.1 Security staff involved with data security (or not)

The *Data Custodian* may report to security or IT. They are responsible for protecting the information. This includes data backup/restore, verifying that backups are valid, and documenting actions related to the data.

7.2 Design: Classifying Data for CIA

Simplicity in security design enables people to easily design, understand, and implement security. Security classifications are one way to achieve such simplicity and minimize the complexity of implementation. Information security uses two classification systems: *Sensitivity Classification* relates to confidentiality and integrity, whereas Criticality Classification relates to availability [4]. Sensitivity Classes usually include 3–5 classes. Table 7.1 shows an example of how skeleton text in the Security Workbook was modified to describe sensitivity classes for Einstein University. For the university, three classes look useful, but the Proprietary class can be dropped. For the Confidential class, the Description column text is modified to explicitly refer to privacy laws and standards. The government includes the sensitivity classes: Top Secret, Secret, and Classified [5].

Table 7.1 Sensitivity classes for Einstein University

Sensitivity classification	Description	Information covered
Proprietary	Protects competitive edge. Material is of critical strategic importance to the company. Dissemination could result in serious financial impact	
Confidential	Information protected by FERPA, PCI DSS, HIPAA and breach notification law. Shall be available on a need-to-know basis only. Dissemination could result in financial liability or reputation loss	Student info & grades, Payment card info., Employee info.
Private	Should be accessible to management or for use with particular parties within the organization. Could cause internal strife or divulge trade secrets if released	Professor research, Student homework, Budgets
Public	Disclosure is not welcome, but would not adversely impact the organization	Teaching lectures

As defined in the Business Continuity chapter, the *Criticality Classification* relates to availability. This classification scheme categorizes data by how long the company can survive without automated or computerized access to the data. Classes include:

- *Critical:* Cannot be performed manually. Tolerance to interruption is very low,
- *Vital:* Can be performed manually for very short time,
- *Sensitive:* Can be performed manually for a period of time, but may cost more in staff,
- *Nonsensitive:* Can be performed manually for an extended period of time with little additional cost and minimal recovery effort.

Not all data in the organization needs to be explicitly classified—however, the most important data should be. This classification scheme defines the controls used to protect confidentiality and availability, including how data is marked, distributed, handled, stored, transmitted, archived, and disposed of. Table 7.2 shows suggested handling for various sensitivity classes, amended in script for a university environment (mainly involved in teaching). It is important that all staff understand the classification process and how data should be handled.

Labeling It is possible to use a "Confidential" label as a header or footer on all pages, as well as the title page. The U.S. government uses cover sheets with various colors to reflect sensitivity classes [5].

Disk Storage and Archive Two issues to be resolved include length of period to hold data, and how to store data. Security regulations often specify a length of time to store data. For HIPAA, data shall be retained for 6 years. For Sarbanes–Oxley, audit papers must be retained for 7 years, and records used to assess internal controls over financial data shall never be disposed of [6].

Table 7.2 Handling of sensitive information

	Confidential	Private	Public
Access	Need to know	Need to know	Need to know
Paper Storage	Locked cabinet, locked room if unattended	Locked cabinet, locked room if unattended	Locked cabinet or locked room if unattended
Disk storage	Password-protected, encrypted	Password-protected, Encrypted	Password-protected
Labeling and handling	Label 'Confidential', Clean desk, low voice, No SSNs, ID required	Clean desk, low voice	Clean desk, low voice
Transmission	Encrypted	Encrypted	
Archive	Encrypted	Encrypted	
Disposal	Degauss and damage disks Shred paper	Secure wipe Shred paper	Reformat disks
Special notes	*Grades*: When a student asks, email of grades for one student/one course is permitted with email security notice appended		

Encryption is the best technique to store sensitive data. Encrypted disks are considered safe under the State Breach Notification Laws. Therefore, if you store any protected information (formally known as Personally Identifiable Information or PII), it should be encrypted, whether it is on disk or backup. It is possible to encrypt specific files or the whole disk. This is a low-cost control with the only precaution that if the encryption key is lost, your data cannot be retrieved. Encrypting a disk is not entirely safe: when you power up your computer you enter the encryption key. Any subsequent accesses through the operating system, e.g., by you or a hacker, will enable either of you to see the data. The data is safely encrypted, however, if a powered-down encrypted laptop or encrypted backup disk/tape is lost or stolen.

The issue remains of how to protect decrypted data after power up. Access control, which adheres to need-to-know and least-privilege concepts, ensures that only authorized people have access. Then, it may be important to prevent even authorized people from writing sensitive data to portable storage. It is possible to install only CD readers, instead of CD reader/writers, and disable USB drives. These actions would have prevented one Wikileak covert data exfiltration in 2010, when a Private overwrote a Lady GaGa CD daily with proprietary U.S. government information [7].

Transmission Encryption is important to protect data being transmitted. Encryption can occur on an application basis, or link basis affecting all transmissions. Email is normally not encrypted, but Secure Shell (SSH) and Secure File Transfer (SFTP) are two applications that enable encrypted remote login and file transfer respectively. Further discussion of encryption transmissions are addressed in the next chapter on Network Security.

Repair and disposal These should be carefully handled, since a criminal technique, *dumpster diving*, is messy but seriously useful in obtaining confidential information.

For repairs, disks can be removed before shipment to safeguard disk data. Disks to be discarded should not simply be reformatted; this usually wipes clean only the disk's header index directory, which is similar to clearing out the table of contents for a book, but leaving the rest of the book intact! A *secure wiping* process writes a pattern over the entire disk, which is better since it is the equivalent of overwriting the entire 'book'—but in very secure situations magnetic traces of the previous data may still remain. Damaging the disks, by disassembling them and taking a hammer to them is a low cost technique that when added to secure wipe can be effective for mid-level security data. Alternative means may include incineration or for paper, pulping. For highly secure information, it is useful to demagnetize a disassembled disk, which is known as *degaussing* [5].

Peripheral memories, such as DVDs, CDs, diskettes and tapes, should be similarly cleaned or destroyed. In these cases, shredders, grinders, incinerators or disintegrators may all be useful in destroying the media. Demagnitizing works on magnetic diskettes and tapes, but not on optical DVDs, CDs or electronic flash (thumb) drives.

Other non-technical controls, such as physical controls, will be addressed in the Physical Security Chapter. This later chapter will also be important for addressing availability and its criticality classes.

After you have defined how each of your sensitivity classes should be handled, the next step is to create an Information Asset Inventory. This table (e.g., Table 7.3) defines each important asset, its sensitivity and criticality class, people who help to secure it, and people or roles who have access to it.

In this Course Registration example, Granted Permissions briefly lists who has access to this application, without being specific as to what they may or may not access within it. A more detailed definition of permissions and authentication/ accountability controls will be our next steps.

Role-Based Access Control defines various roles in the organization, and then allocates permissions to the various roles [4, 8]. Users are allocated a role (e.g., June

Table 7.3 Information asset inventory: course registration

Asset name	Course registration
Value to organization	Records which students are taking which classes
Location	IS Main Center
Sensitivity and criticality classifications	Sensitive, Vital
IS system/server name	Peoplesoft
Data owner	Registrar: Monica Jones
Designated custodian	IS Operations: John Johnson
Authentication and accountability controls	Login/Password Authentication: Complex passwords, changed annually Logs: Staff access to student records
Granted permissions	Department Staff, Advising: Read Students, Registration: Read, Write Access is permitted at any time/any terminal

is an Accountant) and the role has permissions (Accountant has access to files or records A–C). Permissions can be set at the application, file, form or attribute-within-form basis. Permissions can be allocated for Create (C) as in create a new customer or transaction, Read (R) e.g., read a record, Write (W) or change/edit a record, Execute (X) as in run a program, and Delete (D). Below, Fig. 7.4 defines three roles for a university, and Fig. 7.5 defines permissions. These examples are short for demonstration purposes only—a complete security must consider the full scenario, at least within a defined scope.

7.3 Selecting Technology and Implementation Options

In this section we consider authentication, access controls, and accountability. The first two enable entry to a computer and applications, while accountability makes you responsible for your actions. *Authentication* refers to identifying yourself to a computer (e.g., Terry Dinshah) often via login/password, whereas *access control* determines which permissions the known user (Terry Dinshah) can do. There are four levels of controls: access to the network, the computer, the application, and various packages or subsystem/servers used by the application, such as a database system. *Accountability* ensures that you are responsible for your actions, by logging your actions.

7.3.1 Authentication: Login or Identification

Authentication is the mechanism of identifying users to enable access to a system. The traditional method of authentication is login and password, where the login identifies who you are, and the password is the secret that only you know. The password mechanism is inadequate because passwords can be guessed (via social engineering, dictionary attacks or brute force) and password files can be copied to be repeatedly attacked elsewhere. In the worst case, password guessing is extremely easy when the default password for a device was never changed.

Some precautions can help to protect the login-password method. For every device, passwords shall always be changed from the default and should never be written down or retained near the terminal or in a desk. It is best to configure operating systems to require complex passwords, periodic password changes, and retention of a password history. Passwords should be long and complex, including 2–3 of: alpha, numeric, upper/lower case, and special characters. While the 'recommended' length is at least 8 characters, using a 12- or 16-character password is much safer, providing more protection than complexity. Passwords should not be identifiable with the user, for example, a family member or pet name. Preferably passwords are changed as often as possible: every 30 days or less for very high security applications, quarterly for high security applications, and annually otherwise. The password history feature ensures that a password cannot be reused during a period, for example 1 year. Password characters should never be displayed when typed, except via asterisks: ***.

The login-password combination is known as *single factor authentication*, since it relies on 'something you know'. Identification can include other factors, such as 'something you are or do': biometrics, and 'something you have' such as badges or identification cards [4, 8]. *Multi-factor authentication* includes two or more forms of ID, and is considered superior to the simple login/password combination. Thus a two-factor authentication might include login + password + fingerprint, which is something you know and are. A three-factor authentication would include each something you know, have, and are/do.

7.3.1.1 Biometric Systems

Biometrics can be used to recognize 'something you are' such as fingerprint, face, hand, iris and retina, or 'something you do', such as signature and voice [8]. Biometric systems are evaluated by user acceptance, accuracy, reliability, and cost/storage requirements. For example, retina matching is highly accurate, but deemed invasive since a person needs to stand 1–2 in. away from a device for a good read. Palms, hands, and fingerprints are more socially acceptable, but do require physical contact with a reader, which may get slimy. Also physical injuries may affect accessibility. Iris readers do not require physical contact and are socially acceptable, but require large storage and are high cost.

Biometric systems do not provide 100 % accuracy. Their accuracy is measured by percentage using a *False Rejection Rate (FRR)*, which is the rate of valid users rejected due to no recognition and *False Acceptance Rate (FAR)*, which is the rate of invalid users accepted due to false recognition. The biometric devices are tuned to minimize both types of errors, when FRR = FAR, which is known as the *Equal Error Rate (EER)*.

While biometrics can provide more reliable authentication, it does need to be securely installed and handled. Biometric data must be stored, backed up and transmitted in an encrypted way. There should be a backup authentication method, if this method fails. Biometric devices must be physically protected: if a door entry device can be screwed off a wall, it provides no security. Finally, there should be adequate documentation and testing to help people use the device and validate its operation.

7.3.2 Access Control: Permissions

Assuming the computer user has successfully authenticated (or logged in), access control will decide what the user can do on the computer. The type of access control used in the workbook (and Tables 7.4 and 7.5) is Role-Based Access Control

Table 7.4 Partial table of roles for university

Role name	Role description	Current staff (example or complete staff)
Student	Registers for courses, work-study, and scholarships. Examines personal grades and grade history. Accesses university resources: library, courses (D2L). Pays bills	Includes undergraduate and graduate students, full and part-time
Instructor	Observes registration and creates grades for personally-taught classes in registration system. Submits files (notes, homework), quizzes, and grades to D2L, reads student homework and quiz submissions	Includes adjuncts, instructors, and professors
Registrar	Organizes courses, school calendar. Runs grades	Anita Jones, John Robin
Advisor	Reads student transcripts and grade reports for personally-designated advisees and students in own major. Can write advising notes for same students	Includes Advising department, Advising staff outside Advising department, Faculty who advise

Table 7.5 Partial role-based access control for university

Role name	Information access (e.g., record or form) and permissions (e.g., RWX)
Instructor	Student Records: Grading Form (for own courses) RW Student Transcript (current students) R Transfer credit form R Desire2Learn System: All parts (RW) except students grades (R)
Advising	Student Records: Student Transcript (current students in major area) R Fee Payment R Transfer credit form R
Registration	Student Records: Fee Payment RW Transfer credit form RW

(RBAC). This technique allocates permissions by role. Other forms of access control include [4, 8]:

Mandatory Access Control (MAC) MAC is system-determined access control. It is often used within operating systems to control access to files. Terry is allowed to read File A and File B, can read or write to File C, but cannot access File D. In the UNIX-style MAC example in Fig. 7.2, John has read, write, execute (rwx) permissions for File A, while the Mgmt group has read, execute (r x) permissions. Also, in Table 7.3, the "Granted Permissions" entry defines who has access to the file, without worrying about form-level access. Users are allocated to a MAC group according to any definition.

Discretionary Access Control (DAC) DAC enables a user with permissions to distribute those permissions. In this case, John has permissions to records A–F, and he give June permissions for A–C, while May gets permissions for D–F. These two

Mandatory Access Control

File	User	Group	Permi...
A	John	Mgmt	rwx, r x
B	June	Billing	, r
C	May	Factory	r x, r x
D	Al	Billing	
E	Don	Billing	

Role-Based Access Control

Login	Role	Permission
John	Mgr	A, B,C,D,E,F
June	Acct.	A,B,C
Al	Acct.	A,B,C
May	Factory	D,E,F
Pat	Factory	D,E,F

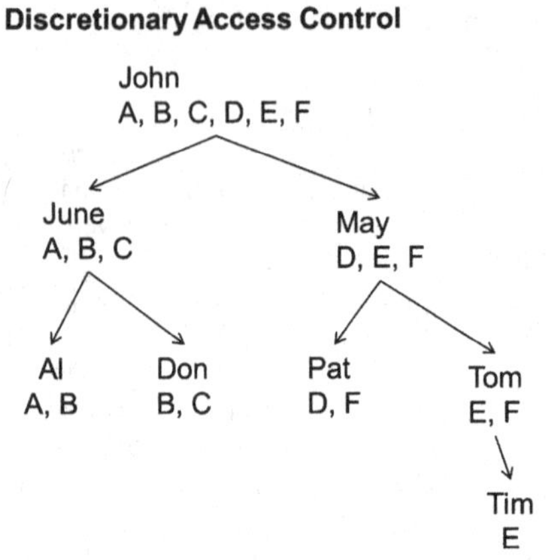

Discretionary Access Control

John
A, B, C, D, E, F
June
A, B, C
May
D, E, F
Al
A, B
Don
B, C
Pat
D, F
Tom
E, F
Tim
E

Fig. 7.2 Various examples of access controls

persons, June and May, can then divvy out permissions to other people within the permissions they have. Thus, June can give permissions to A, B, or C, but not D. DAC may be used within databases.

Physical Access Control This technique provides or prevents access to physical locations, via keys, badges, biometrics, locks, and fences.

7.3.3 Logs: Accountability

For secure applications, for example performing financial transactions, handling payment cards or writing medical prescriptions, people must be accountable for their actions. The best way to ensure accountability is to log or record transactions using login IDs: Who did what when? Periodic review helps to find accesses with excess authority and track fraud. HIPAA health regulation requires such audit trails. Audit trails should be sensitive to privacy: protected information should be encrypted. Logs should also record access violations to the computer, network or data files, such as login successes and failures.

Intruders in a computer system often want to change the audit trail to hide their tracks. Therefore, logins must be unique and logs can never be changed. The best log mechanisms use write-once devices or are signed with digital signatures. Segregation of duties is important with logs. Preferably security personal would configure system logs while system administration performs jobs which create the logs. Security and systems admins and managers have READ-only access to logs. After a sufficiently long period logs can be deleted. PCI DSS requires logs to be retained for 1 year, with logs from the last 3 months quickly accessible [3].

Monitoring audit trails is an important tool to recognize intruders. Log monitoring is required by security regulation/standards such as HIPAA and PCI DSS. PCI DSS requires daily review of security, payment card and other critical devices or systems. However, audit logs are proliferous, and require professional IT staff to monitor. Audit Reduction tools filter important logs and analyze log trends. Such tools are known as *Security Information and Event Management (SIEM)* [9]. Two methods such log analysis tools use include:

- *Attack/Signature Detection*: A sequence of log events may signal an attack (e.g., 1,000 login attempts).
- *Trend/Variance-Detection*: Notices changes from normal user or system behavior (e.g., login during night for daytime employee).

7.4 Audit

During an internal or external audit, an auditor should be concerned that information security policies and procedures are thoughtfully documented and implemented, including that authorization is documented and matches reality and that access follows need-to-know. Workers (employees and volunteers) should be aware of security awareness and their security responsibilities, through regular training. Data owners and data custodians must be implementing their responsibility for safeguarding data, and Security Administrators should be providing adequate physical and logical security for the information security program, data and equipment, and monitoring logs.

7.5 Advanced: Administration of Information Security

An attacker needs two pieces of information to obtain entry: a login ID and a password. Commonly named login IDs such as Guest, Administrator or Admin should be removed or renamed. Very often an attacker will know the login identifier if they know someone's email name. To prevent this, login IDs should follow a confidential internal naming rule.

A password dictionary or brute force attack will lead to multiple incorrect password guesses. When 5–6 incorrect guesses in a row occur, the account should be locked out and a log (or alarm) written. The account can be automatically reinstated some period later (e.g., 1 hour or 1 day). This will slow down and discourage the attacker, as well as notify the administrator that an attack is occurring. The only accounts that should never be locked out, is the locally-accessed administrator account. Local administrators—who are on-site—should always be able to get in!

If an attacker becomes an Administrator, they can do anything. If they cannot easily guess an administrator password, perhaps they can get an admin to open an

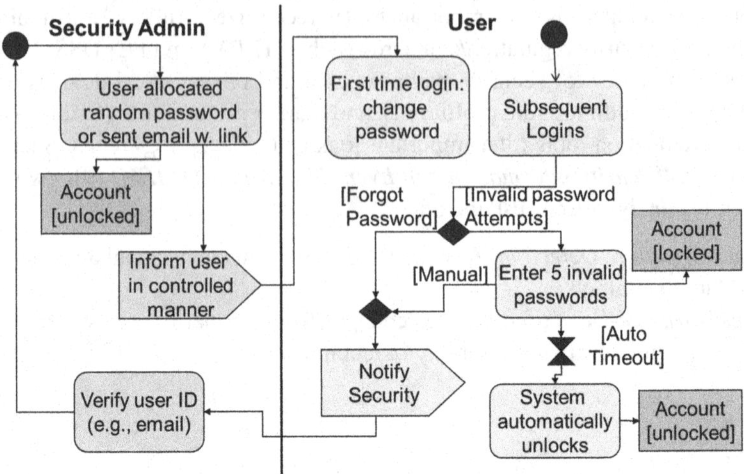

Fig. 7.3 Password lockout algorithm

attachment or run an executable on a web page. This gives the attacker one-shot admin permissions to perhaps copy a password file or install a backdoor for further entry. To prevent this, minimize the number of admin accounts on every system. If you are an administrator, never check your emails or search the web using an admin account. Never share your admin account password. The admin password can be kept in a locked cabinet within a sealed envelope, where a manager has the key.

Attackers who are physically present can gain entrance when a victim walks away from their computer without locking it. To minimize this, sessions should timeout and require password reentry after a period of 10–15 min.

Just in case the attacker is successful in entry, passwords need to be protected in a system. The password file should only be readable by an administrator, and stored passwords should be strongly encrypted using a one-way algorithm.

Figure 7.3 is an Activity Diagram that shows a workable user lockout algorithm. This activity diagram is a type of flow chart that begins at the black dot on the upper left side. There are two swimlanes showing the actions of the security administrator on the left, and the end user on the right. Rectangles with rounded edges are actions, and a black diamond indicates a decision point or decision connection point. To follow the logic, start at the black dot and follow the actions and their arrows. Rectangles with squared edges are data. They indicate a change in status of the account: unlocked or locked. The block arrows indicate a communication between the security admin and the user; emails should never contain passwords.

Single Sign-On is a feature where a user uses only one password to access all systems [8]. This is achievable using a single authentication database, which all systems use to verify logins. This is a preferred technique because of its obvious advantages: one good password replaces lots of passwords and IDs consistent throughout system(s). Single sign-on reduces the possibility that people will write down passwords. Another benefit is that it leads to reduced administrator work in setup and forgotten passwords. The obvious disadvantage is that a single authentication database is a single point of failure, which can result in a total compromise if one single system password becomes known. It is also a complex implementation since it requires reconfiguration of many systems; it may even require software development to implement compatibility. This extra configuration work makes single sign-on time consuming and more expensive.

7.6 Advanced: Designing Specialized Information Security

This section considers two applications: big data and highly secure applications.

7.6.1 Big Data: Data Warehouses

Information is worth money, since it is often sold or harnessed to optimize decisions. This has led to data analytics on large databases. This may lead to good things: (e.g.,) medical discoveries, weather analysis, and increased profits, but it can also lead to data breaches and identity theft.

Data quality is the usefulness of data for a consumer [10]. It measures the accuracy and completeness of the data. Data can be ill-calibrated and flawed: statistics may be used to present false information in order to make a sale or gain economic advantage. Data quality should be the measure of confidence the user has in the data. However, the data a consumer wants may not match the data a provider is willing to provide, for security risk reasons.

The privacy requirements of data are related to *trust* [10]: how comfortable is a provider of data in sharing data with a consumer of data? Medical, financial and government institutions (such as police, military) rely on consultants and their own employees to perform certain tasks or share data. Thus there is a need to hide certain data, while allowing the use of other data for a specifically defined purpose. Statistical data may be permitted, while the personal information upon which it is derived may not. However, even statistical data can divulge excessive information if the sample size is small.

One way to hide details is to anonymize the data, using *data obfuscation*. It is possible to blacklist specific data fields (e.g., name, address), which prevents their disclosure, and whitelist other data fields, which permit disclosure. One may classify certain fields like zip code or age into categories. Data can be randomized using a Gaussian statistical distribution, so that any particular value is not accurate, but that statistical means and variances are generally accurate [11]. This masking can happen in a static way—at data provision—or dynamically, so that privileged users may see the accurate data, while others see obfuscated data. Data obfuscation is a way to balance a data provider's risk, while providing the client permissible data quality—but the means of anonymizing the data must be done very carefully to ensure privacy.

Two approaches to planning data warehouses include collecting it all and sorting later, or deciding what problem you want to solve and then aggregating that. The second method is superior to the first because it considers the business need for the data. Carefully evaluating the actual needs of data analysis may ensure that minimum data is actually retained in a data warehouse [12].

Once the Big Database is built, security for big data should minimally include [14]:

- Encryption: Stored and transmitted data should both be strongly encrypted. A vault securely manages certificates and keys.
- Authentication and Access Control: Finely grained access control supports permissions at the field and record level.
- Firewall: Restricted access to only certain types of messages, potentially from certain locations.
- Security Intelligence: Tool provides alarms regarding potential intrusions. Advanced tools might have a real-time security status display, similar to a SIEM.

A simple approach is to aggregate the data into one collection, then protect that extremely securely [12]. A complex but possible more secure approach fragments data in a distributed way, so that no one location provides any meaningful information. An example implementation is the RAID-type configuration, where a record could be distributed over four databases [15]. Alternatively, data can be divided up logically across databases, so that (for example) contact information, credit card number/expiration, and CVV are retained in three different databases [16]. This is effective in independent attacks, but not if an attacker manages to penetrate an account.

HIPAA allows for data aggregation, which combines information from multiple health providers [17]. One method of data analysis is the "limited data set", which excludes all identifying information such as name, address, contact information, health plan/account numbers, certification/license numbers, vehicle information, device/serial identifiers, internet (IP/URL) information, biometric and facial images. The advantage of this technique is that even if an account is penetrated, data is obfuscated.

7.6.2 Designing Highly Secure Environments

Consider that you may want to purchase something on the Internet. You can use your debit or credit card or mail in a check. You may use your work computer, your home/children's computer, or the public library computer. These various options likely evoke different levels of confidence from you that the security of your payment card is safe. You may trust some options more than other options. Some environments, such as banking, government and defense, require more substantial levels of trust than other applications, since they demand extremely secure data classifications and suffer greater risks. A component can be trusted when it has verified security mechanisms, which cannot be disabled or subverted.

This section addresses how to achieve trust, when implementing multiple levels of security. The Bell and La Padula Model describes security policies that help to build trust.

7.6.2.1 Bell and La Padula Model (BLP)

The Military follows the Bell and La Padula Model [4]. In the traditional model, objects are assigned a security class. In the BLP model, people also are assigned an Authorization Level or a Level of Trust. The Property of Confinement states that a person can write to a classification level at their level and above (Write Up); and can read at a classification level at their level and below (Read Down). Figure 7.4 shows Joe with a Secret classification, which is shown in parenthesis. Joe can thus write to the Secret and above classification levels, and read from Secret or below classification levels.

There can be issues where a high-level person needs to write orders for lower level persons. The Tranquility Principle states that an Object's class cannot change, while the Declassification Principle enables a Subject to lower his or her own class, as an exception to the Write Up rule.

People and objects can also be assigned a subject or domain area. Security classes can then be documented as: (S, D) = (sensitivity, domain) for a subject [5]. The Confidentiality Property states that a subject can access an object if it dominates the object's classification level. In Fig. 7.5, the female is assigned a security class of (Secret, Engineer). She can read any code, email, and user documentation within the engineering group.

Fig. 7.4 BLP: Property of confinement

(Confid., Finance)

(Secret, Eng)

Class	Finance	Engineering	Personnel
Top Secret	Customer list	New plans	
Secret	Dept. Budgets	Code	Personnel review
Confidential	Expenses	Emails	Salary
Non-Classified	Balance sheet	Users Manuals	Position Descriptions

Fig. 7.5 BLP: Confidentiality property

The BLP model defines security policy, which must be built into secure computing. A *Trusted Computing Base (TCB)* is a theoretical model for a high-security computer. It has desirable characteristics of being verified to adhere to security policy, which cannot be evaded or tampered with [5]. The TCB must start with trusted hardware, upon which a trusted operating system is installed [18]. Each application must then be trusted as well. Thus hierarchical levels are defined, where each layer must be trusted. If each layer is individually constructed, security policy implementations would be duplicated. TCB subsets enable processes to share verified security policy implementations, such as authentication and access control aspects. This is implemented by having applications use TCB security implementations offered by operating systems. This hierarchical layer sharing, using *encapsulation* of security software, enables applications to achieve shorter time to market through less development and validation, and enables apps to inherit high security features from the O.S. [19].

However, security must be built in not only vertically, but horizontally. A Top Secret application cannot depend upon a Confidential communications network or a Non-Classified server. A network is a system with many parts. To achieve higher levels of security, all components of a high-security transaction must meet the same security class or level. Hierarchically, a Secret user must use a Secret-level computer with Secret-level applications and operating system. Vertically, the network must also be at the Secret level: routers, switches, transmissions lines, firewalls, and more. These are called *dependencies*: any operation at one security class depends upon all parts of the process being at that security class [13]. It is recommended to diagram the dependencies of operations or transactions in implementing security.

One example of dependencies may be that a system administrator normally performs email operations as a regular user, but logs into a secure account from the user account, as necessary to perform administrator duties. Simply logging into an administrator account from a user account is dangerous: user accounts are more likely to be infected with spyware, such as keystroke loggers, which copy password credentials [13]. Storing administrator passwords in a user account file is even more dangerous. These situations demonstrate that extreme care must be taken to ensure all components of a system meet a particular security class.

7.7 Questions

1. *Vocabulary.* Match each meaning with the correct vocabulary name.

Access control	Biometrics	Mandatory access control
Secure wiping	Integrity	Discretionary access control
Process owner	Data owner	Multifactor authentication
Authentication	Availability	Sensitivity classification
Defense-in-depth	Least privilege	False acceptance rate
False rejection rate	Confidentiality	

   a. Persons have the ability to do their primary job and no more.
   b. The security goal that data shall remain secret except to qualified persons.
   c. The probability that a biometric system incorrectly identifies an unenrolled user.
   d. A data owner can configure permissions to users as a subset of their own permissions.
   e. The security goal that data is accurate.
   f. A cracker would need to penetrate multiple security controls to succeed in an attack.
   g. Overwriting disk contents with a pattern to hide confidential information before disk disposal.
   h. A person authorized to distribute permissions.
   i. The set of categories defining the level of confidentiality of business information.
   j. The security goal that data is accessible when needed by authorized persons.

2. *Workbook Solution for Specific Industry*. Consider an industry you currently work in or would like to work in. Assume the company is in your geographical region. You may use the Security Workbook, Information Security Chapter to complete the tables. For each table, include five or more information or asset types, and at least three roles.

   a. Create a Sensitivity Classification Table, similar to Table 7.1.
   b. Create a Handling of Sensitive Data Table, similar to Table 7.2.
   c. Create an Asset Inventory Table, similar to Table 7.3.
   d. Create a Table of Roles, similar to Table 7.4.
   e. Create a Role-Based Access Control Table, similar to Table 7.5.

3. *SIEM*. Look up websites for three different Security Information and Event Management tools. What security services do they appear to provide and for what price?
4. *Biometric Devices*. Look up websites for three different biometric tools. What security services do they provide and for what price?

7.7.1 Health First Case Study Problems

For each case study problem, refer to the Health First Case Study. The Health First Case Study and Security Workbook should be provided by your instructor or can be found at http://extras.springer.com.

Case study	Health first case study	Other resources
Designing information security	√	Security workbook, Health first requirements doc (optional)

References

1. Macy J, Brown MY (1998) Coming back to life. New Society Publishers, Gabriola Island, p 41
2. Gottshall JY (2013) Security, privacy, and whistleblowing. In: SC congress Chicago, IL, 20 November 2013
3. PCI Security Standards Council (2013) Requirements and security assessment procedures, v 3.0, November 2013. www.pcisecuritystandards.org
4. Harris S (2013) All-in-one CISSP® exam guide, 6th edn. McGraw-Hill Co., New York, NY, pp 109–112, 120–124, 219–226, 369–371
5. Smith R (2013) Elementary information security. Jones & Bartlett Learning, Burlington, MA, pp 773–780
6. Grama JL (2011) Legal issues in information security, 2nd edn. Jones & Bartlett Learning, Burlington, MA, pp 188–213
7. Liulevicius VG (2011) Espionage and covert operations: a global history. The Great Courses, Chantilly, VA, lecture 24
8. ISACA (2010) CISA review manual 2011. ISACA, Arlington Heights, IL, pp 320–326, 337–342
9. Stephenson P, Hanlon J, O'Connor K (2014) Product section: SIEM. SC Mag, Haymarket Media 25(3):35–49
10. Bisdikian C, Sensoy M, Norman TJ, Srivastava MB (2012) Trust and obfuscation principles for quality of information in emerging pervasive environments. In: The 4th international workshop on information quality. Inst. for Electrical and Electronics Eng. (IEEE), http://ieeexplore.ieee.org, pp 44–49
11. Chakraborty S, Raghavan KR, Srivastava MB, Bisdikian C, Kaplan LM (2012) Balancing value and risk in information sharing through obfuscation. In: 2012 15th International Conf. on Information Fusion (FUSION). IEEE, pp 1615–1622
12. Novak K, Gottshall, JY (2013) Security, privacy, and whistleblowing. SC Congress Chicago, IL, 20 November 2013
13. Johansson JM (2014) Security watch island hopping: mitigating undesirable dependencies. http://technet.microsoft.com/en-us/magazine/2008.02.securitywatch.aspx. Accessed 14 Feb 2014
14. http://Big Data (2014) Big risks: secure your data before it's too late. pp 1–4. http://enterprise-encryption.vormetric.com/rs/vormetric/images/CSO Vormetric Big Data Security Whitepaper.pdf. Accessed 4 Dec 2014
15. Dev H, Sen T, Basak M, Ali ME (2012) Approach to protect the privacy of cloud data from data mining based attacks. In: 2012 SC companion: high performance computing, networking, storage and analysis. SC Magazine, pp 1106–1115

16. Subashini S, Kavitha V (2011) A metadata based storage model for securing data in cloud environment. In: 2011 international conference on cyber-enabled distributed computing and knowledge discovery. IEEE, pp 429–434
17. HHS (2013) HIPAA administrative simplification regulation text. U.S. Department of Health and Human Services Office for Civil Rights. March 2013, pp 59–115
18. Li Y, Zhang X (2010) A trust model of TCB subsets. In: IEEE proc. 9th international conf. on machine learning and cybernetics. IEEE, pp 2838–2842
19. Vetter L, Smith G, Lunt TF (1989) TCB subsets: the next step. In: Fifth annual computer security applications conference. IEEE, pp 216–221

Chapter 8
Planning for Network Security

> There is a reason why BlackBerries and iPhones are not allowed in the White House Situation Room. We know that the intelligence services of other countries – including some who feign surprise over the Snowden disclosures – are constantly probing our government and private sector networks, and accelerating programs to listen to our conversations, and intercept our emails, and compromise our systems. (Pres. Barack Obama, Jan. 17, 2014. [1])

The Internet allows an attacker to attack from anywhere in the world from their home desk. They just need to find one vulnerability, while a security analyst needs to close every vulnerability. If that sounds nearly impossible to defend, then implement defense in depth, which requires an attacker to penetrate multiple layers of security to succeed.

In Chap. 7 on Information Security, we classified information assets and defined how each class of assets should be protected. In this chapter, we implement that classification system into the network.

8.1 Important Concepts

Network security builds on the concepts introduced in the Information Security chapter, including Defense in Depth and Least Privilege. A defense in depth should have many layers, similar to an onion. The multiple layers in an IT network should include: firewall, antivirus, authentication, strong encryption, access control, logged problems, etc. To achieve least privilege, firewalls, servers and computers should be configured to support the minimum required applications and no more (providing less features to attack!)

It is important to understand how hackers attack, to better defend against them. The next section defines how attacks to computer systems and networks occur. The first line of defense for network security is the packet filter, which will be explained before starting the design. Additional controls to establish defense in depth are defined later in the chapter.

S. Lincke, *Security Planning*, DOI 10.1007/978-3-319-16027-6_8

8.1.1 How Crackers Attack

Stages of an attack can include [2–4]:

1. Target Identification: Attackers may choose to perform an opportunistic or targeted attack. An *opportunistic attack* focuses on any site that may be easy to break into; a *targeted attack* has a specific victim in mind, and searches for a vulnerability that will work.
2. Reconnaissance: Like a bank robber who might case a bank before an attack, a cracker may investigate an organization before attacking. Social techniques include: dumpster diving, web searches for additional information (Google, news, web sites), and social engineering. Example network investigation techniques include:

    - *WhoIs Service*: Enquiring into this database to find system administrator and Internet information relating to a specific organization.
    - *War Driving*: Driving (or walking) around to find an internal wireless local area network to connect to. This may include *MAC spoofing*, where a criminal adopts another person's WLAN or MAC identification, to connect to the network, and *hijacking* where they could take over that person's connection.
    - *Routing attack*: Using spoofing, a machine changes network address, to either entice transmissions toward it or give inappropriate orders to victims. One such router command can be a router redirection.
    - *War Dialing*: An intruder dials phone numbers associated with an organization to find a modem to connect to.
    - *Protocol Sniffing*: Observing packet transmissions—easy with unencrypted or poorly encrypted wireless LANs. When transmissions are encrypted, *traffic analysis* can indicate patterns of transmission volume to disclose proprietary information.
    - *Network Scanning*: Polling computer IP addresses to determine which devices exist, and for each device, the type of computer (e.g., server, point of sale, user terminal) and its operating system and applications (TCP/UDP addresses). *Enumeration* includes scanning each port (or application) on each computer to learn which applications exist and respond to connection requests.
    - *Domain Name Server Interrogations*: Abusing the IP name translation system to obtain information about a network.

3. Gaining Access: In this stage the cracker gains entrance into a computer via social engineering or hacker tool attacks. Once they achieve access in an internal system, the crackers may launch attacks toward their intended target, such as a server or point of sale device. Often, the initial access is obtained via spear phishing (directed fraudulent email) [4]. Other initial or progressive attacks include:

    - *Watering Hole attack*: Criminals take advantage of unpatched software in public websites to infect those websites with malware.
    - *Man-in-the-Middle attack*: An attacker spoofs (or pretends to be) the desired destination. The spoofer forwards all communications between victim

and desired endpoint, hiding the attack but gaining valuable information. For example, an attacker may create a wireless local area network access point that pretends to be an organizational access point. The rogue access point forwards information between the victim and the real access point, copying credentials and other information.

- *SQL Injection attack*: Attackers manipulate web form input to modify the database commands implemented within the form. Database manipulations may include adding commands (e.g., delete file or show all) or modifying commands (e.g., to make an invalid password look like a valid one).
- Password Guessing: Attackers may use password dictionaries or brute force attacks to guess login credentials.

4. Hiding Presence: A rootkit is a set of malware that hides the attacker's actions. System utilities or the operating system are modified to hide the attacker's actions; logs are modified or the rootkit prevents writing certain alarms.
5. Establishing Persistence: Attackers install Command and Control software, which enables them to remotely control the computer. The attacker may weaken security by establishing a backdoor, which is a mechanism for entry into a system. Often they escalate their access capabilities by installing a keystroke logger or copying the password file.
6. Execution: Intruders may include criminals, state-affiliated groups, or hacktivists, who target financial information, trade secrets, or organizational information, respectively. Exfiltration of sensitive data can be concealed, as a *covert channel*, by transmitting the data within an innocuous data stream, such as web output or hidden within a video transmission. In addition to copying information, the attacker may use the new 'acquire' as a bot or launch one or more attacks on an internal system or someone else's system (e.g., Distributed Denial of Service).
7. Assessment: What went right and wrong? Learn from mistakes.

8.1.2 Filtering Packets to Restrict Network Access

The concept of Least Privilege extends to network security. *Firewalls* and *routers* have a filtering capability that should be configured to permit only approved applications or services to enter the network. This is called a *default deny* policy. Figure 8.1 shows a network filter permits only packets for certain applications, source/destination addresses, and packet types (requests versus responses). Source/destination address filtering occurs using the Internet Protocol (IP) address, while applications are filtered using the Transport Control Protocol (TCP) or User Datagram Protocol (UDP) address. When these routing devices fail, such as potentially during a DOS attack or during power down, they can either pass packets indiscriminately or fully restrict access. A *fail safe* or *fail secure* implementation ensures that no packets pass through, protecting the network from additional attacks. Firewalls often support additional capabilities, which will be discussed in the Advanced section in the chapter.

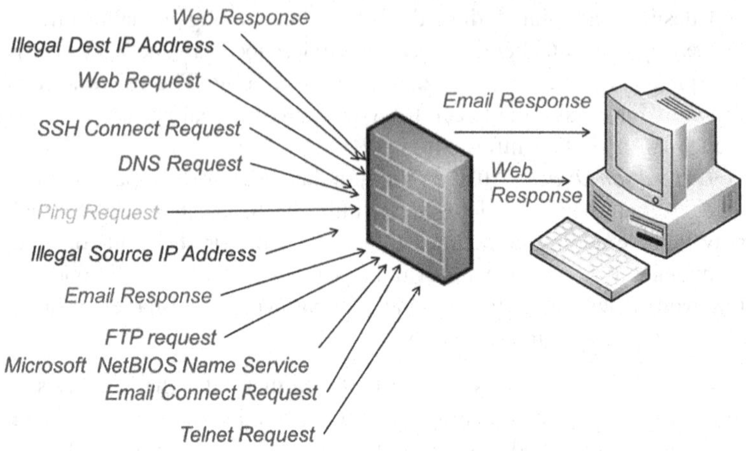

Fig. 8.1 The role of the network filter

8.2 Defining Network Services

As part of the network security design, we first need to establish what legal transactions are. Then we build the network with sufficient filters (or firewalls) to allow legal transactions and detect and reject illegal transactions.

8.2.1 Step 1: Determine Services: What, Who, Where?

We want to permit only legal transactions in our network. We consider:

- Which services will we support in our network?
- Which internal services can be accessed from the outside (i.e., Internet)?
- Which external services (in the Internet) can be accessed from the internal network?
- Who and where (from the inside and outside) can access these permitted services?

In Fig. 8.2 is an informal diagram showing who can access the basic services of a university. The big gray circle represents the campus; faces outside the circle are off-campus. Databases are shown as cylinders, which are color-coded to reflect their sensitivity class: black = confidential; gray = private; and white = public. Faces represent different people, and arrows point in the direction that the service will be requested. This informal diagram shows that only on-campus nurses have access to the nurse database. Students and instructors have access to Desire2Learn and the Registration system, but on-campus students can also access the lab and library resources.

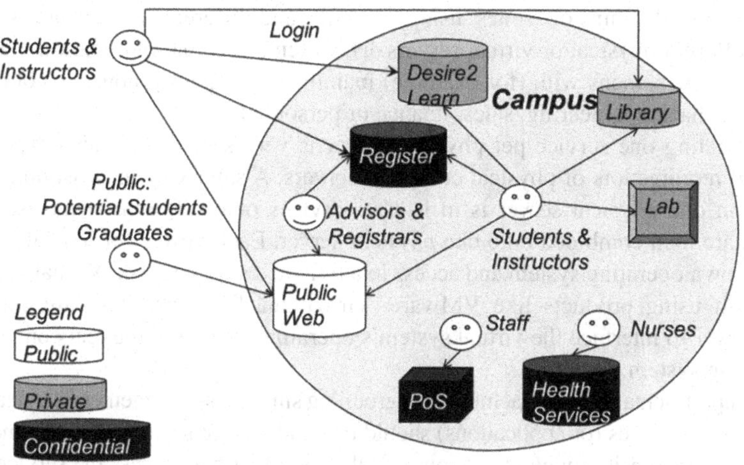

Fig. 8.2 Informal sketch of logical access

Table 8.1 Identifying sources and destinations for services

Service (e.g., web, sales database)	Source (e.g., home, world, local computer)	Destination (local server, home, world, etc.)
Registration, Desire2Learn	Students and Instructors: Anywhere in the World	Computer Service Servers
Registration	Registrars and Advisers: On campus	Computer Service Servers
Library databases	On campus students and staff Off-campus requires login	Specific off-site library facilities
Health Services	On campus: nurses office	Computer Service Servers
External (Internet) web services	On campus: Campus labs, dorms, faculty offices	Anywhere in the world

From this information we have determine who can access what from where

Off-campus students may access library resources via login. This diagram does not show that students and instructors can access any web sites on the Internet; however, that is reflected in the last row of Table 8.1. Table 8.1 is the table which documents an informal sketch of logical access.

8.2.2 Step 2: Determine Sensitivity of Services

If hackers break into one computer in a network, they are likely to escalate their attack to other servers in that network's region. Similarly if a hacker breaks into one service, they are likely to break into other services on that same physical server. *Compartmentalization* or *Separation* partitions a network and services to provide protection between them. To achieve compartmentalization, a network is segmented into regions, domains or 'zones' using firewalls, and different services are isolated onto different physical or virtual servers. The intention is that by separating different services, persons with (for example) manufacturing permissions cannot easily access or hack engineering, sales, finance or personnel data.

Allocating one service per physical server is very secure—but also expensive since it requires lots of physical computer servers. A safer way to consolidate services on one physical server is to isolate services onto different *virtual* servers, which are then combined onto one *physical* server. Each virtual (or logical) server has its own operating system and access to a limited section of disk. Virtual systems are built using products like VMware. Virtual machines use software called a *hypervisor* to interface the virtual system's operating system to the real computer's operating system.

Compartmentalization is achieved by grouping similar assets together. The decision of whether services (or applications) should be combined or separated must consider: (1) the data's sensitivity classifications, (2) the roles that may access the service, and (3) the probability of any specific service being attacked. For example, email is a service highly likely to be attacked, and should not be housed with sensitive services. A good network architecture will *encapsulate* one main function within each compartment, creating *simplicity in design* through *modularity*. In fact, PCI DSS requires and tests that each virtual system support only one primary function [5].

In Table 8.2, university services will be divided out by their sensitivity roles. Confidential services are protected by law, and should be in a separate network region/zone from other services. Public services, such as public web, email, and DNS, are susceptible to attacks from the world and should be separated from any internal (Private) services. Registration and Health Services are both Confidential, but are accessed by very different roles. Therefore, they should be separated into different network zones or servers. Here they will be hosted on separate physical servers. Different web services, however, could be hosted on different virtual servers on the same physical server.

Table 8.2 Partial service classifications and roles for a university

Service name (e.g., web, email)	Sensitivity class (e.g., confidential)	Roles (e.g., sales, engineering)	Server (* = virtual)
Desire2-Learn	Private	Current Students, Instructors	StudentScholastic
Registration	Confidential	Current Students, Registration, Accounting, Advising, Instructors	Student_Register
Health Service	Confidential	Nurses	Health_Services
Web Pages: activities, news, departments, …	Public	Students, Employees, Public	Web_Services*
Sales	Confidential	Sales staff and management: Cafeteria, registration; E-commerce service provider handles on-line sales	None: PoS Devices

8.2.3 Step 3: Allocate Network Zones

A network is compartmentalized into regions called *zones*. Each region will correspond to a related Sensitivity Class, access roles, and accessibility. Accessibility refers to the probability of being broken into: networks with wireless access, the Internet, and public services are higher risk. A *Demilitarized Zone (DMZ)* is a region in a network that is accessible to the public, e.g., for web and e-mail services. A *Private Payment Card Zone* is a special PCI DSS zone where payment card systems are used, such as Point-of-Sale or ATM machines [6]. One or more private zones restrict public access. Larger organizations have (at least) one zone per functional area: e.g., manufacturing, engineering, personnel. In Security Workbook Table 4.2.3, you may add or delete zones as necessary.

Firewalls/routers serve as the guards between zones. They limit or filter application transactions that enter and leave individual network zones. Many firewall/routers can handle a set of zones.

Table 8.3 lists a set of zones for the University configuration. The Confidential Zone has grade and health information, but is separated from the point of sale machines in the Payment Card Zone. Wireless and Internet zones are both very high risk, and are given strong filters. Private user and server zones are separated, since user zones will periodically acquire malware, and server zones need to be well-protected against them.

Technical experts can take this table, learn more about the normal operations of each application, and configure firewall(s) to permit only legal packets per zone.

8.2.4 Step 4: Define Controls

Four types of network controls are shown in Fig. 8.3. In these mini-diagrams, Joe sends information to Ann, but attacker Bill interferes. They include:

- *Confidentiality* ensures unauthorized parties cannot access information. Example controls include: Secret Key Encryption.
- *Authenticity* ensures that the actual sender is the claimed sender. It counters masquerading or *spoofing*, where the sender pretends to be someone else. Example controls include: Public Key Encryption and Digital Certificates.
- *Integrity* ensures that the message was not modified during transmission. Example controls include: Hashing, SHA-2, and HMAC.
- *Nonrepudiation* ensures that the sender cannot deny sending a message at a later time. Nonrepudiation is important in signing contracts and making payments. Example controls include Digital Signature.

Table 8.4 adds controls for each zone or service. Controls for each control type are described in the next section. An IT professional should configure the firewall/router based on this table.

Table 8.3 Creating zones

Zone	Services	Zone description (you may delete or add rows as necessary)
Internet (external)		This zone is external to the organization
De-militarized zone	Web, Email, DNS	This zone houses services the public are allowed to access in our network
Wireless Network	Wireless local employees	This zone connects wireless/laptop employees/students (and possibly crackers) to our internal network. They can access select university databases, any Internet web site, email, and personal files
Private Server Zone	Databases	This zone hosts our student learning databases, faculty servers, and student servers
Confidential Zone	Health, grades info	This highly-secure zone hosts databases with payment and other confidential (protected by law) information
Private Payment Card Zone	Credit card sales	This zone hosts our credit card point-of-sale machines at registration office and cafeteria
Private user Zone	Wired students/employees	This zone hosts our wired/fixed employee/classroom computer terminals. They can access select university databases, any Internet web site, email, and personal files
Student Lab Zone	Student labs	This zone hosts our student lab computers, which are highly vulnerable to malware. They can access select university databases, any Internet web site, email and personal files

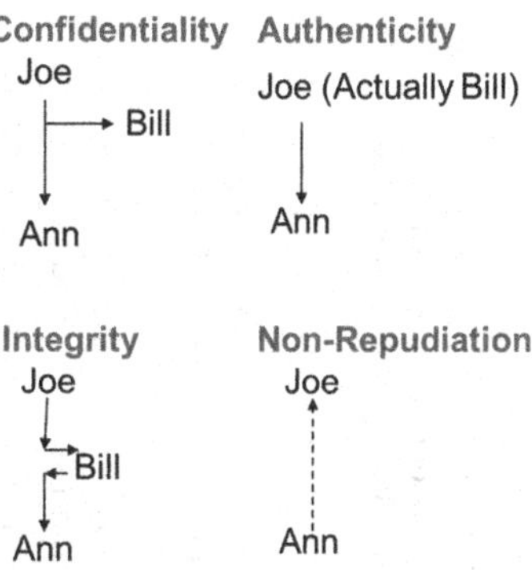

Fig. 8.3 Objectives for network controls

8.3 Defining Controls

Techniques for each of the four network controls, Confidentiality, Authenticity, Integrity, and Nonrepudiation, in addition to hacker-recognition tools, are described in turn next.

8.3.1 *Confidentiality Controls*

Encryption provides confidentiality, by transforming data into an unreadable form to anyone without access to the encryption key. Encryption is critical for safely sending credit card and other private information and securing organization secrets. The security of encryption algorithms depends heavily on both the length and complexity of the key (in bits) and the complexity and number of encryption algorithms performed (in rounds).

Encryption algorithms are categorized into Secret-Key and Public-Key types. These encryption algorithms are then used in specific protocols to protect applications such as web, file transfer, remote login, etc. This section reviews the two types of encryption algorithms, introduces popular algorithms for each, and then reviews the encrypted application protocols.

Secret Key Encryption Both sender and receiver share a common, secret key. These encryption algorithms are very efficient and popular. The issue is how to share the common secret key without also telling others the key. Popular algorithms include [3, 7]:

- *Advanced Encryption Standard (AES):* This encryption standard is more secure than 3DES and sufficient to protect sensitive but unclassified U.S. government information. Key sizes include 128, 192, and 256 bits with 10–14 rounds of encryption.

Table 8.4 Controls for services

Zone	Server (* = virtual)	Service	Required controls (Conf., Integrity, Auth., Nonrepud., with tools: e.g., encryption/VPN, hashing, IPS)
Internet (external)			
De-Militarized Zone	Web_Services*, Email_Server, DNS_Server	Web, Email, DNS	Hacking: Intrusion Prevention System, Monitor alarm logs, Antivirus software within Email package
Wireless Network		Wireless local users	Confidentiality: WPA2 Encryption Authentication: WPA2 Authentication
Private user Zone		Faculty, Classrooms, Employees	Confidentiality (Instructor/employee computers): Encrypted disks. Secure protocols: SSH Hacking: Antivirus software
Student Lab Zone		Student Labs	Hacking: Recently imaged computers for labs
Private Server Zone	StudentScholastic Student_Files Faculty_Files	Classroom software Faculty & student storage	Confidentiality: Secure Web (HTTPS), Secure Protocols (SSH, SFTP) Authentication: Single Sign-on through TACACS Hacking: Monitor logs
Confidential Zone	health, grades info	This highly-secure zone hosts databases with personal confidential (protected by law) information	Confidentiality: Encrypted disks, Secure Web (HTTPS), VPN for health services Authentication: Public Key Infrastructure Integrity: SHA-2 checksums on all info. Hacking: Intrusion Prevention System, Monitor logs
Private Payment Card Zone	Mastercard, Visa, American Express	This zone hosts our credit card point-of-sale machines at registration office and cafeteria	Bastion host implementation includes antivirus, encrypted storage & transmission Intrusion prevention; Monitor logs; Quarterly scans and annual penetration test (Additional PCI DSS requirements in other sections)

- *Triple Data Encryption Standard (3DES):* The 1977 DES algorithm is insufficient, but when three DES operations use three different 56-bit keys, the result is safe encryption. The DES-EDE3 algorithm encrypts the plaintext packet using key 1, decrypts the result using key 2, and encrypts again using key 3, to obtain the ciphertext:

$$\text{Ciphertext} = \text{Encrypt}(\text{Key3}, \text{Decrypt}(\text{Key2}, \text{Encrypt}(\text{Key1}, \text{Plaintext}))) \quad (8.1)$$

The EDE3 name is abbreviated from 'Encrypt, Decrypt, Encrypt using 3 keys'. Other algorithms similarly abbreviated include: EEE3, EEE2, and EDE2.

- *International Data Encryption Algorithm (IDEA):* A European encryption algorithm that uses a 128-bit key, meant to replace DES.
- *RC4 or ARC4:* This is a Stream Cipher, where a key is used to generate a random bit pattern, which is exclusive-ORed (XOR) with the data. RC4 is used in SSL/TLS and WPA protocols.

Public-Key Encryption The sender and receiver keys are complimentary, but not identical. Every entity (person or organization) has their own public and private keys. The public key can be advertised to the world; the corresponding private key is never shared. The property of public-key encryption is that plaintext encrypted with public keys must be decrypted with private keys, and vice versa: plaintext encrypted with private keys must be decrypted with public keys:

$$\text{Plaintext} = \text{Decrypt}(\text{Key}_{\text{Pub}}, \text{Encrypt}(\text{Key}_{\text{Priv}}, \text{Plaintext}))) \quad (8.2)$$

$$\text{Plaintext} = \text{Decrypt}(\text{Key}_{\text{Priv}}, \text{Encrypt}(\text{Key}_{\text{Pub}}, \text{Plaintext}))) \quad (8.3)$$

Therefore, people who know your public key can send you encrypted messages which only you can read. This is highly advantageous, because it eliminates the need to privately communicate a secret key between two users, which is a flaw of secret key encryption. However, public-key encryption is extremely processor-intensive. Thus, it is less attractive for large-scale encryption purposes, such as a file transfer or web session. Therefore, public-key encryption is used to encrypt only small amounts of data. For example, it is used in *key exchange*, to communicate a secret key to be used during one temporary communications session.

Popular algorithms include: Diffie–Hellman, RSA (Rivest, Shamir, Adleman), El Gamal, and Elliptic Curve Cryptosystems [7].

Protocols that support cyphering include upper-layer app-oriented encryption versus lower-layer media-oriented encryption. App-oriented encryption protocols include [3, 7]:

- Secure Web (*S-HTTP*): Encrypts single web message(s).
- Secure Web: *HTTP over SSL (HTTPS):* Protects a web session (or conversation) using the SSL/TLS protocol.

- *Secure Sockets Layer (SSL)/Transport Layer Security (TLS):* provides confidentiality (key exchange, data encryption), integrity, and authentication (server and optional client).
- *Secure File Transfer Protocol (SFTP):* Encrypted file transfer using the SSH protocol.
- *Secure Shell 2 (SSH2):* Remote login to UNIX or LINUX systems. Supports configurable confidentiality (key exchange, data encryption), integrity (HMAC-SHA-1, HMAC-MD5), and in the commercial version: authentication (public key certificates).
- Email: *Pretty Good Privacy (PGP):* Users establish a web of trust, where they informally share public keys. The private key is stored on a disk drive, protected by a pass phrase. This protocol then supports configurable confidentiality (key exchange = RSA, data encryption = IDEA), integrity (MD5), authentication (public key certificates) and non-repudiation (digital signature).
- Email: *Secure/Multipurpose Internet Mail Extension (S/MIME):* Enables the signing and encrypting of email and attachments, using encryption (3DES, ElGamal), integrity (SHA-1), authentication (public key certificates) and non-repudiation (digital signature).
- Client/Server: *Kerberos*: This tool authenticates clients and servers, and supports confidentiality through key exchange and encryption. It is commonly used in the Windows, UNIX/LINUX and Mac networks, particularly for single sign-on environments. It is highly configurable, which may result in compatibility issues.

Lower-layer media-oriented cipher protocols encrypt all packets, regardless of application. However, this encryption may not occur along the entire network path from source to destination. Therefore, for certain applications, such as payment cards, it is important to select cipher protocols that protect across the entire network [5].

- *Virtual Private Network (VPN).* VPN encrypts all application packets between two endpoints. Both endpoints need to be configured to support the VPN protocol. VPNs are easy to use and inexpensive, but are difficult to set up and troubleshoot. VPNs do not solve malware problems or unauthorized actions—they just encrypt them. Often an organization's router or firewall is a VPN endpoint, which decrypts the VPN messages. VPN protocols include:
  - *IPSec Protocol:* Supports an Authentication Header, which supports source authentication and integrity, or optionally an Encapsulating Security Payload (ESP), which provides authentication, integrity and confidentiality. The algorithms used are configurable and negotiated.
  - *Point-to-Point Tunneling Protocol (PPTP):* Provides encryption (RC4).
- *Wi-Fi Protected Access (WPA or WPA2):* A secure wireless local area network (WLAN) implementation. Every person who drives by your office potentially has access to your computer systems unless you have a well-configured WLAN that includes authentication and encryption. WEP protocols offer insufficient encryption. The sufficiency of WPA/WPA2 to protect is based on the length and complexity of the password.

WPA uses a 128-bit key and the MAC address to provide unique encryption per device [8]. The Temporal Key Integrity Protocol changes the key about every 10,000 packets. The key exchange process includes authentication of both client and access point.

WPA-2 includes optional enhancements, including integration of Kerberos and Radius. It also uses AES encryption.

8.3.2 Authenticity and Non-repudiation

Kerberos, discussed in the Confidentiality section, is also a key method of Authentication. Other authentication and non-repudiation techniques include [3, 7, 9]:

Centralized Access Control supports centralized servers that authorize credentials and indicate access control capabilities for single-sign on. They can also provide accounting/audit service to track usage. Products include: RADIUS: Remote Access Dial-in User Service, and TACACS: Terminal Access Control Access, which is a family of products.

Authentication is best performed using two-factor authentication or better. A second factor can include a token, such as smartcard, flash drive, or RSA flash drive that displays a synchronized random number. Other second factors can include biometrics or a SMS passcode, sent to a cell phone providing a one-time (or single use) password.

Public Key Infrastructure (PKI) is a set of standards approved by the International Standards Organization (ISO). PKI provides an infrastructure to support confidentiality, integrity, authenticity and non-repudiation in a flexible, configurable way. Every user (e.g., John) of PKI must register with a Registration Authority, who verifies that entity's identity. John then obtains a Digital Certificate, which is maintained with a *Certificate Authority* (CA). The *Digital Certificate* includes information about John, including his public key. When Joan wants to communicate with John, with assured authentication, Joan requests John's Digital Certificate through the CA. The CA is a trusted organization that effectively vouches for John. When Joan has John's public key, she can verify his digital signature and/or perform key exchanges with him.

Digital Signatures provide non-repudiation for contractual compliance. To create a digital signature, a message is hashed for integrity. The hash is then encrypted using the sender's private key. When the receiver receives the message-plus-encrypted-hash, they use the sender's public key to decrypt the received hash. If the decrypted hash matches the hash calculated over the received message, then the message was authentically sent by the sender and not modified during transmission. For secure applications, such as payment cards, only such trusted keys and digital certificates should be accepted [5].

The Digital Signature Standard is defined by NIST to use a 160-bit SHA hash and RSA or elliptic curve encryption.

8.3.3 Integrity Controls

Hashing or *Message Digests* provide integrity, by adding a sophisticated form of checksum, which is calculated using a secret key and multiple, complex operations across each segment of a data stream. Algorithms recognized as safe include [3, 7]:

Secure Hash Algorithm (SHA) SHA incorporates a secret key into the hash algorithm. Figure 8.4 (top algorithm) shows that both the receiver and sender calculate the hash value (H) using a key (K) and the sender appends the hash to the data for transmission. The receiver compares the received and calculated hashes. SHA-2 consists of SHA-256, SHA-384, SHA-512, where the number in the name reflects the hash size. Larger numbers also reflect higher security levels, and the 384 and 512 algorithms can also be used for larger packets (>264). Recently proposed SHA-3 supports higher level of security at increased efficiency. SHA is used by Digital Signatures and the U.S. government.

Hashed Message Authentication Code (HMAC) An HMAC creates a hash based on the message concatenated with a secret key (see Fig. 8.4). The message and hash are transmitted to the remote side. The receiver also concatenates the secret key to the message to calculate a hash. The calculated hash is compared to the received hash. HMAC is used in IPsec, TLS/SSL, and SET protocols.

Outdated algorithms include MD2 and MD4. MD5 and *SHA-1* are still used but are vulnerable.

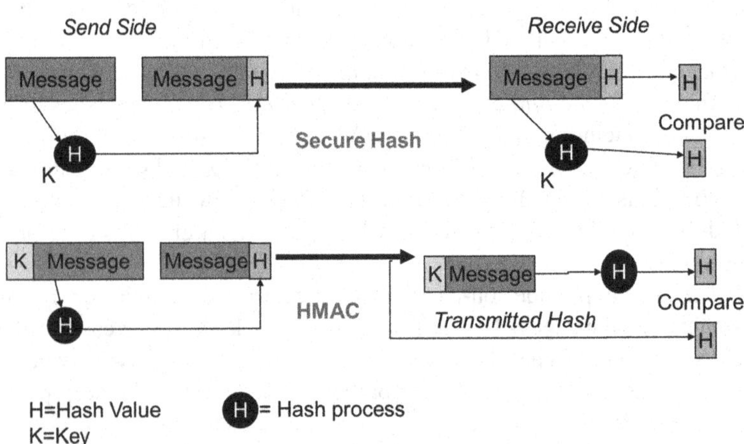

Fig. 8.4 Secure message authentication code calculations

8.3.4 Anti-hacker Controls

It is always important to have anti-hacker tools in your network [3, 7]. This section describes additional security controls. *SC Magazine* evaluates security products monthly in their Product Section and is a great source for further information on specific products. Table 8.5 lists ranges of prices for current products, as recently evaluated by *SC Magazine*. The remainder of this section describes simple/individual security components before building up to multi-featured tools.

Bastion host is a computer that is attack-resistant. All but the necessary applications are turned off, the security configuration is optimized, and the operating system and all applications are recently patched.

Antivirus and *antispyware* is software that controls the content of application data entering a network for malicious data (or malware). Antivirus software can be configured as part of a sophisticated firewall, email server, and/or hosted on end-user machines.

Endpoint security features antimalware and firewall capabilities, but in addition this end-user product prevents data leakage by controlling access to files, folders and removable media. It may provide centralized control to automate enforcement and monitoring of organizational policies.

Email security management tools, commonly implemented on an email server, supports antimalware, antiphishing and spam control. They can encrypt email, enforce email policies for regulatory or internal compliance, and prevent data leakage in outgoing email.

Table 8.5 Security products

Product	Price range
Application firewalls types: Database firewall, web firewall	$7,000–41,000
Authentication types: Flash drive token, RSA token, fingerprint, voice/facial recognition	$1.30–46 per user OR $650–11,000 per site
Email security management	$15 per user to $17,000 per site
Endpoint security	$20–93 per user
Mobile device security	$25–60 per user
Risk and policy management	$485–45,000 per site OR $10–50 per endpoint
Security Information and Event Management (SIEM)	$800–48,000 per site
Unified Threat Management (UTM)	$700–31,000 per unit
Virtual security solutions types: Cloud support, compliance, encrypted memory	$50 per virtual server to $64,000 per site
Vulnerability assessment tools	$2,500–40,000 per site

Mobile Devices and *Bring Your Own Device (BYOD)* are a threat since merging technologies, such as smartphones, are immature in regards to security. When mobile devices are used for both business and pleasure, these devices can expose the internal network to malware, and imperil confidential or proprietary secrets when company data is accessed. A secure policy is to insist that employees not use personal devices to access company data or company devices to access personal data.

Mobile device management apps enforce organizational policy, such as applying authentication/password requirements, allowing viewing but no storing of company data, and blacklisting (forbidding) or whitelisting (permitting) only certain software installations. It also features antimalware, remote wiping, browser content filtering, and possibly two-factor authentication. Some versions enable the device to be split, using containers, to isolate personal and company data [10, 11]. A 'container' can encrypt the business side of the device, and enable secure wiping of that side only [11].

Event Logs are generated by applications, operating systems and other system software to issue a warning or error or record that an action was performed (e.g., clearing of log file). Logs are important to monitor to detect attacks or risky behavior. Operating systems allow the configuration of logs specifically for an organization (via enable/disable mechanisms). A large quantity of logs provides information in detecting and analyzing intrusions, but requires a large amount of storage. Regulations and standards such as HIPAA and PCI DSS require regular log monitoring.

Security Information and Event Management (SIEM) tools assist in log reduction (or summarization), prioritization and correlation. In addition to saving administrator time daily in pouring over hundreds of logs, they collect metrics for risk purposes, generate reports for compliance and help in forensic analysis of log data. They may collect logs from user, server and/or network devices.

Application Firewalls protect either a web server or database, by monitoring activity, detecting attacks and reporting on both. They are also useful in preventing data leakages and countering DDOS attacks.

Intrusion Prevention System (IPS) or *Intrusion Detection System (IDS)* is an advanced tool to recognize attack packets, actions or patterns. Detection systems log or report unsafe behavior to administrators, while prevention systems actually halt unsafe behavior. The major issue is whether unsafe behavior can be accurately determined. There are two ways that intrusion systems can be hosted in a network:

- *Network IDS/IPS*: This is a networked device which examines packets traversing a network or zone for attacks, such as worms, viruses, or scanning attacks. A NIPS would block dangerous packets, while a NIDS would simply report or log unsafe packets for the administrator.
- *Host IDS/IPS*: Examines actions or resources on one host computer or server for unusual or inappropriate behavior. For example, it may detect modification or deletion of special files.

There are three ways for intrusion systems to find attacks. Attacks may be recognized via a signature-based algorithm, or exact pattern match. This is commonly used in antivirus software to match for a worm or virus. Statistical-based algorithms recognize deviations from a norm. For example, most work occurs from 8 AM to 6 PM and high server uses at 3 AM in the morning could raise a red flag. Neural networks recognize deviations from patterns using a statistical-based algorithm combined with self-learning (or artificial intelligence). High security industries recognize that if traffic volume for a particular type of data suddenly balloons to ten times its normal volume, this is a sure sign that the event should be investigated right away. IDS/IPS tools must be properly configured by security staff to recognize attacks. This may be is difficult, since illegitimate behavior may look like abnormal but legal behavior. For example, heavy use of a server at 3 AM in the morning is normally unusual and potentially deviant, except when a scheduled deadline occurs.

Unified Threat Management (UTM) tools combine firewall, IPS, antivirus, spam/email protection, web content filtering, application control and VPN capabilities into one super-firewall device. Important concerns should be redundancy and bandwidth.

It is prudent to restrict access to particular web sites, such as social and email sites, to minimize threats of malware. It is better yet to permit access to only a limited set of Internet sites.

Vulnerability Assessment tools scan the network and/or operating systems for vulnerabilities. Hacking tools used for reconnaissance to penetrate a network are also required to find and patch vulnerabilities. Periodic scans may be required by regulations and PCI DSS. Sophisticated tools will automatically run on schedule, update themselves for new vulnerabilities, and produce reports. Some tools may support penetration testing or auto fixing of vulnerabilities.

Risk and Policy Management tools are database systems to support risk analysis, risk treatment, policy enforcement and incident tracking. The policy management aspect may track patch implementations and enforce/monitor other configuration policies on end-user and/or network devices. This may help in managing and reporting for regulatory compliance.

Honeypot/Honeynet is a system or network that is meant to attract and catch attackers. A honeypot system has no other functions except for a special application which appears easy to break into. All traffic going to honeypot/net should be regarded as suspicious. Honeypots/nets must be carefully monitored, because if this system is successfully penetrated, the attackers will have a convenient launching pad for further attacks.

8.4 Defining the Network Architecture

Now it is time to put all the pieces together. Figure 8.5 shows a diagram of a network, where different colors reflect confidentiality levels: black = proprietary or confidential, gray = private, and white = public. There are three zones: the Demilitarized Zone, where anyone can send us email, access our web, or translate Internet names to IP addresses; the Private Payment Card Zone, where we handle payment cards; and the Internal Network Zone, which is where our employees do their thing.

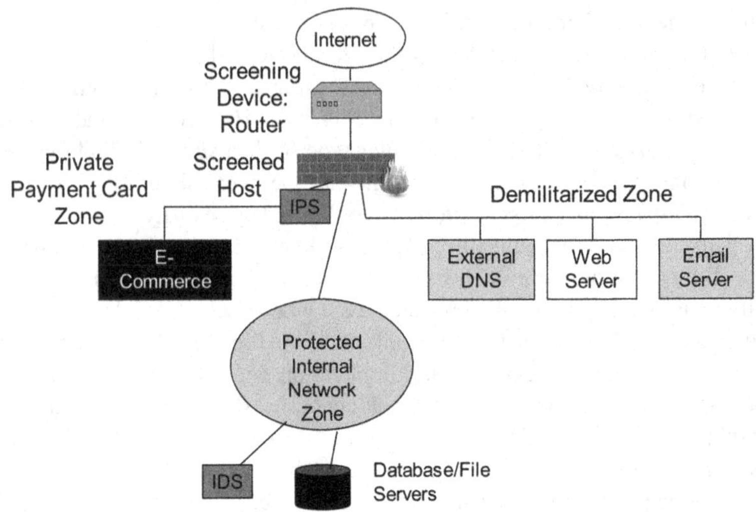

Fig. 8.5 Fundamental network architecture

Since this firewall supports three (or more) zones, it is a multi-homed firewall. There is a screening device, a Border Router, which screens obvious attack packets. This allows our firewall (a 'screened host') to spend more time checking remaining, maybe-safe packets. A border router is a regular router put at the border between our network and the Internet. It screens for illegal applications (port numbers), and invalid source and destination IP addresses, similarly to what is shown in Fig. 8.1.

The firewall and Intrusion Prevention System (IPS) could be separate or a combined device. A Unified Threat Management device can do both functions. The firewall may perform circuit-level screening to verify proper connection sequencing, while the IPS searches throughout each packet for attack signatures (malware) and finds attack patterns across packets. An Intrusion Detection System (IDS) observes and reports attack packets in the Internal Network Zone. It cannot block packets, the way an IPS can.

A system for logs is not shown in this figure. For secure networks, logs may be transmitted to a central database. In highly secure networks, the transmission lines for these logs would be separated from the regular network, to reduce the probability of a Denial of Service attack.

It is also possible to have dual in-line firewalls, to doubly-screen input. For example, there could be border router, firewall, DMZ, firewall, Internal Network Zone. In this case of a screened subnet, packets going to the Internal Network Zone would pass through the DMZ, and be filtered through two (dual) sequential (in-line) firewalls. Figure 8.6 is an example of this. This configuration has the advantage of defense in depth and redundancy.

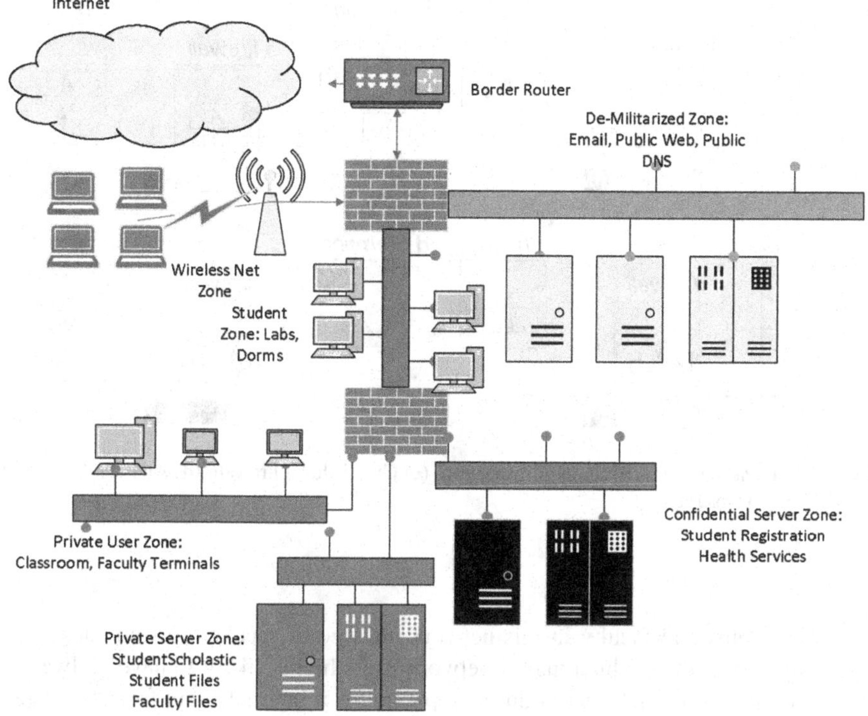

Fig. 8.6 Network diagram for simplified university scenario

8.4.1 Step 5: Draw the Network Diagram

It is now time to draw the complete network, so we can evaluate it for various paths of logical access. A *Path of Logical Access* is a diagram that shows where transactions can enter the system, where they are security-controlled, and where they are processed. Evaluating such paths can ensure there is sufficient defense in depth. A good text description explains why the network architecture is as shown and can further explain logical paths of access. The diagram can show separated or combined servers, and sensitivity, where servers are colored according to their sensitivity class: Green = Public, Yellow = Privileged, Red = Confidential, Purple = Proprietary—or the black–gray–white version used in this text.

Figure 8.6 shows a simplified diagram for the university scenario. Six internal network zones are shown, and all servers are color-coded according to sensitivity. The servers are not broken out, but instead listed under their zone name. This diagram was drawn with Microsoft Visio, which offers easy diagraming capabilities providing a variety of network icons.

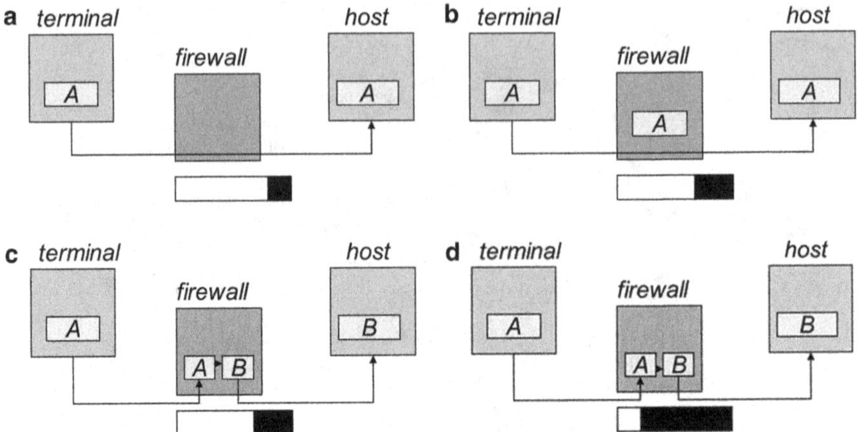

Fig. 8.7 (**a**) Packet filter. (**b**) Stateful inspection. (**c**) Circuit-level firewall. (**d**) Application-level firewall or proxy server

The students and faculty in this network are free to access any web sites and open any email links, which makes network users highly likely to have malware. Therefore it is extremely important to separate even internal users from the data servers, which contain private or confidential information.

The paths of logical access generally enter via the Internet, wireless network, student labs or faculty/classrooms. Notice that to get into the DMZ or student computer labs, packets traverse through one firewall. Filtering through two firewalls is required to enter either of the secure server zones or the faculty/classroom computers. Even internal users go through at least one firewall to get to secure servers.

In the Workbook, Chap. 4 should include your network design, and Chap. 6 should include the firewall and router configurations. Professional network administration personnel should assist in configuring network equipment (firewall, routers) and virtual machines/servers, according to the requirements established in this chapter, and for ensuring detailed network security.

8.5 Advanced: How It Works

This chapter on Network Security is already very technical, but for those who plan on making a career in security, this advanced section will help to explain how different classes of firewalls work [7]. Figure 8.7a–d show four common configurations for increasingly secure firewalls.

The *Packet Filter* (Fig. 8.7a) filters according to TCP and IP addresses, as was shown in Fig. 8.1. The cigarette-looking thing below the firewall shows in black and white the amount of each packet that is evaluated by the firewall. In a Packet Filter, only the (black) TCP and IP packets headers are scanned, and the remainder of the packet, including the (white) application contents, is not filtered. The two 'A's shown on the terminal and host indicate that connection A is established between the terminal and host and the firewall does not participate in or track the connection status.

Stateful Inspection (Fig. 8.7b) is an enhancement of Packet Filtering, since the firewall tracks the state of each connection. (Hence the 'A' now shows up in the firewall.) This means that the firewall can detect if an attacker spoofs a connection, by sending out-of-sequence packets, or sends data packets when no connection is established. The tracking of the connection status means that a little more of the TCP header is now investigated by the firewall, which means that a little more of the packet is shown in black.

With the *Circuit-Level Firewall* (Fig. 8.7c), a connection is established between the terminal and the firewall, and a second is established between the firewall and the host. In this case, the network header is not only inspected, but it is also processed for even greater integrity. This additional processing means that fragmented packets are reassembled before being evaluated for malware and attacks.

The Application-Level Firewall or *Proxy Server* (Fig. 8.7d) performs everything that the other firewalls do, but in addition checks through much of the application data. That is why the packet is mostly inspected (in black) with very little of the packet uninspected (in white).

A network security design and implementation is not complete without a good test [8, 12]. After a network is configured, a network specialist should scan servers, work stations, and control devices to determine service availability and vulnerabilities. Vulnerability scanners can scan for open services, recent patching, and configuration weaknesses. Firewalls and routers can be tested to ensure that filtering and logging occur as designed. Penetration testing uses hacker techniques to try to break into a network. The network should also adhere to policy and standards, such as the implementation and monitoring of network logs and proper reaction to events.

Web servers require special testing to ensure that confidentiality, integrity, authentication and non-repudiation are all properly implemented. They should also be tested for attacks such as SQL injection, cross-site scripting, buffer overflows and proper data processing.

Some regulations/standards require network testing. PCI DSS requires quarterly scans and annual audits, as does FISMA. Sarbanes–Oxley requires regular audits, of which penetration testing should be a component.

8.6 Questions

1. *Vocabulary.* Match each meaning with the correct vocabulary.

Virtual server	Hypervisor	Private payment card zone
Public key	Public key encryption	Secret key encryption
SQL attack	Targeted attack	Man-in-the-middle attack
Nonrepudiation	Authenticity	Intrusion prevention system
Digital signature	Digital certificate	Virtual private network
Secure hash	Bastion host	Public key infrastructure
Honeypot	Demilitarized zone	Unified threat management

a) An attack oriented toward a specific victim.
b) A device or software that provides security functionality, including firewall, antivirus and spam filter.
c) An exploit that manipulates web form input to alter database commands.
d) A service which verifies an entity's identity and provides digital certificate information about the entity.
e) A sophisticated algorithm, calculated over a set of data, provides a result which ensures that the data is not modified in transmission or during storage.
f) A security goal where the sender cannot deny sending a message.
g) This information provides authentication data about an entity, as well as their public key.
h) A hash, encrypted with a private key, serves as a method of nonrepudiation.
i) A section of the network configured specifically to attract and catch attackers.
j) A method of encryption where the sender and receiver share an identical key.
k) A method of encryption where the sender and receiver use complimentary non-identical keys.
l) A security goal where the claimed sender is the actual sender.
m) An attacker pretends to be a desired computer network destination.
n) A method of consolidating services, by allocating different services onto a single physical server. Each service has its own operating system.
o) The software interface between a virtual machine's operating system and the operating system associated with the physical machine.
p) An encryption key that is freely distributed to others.
q) A sophisticated tool that recognizes and mitigates attack packets, actions and patterns.
r) A segment of the network partitioned by a firewall for use by the general public.
s) A segment of the network partitioned by a firewall to handle debit and credit card handling.
t) A configuration where all packets are encrypted between two endpoints.
u) An attack-resistant computer with an optimized security configuration.

2. *Security Design Principles*. How does the design for Einstein University implement the following security design principles: separation of domains, isolation, encapsulation, modularity, least privilege, simplicity of design, and minimization of implementation? For each, give an example of how the technique is used, either from Chap. 7, or this chapter.
3. *Workbook Solution for Specific Industry*. Consider an industry you currently work in or would like to work in. Assume the company is in your geographical region. You may use the Security Workbook, Network Security Chapter to complete the tables. For each table, include five or more services.
   a) Create a 'Sources and Destinations for Services' Table, similar to Table 8.1.
   b) Create a 'Service Classifications and Roles' Table, similar to Table 8.2.
   c) Create a Zones Table, similar to Table 8.3.
   d) Create a 'Controls for Services' Table, similar to Table 8.4.
   e) Design a Network Diagram, similar to Figs. 8.5 or 8.6.
4. *Activity Diagram*. Draw a flow chart or activity diagram showing the stages of an attack. Sample Activity Diagrams include Figs. 5.7, 6.4 and 7.3. Figure 4.1 is an informal diagram.
5. *PoS Infection Example*. Describe a sample scenario of how a criminal cyber team might remotely attack a Point of Sale device.
   a) What stages might this criminal team pursue, and what would the goals and objectives of each phase be?
   b) What security design weaknesses may help the criminal team during the attack? Discuss how a lack of security design principles in the network architecture, including separation of domains, isolation, encapsulation, modularity and least privilege, would make this attack easier.
6. *Virtual Machines*. Virtual Machines are traditionally used to separate one server from another. How could a VM could also protect users' computers from infected email and web accesses, while still enabling some storage from email/web? Consider how this could be implemented.
7. *Product Evaluation*. Select one security product to evaluate: Firewall, IDS/IPS, an encryption package, or Antivirus software. Look up different websites for this one security product, and select three products to evaluate. What security services do they appear to provide and for what price?
8. *Regulation relating to Network Security*. Consider one of the following American security regulations or standards: HIPAA, Gramm–Leach–Bliley, Sarbanes–Oxley, PCI DSS, or FISMA. What requirements do they have related to Network Security? Some websites provide government- or standards-based information, and thus are authentic sources of information. Consider these sites:
   a) HIPAA/HITECH: www.hhs.gov (Health and Human Services) or Chapter 14
   b) Gramm–Leach–Bliley/Red Flags Rule: www.business.ftc.gov (Federal Trade Commission)

c) Sarbanes–Oxley: www.isaca.org or www.sans.org (Organizations for standards/security)
d) PCI DSS: www.pcisecuritystandards.org: Requirements and Security Assessment Procedures v. 3.0
e) FISMA: www.nist.gov (National Institute for Standards and Technology)

8.6.1 Health First Case Study Problems

For each case study problem, refer to the Health First Case Study. The Health First Case Study and Security Workbook should be provided by your instructor or can be found at http://extras.springer.com.

Case study	Health first case study	Other resources
Planning for network security	√	Security workbook

References

1. Crowley S (2014) Obama's speech on N.S.A. Phone Surveillance (transcript). New York Times, 17 January 2014
2. Verizon (2013) Verizon 2013 data breach investigations report. http://www.verizonenterprise.com/DBIR/2013. Accessed 20 Oct 2013
3. Stallings W, Brown L (2012) Computer security: principles and practice, 2nd edn. Pearson Education, Inc., Upper Saddle River, NJ. pp 248–277, 623–726
4. Verizon (2014) Verizon 2014 data breach investigations report. http://www.verizonenterprise.com/DBIR/2014. Accessed 30 June 2014
5. PCI Security Standards Council (2013) Requirements and security assessment procedures, v 3.0, November 2013. www.pcisecuritystandards.org
6. PCI Security Standards Council (2013) Requirements and security assessment procedures, Ver. 3.0, November 2013
7. Harris S (2013) All-in-one CISSP® exam guide, 6th edn. McGraw-Hill Co., New York, NY, pp 800–843, 853–864
8. Walker M (2012) CEH™ certified ethical hacker all-in-one exam guide. McGraw-Hill Co., New York, NY, pp 274–279
9. Stephenson P (2014) Product section: authentication. SC Mag 25(1):36–47
10. Sutherland C, Halle H, Boroff B (2013) Inside, outside, upside-down: staying ahead of the threat, wherever it is. In: Plenary, SC congress Chicago, IL, 20 November 2013
11. Kolappon R (2013) Security content in the changing landscape of the mobile enterprise. In: SC congress Chicago, 20 November 2013
12. ISACA (2010) CISA review manual 2011. ISACA, Arlington Heights, IL, pp 320–326, 337–342

Chapter 9
Designing Physical Security

> ...for now know that every border you cross, every purchase you make, every call you dial, every cell phone tower you pass, friend you keep, site you visit, and subject line you type, is in the hands of a system whose reach is unlimited but whose safeguards are not. (Edward Snowden, CITIZENFOUR trailer.)

Physical security may be overlooked because it is not as complex or interesting as technology security. However the number one threat, at 35 % of forensic-analyzed attacks, was physical attacks and most of them involved ATMs and Point of Sale devices or controllers [1]. Of organization-reported security breaches, the number one cause involved lost, misdelivered or stolen media, documents, and faxes. All of these physical issues involve or could involve data breaches, protected by law.

Physical attacks can impact confidentiality and integrity, and environmental conditions may impact availability. In the Information Security chapter we rated assets using a sensitivity classification that included proprietary, confidential, private, and public classes. In the Business Continuity chapter, we assigned a criticality class to important assets, and rated them critical, vital, sensitive, and nonsensitive, depending on the loss we would incur if the assets or data were not available for a period of time. Instead of re-inventing the wheel, why not continue to use these classification systems, already developed, in our goal of physical security? Basically, we define room classifications, including how each class should be handled—and then we assign each room a classification. This is done in Tables 9.1 and 9.2. In Table 9.1, only two sensitivity classes are shown, but all should be described. In Table 9.2 only the two top availability-related classes (Critical, Vital) need be described, but others can be. Figure 9.1 then draws a map of a floor of a building and assigns a sensitivity and criticality class to each room, where the sensitivity class is color-coded.

The Physical Security Map can be shown in table form (Table 9.3), instead of map form. The advantage of this table form is that specific controls for individual rooms can be described. In the case of the university, there are more individual room situations than easily fit into the three defined sensitivity classes. Thus, there is a choice between defining more sensitivity classes (e.g., Protected, Private), or allocating descriptions for individual rooms. Defining too many sensitivity classes

S. Lincke, *Security Planning*, DOI 10.1007/978-3-319-16027-6_9

Table 9.1 Sensitivity class handling (partial listing of classes)

Sensitivity class	Description	Special treatment
Confidential	Room contains confidential information storage	Guard key entry Badge must be visible Visitors must be escorted
Privileged	Room contains end-user computer equipment, PoS devices or controlled substances	Computers, PoS devices are physically secured using cable locking or other lock-down mechanism PoS devices inspected daily for tampering/replacement Controlled substances locked in cabinets Doors locked between 9 PM and 7 AM, and weekends unless class in session. (Specific rooms may have other lock hours, unless attended by owner.)

Table 9.2 Criticality class handling

Criticality class	Description	Special treatment (controls related to availability)
Critical	Room contains critical computing resources, which cannot be performed manually	Availability controls include: Temperature control, UPS, smoke detector, fire suppressant
Vital	Room contains vital computing resources, which can be performed manually for a short time	Availability controls include: surge protector, temperature control, fire extinguisher

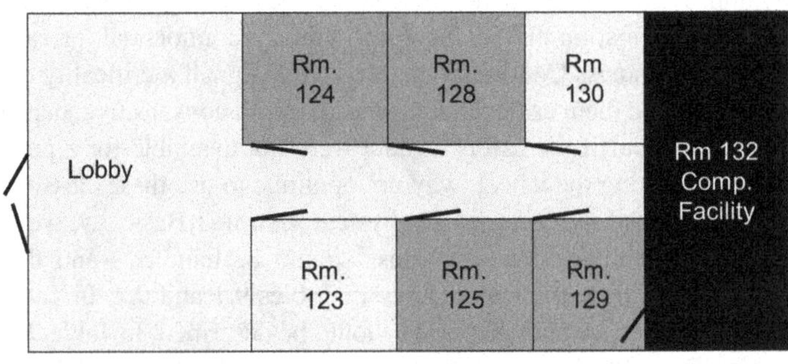

Fig. 9.1 Physical security map

can make the classes difficult to remember. Table 9.3 can list all non-public rooms, or list only special handling requirements. For ease of use, Table 9.3 may be separated into two tables: one each for Sensitivity and Criticality, since guards need to be concerned only with the Sensitivity class controls.

Table 9.3 Allocation of assets

Room	Sensitivity and critical class	Sensitive assets or info	Room controls
Rm 123	Privileged, Vital	Computer Lab: Computers, Printer	Cable locking system Doors locked 9PM–8AM by security
Rm 125	Privileged, Vital	Classroom: Computer & projector	Cable locking system Teachers have keys to door
Rm 132	Confidential, Critical	Servers and critical/ sensitive information	Combination-keycard entry logs personnel. Badges required
Cafeteria	Privileged, Vital	Point of Sale Terminals	Security gate locked when cafeteria closes sales

Physical security designs should continue to develop the Defense in Depth concept. When evaluating physical security controls, we should consider both quantity, including cascading controls (multiple sequential defenses) as well as quality, including whether controls are preventive, detective or corrective in nature. Now that you have a good idea how to design physical security, let's discuss the different types of controls you can select from concerning availability, then confidentiality/ integrity.

9.1 Selecting Availability Controls

Problems with electricity can include lost, reduced, or unsteady electrical currents [2]. A blackout is a total loss of power, which can occur for short or longer durations. Irregular power levels can cause damage to computer equipment, including crashes. Such power fluctuations include a brownout, which is a consistently reduced power level; or sags, spikes and surges, which are momentary changes in electrical levels. Power levels may fluctuate due to high period use (e.g., very hot days); electromagnetic interference (EMI) caused by electrical storms; or by sharing electrical circuits with departments who vary their electrical usage [3]. Therefore, it is a good idea to have data centers on their own circuits.

Fortunately, equipment to protect computers are relatively cheap. A *surge protector* regulates electrical surges for durations measured in milliseconds, by sending excess current to ground [2, 3]. *Voltage regulators* or conditioners provide a nice steady power stream. A *Universal Power Supply* (*UPS*) provides regulated power with battery backup for up to 30 min. More expensive *power generators* are required to extend electrical power beyond 30 min, including for hours or days.

An Information Processing Facility (IPF or computer room) should have a number of additional availability controls [2, 3].

Smoke detectors can warn of fire, and should be placed above and below ceiling tiles, and under the room floor. Detectors are placed at the highest point in each enclosure (e.g., attached to the underside of the floorboard). Manual fire alarms and fire extinguishers should also be available within 50 ft of electrical equipment.

Fire extinguishers should be tagged and inspected annually. Alarms should sound locally, at any monitored guard station, and preferably at the fire department.

Water detectors are useful if natural or manmade flooding is possible or if water is used as a fire suppression system anywhere in the building. Water is particular dangerous in an IPF due to electrical shock; people should be trained for handling such risks. Water detectors should be placed under raised floors at the lowest point in that enclosure (e.g., on the ground below the floorboard) and their locations should be marked on the floor.

An *emergency power-off switch* is useful to turn off power to all equipment, if a fire or flood occurs. There should be a switch both inside and outside the IPF room.

Air conditioning prevents computer overheating, which can result in computer malfunctioning in the short term, and shorter equipment lifespan over the long term. Your equipment manufacturer can provide exact specifications for your computer equipment, but ASHRAE standards currently recommend that computer equipment be maintained between 64.4–80.6 °F temperature and 20–80 % relative humidity [4]. High and low humidity can cause corrosion or electric static, respectively. Antistatic bags and flooring can protect electrical equipment from these electrical surges, when equipment is carried around [3].

Some fire suppression systems are safe and some are dangerous—to equipment or human beings. The safe suppression systems include those that don't kill people or damage equipment, like *FM-200* or *Argonite*. FM-200 foam cools equipment down, lowering the risk of combustion, while Argonite is a life-friendly gas. Fire suppression systems that are dangerous to humans include carbon dioxide and halon. While these gas systems do not damage equipment during a fire, they do replace oxygen and thus require lead time for people to exit. Halon was also banned due to its damage to the ozone layer.

Water sprinklers are popular but water tends to damage computer equipment. Although water is safe to humans, water conducts electricity well. Therefore, power should be turned off before a water sprinkler is discharged [3]. Air conditioning should simultaneously be turned off, since oxygen fuels fires. With *Wet Pipe* or *Charged* water sprinklers, pipes always carry water and can break or leak, while *Dry Pipe* systems carry water only when a fire is detected. Thus, Dry Pipe is safer in northern environments, where pipes could freeze.

The computer room is best located on a middle floor [2]. If the floor is too low, it is prone to break-ins and flooding, while if it is too high, the fire department cannot easily reach the floor to put the fire out. The fire department should inspect the room annually. Policies should state that there is no smoking, food or water in the IPF. The IPF should be configured with fire-resistant walls, floor, ceiling, furniture, and electrical panel and conduit. Walls should have a 2-hour fire resistance rating. In general, thicker walls have better ratings [3]. Redundant power lines reduce the risk of environmental hazards.

An auditor would observe that some sample controls are in place [2]. They should test sample batteries, handheld fire extinguishers, and ensure the fire suppression system is to code. They may inspect documentation, including policies and the physical security plan.

9.2 Selecting Confidentiality/Integrity Controls

Confidentiality controls include controlling access (or access control) to buildings, rooms, computer and other equipment, and documents. Least privilege dictates that people should have access to information or equipment only if their primary job responsibilities require them to have access. However, some organizations are in the business of serving the public—and they offer the public access to payment card readers, computers, or IT networks, such as gas stations, stores, libraries, schools, and Internet cafes. They need additional physical protections. We review each of these in turn.

9.2.1 Building Entry Controls

A few general rules of security are to ensure that your vicinity and grounds are safe and that you screen all entrants into your building/office area [3]. Your vicinity can be selected to be reasonably close to police, fire department, or a hospital, if your industry is prone to require any of them. You can select the location to be in a quiet spot with limited access or a busy spot with high public visibility. The grounds should be well lit at night where you want people to walk. You should guide people to one, or a limited number of entrance(s), where you can screen people and have visitors log in and out. It is possible to establish a map with security zones of your grounds: controlled, security, and public [3].

Crime prevention is subtly used to guide—and manipulate—people to proper behavior in external security. To prevent crime, security uses the defenses of good visibility and public observation. For example, secured doors/windows should be sufficiently well-lit at night to discourage attackers. Avoid using trees and higher bushes around any doors, which could enable hiding. Clearly observable CCTV cameras, public benches and picnic tables in key locations provide unwelcomed witnesses to potential criminals. Similarly, office windows when they overlook the parking lot help to prevent crime.

Friendly props, labels and sidewalks can be used to guide people to front entrances and away from side entrances or windows. For example, the use of shrubs, flowers, and other landscaping tell people "do not walk here", while sidewalks announce "please walk here". Shrubs should be sufficiently low, below 2.5 ft (or less than 1 m), to ensure visibility. Parking is best located just outside the front door. Signs can be used to attract the public, while the lack of signs tells the public "boring – ignore me."

Creating a friendly atmosphere gives the location a community feeling, where people feel responsible for each other and will help each other, if necessary. People need to feel safe, and good lighting and visibility helps to achieve that. Trees are pleasant and can help to provide the community feeling, but should not hinder visibility where security is an issue.

9.2.2 Room Entry Controls

Considering a defense in depth, let us assume an intruder has social engineered her or himself past the front desk, for example by saying he is a computer repair person. The uninformed guard told him where the computer room is, without calling an IT representative first. Let's look at room controls.

Some door locks are better than other door locks. For example, a key lock cannot track entrants; lets people in regardless of time of day; and can easily be circumvented by stealing or copying a key. Other types of door locks include electronic (key card), combination (numbers), and biometric (discussed in the Information Security chapter). The best systems are two or multifactor. Issues to consider with door locks include [2, 3]: can it track who entered at which times? Can it prevent entry by time of day to particular persons? Is it prone to error, theft, or impersonation? How expensive is it to install and maintain? If power fails, should it fail open or closed? A fail secure policy fails locked, but if there is a fire, people must exit. The decision should be considered carefully.

Piggybacking is a means whereby our intruder gains entry by following along with someone who is credentialed (by pretending to be credentialed and/or to be a friend of someone credentialed). *Deadman* or *mantrap* doors are an especially safe way to prevent piggybacking [2]. These include a double set of doors, where the space between the doors can only hold one person. A person enters the first door and must shut it before the second door can open.

Additional room entry controls may include walls, security cameras, motion sensors, security alarms, guard or patrols. For very high security applications, windows can be reinforced [3]. Tempered glass, acrylics, and wired glass are stronger than regular glass. Regular glass can be made somewhat stronger by applying a film to darken windows and reduce shattering. Door hinges should also be attack-proof. Room entry control procedures may include escorted visitors and employee badges.

To continue our intruder story, unfortunately our organization can't afford guards or security cameras for the IT data center. The intruder hides out and waits for 7 PM, when most people have left. Then he bypasses the door locks by using climbing equipment to enter the computer room through the ceiling panels. Hopefully we have good computer controls.

9.2.3 Computer and Document Access Control

This section discusses controls you may take if your equipment is generally handled by employees or trusted volunteers. The suggestions in this section are requirements for confidential information, and many are requirements for HIPAA adherents.

Computer access controls include engraved serial numbers, encrypted disk drive(s), encrypted copiers, and disabled disk or USB/disk interfaces. All organization equipment over a given price should be labeled with serial numbers and tracked in a database or spreadsheet. Serial numbers can be engraved or labeled with tamper-resistant tags specifying the company name (see Fig. 9.1). An equipment inventory should be taken regularly.

Device theft recovery solutions can be installed on computers, which enable law enforcement to quickly locate stolen computer equipment. If your computer is stolen, you log into the vendor's web site and turn on the activate function. According to web pages, features may include: using the computer's camera to record the image and voice of the next person to use the equipment, or locking out the thief and erasing all data. This software may also provide location information, if not an IP address that law enforcement can track. Not only do you get your computer back, but the thief gets prosecuted!

Encrypted disk drives (and their backups) are required to protect personal data, as described in the chapter on Information Security. Laptops and other mobile devices are especially prone to loss and theft. If disks are not encrypted, then specific files can be encrypted. However, the password cannot be forgotten, or the file(s) may be lost forever… This is also a problem if the person who created the encrypted files leaves the organization.

Commercial copy machines, which can make multiple copies of large documents, contain disk storage sufficiently large to retain many documents. These digital copy machines store documents when they copy, scan, fax, print and email documents. This retention of data is a concern when data is sensitive, since copy data may be accessed via the Internet or if the disk is stolen. In this case, the Federal Trade Commission recommends using copiers with extra security features, including encrypted disks and an overwrite feature [5]. The overwrite feature writes random data over copy files either upon a schedule (e.g., daily or weekly) or after each job run. Remember that encryption is a viable defense for state breach laws, in case your copy machine disk disappears with confidential data. An alternative or additional control is to specify in the copy machine contract that when the copy machine gets returned, either your organization keeps the disk(s) or the disk(s) are securely destroyed. A notice to this effect should be stuck on the copy machine. Accessing copy disks should be done by a professional, since they are often closely integrated into the copy machine. Improper handling can break the machine.

Computers should be protected so that passers-by cannot access other employee's terminals—potentially by viewing, keyboarding, and/or saving data off to a USB flash drive. Controls to prevent on-lookers include monitor hoods or privacy monitors, or simply placing the terminals where they cannot be easily viewed by visitors. Lockout function keys or screensaver timeouts can force an employee to login after not using the computer for a period, such as when walking away. USB flash drives and CD/DVD drives can be disabled. If USB drives are not disabled or the computer is portable, antivirus software is important to minimize the probability of malware [6].

Sensitive documents should be shredded upon disposal. A clean desk policy and locked files can ensure that proprietary or confidential papers will not be lying around for on-lookers to see.

To finish the intruder story, our intruder has entered the computer room and is looking for the proprietary information server. The servers are in cabinets, which are not locked—hooray! He powers servers down, and uses a prepared CD and USB flash drive to reboot different computers to the operating system provided on the CD or USB (whichever will work). In some cases he succeeds, and then begins to peruse the server disk contents. Darn, the contents are encrypted and he can't get in [6]!!! It probably isn't worth taking the disks, since most likely the disk he is looking for will be encrypted. The whole trip may be wasted! No, he may still succeed... He installs a wireless access point and connects it to an internet outlet, testing it out before he leaves. Yes, internal access! He also leaves around some unmarked DVDs and flash drives with Trojan horses on them. For sure someone will pick them up and want to see what is on them... Stay tuned for tomorrow's episode.

9.2.4 The Public Uses Computers

Some organizations may have rooms open to the public that contain computers—either employee computers or computers available for use by the public. In addition to the controls specified in the previous sections, additional precautions can prevent theft and malware takeovers.

Theft results when the whole or parts of computer(s) disappear. Figure 9.2 shows how a padlock can be used to lock the backside of a computer, preventing important computer cards or other components from 'walking away'. If the lock is used in combination with a bike cable, the computer can be physically tethered to a permanent fixture in the room.

Fig. 9.2 Computer is padlocked and tethered

Publicly-used computers are very prone to malware. Computers can be *imaged* where all stores to disk (if available) are temporary. In this scenario, every power up results in the same unmodified standard configuration. While this does not prevent malware infestations, it clears the malware every time the computer is rebooted. One issue is that if the imaged computer can be broken into via the Internet, the malware can be reinstalled day after day. This could occur if the computer is not configured properly for security or a login-password becomes known.

Ensuring that the image is recently patched will help to prevent intrusions. For example, Microsoft Windows ordinarily releases patches on the second or fourth Tuesday of each month (on "Patch Tuesday"), but may release a critical patch on an unscheduled basis.

9.2.5 The Public and Point of Sales Devices

In years back, identity thief Gonzalez would encode PINs onto forged debit card magnetic strips, and take as much money as he cared to out of ATM machines [7]. This is a good example of the security maxim: "The problem with common sense is that it is not all that common." [8] With better security, during the last year of this writing: Target, Staples, Home Depot, JPMorgan, P F Changs, Neiman Marcus, UPS, Michaels, Goodwill Industries, Supervalu and Community Health Systems were breached for customer data.

ATM and Point of Sale (PoS or payment card) machines at banks, gas stations, and other retail stores are attacked physically using skimmers, or via the Internet by installing spyware. ATM/PoS attacks make up 91 % of physical security attacks investigated by forensic experts [1]. Skimmers come in all sizes and colors to match their intended targets. They are even being produced by 3D printers. The skimmers record magnetic strip information, while pinhole cameras record PIN codes. They are installed in seconds. They are most often installed by outsiders, and most frequently at an ATM machine. However, they can be installed by insiders, including waiters, cashiers and bank tellers, who may be solicited to record, skim or install skimmers as fraud collusion [1]. Alternatively, PoS devices can be quickly replaced by an identical device with a skimmer installed; then the stolen PoS device is also altered and put into service elsewhere. A partner 'customer' distracts the attendant while the skimmer is installed [9]. Sophisticated criminals then collect the data wirelessly.

Properly installing devices in a tamper-proof way according to recommended directions can thwart physical abuses. Installation should also prevent booting from an infected CD [10]. PCI DSS requires that organizations inventory PoS/ATM devices, listing make, model, serial number and location [11]. There should be policies to inspect devices periodically, and more frequently in public places. Employees should recognize tampering and substitution, and should report suspicious actions like unplugging devices or intimidation. Recognizing tampering is easier when the procedure includes a picture and recorded serial numbers. Employees and managers shall also check for loose parts. Alternatively, the device can be marked with an ultraviolet light marker.

PCI DSS requires that entry to sensitive data centers that process or store payment card data be monitored [11]. Logging individual access via keycard or biometric identification, video, or Close Circuit TV (CCTV) can help in prosecuting attacks. Anyone claiming to be a PoS/ATM maintenance person should be authenticated with extra care to avert a social engineering attack.

A PoS smash-and-grab attack does not require physical presence, since criminals instead attack via the Internet [9]. They may use social engineering to establish a foothold in the network, then launch a brute force password guesser to obtain access to the PoS device. Alternatively, they may scan a network for remote access to a PoS machine and then use a password guesser [12]. Upon login, they install spyware such as PIN keystoke loggers and RAM scrapers, to record payment card information.

To avoid smash-and-grab attacks, restrict remote access, use antivirus software and mandate strong authentication for PoS/ATM devices. Two-factor authentication mandates what-you-know: a long and different password for each device [9]; combined with what-you-have: a one-time password, when remote access is required [12]. Also, ensure that these devices are recently patched from OS to PoS application; remove other applications; and prevent any use of these devices for other purposes [11]. Finally, encrypt all customer data [12].

Europay–Mastercard–Visa (EMV) smart payment cards have installed chips. They are difficult to counterfeit. Payment card companies have a target date of October 2015 for updating PoS devices to accept EMV cards [12].

When all other prevention and detection mechanisms fail, Common Point of Purchase (CPP) analysis queries fraud victims for their spending habits, and then finds common points of purchases to determine where the crime originated [1].

Auditors reviewing PoS devices should determine whether any information is stored in the device. If so, strong encryption is essential. Policies and procedures for PoS and ATM devices must be comprehensive, outlining overrides and balances, security controls, incident response, disaster recovery, maintenance, and audit trails and their review [2]. If the organization issues PINs, policies and procedures must safeguard those processes. Devices should adhere to the latest standards of PCI compliance for payment machines. Additional PCI DSS requirements apply if your organization develops its own payment card implementation [11]. This is further described in the chapter on Secure Software Development.

9.3 Questions and Problems

1. *Vocabulary.* Match each meaning with the correct vocabulary.

Voltage regulator	Universal power supply	Emergency power off switch
FM 200	Deadman door	Wet pipe

   a) A double set of locked doors prevents piggyback entry.
   b) A device which eliminates power sags and surges.

   c) A fire suppression system that sprays water, but may freeze in cold temperature climates.
   d) A fire suppression system that sprays a life-friendly foam, which cools equipment down and lowers the rate of combustion.
   e) A technique to turn off power to all equipment.
   f) A device which provides regulated power with battery backup for about 30 min.

2. *Workbook Solution for Specific Industry*. Consider an industry you currently work in or would like to work in. Assume the company is in your geographical region. You may use the Security Workbook (at http://extras.springer.com), Physical Security Chapter to complete the tables. <u>For each table, include five or more information or asset types, and three roles.</u>

   a) Create a 'Sensitivity Class Handling' Table, similar to Table 9.1.
   b) Create a 'Criticality Class Handling' Table, similar to Table 9.2.
   c) Create a Map, similar to Fig. 9.1. This map may be small but contain representative types of rooms that would be used in this industry.
   d) Create an 'Allocation of Assets' Table, similar to Table 9.3.

3. *Product Evaluation*. Select one security product to evaluate: CCTV, UPS/voltage regulator, fire suppression system, location-based software, encrypted copy machine, door locks, and point-of-sale devices. Look up different websites for this one security product, and select three products to evaluate. What security services do they appear to provide and for what price?
4. *Regulation relating to Physical Security*. Consider one of the following security regulations or standards: HIPAA, Gramm–Leach–Bliley, Sarbanes–Oxley, PCI DSS, or FISMA. What requirements do they have related to Physical Security? Some websites provide government- or standards-based information, and thus are authentic sources of information. Consider these sites:

   a) HIPAA/HITECH: www.hhs.gov (Health and Human Services) or Chap. 14
   b) Gramm–Leach–Bliley/Red Flags Rule: www.business.ftc.gov (Federal Trade Commission)
   c) Sarbanes–Oxley: www.isaca.org or www.sans.org (Organizations for standards/security)
   d) PCI DSS: www.pcisecuritystandards.org: Requirements and Security Assessment Procedures v. 3.0.
   e) FISMA: www.nist.gov (National Institute for Standards and Technology)

9.3.1 Health First Case Study Problems

For each case study problem, refer to the Health First Case Study. The Health First Case Study and Security Workbook should be provided by your instructor or can be found at http://extras.springer.com.

Case study	Health first case study	Other resources
Designing physical security	√	Security workbook HIPAA notes

References

1. Verizon (2013) Verizon 2013 data breach investigations report. http://www.verizonenterprise.com/DBIR/2013. Accessed 20 Oct 2013
2. ISACA (2010) CISA review manual 2011. ISACA, Arlington Heights, IL, pp 189–192, 381–386
3. Harris S (2013) All-in-one CISSP® exam guide, 6th edn. McGraw-Hill Co., New York, NY, pp 427–499
4. ASHRAE (2011) Thermal guidelines for data processing environments – expanded data center classes and usage guidance. American Society of Heating, Refrigerating and Air-Conditioning Engineers, Inc, www.ashrae.org
5. FTC (2010) Copier data security: a guide for businesses. Federal Trade Commission, pp 1–6. business.ftc.gov. November 2010
6. Conklin WA, White G, Williams D, Davis R, Cothren C (2011) CompTIA security+ all-in-one exam guide, 3rd edn. McGraw-Hill Co., New York, NY, USA, pp 581–595
7. Anon (2010) U.S. department of justice; leader of hacking ring sentenced for massive identity thefts from payment processor and U.S. retail networks. Biotech Business Week, 12 April 2010
8. Johnston R (2011) Security maxims. http://www.ne.anl.gov/capabilities/vat. Accessed 20 March 2011
9. Verizon (2014) Verizon 2014 data breach investigations report. http://www.verizonenterprise.com/DBIR/2014. Accessed 30 June 2014
10. Internet security threat report 2014, vol 19. April 2014. Symantec Corp.
11. PCI Security Standards Council (2013) Requirements and security assessment procedures, v 3.0, November 2013. www.pcisecuritystandards.org
12. Perlroth N (2014) U.S. finds 'Backoff' hacker tool is widespread. New York Times, 22 August 2014

Chapter 10
Organizing Personnel Security

> ...it is not how good a check looks but how good the person behind the check looks that influences tellers and cashiers. (Frank W. Abagnale, ex-con man, Catch Me if You Can, p. 120 [1]).

What does computer security have to do with personnel? Well, security experts are not likely to make simple security mistakes, whereas ordinary staff are. If a social engineer pretends to be system administrator and asks an employee to do some suspicious actions, the security staff will not likely be fooled, but some ordinary staff could. Since security is only as strong as the weakest link, all links must be made strong! Therefore, a major goal of personnel security is to ensure that all staff understand policies, know their security responsibilities, and are sufficiently trained to perform these security responsibilities. Thus, it is useful for the security designer (you) to have completed all of the previous chapters in the book. How can you assign security responsibilities and design security training unless you understand what each role involves?

Documentation serves as a contract to manage both employees and contractors. A second goal of this chapter is to discuss documentation aspects of managing projects, enforcing accountability, and tracking internal documents: Configuration Management and Change Management, as well as the development of external contracts: Service Level Agreements.

Another major goal of Personnel Security is fraud prevention. While Merton's Maxim is: "The bad guys don't obey our security policies" [2], it is still better to have clear policies and educate about them. Approximately 14 % of breaches are attributed at least in part to internal employees. Employees about to leave or who have left the organization cause 70 % of internal information theft [3]. This can be caught by monitoring changes in access patterns to information. Much of this can be prevented by disabling all corporate accounts and access permissions for terminating employees. In this chapter, we will look at this problem of fraud, first.

S. Lincke, *Security Planning*, DOI 10.1007/978-3-319-16027-6_10

10.1 Controlling Employee Threats

Personnel and customers are both a potential weakness in the security defense system, as well as a potential source of fraud. Many of these threats are industry specific. For example, a bank would be susceptible to the sale of credit card numbers, and creation of fake accounts with transferred money. Table 10.1 on Personnel Threats lists example threats to Einstein University that could be subverted by staff. This table considers which roles are most likely to involve this fraud or security vulnerability, and the potential liabilities.

While this task is somewhat repetitive with risk management, it is amazing what new important ideas come up when we focus on staff, instead of the external threats we tend to emphasize during risk analysis. Therefore, it is a good idea to think of threats independently now, then copy over any employee-related threats from the Risk chapter (and perhaps the new threats to the Risk chapter!)

Our next job is to consider controls for these risks. The most significant control is Segregation of Duties, which was introduced in Chap. 2. Here we will apply the concepts. Remember that good management ensures that no one person can defraud the system. Roles are categorized into Origination, Authorization, Verification, and Distribution, which originate, approve, double-check, and act on, respectively. These will be implemented in the computer system using authorization (logins, forms) and access control (permissions).

Figure 10.1 shows business relationships in a larger organization, which includes software development [4]. Notice that Security/Compliance would tend to 'authorize'

Table 10.1 Personnel threats

Threat	Role	Liability or cost if threat occurs
Divulging private info	Employee	FERPA violation = loss of federal funds
Skim payment cards	Salesperson	PCI DSS, state breach violation
Grant abuse	Employee with grant	Loss of funds from US granting agencies
Abuse of student	Employee, student, visitor	Bad press—loss in reputation May incite lawsuit

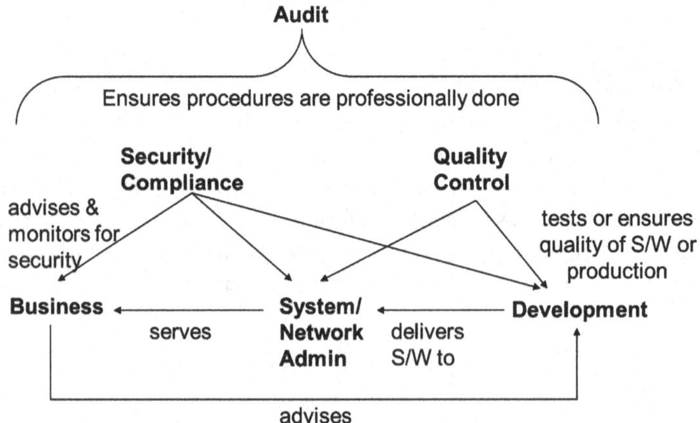

Fig. 10.1 Business relations for segregation of duties

aspects of software development, while quality control 'verifies' software development. System/network admin 'distributes' software to business, who is the user. Audit 'verifies' all other systems at a high level, by verifying their processes are defined safely and adhered to. These authorization/verification types of activities add a layer of approval.

If separation of duties is not possible to attain due to organization size, job rotation and mandatory vacations are compensatory controls. Techniques that help to prevent security breaches and fraud and/or shorten the duration of undetected fraud include preventive and detective/deterrence controls, such as [4–7]:

10.1.1 Preventive Controls

Chief Information Security Officer Naming a CISO (or maybe at least a Security Manager for small companies) makes someone responsible for security. A dedicated person allocated to the security function (whatever the title) is a requirement for HIPAA, Gramm–Leach–Bliley, PCI DSS and FISMA. Other important personnel functions include (defined elsewhere):

- *Data Owner, Process Owner*: Allocates permissions, defines safe processes.
- *Info Security Steering Committee*: Management with knowledge of business and/or security functions defines security (e.g., working with Security Workbook).
- *Incident Response Management/Team*: Decides or performs functions related to incident response.
- *Security Analyst, Security Administrator*: Security staff to design or implement security functions.

Security awareness training Discussion of organization policies, legal compliance, appropriate password selection, appropriate use of computer, appropriate handling of payment card information (if appropriate), and recognizing and reporting security events.

Training and written policies and procedures Include appropriate skills and knowledge of standards to do job. Payment card policies regarding handling and security are necessary for those handling sales. Training to recognize and report fraud can be geared towards employees and management.

Signed agreements Lists job responsibilities, security requirements, confidentiality agreement, proper computer (e.g., email) use. Three recommended policies for employees and one for contracts include [8]:

- *Code of Conduct*: Describes general ethical behavior requirements. (See Workbook for example).
- *Acceptable Use Policy*: This should address what, when, where, how and why company data can be accessed. If a mobile device is used for business purposes, it should address who can use the device: children are off-limits. It should address what is an allowable device for accessing organizational data (e.g., personal devices).

- *Privacy Policy*: Defines proper behavior in regards to company confidential information, such as regulatory requirements. Includes policies on password quality and secrecy, maintaining physical security, locking terminals, and reporting security issues.
- *Service Level Agreement*: This contract specifies required levels of service between a customer and provider. There is a separate subsection on this later in this chapter.

Ethical Culture To combat fraud, it is not sufficient to merely write policies; management must live, mentor and insist on ethical behavior.

Employee Support Programs Help employees cope with personal and financial problems before they become unmanageable.

Background checks Background checks are important for any employee who handles protected identifiable information (PII) or payment cards. It is also a good idea to screen security and system administrators since they are effectively god on a computer (i.e., have extremely high privileges).

Need to Know/Least Privilege As per the information security chapter, defines the minimal permissions per role to information. PCI DSS requires a documented list of roles with business reasons for the need to view or access payment card primary account numbers [7].

10.1.2 Detective (and Deterrence) Controls

Fraud reporting or hotline mechanism Customers and employees can discreetly (and preferably anonymously) report potential fraud to internal audit, an ethics officer, or an independent agent. This may include rewards for whistleblowers.

Identification badges Badges help to distinguish between onsite employees, contractors and visitors. All badges should be strictly controlled, with visitor badges expiring and surrendered daily. The visitor log should be retained for 3 months or more [7]. Badges are required by PCI DSS for sensitive areas where cardholder data is processed or stored.

Logged transactions Some transactions should be logged, providing the potential for review. Computer systems normally log important events like clearing the logs, changing log or security configurations, logging on or off a system, installing software, etc. HIPAA requires personnel to log medical transactions. Any adjustment of financial or monetary transactions should also be logged. Some of these transactions should be authorized by a manager before implementation.

Internal Audit Department and Surprise Audits: These are effective means to detect and deter fraud, and ensure compliance.

Mandatory vacations or job rotation Inappropriate performance will eventually be recognized.

Table 10.2 Example personnel controls for Einstein university

Threat	Role	Control
Divulging private info	Employee: instructor, advisor, registrar, administrator	FERPA training: annual quiz, new employee training
Grant abuse, travel abuse	Employee with grant or funding	Financial controls: employee's administrator and financial office double-check expense
Abuse of student or financial information	Instructor, advisor, or any employee who deals with students Salespersons with access to PoS	Background check at hiring. Policy of suspension, review and termination upon substantiated suspicion

10.1.3 Corrective Controls

Employee Bonding Insurance protects against losses due to theft, mistakes and neglect. (This is illegal in some countries.)

Fidelity Insurance Insurance against fraud or employee misdeeds is useful for rare but expensive risks.

Table 10.2 considers how specific threats from Table 10.1 can be controlled using segregation of duties or another control listed above.

At this point we have (hopefully) thoroughly considered all threats caused by insiders. We can now proceed to our second major personnel goal: coordinating responsibilities and training across our staff. This is a coordinated effort which considers all the other chapters in the Workbook, including: policy, risk, business continuity, information security, network security, physical security, incident response, personnel security (previous tables), and metrics.

In Table 10.3, two positions have Workbook-suggested job responsibilities (in type) while university-specific responsibilities are shown via handwritten script. In the table below, it may be useful to specify a name next to a role, such as a manager or department name. This table will turn into a description of security job responsibilities for each position. Note that these descriptions are simply suggestions, and you may edit them in the Security Workbook as you like.

It is highly recommended that someone acts as a Chief Information Security Officer. In larger organizations it should be a full time position.

10.2 Training for Security

Now that we have an idea of the security roles and responsibilities, we need to make sure that employees are trained to do their security responsibilities—and consider which documents and written procedures will help them to perform each role.

Table 10.3 Responsibility of security to roles

Role	Responsibility
Chief Info Security Officer: John Doe	Lead Info Sec. Steering Committee and incident response teams Lead efforts to develop security policy, security workbook Manage security projects, budgets, staff Lead security training for required staff on FERPA, PCI DSS, HIPAA, state breach Maintain security program: metrics, risk, testing, and policy revisions
Personnel: Alice Strong	Participate in Information Security Steering Committee Tracks and documents theft (to determine pattern) Prepare/manage contracts with Third Party contracts, establishing expectations relative to security At hiring: Perform background check for persons handling confidential info/major assets or interfacing with students. Write job description considering segregation of duties, security responsibilities Employee: Signs Acceptable Use Policy; Takes security awareness training including compliance, policy training At termination: Revoke computer authorization, return badges/keys and equipment, notify appropriate staff
Security Admin	Monitor logs for secure systems daily Enable/disable permissions according to data owner's directions Configure security appliances; audit equipment Rebuild computers after malware infection Investigate incident response, collect security metrics
Registrar	Establish FERPA training Data Owner: student scholastic and financial information Oversee FERPA adherence in Registration dept.
Office Admin., Advisor	Adhere to FERPA; attend training Retain locked cabinets with student info
Managers of staff handling payment card sales	Ensure sales staff is trained in pertinent PCI DSS requirements Inspect PoS machines daily

Training can be required before hiring, taught at hiring, and thereafter performed periodically.

There are three types of security training: security awareness for most employees, security training for people involved with security, and security education for security specialists. Security awareness and other training is a requirement of most security regulations.

Security Awareness This training is important for nearly everyone in the company, including anyone who uses a computer, handles payment cards, or accesses protected information or PII. Training can include contractors, vendors and partners. This training makes staff aware of organizational policies and trains them in permitted use of computers. Training occurs through single classes, meetings, web or video training, newsletters, quizzes and posters [5]. PCI DSS requires that training occurs at hiring and at least annually thereafter. PCI DSS also requires that two mechanisms are used for training and that appropriate employees sign that they have understood the security policy [7].

Selections from chapter one and two of this text—which relate to your business—provide the kind of knowledge that all staff should be aware of. Specifically this training should include smart computer use, including choosing passwords, avoiding email and web viruses, recognizing potential malware issues, and (potentially) backing up work-related files; and recognizing or preventing fraud through recognizing social engineers, reporting security incidents, and securing confidential information in paper or other media form [5]. People should understand why the policy is in place and the consequences of non-adherence.

Security awareness training is important, but can be totally ineffective. Measuring that staff (1) understand and remember security policies, and (2) implement security, can help to determine the effectiveness of the training.

Security Training Certain staff, such as medical staff, human resources, management, software developers, and IT, need security training specific to their responsibilities. This training is often received through workshops or conferences.

Security Education Education is extended training used to prepare people whose primary responsibility involves security, such as auditors, risk managers, security analysts and security administrators. Education develops both core skills and a high level understanding. It is taught through a formal course, book learning and/or through informal coaching. A list of topics deemed relevant to information security professionals is called the Common Body of Knowledge (CBK), and security certifications focus on these topic areas.

Continuing education is important for those whose jobs involve a high level of security. Security is one of the fastest moving fields, even compared to the fast-moving computer field. Security and incident response personnel must have annual security training. Most security certifications require annual training to remain certified.

Security personnel need continual training to maintain certification. Table 10.4 shows the annual training requirements for various security certifications, given in hours of training required.

Table 10.5 describes the training and documentation requirements needed for various roles with security functions. Table 10.5 has Workbook-suggested text for three positions, and a few university-specific roles.

A final reminder is that to perform this chapter correctly, it helps to review all previous chapters to ensure that all security functions have been integrated into this Personnel chapter. You will also need to do that for our next chapter on Metrics. Also, you will find that your evolved security understanding will help to improve your earlier chapters work.

Table 10.4 Continuing education requirements for security certification

Security certification(s)	Minimum 1-year requirement	Minimum 3-year requirement
CISSP, CISA, CISM, CRISC, CEH	20	120
SSCP, CAP, HCISPP	10	60
Security+	–	50
Other CompTIA certificates	–	20–75

Table 10.5 Requirements for security roles: training and documentation

Role	Requirements: Training, documentation
Chief Info Security Officer	Training: Security certification required at hiring Annual security maintenance training: 40 hours/year Documentation: Development of Security Workbook, legal compliance checklist
Security Administrator	Training: Security certification required at hiring Annual security maintenance training: 17 hours/year Documentation: TBD
Registrar	Training: FERPA experience in hiring Training every 3-5 years at national conference or workshop Training to adhere to PCI DSS annually
Employee handling student data	Training: FERPA annual quiz Documentation: University FERPA web page, signed acceptable use policy

10.3 Tools to Manage Security

An important tool to manage IT people, projects, and security is documentation. Whether the document is for internal use as a security plan, design, or code implementation, or for external use as a contract, an agreed upon version establishes a golden artifact, that serves to guide further personnel actions. Configuration Management, Change Management, and Service Level Agreements help achieve these goals.

10.3.1 Configuration Management and Change Control

Important documents need to occasionally be recorded at specific moments in time, since they often serve as a contract within or between organizations. Documents evolve, and thus multiple versions of documents will need to be recorded and managed. This is the function of Configuration Management [9].

A *configuration management* system is a central repository, which is similar to an electronic library document management system. Important documents are maintained in this repository. For software development teams, this includes requirements, design and test documents, program code and project, audit and security plans. The repository holds a snapshot of different versions for each document, thereby maintaining a history, so that any version can be retrieved at any time.

This document management system does permit users to checkout a document; edit, review or approve the document; and check it back in. Revised documents are allocated an increased version number. The revision-author and reason for revision is recorded at check-in and is later available as part of the version history.

Change management is the process that creates different configuration management versions. Change management usually starts with a change proposal: (1) a Change Request, which may be (2) analyzed and approved by management for implementation. The change is then (3) implemented (e.g., programmed or acted upon) and this change may be (4) tested and approved, when the change is ready for deployment. Documentation for each of these stages is maintained in a change management or configuration management repository, and emails may notify stakeholders of changes of status.

10.3.2 Service Level Agreements

A Service Level Agreement (SLA) is a contract to outsource any IT or other sensitive service, potentially including networking, business continuity, security or information security. An SLA should cover the following sections, to ensure that performance, security, legal compliance, and payment are agreed upon [9]:

- Introduction and Scope of Work
- Performance, Tracking and Reporting
- Problem Management
- Compensation
- Customer Duties and Responsibilities
- Warranties and Remedies
- Security
- Intellectual Property Rights and Confidential Information
- Legal Compliance and Resolution of Disputes
- Termination of Contract
- Schedules and General
- Signatures

Note that most regulations (e.g., HIPAA, FISMA, Gramm–Leach–Bliley) and PCI DSS require that contractors meet these regulations to the same level as the contracting company. These contracts must ensure competence and full adherence to regulation when confidential information is involved. PCI DSS requires that a list is maintained of all such service providers, detailing specific services, and that they are annual monitored for compliance [7]. More information on SLAs can be found on-line at www.service-level-agreement.net.

10.4 Questions and Problems

1. *Vocabulary*. Match each meaning with the correct vocabulary.

Security education	Acceptable use policy	Service level agreement
Security training	Change control	Configuration management

   a) A document addressing what, when, where, how and why company data may be accessed.
   b) A contract which specifies required standards of service between a customer and provider.

c) Comprehensive training for people whose primary role is security.
d) Security training for a particular role or function.
e) A central repository for document management.
f) A process to track and record modifications to equipment, software or documentation.

2. *Segregation of Duties.* Consider an industry you currently work in or would like to work in. Draw a Segregation of Duties diagram, similar to Fig. 10.1, for this industry. Include roles and labels for each arrow relationship. Describe in text how segregation of duties is implemented (or not) for this industry. If it is not implemented, describe some options of how it could be, or how compensating controls (mandatory vacations or job rotations) could help.
3. *Workbook Solution for Specific Industry.* Consider an industry you currently work in or would like to work in. Assume the company is in your geographical region. You may use the Security Workbook Personnel Security Chapter to complete the tables. For each table, add at least 3–5 entries.

   a) Create a 'Personnel Threats' Table, similar to Table 10.1.
   b) Create a 'Personnel Controls' Table, similar to Table 10.2.
   c) Create a 'Responsibility of Security to Roles' Table, similar to Table 10.3.
   d) Create a 'Requirements for Security Roles: Training and Documentation' Table, similar to Table 10.5.

4. *Security Certifications.* Do research on three of the following security certifications: Security+, CISSP, SSCP, HCISSP, CISA, CISM, CRISC and CEH. What does each certification strive to achieve? Develop a table which shows subject areas that each covers. The subject areas can be the chapter topics of this book: Security Awareness/Malware, Fraud, Regulation, Risk, Business Continuity, Security Governance, Information Security/Authentication/Access Control, Network Security/Wireless, Physical Security, Personnel Security, Incident Response, Metrics, Audit, Software/Application Security. You can learn about the certifications by looking at the certification website or a table of contents' chapter headings of study guide books for each. Do you see differences in expertise between them?

10.4.1 Health First Case Study Problems

For each case study problem, refer to the Health First Case Study. The Health First Case Study and Security Workbook should be provided by your instructor or can be found at http://extras.springer.com.

Case study	Health first case study	Other resources
Organizing personnel security	√	Security workbook HIPAA notes or slides
Update requirements document to include segregation of duties	√	Health first Requirements document

References

1. Abignale FW (1980) Catch me if you can. Broadway Books, Broadway, NY, p 120
2. Johnston R (2011) Security maxims. http://www.ne.anl.gov/capabilities/vat. Accessed 20 March 20 2011
3. Verizon (2013) Verizon 2013 data breach investigations report. http://www.verizonenterprise.com/DBIR/2013. Accessed 20 Oct 2013
4. ISACA (2010) CISA review manual 2011. ISACA, Arlington Heights, IL, pp 105–106, 117–119
5. ISACA (2011) CISM® review manual 2012. ISACA, Arlington Heights, IL, pp 161–162
6. ACFE (2014) Report to the nations on occupational fraud and abuse: 2014 global fraud study. Association of Certified Fraud Examiners (ACFE)
7. PCI Security Standards Council (2013) Requirements and security assessment procedures, v 3.0, November 2013. www.pcisecuritystandards.org
8. Cammarata C, Wilcox AS (2013) Going mobile. In: SC congress Chicago, IL, 20 November 2013
9. Gregory P (2008) IT disaster recovery planning for dummies. Wiley Publishing, Inc., Hoboken, NJ, pp 158, 257–258, 311–312

Chapter 11
Planning for Incident Response

> Ceremonial Security (a.k.a. 'Security Theater') will usually be confused with Real Security; even when it is not, it will be favored over Real Security. Comment: Thus, after September 11, airport screeners confiscated passengers' fingernail clippers, apparently under the theory that a hijacker might threaten the pilot with a bad manicure. At the same time, there was no significant screening of the cargo and luggage loaded onto passenger airplanes. [1]

What should you do? A hacker has penetrated your network and turned a server into a bot. You have a choice of closing the firewall down, closing the inner network down, closing the server down, or keeping everything up. Except the last, each of these might stymie the attacker, but what is it also doing to your organization's business?

If your business is a pharmacy, bringing the network down might make it impossible for customers to get lifesaving prescriptions. Leaving it up might enable the attacker to change multiple prescriptions, potentially killing someone.

If your business is a bank, the intruder may walk away with millions of credit card numbers and Social Security numbers. Closing the network down might prevent all banks from operating.

Your business could be a search engine, an airline serving thousands of passengers daily, an automated factory producing goods. The decision of how to react to an intrusion is a decision that may impact customer service, customer security, organizational sales, and legal liability. This decision cannot be made lightly, and should be made at the highest levels of the institution—well before an attack actually occurs. Therefore, it is highly important that top management make strategic decisions about what should happen when an intruder is poking around sensitive organizational data. But this top management should be aware of the full implications of their decision—including security costs and regulation liability.

S. Lincke, *Security Planning*, DOI 10.1007/978-3-319-16027-6_11

11.1 Important Statistics and Concepts

A security *incident* is defined as a series of events that impact an organization in a adverse way. NIST SP 800-61 defines an incident as "a violation or imminent threat of violation of computer security policies, acceptable use policies, or standard security practices." Examples of incidents may include a social engineering, fraud, hacker or terrorist attack, or data exposure. The difference between Business Continuity and Incident Response is that with Business Continuity, incidents often relate to failed IT systems, whereas with Incident Response, incidents relate to security threats to systems, networks and data. Incident response issues may include loss of data confidentiality and non-repudiation. Since a security incident could result in temporary loss of IT, the Incident Response Plan should build upon or be integrated with the Business Continuity Plan, adapted for security incidents.

So why is it important to plan for security incidents before they actually happen? Why, to save money and reputation, of course! The bad news is that it is REALLY expensive if you experience a data breach (see Table 11.1). Typical expenses after a data breach include hiring forensic experts to determine the full extent and reason for the breach, and supporting your customers via hotline, free credit monitoring subscription, and discounts for future services [2]. While these costs are expensive, they average only half the cost of customer maintenance after a breach, which includes loss of reputation, abnormal churn of customers, and increased customer procurement activities.

Unfortunately incidents can take a long time to detect, and are often detected by outsiders. Statistics show that 66 % of incidents took a month or more (even years) to discover, and 82 % of incidents were detected by outsiders [3]. These outsiders included internet service providers, Information Sharing and Analysis Centers (ISAC) or other organizations, who often recognized communications with known suspicious sites (e.g., an attack is originating from your network). Therefore, it is highly important to emphasize detective techniques, in addition to preventive techniques, to recognize intrusions and data breaches as early as possible.

Some good news is that 78 % of the initial intrusions were rated as low difficulty. As the Verizon Data Breach Investigation report states: "Some interpret attack difficulty as synonymous with the skill of the attacker, and while there's some truth

Table 11.1 Incident response costs, Ponemon Institute's 2014 Cost of Data Breach Study: United States, Sponsored by IBM

Expenses following a breach	Average cost
Detection and escalation: Forensic investigation, audit, crisis management, board of directors involvement	$420,000
Notification: Legal expertise, contact database development, customer communications	$510,000
Post breach response: Help desk and incoming communications, identity protection services, legal and regulatory expenses, special investigations	$1,600,000
Lost business: Abnormal customer churn, customer procurement, goodwill	$3,320,000

to that, it almost certainly reveals much more about the skill and readiness of the defender." [3 p. 48] So if you do a good job with planning—and implementing—security, you may have a much lower probability of an incident occurring… but be sure that third party outsourcers and business partners are equally protected, because 40 % of data breaches occur due to third party error.

The chapter on Risk provides statistics on breaches and indicates the average cost per breached record is $201. With good preparation, you can encounter lower costs if a breach occurs. The Ponemon Institute's Data Breach Study [2] found that you can reduce the average cost per record of a data breach if your organization has a formal Incident Response Plan ($17), a strong security program ($21), a Chief Information Security Officer ($10), and/or involves a Business Continuity management team ($13). But of course, if you can prevent a data breach, the entire cost goes away.

The *Incident Management Team* (*IMT*) is the managerial team that designs the Incident Response Plan (IRP) [4]. The Information Security manager works with business management to prepare the IRP. Together, they strategize over how various security incidents should be handled and how incidents should affect business, IT, business continuity and risk management. The Information Security manager leads this team, which in a larger organization includes members from the Security Steering Committee and Incident Response Team. This management team also discusses budgets, evaluates schedules and performance, and reviews incident postmortem reports.

The *Incident Response Team* (*IRT*) is a technical team that handles the specific incident [4]. This team has technical knowledge relating to security, network protocols, operating systems, physical security issues, and malware. While these incident handlers and (if possible) investigators are the main members of the team, representatives from business management, legal, public relations, human resources, physical security, risk and IT also have important roles relating to their expertise, following an incident. In most organizations, forensic expertise is not available in house. In these cases, the function must be outsourced using a qualified security/forensic organization, that is preferably local. For incident response purposes, external consultants will need full and timely Internet and physical access for their investigation, and will make quicker progress if internal technical staff is present to help [5].

11.2 Developing an Incident Response Plan

An *Incident Response Plan* (*IRP*) addresses each stage of incident response. The stages of incident response [4, 6] are shown in Fig. 11.1. The first stage is Preparation, where the Incident Response Plan is developed. This occurs BEFORE any incident occurs (hopefully). An incident triggers the Identification Stage. An employee may recognize a social engineering event, a system administrator may recognize an attack in system logs, or an intrusion detection device may recognize an attack signature. Once the attack is recognized, it is important to contain the incident: the intruder should not be able to expand the attack or do more damage. Defensive actions may

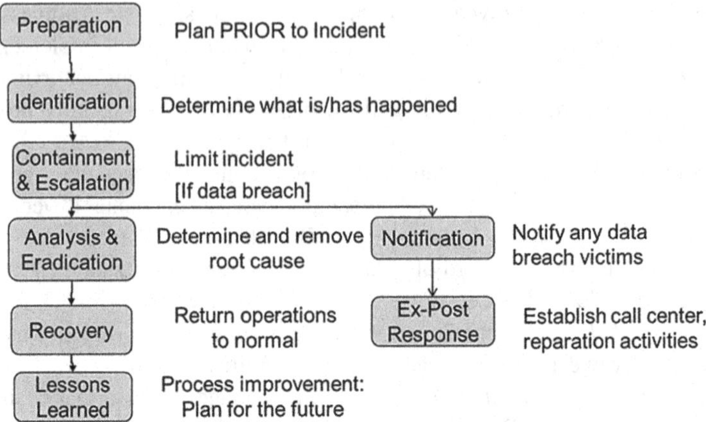

Fig. 11.1 Stages of incident response

include bringing the application, system, and/or network down, or modifying firewall access control to reject the connection (which will only delay further attacks). In the Analysis and Eradication Stage, the root cause of the attack is determined and attack software is recognized and removed from the network. After testing ensures the rebuilt system is ready for operation, the Recovery Stage brings the system back online again. If a data breach occurred, two additional stages are added: Notification and Ex-Post Response, which is where we notify victims and offer redress. The Lessons Learned Stage reviews how the organization did as part of incident response, and how the procedures could be made clearer, faster and more effective. The next sections elaborate on each of these stages in detail, to help you plan for incident response.

11.2.1 Preparation Stage

The purpose of the Incident Response Plan (IRP) is to decide in advance [4, 5]:

- Strategy: How will we detect incidents? What shall we do to prevent or discourage incidents from occurring (e.g. policies and warning banners at computer logon)?
- Containment: What should we do when different types of incidents occur? The BIA can help in determining critical assets and how incidents can be handled. When can the IRT confiscate or disconnect an employee's computer? If we may call the police, what actions do they recommend us taking before they arrive?
- Escalation: When is the incident management team called? How can governmental agencies or law enforcement help? When do we involve law enforcement, and who can call them?
- Preparation: What equipment do we need to handle an incident? Where on-site and off-site shall we keep the IRP?

Security threats that should be considered include: malware, unknown or unauthorized user, compromised server, lost or stolen equipment, divulged secrets/files, (distributed) denial of service, written threats to IT, unidentified network objects (e.g., wireless, hosts), and modified information [5, 7]. *Attack vectors* (or source methods) may include removable media, flash drive, email, web, improper use, loss or theft, physical abuse, social engineering, etc.

To detect an incident, an organization must have detection and monitoring capabilities. The sooner the attacker can be found, the more limited the scope of the attack will be. Proactive detection mechanisms include [4, 5, 7]:

- *Antivirus software*: Detects malware infections and may fix some infections.
- *Endpoint Security Suite*: Enterprise-level software includes antivirus/antispyware software and firewalls, but in addition verifies that operating system software is recently updated, and that only whitelisted (permitted) applications are installed or blacklisted (not allowed) software is not installed [8]. This software sends alerts or emails to a centralized system when problems are detected.
- *System baseline*: Knowledge of normal terminal configurations, including processes and communications, can help to distinguish abnormal, suspicious configurations. A normal configuration is saved as a system baseline for future comparisons.
- *Log management*: Log management is required as part of comprehensive security regulations (e.g., HIPAA, FISMA, PCI DSS, SOX-COBIT). It is important to consider which computer logs will best help to detect and analyze an attack, and how much storage is needed for this. Since it is important to correlate logs between different network and computer equipment, the Network Time Protocol ensures the network agrees on a precise time. Log management requires extensive time and technical expertise. For larger organizations, a SIEM tool collects system logs network-wide, coordinates and co-relates logs, and tracks the status of incidents to closure. See Fig. 11.2 for important logs to collect.

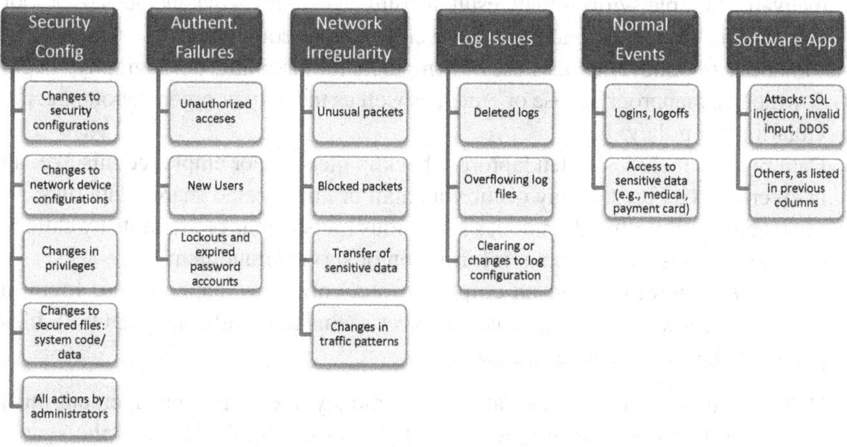

Fig. 11.2 Important logs to collect [8, 9]

- *Vulnerability testing*: Periodic automated or manual testing ensures that servers and network equipment are configured to withstand common attacks, including that servers are patched, and security configuration options are adequate. PCI DSS requires quarterly testing. It is recommended that vulnerability tests are automatically run daily, with results compared with known good results [8].
- *Protocol sniffer*: These tools record and decipher packets traveling across the network. A professional knowledgeable about network protocols will be able to inspect and search through packets, when an incident is suspected. Inspecting 3 h of unusual traffic per week may discover an intrusion [8].
- *Intrusion detection/prevention systems*: Network Intrusion Detection/Prevention Systems (NIDS/NIPS) and Host Intrusion Detection/Prevention Systems (HIDS/HIPS) automatically recognize attack signatures and abnormalities. These tools are often configured to recognize exfiltration, or the copying of sensitive data, and unusual patterns of data access.

Slower but effective mechanisms include human (employee, customer, vendor) report of unusual or suspicious activity. For this to be an effective means of incident detection, security awareness training should educate employees to recognize attack symptoms and tell them how to report an incident that they personally observe or hear from customers or vendors. There needs to be a way for people to submit incidents anonymously [5].

Symptoms that should be investigated by IT professionals include: a device (firewall, router or server) issues one or more serious alarms, an intrusion detection system recognizes an irregular pattern (e.g., unusually high traffic, inappropriate file transfer, changes in communications protocol use), and unexplained system crashes or connection terminations. Even if an IDS is not available, heavy usage through firewall or at server should be a concern. Finally, when reported network or computer activity does not match actual activity, a hidden rootkit can explain the discrepancy [7].

Events that employees should report include [10]:

- Malware: includes ransomware, suspicious emails, or antivirus software reports malware. "Simple" viruses may result in criminal escalation that includes backdoor entry, data copying, and additional attacks on other computers.
- Violations of policy: includes use of computers for gambling, pornography, illegal downloads, inappropriate use of email, as well as industry or organization-specific violations of policy.
- Data breach: includes stolen laptop or backup memory, or employee mistake: an inadvertent data breach may occur via email or unprotected shared data files.
- Social engineering/fraud: includes suspicious transactions or attempts by callers, e-mailers, or visitors to obtain information or service fraudulently.
- Unusual/suspicious event: an employee recognizes an inappropriate login, a system aborts without good cause, a server seems unusually slow (DOS?), files get deleted, or the website is defaced.

Detection tools and implementations cost money. Executive management must be convinced that this money is well spent. Hopefully, Table 11.1 and the source

Table 11.2 High-level planning for incident detection and handling

Incident	Description	Methods of detection	Procedural response
Intruder accesses internal network	Firewall, database, IDS, or server log indicates a probable intrusion	Daily log evaluations, high priority email alerts	IT/Security addresses incident within 1 hour: Follow: Network Incident Procedure Section
Break-in or theft	Computers, laptops or memory is stolen or lost	Security alarm set for off-hours; or employee reports missing device	Email/call Management & IT immediately. Management calls police, if theft. Security initiates tracing of laptops via location software, writes Incident Report, evaluates if breach occurred
Social Engineering	Suspicious social engineering attempt was recognized OR information was divulged that was recognized after the fact as being inappropriate	Training of staff leads to report from staff	Report to Management & Security Warn employees of attempt as added training Security evaluates if breach occurred, writes incident report
Trojan Wireless LAN	A new WLAN masquerades as us	Key confidential areas are inspected daily for WLAN availability	Security or network administrator is notified immediately. Incident is acted upon within 2 hours

Verizon and Ponemon references [2, 3] will help to inform management of the true costs of a data breach. In addition to detection tools, redundant configurations including redundant computers or alternative routing may carry part of the load following an incident, after infiltrated equipment is removed.

Table 11.2 documents methods of detection and procedural responses for various types of incidents. The social engineering and theft events include brief descriptions of how the incidents should be handled. The 'Intruder accesses internal network' event is more complex and cannot be fully described in the Procedural Response section. Should the network/server be brought off-line? They type of alarm generated may indicate which specialist technician should handle the event and dictate the event's priority. Therefore, the incident itself may be further divided into a number of incidents. Because this incident's Procedural Response is lengthy, this table entry simply refers to a procedure. This extended procedure is divided into sections by incident stage: Identification, Containment, Analysis, etc., and a sample is demonstrated later, as Table 11.3.

In addition to having an incident response plan, each organization shall have an incident response form. Fields that may be included in such a form include: date/time the incident was detected, date/time the incident occurred, contact info for the reporting person, reported suspicious observation, the incident type, affected systems and applications, impacted accounts, any police report, and all incident details, summary, and observation snapshots as noted by the incident response team [7].

Table 11.3 Incident handling response procedure

Incident Type: Malware detected by Antivirus software
Contact Name & Information: Computer Technology Services Desk: 262-252-3344(O)
Emergency Triage Procedure: Disconnect computer from Internet/WLAN. Do not reconnect. Allow antivirus to fix problem, if possible. Report to IT first thing during next business day
Containment & Escalation Conditions and Steps: If laptop contained confidential information, investigate malware to determine if intruder obtained entry. Determine if Breach Law applies
Analysis & Eradication Procedure: Security investigates problem If confidential information was on the computer (even though encrypted), malware may have sent sensitive data across the internet; encryption was ineffective and breach law may apply. A forensic investigation is required After this is resolved, determine if virus was dangerous and if user had admin privileges: Type A: return computer. (A=Virus not dangerous and user not admin.) Type B: Rebuild computer. (B=Either virus was dangerous and/or user was admin.) Password is changed for all users on the computer
Other Notes (Prevention techniques): Note: Antivirus should record type of malware to log system

11.2.2 Identification Stage

In this stage, the attack has landed—or may have. Anyway, something looks very—or kind of—suspicious. An incident has been reported and it is time to look into it. It could be a real problem or a false positive (i.e., looks threatening but is ok). The questions that need to be answered during the Identification Stage is: What type of incident just occurred? What is the severity of the incident? Who should be called? The severity may increase if recovery is delayed. When an incident is suspected, the appropriate incident response person should be called immediately to determine whether the cause for concern is real or a false positive. This investigator and other incident response team members will need written permissions in policy to access and monitor accounts. This elevated permission may be kept in secured storage for security incidents [7].

Triage is the function of naming and categorizing the incident, prioritizing it, and assigning the handling of the incident to an appropriate handler [4]. In a hospital, triage is what they do in at the emergency room front desk to stop the bleeding, write a preliminary report, prioritize patients, and schedule the right doctor (according to how quickly people are dying). Triage for a network attack may be for the firewall to disconnect problem connection(s) and notify the network administrator via a high-priority alarm that a certain type of attack is underway. The IRT has a preconfigured jumpkit with all tools, including forensic software utilities, to investigate the incident. All communications about the incident should be off-net, using cell phones or external email accounts, to combat any listening attacker [7].

The full set of functions during this stage include: Sort, Categorize, Correlate, Prioritize and Assign [4]. Sorting may be important when multiple events occur simultaneously as part of one or more incident(s). Documenting a snapshot of the known status of all reported incident activity is important to properly identify and categorize the event. This documentation will also be important in later Analysis stages and to establish a chain of custody for evidence. Categories for attacks may include: DoS, malicious code, unauthorized access, inappropriate usage, or a combination of components. Prioritization is important when there is limited time and staff. Higher priority should be allocated to services at higher class levels for confidentiality, integrity, and/or availability [5], as defined by Business Continuity and Information Security sections. However, once Containment is completed, priorities may change. Assignment of staff may consider who is free or on duty, and who is competent in this area.

Evidence must follow *Chain of Custody* law to be admissible in court [4]. If the incident may ever be prosecuted, chain of custody must start immediately and proceed through this and all subsequent stages. This includes documenting all actions, working with a witness, and avoiding modifying the evidence. Most technical people do not know what they can and cannot do in evidence handling. If prosecution is to remain an option, it is important to employ specially trained staff as soon as possible, such as calling an outside forensic expert and legal counsel, law enforcement, or your own security response team. In the case of a data breach, the advantage of hiring outside legal council is the attorney-client privilege, but eventually you will need to notify customers, and in the U.S., possibly the Attorney General or a state authority [11]. In Europe, you may need to report the breach within 24 h, as part of following the European Unction Directive 2002/58/EC and the Council of 12 July 2002 [7].

In the United States, the FBI recognizes cyber incidents as an exponentially growing threat, and treats cyber incidents as priority number 3, just after terrorism and foreign espionage [12]. The typical FBI response to a threat involves interviewing key personnel, isolating compromised systems, performing live response, creating forensic images, and copying related logs and relevant evidence. They will leave your equipment in tact as much as possible. They need to be notified as soon as possible, and are willing to deal with some false alarms.

Regardless of whether your organization decides to hire consultants, bring in law enforcement, and/or do much of the forensic work yourself, evidence collection is very tricky work. It is further described in the Computer Investigation and Forensics section later in this chapter.

However, it is also important to react quickly to minimize damage. A system administrator can retrieve information to identify an incident, determine the scope and size of the impacted environment (system/network), establish the degree of loss or damage, and uncover the possible path of attack [4]. While it is important to clearly identify the incident, it can be a good idea to begin to contain the incident, even if the incident is not yet fully identified.

11.2.3 Containment and Escalation Stage

In this stage, the Incident Response Team is tasked with containing the threat. During Containment, the problem is isolated so the attacker becomes confined and controlled. Containment options may include [10]:

- Halting connections: disconnect attacker by reconfiguring firewalls or routers to not service particular IP addresses or port numbers. This is a temporary fix, since most attackers can easily change their IP address. The Internet Service Provider may be able to help in filtering an attack pattern.
- Disabling server communications or network zone: disconnect the computer or server from the network by effectively removing or disabling the Network Interface Card (NIC) from the infiltrated machine. It is also possible to break access to a zone or router region, by disconnecting network connections or powering down routers.
- Disabling user access: revoke privileges to internal users who violate policy. Management actions may include scolding, additional training or termination.

It is never appropriate to attack the attacker. This usually violates law and can escalate the confrontation.

Technical staff will need to collect system data and analyze this data and log files. They may require additional technical assistance from other staff. To further contain the incident, they may deploy patches and workarounds. The attack itself or a disabled service may affect other parts of the business. Management will need to be notified of the attack and any implications, such as temporarily unavailable services. Finally, if the incident is ever to go to court, the forensic staff must continue to obtain and preserve evidence according to strict legal rules.

Escalation is required for certain attacks, such as data breaches. During escalation authorities are notified, such as the incident management team, executive management, board of directors, and possibly law enforcement [6]. Legal counsel should advise on issues related to investigation, prosecution, liability, privacy, regulation and nondisclosure. Forensic experts may be hired to investigate a breach.

11.2.4 Analysis and Eradication Stage

The intruder found some way to initially gain entrance into the network, and could do it again if this entry is not repaired. In addition, they most likely installed new backdoors into infiltrated systems. Therefore, the main function of the Analysis stage is to determine the *root cause* of the incident. This means analyzing the vulnerabilities that enabled the attack and why those vulnerabilities existed. To determine the root cause, it is important to start to understand what damage occurred and why. Computer Emergency Response Team (CERT) centers gather basic statistics per incident, including [3]:

- Actors: Who perpetrated the incident?
- Assets: Which assets (equipment, data) were affected?
- Actions: What happened during this incident?
- Attributes: How were the assets affected?

An extended set of questions asks about the initial attack: What vulnerability enabled the original attack? When did this initial attack occur? Where did the attack originate from? What is also important is what happened during the attack: How did the attack happen? Who was affected? What was the motivation for the attack? The origin may be in a programming or configuration error or other vulnerability.

To acquire root cause information, it is important to find the indicators (or symptoms of abnormal behavior) for the incident. Methods of analysis include using forensic tools, as discussed later in the Computer Investigation and Forensics section. Logs will need to be analyzed from different devices: operating system logs should indicate which accounts were accessed and when; and network devices may indicate any unusual ports. Internet Service Providers can assist by providing their logs regarding your network connection(s). The company whose software was attacked may be able to answer questions about error messages and codes, and provide help regarding their experience. Comparing baselines between a known good and attacked computer can pinpoint changes, by comparing expected files, file sizes, and file hashes for important files, and/or the set of active processes and connections when powered up. A forensic expert team (usually a private agency, but possibly law enforcement) can help to determine the scope of the attack and set of probable victims.

CERT centers monitor incidents and are good sources of information for common and emergent threats. By working with these centers, your organization helps not only yourself but other organizations who encounter similar threats [5]. Agencies include for U.S.: www.cert.org and www.us-cert.gov, and for Europe: www.enisa.europa.eu/activities/cert.

Once it is clear what happened, it is possible to remove the root cause. This will include rebuilding affected systems, updating the systems with recent patches and antivirus software, and fortifying defenses with enhanced security controls. Employees who were or may have been impacted should change their passwords on all their accounts. Finally, the rebuilt systems should be retested using vulnerability analysis tools.

Table 11.3 shows an incident response procedure to handle malware detected by antivirus software. Some malware may simply install a backdoor, enabling the hacker to enter at will. Antivirus software may be smart enough to remove the backdoor. However, it certainly cannot predict what the attacker installed in the window of opportunity between the installation of the backdoor and the detection of malware by antivirus software. Therefore, it is important to understand the severity of the malware infection and who got infected—the administrator or a low-privileged user. It is also important to understand whether the computer held protected confidential data, to determine whether the breach law may apply: even if the disk was encrypted, the operating system probably decrypted the data for the virus.

11.2.5 Notification and Ex-Post Response Stages

If a data breach of privacy has occurred, victims will need to be notified in an 'expedient' way [13]. According to Breach Notification Laws, protected information (or PII) includes for most states: social security number, driver's license number, state identification card number, financial account number or credit or debit card number, or a financial number combined with any security/access code or password. Some states or HIPAA regulation also protect medical or health insurance information, genetic information, birth date/place, and some login/passwords. In addition, organizations adhering to FISMA must report incidents to US-CERT and keep data for three years [5]. It is required or recommended to report any breach to the state's Attorney General, who will issue a lawsuit against any organization who does not notify in a timely manner [11].

There are many financial issues related to breaches, beyond the state's Attorney General. The Federal Trade Commission (FTC) has brought civil suits against companies who do not provide sufficient privacy/security for their customers, resulting in an avoidable breach. This lawsuit generally argues that you advertised a privacy policy for your customers, which you did not follow up on [11]. In addition, class action lawsuits are emerging, to compensate customers and/or shareholders (e.g., for disclosures not fully reported). Finally, breach of contract civil suits may apply.

For a data breach, a contact database of probable victims must be created. Notification may be delayed by law enforcement if an investigation is in progress. Using a consultant with experience in data breaches may save companies money, as it did in 2013 [6]. Working with a legal advisor can ensure that the law is fully met in developing and sending the breach notification letters to victims and regulators. Adopting a good public relations plan can also help to minimize customer churn, a major cost after a data breach. This often requires specialized training for remediation and call centers [3].

Following the Notification stage, the Ex-Post Response stage is concerned with redress or reparation [6]. Activities may include: implementing a call center, reissuing new (e.g., financial) accounts, offering discounts, and paying for identity protection services and/or credit report monitoring [6]. Because of increased customer churn, organizations often take actions to repair their image and acquire new customers.

11.2.6 Recovery and Lessons Learned Stages

During the Recovery Stage, we restore operations to normal. The restored system should be fully tested before resuming operation.

Once all is returned to normal, it is smart to learn from mistakes as part of the Lessons Learned stage. This stage should occur for major incidents, and perhaps quarterly or at least annually for minor events. What worked or caused problems during the incident response? Should the organization invest in additional detection or forensic analysis tools or training? Procedures can be corrected and expanded as part of process improvement. Security personnel should prepare a full Incident Report, which should include lost hours and incident costs, including costs of loss and handling. The report should be reported to stakeholders.

Companies who have encountered data breaches consistently report implementing the following preventive controls (with perfect hindsight): implementing end-point security software, training for security awareness, expanding use of encryption, improving security documentation and controls, adding tools for data loss prevention, identity/access control and/or security intelligence, etc. [2]

11.3 Preparing for Incident Response

The most common reason for failure in incident response is lack of management support. Hopefully, with the easy method provided by this book, this will not be your problem. Let's assume your IRP is written and approved by management. Congrats! However, there are still some things to do to prepare for an incident, including training, testing, revising the IRP, and (periodically) audit. There should be introductory training at or before the first day of IRT/IMT membership. Other forms of training may include mentoring via a senior member, formal training, periodic training exercises and on-the-job training. Re-training is important when the IRP changes.

A *penetration test* is where a (friendly) ethical hacker is hired to attempt to penetrate a network through hacking, social engineering, and/or physical attacks. Such hackers are credentialed with the SANS GPEN, Offensive Security's OSCP, or Infosec's CEH certifications. They evaluate firewalls, servers, wireless and web technologies for common high-tech vulnerabilities; and use phishing, tailgating, social engineering phone calls (etc.) for low-tech vulnerabilities [14]—and then use street smarts the same way a criminal would to see what else might work. Finding vulnerabilities through an ethical hacker is a lot cheaper than through a criminal stealing confidential data (and paying subsequent costs to forensic experts). The main difference between an ethical hacker's 'pen' test and a criminal attack is written permission—and of course, consequences. Here are some different types of penetration tests [15]:

- *External Testing*: Penetration tester tests from outside network perimeter.
- *Internal Testing*: Tester tests from inside the network.
- *Blind Testing*: Penetration tester knows nothing in advance and must do web/news research on company.
- *Double Blind Testing*: System/security administrators are not aware of the penetration test, in addition to the penetration tester having no previous knowledge. This test is useful for determining how effecting internal security is at recognizing and handling attacks.
- *Targeted Testing*: Penetration tester has internal information about a target, and may have access to a user account.

A penetration test is a wonderful method of audit. PCI DSS requires a qualified tester to perform an external and internal penetration test annually, as well as an incident response test to determine how the organization would respond to a serious attack [9]. Other ways to audit incident response is to ensure that the IRP is complete, approved and updated annually, that IRT/IMT members are comfortable and knowledgeable about their roles and responsibilities, and that incident response testing has been recently performed.

For larger organizations, metrics help to evaluate incident response and the security organization's effectiveness. Recommended metrics include [4]:

- Number of reported incidents (via human or external reports)
- Number of detected incidents (via IT/security tools)
- Average time to respond to incident (attain Containment Stage)
- Average time to resolve an incident (attain Recovery Stage)
- Total number of incidents successfully resolved
- Proactive and preventative measures taken
- Total damage (costs) from reported or detected incidents
- Total damage if incidents had not been contained in a timely manner

11.4 Advanced: Computer Investigation and Forensics

If a case will ever succeed in court, any hacking or fraudulent crime must be properly handled according to law enforcement procedures. This section introduces the required precautions and court procedures. However, law enforcement or experienced forensic experts are necessary to ensure all details are correctly handled.

Authenticity of evidence is concerned with the true history of the investigation. Authenticity requires that the evidence is from the system under investigation, and the evidence was not altered [16]. Chain of Custody tracks who handled the evidence from minute to minute and ensures that the evidence was properly sealed and locked away with extremely limited access. A chain of custody document tracks the case number, the device's model and serial number (if available), when and where the evidence was held/stored, and the name, title, contact information and signature for each person who held or had access to the evidence at every time point and why they had access [5, 17]. It is useful to have a witness at each point (see Fig. 11.3.) Evidence is stored in evidence bags and sealed with evidence tape.

Forensic examiners travel with a jumpkit, which includes a laptop preconfigured with protocol sniffers and forensic software, and network taps and cables [5]. Often, the initial part of an investigation will be to get a full memory and disk image snapshot, which includes a record of network connections, open files, and in progress processes. Since the attacked computer may have a corrupted operating system, the jumpkit provides reliable tools to obtain valid data. After an investigator photographs an active screen and records memory contents, the computer may be powered down. Photos are taken of inside and outside of the computer, to document

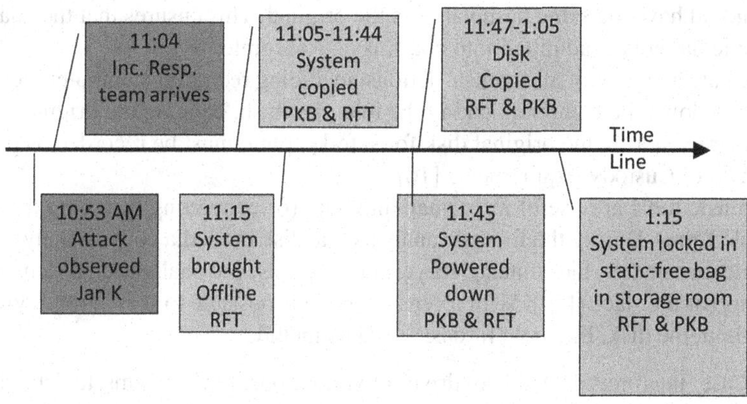

Fig. 11.3 Chain of custody timeline

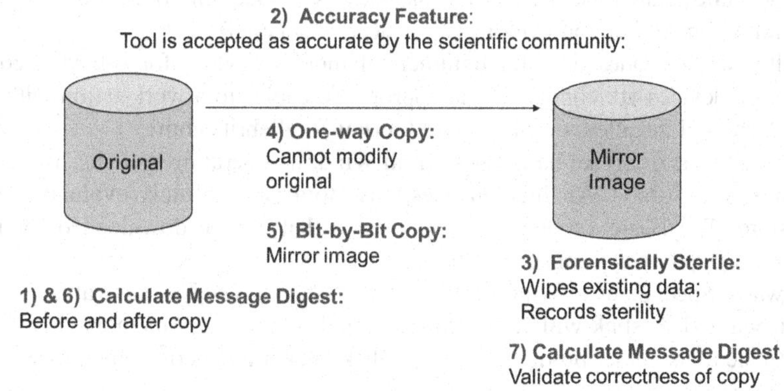

Fig. 11.4 Creation of an identical disk copy for forensic analysis

the full hardware configuration of the computer. The investigator must be careful to not taint the evidence. For example, if a cell phone is left on to retain evidence, it must be kept in a Faraday bag, which will shield the phone from connecting to other networks [19].

As part of a forensic investigation, it is important to analyze disk contents. In the computer forensic field, a disk admitted as evidence must be original and unmodified. Thus, the analysis must be done with a copy of the disk, and not the original. It is recommended that two copies of any evidence be made: the first is for analysis, and the second is admitted as evidence, along with the original [16]. Figure 11.4 shows how a copy is created. To ensure the original disk or media has not been modified, an integrity hash is calculated over the entire original disk or media. Replicas are created by copying bit-by-bit from the original, using an approved-for-court media copy tool. When an integrity hash is calculated over the replicas, they should have the same hash value as the original. This ensures that the analysis of the media replica, admitted into court, is also accurate.

The date and time of all forensic actions, including recording computer memory, powering down the computer, taking the integrity hash, copying the original disks, and securely storing the original disk for safe-keeping, must be recorded as part of the Chain of Custody requirements [16].

Forensic tools are useful in normalizing data (or converting disk data to easily readable form). During the forensic analysis, the disk or media copy is analyzed for logs, file timestamps, file contents, recycle bin contents, and unallocated disk memory contents (or file slack) [16]. With forensic tools it is possible to search for keywords throughout the disk. Example forensic toolkits include:

- EnCase: Interprets data of hard drives of various operating systems, tablets, smartphones and removable media for use in a court (www.guidancesoftware.com).
- Forensic Tool Kit (FTK): Supports Windows, Apple, UNIX/Linux operating systems including analysis of volatile (RAM memory and O.S. structures) and nonvolatile data for use in a court. Disk analysis includes interpretation of popular Windows and other applications (www.accessdata.com).
- Cellebrite: Decodes data for commercial mobile devices for use in a court. Mobile devices are connected via appropriate cables to a workstation with the forensic tool installed, or via a travel kit (www.cellebrite.com).
- ProDiscover: Analyzes hard disks for all Windows operating systems, as well as Linux and Solaris. An Incident Response tool can remotely evaluate a live system. The Basic version is a test version that can be downloaded for free (www.techpathways.com).
- X-ways: Specializes in Windows operating systems. X-ways can evaluate a system via a USB-stick without installation, and requires less memory than other forensic tools. Other products include a disk imager and permanent disk erasure (www.x-ways.net).
- Sleuthkit: This open-source tool evaluates Windows, Unix, Linux and OS-X operating systems. It is programmer-extendable. The Sleuth Kit (TSK) is a command-line took, while Autopsy provides a graphical interface (www.sleuthkit.org).

In some cases, an investigator will want to see how an application behaves. The investigator launches the application on a virtual machine, running identical versions of operating system and software packages. Virtual machines have an advantage that snapshot images can be taken while a process is occurring, allowing for a detailed examination of that process [18].

When the case is brought to court, the disk copy tool and forensic analysis tools must be standard and qualified for court. Also the investigator's qualifications, including education level and forensic training, will be subject to scrutiny [19]. Forensic Examiners should be certified, either through forensic software vendors (e.g., EnCase, FTK) or through independent organizations (with sample certs: Certified Computer Forensics Examiner or Certified Forensic Computer Examiner). Some states require a private detective license.

The Investigation Report will need to describe the details of the incident accurately. It will need to provide descriptive details of all evidence and forensic tools used in the investigation. All evidence must be easily referenced and provided in full detail, including interview information and communications. Actual data should be provided for forensic analysis results. The report should fully describe how any conclusions are reached in an unambiguous and understandable way. The report shall also include the investigator's contact information and dates of the investigation, and the report must be signed by the investigator [15, 4].

11.4.1 The Judicial Procedure

The Investigation If the investigation is initiated by law enforcement, which is investigating an organization or home, a search warrant is required unless the organization/home gives permission; the crime is communicated to a third party; the evidence is in plain site or is in danger of being destroyed; evidence is found during a normal arrest process; or if police are in hot pursuit [19]. Computer searches generally require a warrant except when a signed acceptable use policy authorizes permission. Also, if a computer is submitted for repairs, the repair person during their normal repair functions may notice illegal activities, such as child pornography [17]. In this case, they can report the computer to law enforcement.

The judicial proceedings begin for a civil case when a Complaint (or lawsuit) is filed, and for a criminal case when someone is arrested. For a civil case, the defendant must send an Answer within 20 days [19]. For an arrest in the United States, the Miranda rights must be read: "You have a right to remain silent…" In some states, a prosecutor then files an Information, detailing the criminal charges. Alternatively, a grand jury issues an indictment if they determine that the alleged charge should proceed.

Discovery During Discovery, the plaintiff, who initiated the lawsuit, and the defendant provide their list of witnesses and evidence to the other side. Each side may then request testimony, files and documents from the other to determine legal claims or defenses [18]. Such documents are called Responsive documents and can take the form of electronically stored information (ESI). The U.S. Federal Rules of Civil Procedure define how ESI should be requested and formatted. E-discovery (or ESI) requests can be general or specific, such as a specific document or a set of emails referencing a particular topic.

Depositions are interviews of the key parties, such as witnesses or consultants [20]. A deposition consists of a question-and-answer session, where all statements are recorded by a court reporter and possibly via video. The deponent, or person who answered questions during the deposition, may correct the transcript before it is entered into court record.

Evidence admissible to a court includes reports or testimony. Witnesses can be fact witnesses, expert consultants, or expert witnesses [18]. Fact witnesses report only on their participation related to the case, generally in obtaining and analyzing evidence. When providing testimony, they must present their qualifications. Email correspondence with lawyers is given attorney-client privilege and cannot be requested during discovery. However, notes, reports, and chain of custody documents are discoverable.

Expert consultants help lawyers in understanding technical details, but do not testify or give depositions.

Expert witnesses are the most qualified with extensive experience [18]. Computer forensic examiners often serve in this role. They provide expert opinions within reports and/or testimony at both depositions and trials. They do not need to have first-hand knowledge of the case, but can interpret evidence obtained by others. Expert witness testimony must be carefully given, because if an expert contradicts himself, the judge may order the jury to ignore the testimony. That expert's mistake can then be brought into question in future cases, and thus can ruin her reputation.

Declarations are written documents, where the declarer states publicly their findings and conclusions [20]. Their name, title, employer, qualifications, and often billing rate are all documented in the declaration. The case is identified and the declarer's role and position are clarified; the declarer signs the document. An affidavit is similar in outline to a declaration, but stronger since the affidavit is signed by a notary. Both declarations and affidavits are limited in breadth to support motions. An expert report can provide opinions, but should do so extremely carefully since every word may be challenged by expert witnesses on the other side [20]. All court reports become public documents unless they are specifically sealed. Any public document can be challenged in the current—as well as future—cases; thus, a witness must be very confident in anything they write in such a report. Providing full references to public documents helps to defend your position and bolster your claims.

Discovery usually ends 1–2 months before the trial, or upon agreement by both sides.

The Trial The four stages of a typical trial include opening arguments, the plaintiff's case, the defendant's case, and closing arguments. In the United States and the United Kingdom [21], case law is determined by regulation, but also by precedence: when regulation is not explicit and must be interpreted, then decisions in previous cases hold weight. To obtain a conviction in a criminal case in the U.S. and U.K., the burden of proof must be "beyond a reasonable doubt" that the defendant committed the crime [21]. In a civil case, the U.K. burden of proof is "the balance of probabilities" or "more sure than not".

11.5 Questions and Problems

1. *Vocabulary*. Match each meaning with the vocabulary.

Whitelist	Endpoint security suite	Event or log management
Triage	Vulnerability test	Incident response plan
Blind test	Incident mgmt team	Incident response team
Root cause	Penetration test	Chain of custody

a) A security tool for user computers, which features a firewall, antivirus and security configuration checking features.
b) A friendly ethical hacker is paid to find vulnerabilities.
c) A test to ensure that networked equipment can withstand common attacks.
d) A tool or process of analyzing computerized alarms or notifications.
e) A team of technical persons who will handle the incident, in combination with designated business management, public relations, legal and physical security persons.
f) A list of approved applications.
g) A penetration tester is given no insider knowledge or credentials before their attack.
h) The legal process of protecting evidence, by documenting all actions, working with a witness, and by not altering the evidence.
i) The stage of naming and categorizing the incident, prioritizing it, and assigning the handling of the incident to an appropriate handler.
j) The plan that guides IT and security about how to handle security incidents.
k) The vulnerability that enabled the attacker to enter the system.

2. *Workbook Solution for Specific Industry*. Consider an industry you currently work in or would like to work in. Assume the company is in your geographical region. You may use the Security Workbook Incident Response Chapter to complete the tables.

   a) Create one 'High-level Planning for Incident Detection and Handling' Table, similar to Table 11.2, listing five incident types.
   b) Create two 'Incident Handling Response Procedure' Table, similar to Table 11.3.
   c) If you refer to a Procedure in b), write a paragraph describing what steps should be taken, instead of writing a full procedure.

3. *Vulnerability Root Cause*. A forensic team is hired to analyze an expected infiltration. The team finds that an employee scanned computers on the local network until she found a Point of Sale device. She found that the password to the PoS was the default password and installed spyware to record credit card numbers. The result was a sudden increase in traffic sent over the Internet. The slowdown caused management to become suspicious. They called in an IT specialist to investigate. The IT specialist saw unrecognizable packets coming from the PoS, and recommended the forensic team.

   a) What is the root cause(s) of the vulnerability?
   b) What mitigation strategies shall be used to fix the vulnerabilities?

4. *Forensic Tool Evaluation*. Select a forensic tool to evaluate. What capabilities does this forensic tool have? What devices or operating systems does it analyze? How much does it cost? Can it be used legally? Write a description of this tool.
5. *Investigate CERT web sites*. What information is available at a CERT website? Look at the links and documents that are available at the site and write a description

of what information is provided, including how you think the information could be used. Here are some sample sites:

a) U.S.: www.cert.org and www.us-cert.gov
b) Europe: www.enisa.europa.eu/activities/cert
c) International: www.sans.org

6. *Recent Incident Reports*. This textbook refers to security reports from the year the book was written. Some statistics have certainly changed by the time you read this. What are some of the most recent statistics, according to Pomenom, Verizon, NIST, or Symantec reports? Search for a recent Breach Report or Security Report and document 15 statistics from that report.
7. *Recent Regulation*: Look up recent news reports on laws from any nation at: www.huntonprivacyblog.com. Your instructor may provide additional resources. What recent legal issues did you find?

11.5.1 Health First Case Study Problems

For each case study problem, refer to the Health First Case Study. The Health First Case Study and Security Workbook should be provided by your instructor or can be found at http://extras.springer.com.

Case study	Health first case study	Other resources
Planning for incident response	√	Security workbook

References

1. Johnston R (2011) Security maxims. http://www.ne.anl.gov/capabilities/vat. Accessed 20 March 2011
2. 2014 cost of data breach study: United States. May 2014. Ponemon Institute LLC, Traverse City, Michigan
3. Verizon (2013) Verizon 2013 data breach investigations report. http://www.verizonenterprise.com/DBIR/2013. Accessed 20 Oct 2013
4. ISACA (2011) CISM® review manual 2012. ISACA, Arlington Heights, IL, pp 221–227
5. Cichonski P, Millar T, Grance T, Skarfone K (2012) NIST special publication 800-61 Rev 2 computer security incident handling guide. National Institute of Standards and Technology, Gaithersburg MD, August 2012
6. Ponemon (2013) Cost of data breach study: United States. May 2013. Pomenon Institute LLC, Traverse City, Michigan, pp 1–22
7. Murdoch D (2014) Blue team handbook: incident response edition, v. 2.0. www.vmit.com
8. SANS (2013) Critical controls for effective cyber defense, version 4.1, March, 2013. www.sans.org
9. Payment Card Industry (2013) Requirements and security assessment procedures, ver. 3.0, November 2013. www.pcisecuritystandards.org
10. Gibson D (2011) Managing risk in information systems. Jones & Bartlett Learning, Burlington, MA, pp 392–418

11. Thompson L (2013) Privacy: the tidal waves of the future. In: ISACA chapter meeting, Rosemont IL, 13 December 2013
12. Brelsford E (2013) 2014: a cyber odyssey. In: ISACA Chicago chapter meeting, Rosemont IL, 13 December 2013
13. National Conference of State Legislatures (2014) Security breach notification laws. http://www.ncsl.org/research/telecommunications-and-information-technology/security-breach-notification-laws.aspx. Accessed 20 Aug 2014
14. Walker M (2012) All-in-one CEH™ certified ethical hacker exam guide. McGraw-Hill Co., New York, NY
15. ISACA (2010) CISA review manual 2011. ISACA, Arlington Heights, IL, pp 379–381
16. Ali KM (2012) Digital forensics: best practices and managerial implications. In: 2012 fourth international conf. on computational intelligence, communication systems and networks, IEEE Computer Society, http://ieeexplore.ieee.org, pp 196–199
17. Brown CLT (2006) Computer evidence: collection & preservation. Charles River Media, Newton Centre, MA, pp 16–17, 28
18. Cowen D (2013) Computer forensics: InfoSec pro guide. McGraw-Hill Co., New York, NY, pp 257–282
19. Grama JL (2015) Legal issues in information security, 2nd edn. Jones & Bartlett Learning, Burlington MA, pp 461–488
20. Philipp A, Cowen D, Davis C (2010) Hacking exposed™ computer forensics, 2nd edn. McGraw-Hill Co., New York, NY, pp 341–368
21. Giles S (2012) Managing fraud risk: a practical guide for directors and managers. Wiley, Chichester, West Sussex, England, pp 255–293

Part IV
Measure, Test and Audit

The four stages in risk management include identify/assess risk, design risk/security plan, implement plan and monitor performance. The previous parts guided the planning and design of the security system. This part focuses on the planning of the fourth stage, measuring security effectiveness: do the controls work? How well do they work?

When a security control is implemented, it must be tested for effectiveness. Executing a test plan can ensure that the control functions as planned: for example, a firewall blocks illegal packets. The security system should then be monitored: e.g., how many illegal packets are traversing our internal network? This monitoring over time results in statistics or metrics that are periodically reviewed, and drive new risk analysis evaluations when security is not performing as desired. Finally, external auditors can verify that the security system is designed and managed properly. This part is about designing the review cycle: metrics and audit. Since testing can use the audit plan outline, the section on audit is useful for designing a proper security test plan.

Chapter 12
Defining Security Metrics

> I walked with him [head of security] outside the store entrance, rooted around in the trash receptacle there, and fished out a receipt. Customers are constantly throwing away their receipts as soon as they leave a store. I examined the receipt and noticed it included a toaster oven. So I went with the security head to the small appliance area and picked out the same model toaster oven. I told the security director, 'Now all I have to do is go to customer service, tell them I just bought this and need to return it, and I've just conned the store'. (Frank W. Abagnale, *The Art of the Steal*, p. 73 [1].)

When an organization establishes a set of metrics, the organization can get a realistic baseline, or view, of how it performs at a point in time. Future metrics then determine whether performance improves with new controls. Thus, metrics are a way for security organizations to regularly monitor how well security controls, the security organization, and the organization as a whole are performing relative to security goals.

There are two popular approaches to metrics: business-driven and technology-driven. The business-driven approach believes that the business has particular risks, as addressed by risk management, and the focus of attention should be concerned with how well the organization is performing relative to these risks [2]. Thus, metrics inform management (and independent auditors) of the effectiveness of the security program. Business-driven metrics have the advantage that they are tailored to the particular circumstances of the organization, and can be designed to measure adherence to control objectives. One thought worth considering is that monitoring achievement of control objective is more important than perfecting security procedures. Following this idea, measuring informs us when we have sufficient or inadequate security, and where improvements must be made.

A technology-driven approach to metrics uses CERT-based forensic data to help understand the current level and types of security threats. The basic idea is: what criminal attacks are emerging that we are prone to? A tech-driven approach would argue that many incidents go undetected for months and are caught by outside organizations—thus, building sufficient security is necessary before assuming any metrics may actually even be valid. The tech-driven approach to metrics can be a checklist of best-practices goals to attain.

S. Lincke, *Security Planning*, DOI 10.1007/978-3-319-16027-6_12

Both ideas are highly relevant and compatible. In fact, CERT data should be used to update risk analysis and drive metrics. Both metric types are discussed in two different sections of this chapter. While metrics are not absolutely necessary for the average small organization, any organization that is subject to regulation (e.g., HIPAA, SOX, FISMA) should take this section very seriously. In fact, most organizations would benefit from a few carefully selected metrics, particularly after a minimum baseline of security is implemented. However, it is good to remember Colsch's (Keep It Simple) Maxim: "Security won't work if there are too many different security measures to manage, and/or they are too complicated or hard to use" [3].

12.1 Considering Business-Driven Metrics

Metrics are part of the Monitoring and Compliance function, and help to indicate whether controls and compliance are effective or not. A programmer or system administrator can help to automate the collection of computer-generated metrics. *Key Risk Indicators* (*KRI*) are metrics that are highly relevant to high priority risks and are capable of indicating a probability or trend of the actual status of risks [4]. KRIs provide organizations a more accurate guide for the future, enabling them to meet strategic goals. KRIs also enable an evaluation of past performance, allowing organizations to learn about their actual risk appetite.

Business management is not interested in the number of attacks handled by each firewall every week—nor are technical people interested in security cost metrics. Therefore, security metrics can be categorized into three levels, depending on the intended audience [2]. Strategic metrics are of interest to executive management, who are interested in risk (ALE), budget, and policy (e.g., regulatory compliance), as well as major results such as disaster recovery test results. Tactical metrics determine the effectiveness of the security program, and include rates of policy compliance/non-compliance, incident management effectiveness, and risk changes resulting from system changes. Operational metrics tend to be technical and of interest to the security staff, and include firewall, IDS, or system log analysis, vulnerability test results, and patch management status.

The reporting interval for metrics varies for each metric category. Strategic metrics may be discussed annually or semiannually. Tactical metrics show trends and may be discussed every 6 months or so. Operational metrics are discussed weekly or monthly, and are preferably automated.

Business-oriented metrics consider the needs of the business first. This three-step process helps consider the most important threats, how to measure those threats, and how to report on them:

Step 1: What are the most important security areas to monitor in your organization? What threats and legislation are you most concerned with? Review your risk section and policies to help define the most important areas to monitor.

Step 2: After listing your most important threats, consider which metrics make the most sense to collect. Since automated metrics are doable in a busy world, is there an easy way to collect these metrics?

Step 3: Consider the three perspectives of strategic, tactical and operational metrics, relative to the three audiences.

Major risks in a university environment include a lunatic gunman, FERPA violation (data breach), a cracking attempt and web failure. Metrics developed from these risks are shown in Table 12.1. Starting with a small number of metrics is useful until metrics generation can be automated.

Table 12.2 shows sample metrics for various categories of a security program [2, 5]. This list of potentially useful metrics includes cost, program, and risk-oriented metrics, and is mainly taken from the CISM® Review Manual [2].

Table 12.1 Selected metrics for Einstein University

Category	Metric	Calculation and collection method	Period of reporting
Strategic	Cost of security/terminal	Information Tech. Group	1 year
	Cost of incidents	Incident Response totals	6 months
Tactical	% employees passing FERPA quiz	Annual email requesting testing	1 year
	% employees completing FERPA training	Two annual trainings with sign-in. Performance review	1 year
	# Hours Web unavailable	Incident Response database	6 months
Operational	# illegal packets in confidential zone	Log management database	1 month
	# malware infections	Incident Response database	1 month

Table 12.2 Example metrics

Risk: The aggregate ALE % of risk eliminated, mitigated, transferred # of open risks due to inaction	Cost effectiveness: Cost of workstation security per user Cost of email spam and virus protection per mailbox
Operational performance: Time to detect and contain incidents Quantity and severity of incidents % of systems audited in last quarter	Organizational awareness: % of employees passing quiz, after training vs. 3 months later % of employees completing training
Technical security architecture: # of malware identified and neutralized Types of compromises, by severity and attack type Attack attempts repelled by control devices Volume of messages, KB processed by communications control devices	Security process monitoring: Last date and type of BCP, DRP, IRP testing Last date asset inventories were reviewed and updated Frequency of executive management review activities compared to planned
Security Management Framework: Completeness and clarity of security documentation Inclusion of security in each project plan Rate of issue recurrence	Compliance: Rate of compliance with regulation or policy Rate of automation of compliance tests Frequency of compliance testing
Secure software development: Rate of projects passing compliance audits Percent of development staff certified in security Rate of teams reporting code reviews on high-risk code in past 6 months	

12.2 Implementing Technology-Driven Metrics

Technology-driven metrics are defensive techniques to counter known attacks. Technology-driven metrics are derived by security experts and tend to be tactical or operational in nature.

One highly respected set of controls with metrics is provided by SANS [6]. The document is called: "Critical Controls for Effective Cyber Defense" [7]. This set of 20 controls was developed to defend against criminal organization attacks and nation-state spying. One goal is to automate daily or weekly checks and metrics. The summary below outlines *minimum* requirements.

1. Inventory of Authorized and Unauthorized Devices: Ensure all devices that are on your network are known, configured properly, and recently patched. Everything with an IP address is inventoried and controlled.
   - Tool: Automate network scanning for daily execution and/or use DHCP reports and passive monitoring. Compare results between daily and known good configurations.
   - Metric: Temporarily place an unauthorized device on the network. It is found within 24 h, isolated within 1 h confirmed by alert or email, and reported every 24 h thereafter by email/alert until the device is removed.
2. Inventory of Authorized and Unauthorized Software: Ensure all software is approved and recently patched.
   - Tool: Use whitelisting tools, where a whitelist defines the permitted list of software. Endpoint Security Suites (ESS) often contain antivirus, antispyware, firewall, IDS/IPS, and software white- and blacklisting. A blacklist defines software that is not allowed on specific systems (e.g., IT tools). ESS tools generate alerts if unapproved software is installed.
   - Metric: Temporarily attempt to install unauthorized software on a device. It is found within 24 h, disabled/quarantined within 1 h confirmed by alert or email, and reported thereafter every 24 h by alert/email until the software is removed.
3. Secure Configurations for Hardware and Software: All devices are hardened using recommended security configurations (beyond the scope of this text). A list of insecure software is not permitted, including Telnet, VNC, and RDP. New software is quarantined and monitored. Any imaged software is maintained in an updated state.
   - Tools: Build secure images, and use configuration checking tools daily.
   - Metric: Temporarily attempt to change a set of random configurations. Changes are reported within 24 h, disabled/quarantined within 1 h confirmed by alert or email, and reported every 24 h by alert/email thereafter until the configuration is corrected.

4. Continuous Vulnerability Assessment and Remediation: Run vulnerability scans on all systems at least weekly, and preferably daily. Problem fixes are verified through additional scans.
   - Tools: Vulnerability scanning tools, which are updated: wireless, server, endpoint, etc.
   - Metric: Vulnerability notification(s) are emailed within 1 h of completion of a vulnerability scan. If the scan does not complete in 24 h, an email notification occurs. Automated patch management tools notify via email when all systems have been patched.
5. Malware Defenses: Antivirus/antispyware is always updated and run against all data, including shared files, server data, and mobile data. Additional controls including blocking social media, limiting external devices (e.g., USB), using web proxy gateways, and network monitoring.
   - Tools: Antivirus/antispyware or endpoint security suites, which have the additional capability of reporting that the tool is updated and activated on all systems.
   - Metric: If benign malware (e.g., security/hacking tool) install is attempted, antivirus either prevents installation or execution or quarantines software, and then sends an alert or email report within 1 h of installation. The alert/email provides notification of specific device and owner. The antivirus software prevents the security team from executing the software.
6. Application Software Security: New application software is tested for security vulnerabilities, including web vulnerabilities: buffer overflow, SQL injection, cross-site scripting, cross-site request forgery, clickjacking of code, and performance during DDOS attacks. Software validates input for size and type checks and does not report system error messages directly. Automated testing also includes static code analyzers and automated web scanning tools. Configuration requirements include application firewalls and hardened databases.
   - Tools: Static code analyzers, automated web scanning tools and automated database configuration review tools; security training for programmers.
   - Metric: An attack on the software generates a log or email within 24 h (or less). Automated web scanning occurs weekly or daily; scan reports are sent within 24 h, or an email indicating a delay occurred is sent daily until the scan completes. When errors are found, they are fixed within 15 days.
7. Wireless Device Control: Wireless access points are securely configured with WPA2 protocol supporting the AES encryption algorithm. Extensible Authentication Protocol-Transport Layer Security (EAP/TLS) provides mutual authentication. Only approved devices are able to connect, which have been registered and follow security standards. Wireless networks are configured for the minimum required radio footprint. Rogue networks are quickly found and removed: a most serious attack occurs when a wireless network is installed in a confidential zone, behind the firewall.

- Tools: Wireless intrusion detection systems detect available wireless access points and deactivate rogue access points. Vulnerability scanners can detect unauthorized wireless access points connected to the Internet.
- Metric: The system can detect a rogue access point or unauthorized device within 1 h, isolate the device with alert or email notification within 1 h, and report on the status every 24 h until the device is removed.

8. Data Recovery Capability: Backups are maintained at least weekly and more often for critical data. Backups are encrypted and securely stored. Multiple staff can perform backup/recovery.

   - Test/Metric: Test backups quarterly for a random sample of systems. This includes operating system, software, and data restoration.

9. Security Skills Assessment and Appropriate Training to Fill Gaps: Security awareness training is required for end users and more so for system owners. Security training is necessary for programmers, system, security and network administrators.

   - Test/Metric: Test security awareness understanding; attempt periodic social engineering tests using phishing emails and phone calls. If employee fails the test, they must attend a class.

10. Secure Configurations for Network Devices such as Firewalls, Routers, and Switches: A configuration database tracks approved configurations in configuration management for network devices. Two-factor identification is used for network devices.

    - Tools: Tools can perform rule set sanity checking for network filter devices, which use Access Control Lists.
    - Metric: Any change to the configuration of a network device is recognized within 24 h, with a log or email alert, and every 24 h thereafter until it is investigated. Changes to either software or configuration are reported.

11. Limitation and Control of Network Ports, Protocols, and Services: The default configuration is to deny packets not specifically allowed. Since configurations tend to loosen over time, allowed services are periodically reviewed for possible restriction.

    - Tool: Automate port scanning for daily execution. Monitor for open services and versions of those services. Compare results between daily and known good configurations.
    - Metric: Temporarily place a secure test service randomly on the network, which will respond to network requests. It is reported via alert or email within 24 h, and re-reported every 24 h by alert/email thereafter until the port is deactivated or approved.

12. Controlled Use of Administrative Privileges: Few people have elevated privileges and these privileged accounts are only used for necessary services. Passwords are complex, changed periodically, never shared, and two-factor authentication

is used. Password files are encrypted and restricted. Different passwords are used for different customers and for elevated privileges.

- Tools: Operating system tools can display running processes; these can be monitored for elevated privileges.
- Metric: When a super-user/admin account is created, an alert or email is generated within 24 h, and every 24 h thereafter until it is approved.

13. Boundary Defense: Establish zones protected by firewall/routers. Filter both incoming and outgoing traffic. Blacklist (or restrict) known bad network (IP) addresses or whitelist (only permit) authorized network addresses.
    - Tools: Sniffers monitoring for a 3-h period once a week may detect unusual packets. Vulnerability scanners and packet-creating tools can trigger an alert by networking equipment.
    - Metric: Unauthorized packets generate an alert or email within 24 h, and the alert is reissued every 24 h until the problem is cleared.
14. Maintenance, Monitoring, and Analysis of Security Audit Logs: Server logs are write-only and archived for months. Anomaly logs are reviewed biweekly. Firewalls log all allowed and blocked traffic. Unauthorized access attempts are logged.
    - Tools: Logs are verbose and sufficient space is allocated for them. SIEM tools help in analyzing alerts.
    - Metric: Logs record date, timestamp, source address, destination address, and details. If a device is unable to write logs (e.g., space filled, server crash), an event or email is generated with 24 h or preferably less time.
15. Controlled Access Based on the Need to Know: Data classification schemes, restrictive firewall configurations, and logging for access to confidential data help to prevent exfiltration of data to potential competitors.
    - Tools: Fine-tuned authentication, access control, and zoning.
    - Metric: Unauthorized accesses generate an alert with 24 h or preferably less time.
16. Account Monitoring and Control: Terminated accounts are removed in a timely manner, via account expiration dates, or as a result of logs of expired password accounts, disabled accounts, or locked-out accounts. Access to deactivated accounts is monitored. For active accounts, failed logins result in lockouts; inactivity results in logged off or locked sessions; and access during unusual hours results in an alert. Data exfiltration is caught by recognition of transmission of keywords.
    - Tools: Operating system tools to generate alerts for the above conditions should be enabled.
    - Metric: A list of valid user accounts is collected every 24 h and automatically analyzed within 1 h for deviations: new or changed status. An alert or email is generated for unusual changes.

17. Data Loss Prevention: Prevent exfiltration: proprietary or confidential information from being transferred outside an internal network. Encryption of mobile and USB devices; disabling of USB.
    - Tools: Tools monitor for transmission of keywords which are part of proprietary data. Data Loss Prevention (DLP) tools can monitor for sensitive data transmissions. Blocked attempts are investigated.
    - Metric: Transmission or copying of a file triggers an alert or email within 1 h, and every 24 h thereafter until the risk is addressed. The alert indicates the affected system and location.
18. Incident Response and Management: An Incident Response Plan defines which roles should perform what under various conditions. The IRP includes contact information for third party contractors.
19. Secure Network Engineering: Separate zones include DMZ, middleware, and private network. Access to the DMZ is through a proxy firewall. Domain Name Servers (DNS) translate IP names into IP addresses at the location where they are needed: DMZ DNS is in the DMZ; internal DNS is in the internal zone, etc. An emergency configuration for restricted network filtering is ready for quick deployment.
20. Penetration Tests and Red Team Exercises: Penetration tests proceed beyond vulnerability testing, like an attacker would. Red Team exercises test incident response team reactions.
    - Tools: Rules of engagement specify the testing times, duration, and overall test approach.

Further details on these 20 recommended controls can be found at www.sans.org. The measures listed tend to be pass–fail tests, but can be quantified by measuring precise durations for vulnerability detection and handling. Since the above list describes the longest tolerable timeframes for discovering and handling vulnerabilities, it is expected that advanced organizations shorten timeframes from 24 h preferably to an optimum of 2 min. Also, some controls do not specify measures, such as for incident response. The Verizon CERT report recommends measuring the 'number of compromised systems' and 'mean time to detection' [8].

If fraud is a factor in your organization, fraud-related statistics include [9]:

- False alarm rate or false positive rate: percent of legitimate transactions that are incorrectly interpreted as fraudulent.
- False negative rate: percent of fraudulent transactions that are incorrectly interpreted as legitimate.
- Fraud catching rate or true positive rate: percent of fraudulent transactions that are correctly recognized as fraudulent.

12.3 Questions and Problems

1. *Business-Driven Metrics for Specific Industry.* Consider an industry you currently work in or would like to work in. Assume the company is in your geographical region. You may use the Security Workbook Metrics Chapter to complete the three questions and one table. For each table, include two or more metrics for each of the strategic, tactical and operational levels.
   a) Step 1 Question: What are the most important security areas to monitor in this organization? What threats and regulation are the greatest concern? Review risk results and policies to help define the most important areas to monitor.
   b) Step 2 Question: After listing the most important threats, consider which metrics make the most sense to collect. Since automated metrics are doable in a busy world, is there an easy way to collect these metrics?
   c) Step 3 Question: Consider the three perspectives of strategic, tactical and operational metrics, relative to the three audiences.
   d) Create a 'Metrics' Table, similar to Table 12.1.
2. *Tech-Driven Metric Alerts.* Review the technology-driven metrics requirements for alerts or emails to be generated. Prepare a list of the required alerts/emails to be fully compliant with the top-20 SANS controls.
3. *Regulation relating to Metrics.* Consider one of the following security regulations or standards: HIPAA, Gramm–Leach–Bliley, Sarbanes–Oxley, PCI DSS, or FISMA. What metrics may help in monitoring for compliance? Develop five metrics that will help test for regulatory compliance. Websites that provide government- or standards-based information as authentic sources of information include:
   a) HIPAA/HITECH: Chap. 15 of this text or www.hhs.gov (Health and Human Services) and search for HIPAA.
   b) Gramm–Leach–Bliley and Red Flags Rule: Federal Trade Commission: http://www.business.ftc.gov/privacy-and-security
   c) Sarbanes–Oxley: www.isaca.org (Organizations for standards/security) Your instructor may provide '*Information Security Student Book: Using COBIT®5 for Information Security*', available at www.isaca.org. Additional information is at www.sans.org, search for 'COBIT'.
   d) PCI DSS: Access information from https://www.pcisecuritystandards.org/security_standards/. Select the PCI DSS link. Register and download 'PCI DSS v3.0'. Skim the Requirements, starting on page 19.
   e) FISMA: www.nist.gov (National Institute for Standards and Technology) and search for FISMA. Specific link: http://www.nist.gov/itl/csd/soi/fisma.cfm. Access FIPS Publication 200 first.

12.3.1 Health First Case Study Problems

For each case study problem, refer to the Health First Case Study. The Health First Case Study and Security Workbook should be provided by your instructor or can be found at http://extras.springer.com.

Case study	Health first case study	Other resources
Defining security metrics	√	Security workbook
Defining security metrics Optional: designing metrics for the requirements doc	√	Health first requirements doc

References

1. Abagnale FW (2001) The art of the steal. Broadway Books, Broadway, NY, p 73
2. ISACA (2011) CISM® review manual 2012. ISACA, Arlington Heights, IL, pp 191–194
3. Johnston R (2011) Security maxims. http://www.ne.anl.gov/capabilities/vat. Accessed 20 Mar 2011
4. ISACA (2012) CRISC™ review manual 2013. ISACA, Arlington Heights, IL, pp 100–101
5. Open Web Application Security Project (OWASP) (2014) Software assurance maturity model, ver 1.0. http://www.opensamm.org/downloads/SAMM-1.0.pdf. Accessed 15 Nov 2014
6. McMillan A (2013) Funding your programs through smart risk and security management. In: SC congress Chicago, 20 November 2013
7. SANS (2013) Critical controls for effective cyber defense, ver 4.1. March 2013. www.sans.org
8. Verizon (2013) Verizon 2013 data breach investigations report. http://www.verizonenterprise.com/DBIR/2013. Accessed 20 Oct 2013
9. Kou Y, Lu C-T, Sirwonwattana, S, Huang, Y-P (2004) Survey of fraud detection techniques. In: IEEE international conference on networking, sensing & control. Inst. Electrical & Electronics Eng. (IEEE), http://ieeexplore.ieee.org, pp 749–753

Chapter 13
Performing an Audit or Security Test

> My crime is that of outsmarting you, something that you will never forgive me for.—Mentor (hacker) [1]

Compliance means that the organization and its actors adhere to applicable regulation and organizational policy and standards. Auditors are professional evaluators who test for compliance and/or that certain objectives are met. Therefore, understanding audit techniques professionalize testing, whether it is done for test or audit purposes. The Certified Information Systems Auditor (CISA) definition of audit is [2 p. 51]:

> Systematic process by which a qualified, competent, independent team or person objectively obtains and evaluates evidence regarding assertions about a process for the purpose of forming an opinion about and reporting on the degree to which the assertion is implemented.

Each of these words was carefully selected. The *qualified, competent, independent team or person* means that the auditor is competent and knowledgeable in the specific audit task that is being evaluated. Professional independence means the auditor is independent in "fact and appearance" as regarded by any typical third party [3]. This tends to mean that every auditor is not related, has no financial ties, is not close friends with, and does not date, flirt, party or normally associate with the individuals being audited. Organizational independence means that the auditor and auditing company does not have any special financial ties to the organization being audited. *Objectively obtains and evaluates evidence* means that the auditor must obtain and analyze objective, reliable, qualified and proven facts. Sources of evidence should include internal documentation, external letters, contracts, interview notes from qualified persons, electronic data, and test results. *Assertions about a process* implies that the auditor cannot certify that no transaction is fraudulent, but is analyzing the process to ensure that precautions have been taken to minimize fraud and implement sufficient controls. *Assertions* are the claims that management is making about the integrity of its process [3]. *Forming an opinion about and reporting on* is about the final result: an assessment report, which depends upon expertise and facts to express a realistic, accurate view as to the validity of the process.

S. Lincke, *Security Planning*, DOI 10.1007/978-3-319-16027-6_13

Auditing/testing can be classified by levels: internal testing, internal audit and external audit. Internal testing occurs when a security group or quality control tests their own security controls. Internal audit occurs when an organization has an audit group, separate from IT/security, which performs in-house auditing of the IT/security and business departments. This internal process prepares an organization for an external audit.

The main purposes of audit are to measure conformance to policy, standards and regulation, and to evaluate organizational risk [4]. External audits are required by FISMA and Sarbanes–Oxley for corporations, and are recommended for nonprofits. PCI DSS requires limited auditing, as described later. During an external audit for SOX, an independent audit organization formally reviews the internal controls and the integrity of an organization's financial statements in order to report the organization's efficacy to external stakeholders (e.g., shareholders of a corporation) [5].

This chapter includes two major sections: the first section is on internal testing or informal audit and the second on external or professional audit. Much of professional auditing is useful knowledge, even for internal testing and auditing. Therefore, the section on professional audits builds on the first section on internal testing/audit, which incorporates simpler audit ideas.

13.1 Testing Internally and Simple Audits

In the perfect world, an organization would fully test all systems, thoroughly, in an automated fashion. However, this is rarely possible. Therefore, shortcuts that make best use of the auditor's test time include scheduling, random sampling, priority [2] and automation. Scheduling is useful to evaluate different components of the organization in different quarters or years; all important sectors or systems get tested eventually, but just not this year. Since it is not possible to test all components, auditors test a random sample incorporating all or most types of components (e.g., transactions, devices, stores). Random sampling is useful, but some components may be more important to test than others based on increased risk. Therefore, risk raises the priority of certain tests, so that they are scheduled sooner and more often. Alternatively, critical components may be randomly tested at a higher rate than other components. Automation enables testing to occur frequently, such as daily or weekly, to safeguard integrity. Random sampling will be discussed in the professional audit section.

Scheduling and priority should be considered for all test and audit planning. Factors for short-term planning (i.e., this year) include [2]:

- Risk: Some aspects of business are more susceptible to risk or have recently changed;
- Regulation: Conformance to regulation is high priority, particularly if regulatory requirements have recently changed;
- Tools: new or reconfigured evaluation tools demand testing.

Table 13.1 Audit plan schedule

Audit area	Time-frame	Date of last test	Responsibility
Policies & Procedures for Registration, Advising	1Q	Never	Internal Auditor
PCI DSS audit	2Q	2014	CIO, Security Consultant
FERPA: Personnel interviews	3Q	Never	Internal Auditor
IT: Penetration Test	4Q	2012	CIO, Security consultant

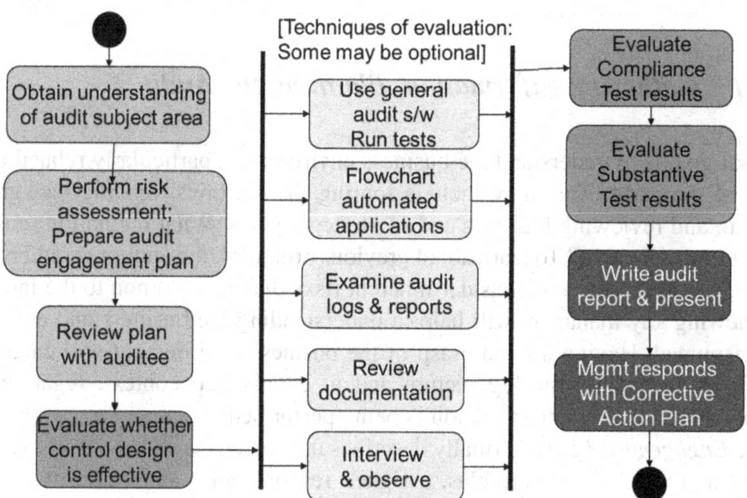

Fig. 13.1 Activity diagram of the audit engagement process

The tests that cannot be accomplished this year can be scheduled for future years, as part of a long-term plan. Table 13.1 shows a short-term audit plan for Einstein University. Timeframes are given in quarters (Q). The date of last test helps to determine the priority. The Responsibility column allocates accountability for the test, and indicates where external consultants will be used. This audit plan should be updated and discussed with upper management annually [6].

An Audit Engagement is a specific audit task, such as one row in the Audit Plan [7]. The steps of a risk-based audit include [2, 8]:

1. *Gather Information, Plan Audit*: Learn about the organization, assess risk, and prepare the audit plan.
2. *Review the Design of Internal Controls*: Determine on paper whether the design of controls is effective to achieve management assertions or policy claims.
3. *Perform Compliance and Substantive Tests*: Validate that the controls are effective and business transactions are processed properly.
4. *Prepare and Present Report*: Write an audit report and present it to agreed-upon parties.

These four steps are covered in the next four subsections. However, a more detailed diagram of functions is shown in Fig. 13.1, which is an Activity Diagram (or flow chart) of the audit engagement process. To read the diagram, start at the top left bullet and follow arrows. The left column represents the first two steps in the four-step audit process. The two thick vertical lines indicate that the lighter-colored middle processes occur in parallel and complete (usually) before the right column begins. The two dark processes on the bottom right are part of the fourth step: Prepare and Present Report.

13.1.1 Gathering Information, Planning the Audit

The first goal is to understand the business environment, particularly related to the scope of the audit. This may include touring the facilities, reading background material, and reviewing business and IT strategic plans. What regulation must the organization adhere to? To learn about previous problems, the auditor should review previous audit reports and consider inherent risks that are common to the industry. Interviewing key managers will help in understanding the business and areas that are outsourced. Having a good grasp of the business environment will enable the auditor to understand the big picture and fit details into context, regardless of whether an internal or external audit is being performed.

The *Engagement Letter* normally describes the objectives and scope of the audit, as well as the set of deliverables, assigned responsibility and authority, budget, timeline, and who the audit report will go to [3]. The *Audit Subject* is the area to be audited, e.g., "Information Systems related to Sales". The *Audit Objective* is the purpose of the audit, such as: "Determine whether Sales database is secure against data breaches, due to inappropriate authentication, access control, or hacking" or "Confirm adherence to regulation X". The *Audit Scope* constrains the audit to a specific system, function, unit, or period of time, such as: "The scope is constrained to headquarters for the last year". This document focuses the audit, and defines the beginning part of the Audit Engagement Plan.

The risk-based auditing approach considers what risks might result in a business disturbance, such as a financial loss, a regulatory infraction, business interruption, and/or loss of public trust. As a result of this risk analysis, the auditor can set priorities to focus the audit and determine how problems might be categorized into different significance levels (e.g., Material Weakness versus a Deficiency) [7].

Risk-based auditing considers the *overall audit risk*, which considers that the audit may not find significant deficiencies that do exist [6]. Audit risk includes the inherent risks, control risks and detection risks for a company [2]. *Inherent Risk* addresses problems that certain companies, industries or components tend to be prone to. For example, a bank's inherent risk is a robber, and a school's inherent risk is student hacking and open systems. *Control Risks* are vulnerabilities that internal controls fail to safeguard against. An example of a control risk would be an IPS that does not catch a proprietary file exfiltration. A *Detection Risk* could occur when an auditor does not detect a problem that does exist. For example, insufficient segregation of duties results in fraud, but is not caught by an auditor. Risk is considered relative to the business, technological factors, national environment, contractual issues, and project [3].

Once risks are considered, the audit engagement plan (or test plan) can be developed [3]. At a minimum the audit objective, audit scope and audit approach should be defined. The *Constraints* section may list limitations imposed to safeguard the auditor or auditee, such as requirements to execute high-volume tests during low-volume times, specify auditor requirements for assistance, or notify the security department before using hacking tools. The *Compliance and Criteria* section describes the regulation, external standards/guidelines (e.g., industry best practice, security standards, audit frameworks) and/or organizational policy that will be used as a standard to benchmark the audit against. The *Risk Analysis* section summarizes the evaluated risk, including where the 'gold' lies in the area under test and the high-risk activities within this network. The *Audit Approach* lists the high-level methodology or summary strategy of the testing that will occur.

An optional *Checklist* provides a detailed list of tests or actions to be taken. The checklist is useful as part of a test plan or internal audit, to carefully plan the detailed audit and to get specific permission for all planned security activities [4]. An ethical hacking tester may use vulnerability, scanning, sniffer and other hacking tools, as well as social engineering techniques [9]. An auditor may in addition or alternatively analyze documentation or audit logs, interview or observe personnel, flowchart applications, and/or use general audit software to generate and perform tests [2]. The audit plan checklist should be detailed, describing for example, who will be interviewed and the specific required documentation.

This document is presented to the auditee organization (and specifically to the persons and managers who will participate in the audit) during the Entrance Conference, so they are aware of what is happening, what is expected of them, and when it will happen [4]. It is important that the people who will participate in the audit be present, to inform them, help in scheduling, and possibly provide important feedback. A manager of the auditee organization should sign the Audit Plan.

More extensive audit plans would include a project plan, including a schedule or timeline, documentation/deliverables, a set of required skills, resources and tools, and a communication plan telling the auditee of the report distribution [3]. Table 13.2 Audit Engagement Plan Example shows a shortened version of an audit engagement plan, showing minimal (test-oriented) sections and sample text. (The figure shows a draft, but actual plans would always be fully typed.)

The most important part of the audit plan is the *Signature* at the bottom, because it gives an auditor or tester permission to perform the specified security tests [4]. It is the auditor's Get-Out-Of-Jail-Card, in case testing results in some undesirable results or news. There have been a number of cases where ethical hackers and *even IT employees* have been prosecuted for hacking when they discovered breaches or

Table 13.2 Audit engagement plan example

Title: 2014 Audit Engagement Plan for Einstein University's Student DB Web Interface
Objective: Determine security of Web interface for student databases
Scope: Penetration test on all web pages related to Student-accessed databases: Registration, Financial Aid, Coursework, and Grading
Compliance and Criteria: State Breach Notification Law, FERPA, PCI DSS
Constraints: Must perform security hacking tests between 1 and 6 AM
Risk Analysis: **Inherent Risks: (Risks organization is predisposed to)** **Data Breach:** student grades, disabilities (FERPA), student health (HIPAA), student and employee financial account and payment card information (PCI DSS, State Breach), student social security number and passport numbers (State Breach). Students must agree to publish contact information annually (FERPA) **Hacking:** University is an open system, with no limitations on installed software and BYOD devices. Student homework must be protected **Control Risks: (Risk that a control has vulnerability(s))** **Insufficient Firewall/IPS Restrictions:** While much of the university network is open, critical databases must be in a secure zone with a high level of restrictive access **Detection Risk: (Risks of auditor not detecting a problem)** **Hacker within Confidential Zone:** This audit may not detect an infiltrated Confidential Zone or critical vulnerability
Approach: Tester has valid session credentials (i.e., is a student) Specific test records are available for attack Test attack on all databases using manual and automated web testing tools Attempt DDOS attack without using credentials
Checklist The following databases & forms will be tested: Registration process, financial aid and payment process, classroom software with homework assignments, submission and grading, accessing grades, advising records, transcripts … The following security attacks will be tested for all databases/forms: invalid input, buffer overflow, SQL injection, cross-site scripting, cross-site request forgery, clickjacking Confidential zone audit: Firewall scan, network sniffing, log analysis of server and firewall
Signatures: Ellie Smith CISO Terry Doe CISA

security problems and tried to report them. An example of an external hacker who handled his discovery poorly follows next, but do know that employees have been treated similarly when they performed, but were not authorized to execute, certain security tests.

"Weev" Auernheimer created a web crawler to access publicly available information on AT&T's Internet, and reported a security breach to the Gawker blog [1]. The breach information included email addresses of 114,000 iPad users, including Mayor Michael Bloomberg, and Rahm Emanuel, then White House chief of staff. His whistleblowing efforts resulted in a prison sentence of 41 months and a $73,000 fine for breach notification damages to AT&T. In summary, be sure to ALWAYS get specific permission before performing any security tests, even if you believe it is in your list of job responsibilities.

13.1.2 Reviewing Internal Controls

The second step is to organize the set of controls to determine whether the internal controls are at least theoretically adequate or whether an enhancement in security design is necessary. Preventive controls are most desirable, but detective and corrective controls also play an important role. During the third stage the auditor will test the controls to validate their implementation, including determining their specific capabilities and configuration.

A control matrix (Table 13.3) is useful in this stage's theoretical analysis to evaluate the design of controls: where controls are weak or insubstantial and where vulnerabilities exist [2]. To prepare a control matrix, list attacks or problems as column headings across the top row of the table. List controls as row headings down the left-most column. Attacks and controls can be added as needed.

Controls are evaluated per vulnerability as strong (***), medium (**), weak (*), or blank for not applicable, appropriate, or available. In addition, controls can be evaluated as Preventive (p), Detective (d), or Corrective (c). Table 13.3 notes Strong Preventive as (ppp). An *Overlapping Control* is two strong controls, and of course that is preferred. A *Compensating Control* is where a strong control supports a weak one. It is recommended that at least one strong control exists per vulnerability and that multiple controls exist. This table may be listed directly within the audit report findings.

The control matrix is only a theoretical evaluation. The actual implementation of the controls is tested during the next stage.

Table 13.3 Audit control matrix

Problem control v	Disk failure	Power failure	Data breach	Fraud	Hack	Malware	Social engineer	Stolen/lost equipment
Access control				p				
Authentication					pp			
Antivirus								
Firewall			d		pp	p		
Logs/alarms								
Physical security			p	p				pp
Strong policies, standards, guidelines, procedures	cc	cc					p	
Security awareness training							ppd	
Vulnerability testing/audit			dd					

13.1.3 Performing Compliance and Substantive Tests

When working with members of the auditee organization, be careful not to antagonize. The auditor should always be polite and never use an accusatory tone or words with the persons they are working with [4]. It is possible to inform by saying "best practices involve …" Avoid using the 'you' term, such as "you should …" Their feedback can be included in the final report, as well as your professional opinion. It is a good to note and include in the final report where the organization is doing things well and who is performing particularly well, in addition to where improvements need to be made … in a tactful way.

An audit or auditor may focus on one or both of compliance or substantive testing. Compliance tests evaluate security controls, whereas substantive tests evaluate that business transactions are properly processed. Figure 13.2 shows that when we think of the defense in depth onion analogy, the onion layers are the security controls (compliance) that protect the (substantive) business data, which is in the core of the onion.

Thus, substantive tests ensure that transactions are valid and not modified or destroyed in processing. For example, a batch processing control validates throughout processing that the total number of transactions, the financial transaction total, and/or a hash total on certain fields remains consistent. Batch controls ensure that any problem transactions are resolved [2]. Another form of substantive testing is input validation [2]:

- Sequence check: Sequence numbers are indeed sequential.
- Range check: Input data is within appropriate lower and upper bounds.

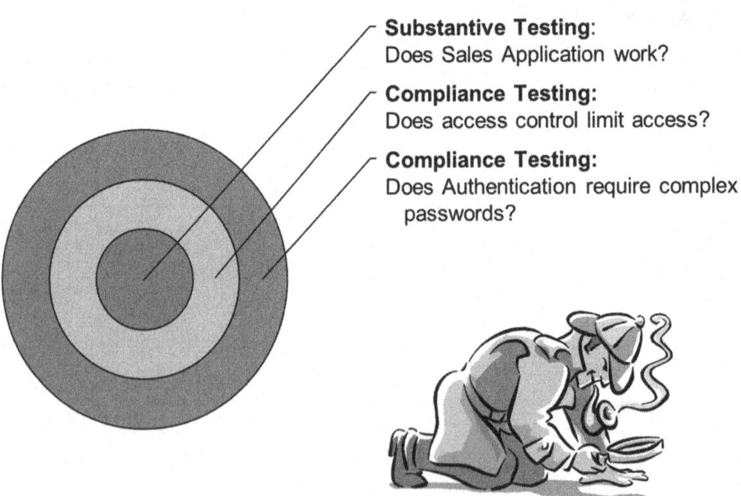

Fig. 13.2 Substantive versus compliance testing

- Validity check: Input can be one of a set of valid entries (e.g., sex = M or F).
- Reasonableness check: The transaction appears normal. For example, an order count is within the normal range of purchases.
- Existence check: All required fields have been input; optional fields need not be entered.
- Key verification: An entry is typed twice to ensure accuracy, e.g., in setting up a password.
- Logical relationship check: Data entered is consistent, e.g., a child of 5 years does not have a driver's license number.
- Check digit: An algorithm on a field is used to generate a check digit, which matches an entered number when the field is entered correctly. This check protects against transcription errors.
- Type check: Entered data is in the appropriate form. For example, a name would not consist solely of numbers; or a quantity field allows only numbers.

The focus of this book is security controls or the compliance arena. A first security test may ensure that servers and user computers are securely configured, with needless services removed, and exposed vulnerabilities resolved that may bring unwanted attention [10]. The test should also validate that all systems are patched, two-factor authentication including strong passwords are used, backups are verified regularly, updated antivirus software is implemented, and users are trained for security awareness.

Continuous Audit is a more advanced stage of audit, which automates the validation of security controls. Regularly (weekly, daily, or more frequent) checking of preventive and detective security controls executes automatically and provides reports and alerts. Many of the top 20 controls, as outlined in the Metrics chapter, require seamless and automated security checks.

An auditor relies upon a number of software tools to perform substantive and compliance tests, including tools which access and analyze data in databases and which perform penetration and vulnerability tests. These software tools are called *Computer-Assisted Audit Techniques* (*CAAT*). They may include utility software, network scanning software, application traces, expert systems, and generalized audit software. The auditor often specifies these tests in the audit plan and report.

13.1.4 Preparing and Presenting the Report

The Audit Report should have a unique title and publish date. The *Objective*, *Scope*, *Period of Audit* and *Compliance and Criteria* sections can be copied from the Audit Engagement Plan. The *Executive Summary* describes, in non-technical language, the auditor's overall opinion about the effectiveness of controls, the risks resulting from any deficiencies, and any reservations or qualifications the auditor holds [2]. The *Detailed Audit Findings and Recommendations* section describes the findings and recommendations, organized in a logical manner by materiality or intended

Table 13.4 Abbreviated audit report

Title: 2014 Audit Report for Einstein University's Student DB Web Interface
Objective: Determine security of Web interface for student databases
Scope: Penetration test on all web pages related to Student-accessed databases: Registration, Financial Aid, Coursework, and Grading
Period of Audit: June 21–28, 2015
Compliance and Criteria: Compliance: State Breach Notification Law, FERPA, PCI DSS Criteria: Top 20 Controls, Certified Ethical Hacker tests related to Web penetration tests
Assertions: As per Audit Engagement Letter, dated Jan 5, 2015, management asserted that: University management has established effective internal controls for accounting and information systems, and is compliant with all laws. Management agreed to provide all necessary documentation for the audit, including policies, procedures and previous audit data; as well as auditor access to the applicable systems as a student user
Executive Summary: It is the opinion of the auditor that there were material weaknesses within the web interface. Web interface A and B were secure, but Web interface C and D need additional security
Detailed Findings and Recommendations: The following attacks were successful on the indicated databases. Also listed are the recommended fixes …
Evidence: Screenshots are attached in Appendix A
Signed: John Smith, CISA CISSP **Date:** 1/13/2015

recipient [2]. It may or may not include minor deficiencies, which can be communicated separately via a letter, depending on management preference. Finally, the document should include the names and signatures of the auditors. The document should be written clearly. Table 13.4 shows an abbreviated Audit Report.

Optional sections may include a distribution list, a list of management assertions, proposed rework dates, statements of responsibility, disclaimers and audit methods used [8]. Assertions, if included, are the auditee management statements indicating adherence to regulation, establishment of internal controls, a lack of awareness of existing fraud, and a promise of cooperation for auditor-requested documentation. Management Assertions can serve as audit Criteria to test against. Both external and internal audits would have many or some additional statements of responsibility, respectively. These statements would detail expectations, mainly of the auditee, in providing the necessary documentation, agreeing to audit criteria, and disclosing any outstanding issues. The report may also include disclaimers to limit auditor liability, for example for undetected fraud and future changes of control use. These sections are not included in Table 13.4, but can be found in ISACA's "IS Audit and Assurance Guideline 2401 Reporting" [8].

The audit report should disclose specific measurement methods used (if multiple options exist), if any deviations from normal measurement practices were used, or if and where any interpretation of data impacted the result.

After preparing the audit report, the auditor *tactfully* presents the report to the persons who participated in the audit as part of an Exit Conference [4]. Some feedback (e.g., reasons or compensating controls) may be provided, which can be added to the final report. The auditor does not change their audit opinion, but they can add the opinion or reasons provided by staff. Then external (and possibly internal) auditors would present their report to upper management. Both presentations should indicate things done well, as well as areas of improvement. The report to upper management should avoid being overly technical.

An audit is useless unless management acts on its findings. Management is responsible for defining how it will address shortcomings in a Corrective Action Plan. Security testers and internal auditors would normally follow-up to ensure that the plan addresses deficiencies, and that those deficiencies are fixed. Alternatively management must take responsibility for not acting [3].

13.2 Example: PCI DSS Audits and Report on Compliance

The document: *Payment Card Industry, Requirements and Security Assessment Procedures*, found at www.pcisecuritystandards.org serves as an excellent baseline security audit plan [11]. At a very high level, PCI DSS requires quarterly scanning tests and an annual penetration test. The pen test should also be performed after any significant change in either hardware, system software or important application change in a critical zone. In addition to high-level requirements, PCI DSS also provides a detailed list of tests for each of the 12 PCI DSS basic requirements; a short sample of which is shown in Table 13.5 [11]. Note that these tests are detailed and explicit, enabling the audit plan to be clearly understood.

A PCI DSS Report on Compliance (ROC) is a form of an audit report. The outline of the ROC is as follows [11]:

1. *Executive Summary*: This summary includes a description of the organization, a summary of quarterly scan reports, a summary of findings for this audit, and a high-level network diagram, showing important devices/components and service connections.
2. *Scope of Work and Approach Taken*: The scope of the audit indicates the parts of the organization that were actually reviewed, including which business environments and network segments were covered and if sampling was used. Of particular interest is whether any wholly-owned entities (e.g., third party), international or wireless environments were included.
3. *Details about Reviewed Environment*: This section outlines a detailed description of the cardholder data environment, including how payment card data is specifically processed, which files are used and how they are secured, and how access is logged. It is important to record all cardholder processing equipment

Table 13.5 Short snapshot of PCI DSS testing requirements [11 p. 73]

9.1 Verify the existence of physical security controls for each computer room, data center, and other physical areas with systems in the cardholder data environment Verify that access is controlled with badge readers or other devices including authorized badges and lock and key Observe a system administrator's attempt to log into consoles for randomly selected systems in the cardholder environment and verify that they are "locked" to prevent unauthorized use
9.1.1.a Verify that video cameras and/or access control mechanisms are in place to monitor the entry/exit points to sensitive areas

and software, their versions, and whether each is PA-DSS compliant. This section also defines any managed service provider or third party access to cardholder data/equipment. The auditor(s) also define what documentation was reviewed and who was interviewed (with rank and organization).

To achieve PCI DSS compliance, it is possible to use sampling. However, sampling must cover all possible business and technological configurations, and be geographically diverse. For example, it is not possible to simply test Sun OS equipment, without testing Microsoft or other used equipment. It is also important to justify, in a documented rationale, how sampling was appropriate and complete.

1. *Contact Information and Report Date*: This describes the period of audit, and how the merchant interface and auditor can be contacted.
2. *Quarterly Scan Reports*: After the first year, the organization must pass all four quarterly scans. Each scan shall cover all externally accessible (or Internet-facing) IP addresses for the organization.
3. *Findings and Observations*: This section follows the 'Detailed PCI DSS Requirements and Security Assessment Procedures' template to provide a detailed description of findings. Any Not Applicable responses or compensating controls must be fully defined.

13.3 Professional and External Auditing

Professional auditing is concerned that the audit follows a defined process and is well documented. Documentation of evidence should use a statistical-based analysis. Problems found by the audit are classified as to severity and follow-up ensures that issues are acted upon.

13.3.1 Audit Resources

To guide auditors in following a professional audit process, ISACA provides a set of standards. Table 13.6 outlines ISACA's IT Assurance Framework (ITAF™) [3], which describes this set of standards and guidelines developed using materials from the IT Governance Institute (ITGI) and other sources.

13.3.2 Sampling

Evidence must be statistically significant to be valid and credible. Rarely can the entire population of data or controls be validated, so sampling is used to reach a conclusion. Sample transactions or units may be selected randomly or systematically,

Table 13.6 ISACA's IT assurance framework [3]

ISACA standards	Description
Section 2200 general standards	Defines guiding principles for IT audit and assurance. Defines terms such as independence, objectivity, management's acknowledgement, proficiency, due professional care, completeness, etc.
Section 2400 performance standards	Audit and assurance must include: Planning and supervision: includes evidence, time and budget, expected report Sufficient evidence: Appropriate quantity, quality, evidence corroboration, documentation Assignment performance: Appropriate knowledge, skills and audit time Representations: Auditee statements of responsibility
Section 2600 reporting standards	The report shall describe: scope and objectives of work, time period covered, professional standards used, auditee/auditor responsibility, conclusions, reservations, restrictions, date of report, signature
Section 3000 IT assurance guidelines	Introduction to assurance guidelines: 3200, 3400, 3600, 3800
Section 3200 enterprise topics	Addresses enterprise-wide issues, and how they may impact the IT department, including: enterprise policies, practices and standards (3210); enterprise assurance initiatives (3230, 3250); additional issues (3270)
Section 3400 IT management processes	Describes IT management and operations common practices, controls and resources related to IT governance (3410), project mgmt. (3420), plans and strategy (3430), processes (3450), risk management (3470), etc.
Section 3600 IT audit and assurance Processes	Focuses on audit approaches, methodologies and procedures, including their issues and pitfalls, including (e.g.,) COBIT (3610), application controls (3650), ERP (3655), CAAT (3670), etc.
Section 3800 IT audit and assurance management	General topics related to the IT audit process, including: planning and scoping (3820, 3830), gathering evidence (3860), documentation (3870), evaluating results (3880), reporting (3890), etc.

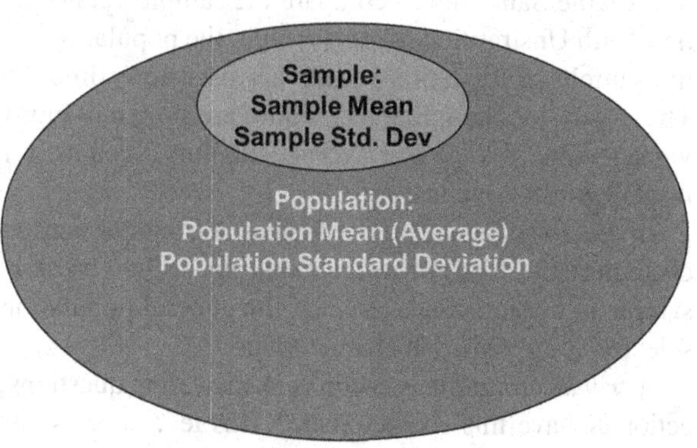

Fig. 13.3 Population sampling

such as every N units [12]. Figure 13.3 shows that the sample population is a small subset of the total population, but the sample is hopefully representative of the population. This *precision* can be measured by comparing the sample and population mean and standard deviation. A *confidence coefficient* is the confidence level or

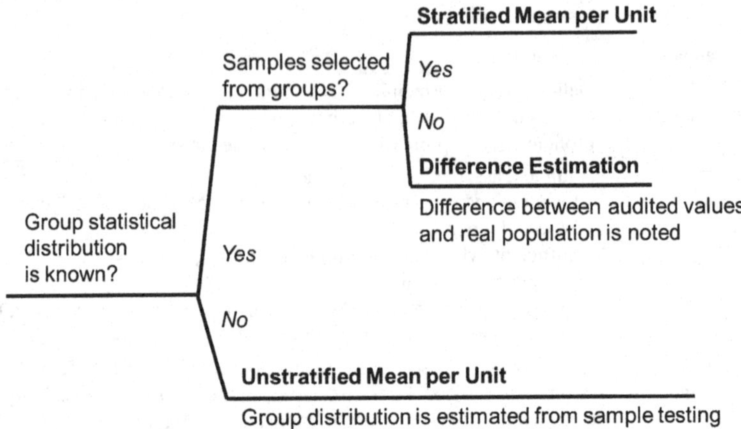

Fig. 13.4 Variable sampling using stratification

probability that the sample truly represents the population. A confidence level of 95 % is considered a high degree of comfort [2]. This type of sampling is called *statistical sampling*, and is useful in reaching conclusions about a population.

Another means of achieving statistical sampling accuracy is by using a similar *stratification* for the sample as exists in the total population [12]. This if it is known that bank transactions are 60 % credit/debit, and 10 % deposits, withdrawals and ATM transactions, and 5 % investments and loans, then sample transactions can be selected to match that stratification, as part of a Stratified Mean per Unit. *Variable Sampling* can estimate the population stratification or determine the appropriateness of the sample in representing the total population [2]. Difference Estimation is a use of Variable Sampling to compare the sample versus population stratification statistics. With Unstratified Mean per Unit, the population stratification is not known, and the sample stratification results are used to estimate the population stratification. These Variable Sampling techniques are shown in Fig. 13.4. Variable Sampling provides results as a total or average quantity, such as in monetary units, and is often used in substantive testing.

In order to evaluate high risk areas, the auditor may choose to oversample a certain characteristic. *Nonstatistical sampling* or *Judgmental sampling* is used when the sample is not intended to match the general population, such as when samples are selected for a high-risk characteristic.

Attribute Sampling is useful is in answering questions such as: How many of transaction X have this characteristic? This technique is commonly used in compliance testing to measure the rate of compliance [2]. An example test might be: How many batches with errors were fully analyzed and properly documented?

The *Tolerable Error* is the maximum problem rate that an auditor will accept before passing a test [2]. In some cases, the observed problem rate may be very close to or exceed the Tolerable Error. Then it makes sense to test a larger sample to better understand the problem. *Discovery Sampling* is useful when the expected problem rate is extremely low (e.g., fraud), and is implemented by first testing some minimal sample. In *Stop-or-Go Sampling*, slightly more testing occurs if any problems are found: If the first 100 have zero errors, then stop; otherwise if the first 1,000 have less than ten errors, stop; and so on.

If sampling sounds complicated to you, then *Generalized Audit Software* (*GAS*) comes to the rescue! GAS is a utility that makes the auditor's life easier by automating sampling and statistical operations. GAS can manipulate files by sorting, indexing, and merging files [2]. It can select and read a set of records to create a sample, and calculate statistical properties (including precision, stratification, frequency analysis) and other arithmetic operations (such as sequence checking, Attribute Sampling) on the sample.

13.3.3 Evidence and Conclusions

Evidence is taken from test results, documentation, interviews, observations and email. Evidence can be insufficient and/or contradictory. The most reliable evidence is external, objective, qualified and timely. External evidence is derived from sources outside the auditee organization, such as contracts, letters or reports. Objective evidence is evidence that is less prone to judgment, such as comparing actual transaction results and reports, compared to what someone might say. Knowledgeable people closest to the operation are more qualified sources than persons less involved. Finally, all evidence should refer to the time period under review.

Problems that can be found during an audit include errors, omissions, irregularities and illegal acts [2]. These problems or *audit exceptions* can be ranked as an Inconsequential Deficiency, a Significant Deficiency, Material Weakness or Pervasive Weakness. An *Inconsequential Deficiency* is insignificant, even when combined with other problems [8]. A *Significant Deficiency* is a significant problem of some consequence. The *Material Weakness* designation may be used when controls are not in place, not in use or are inadequate, or when multiple significant deficiencies result in a significant vulnerability, and whenever escalation is required [3]. A *Pervasive Weakness* indicates multiple material weaknesses. The audit report includes a summary evaluation, which considers the deficiencies in total.

If a potential fraud or illegal action is found during the audit, the auditor should prioritize confirmation and get sufficient details on the problem, then report the finding to an appropriate level of management or the audit committee in an expedient way (i.e., before writing the audit report) [3].

Summary evaluations for audit engagements can be categorized as [8]:

- *Unqualified*: Internal controls were effective.
- *Qualified*: Control weaknesses exist or may exist but are not pervasive. This evaluation may be given when there is insufficient evidence or known material weaknesses.
- *Adverse*: Significant deficiencies result in material weakness and pervasive weaknesses.
- *Disclaimer*: The auditor cannot form an opinion since they cannot obtain sufficient and/or appropriate evidence.

In addition to noting problems, the auditor should suggest fixes or *remediations*. If a fix is not available, mitigation techniques may be suggested.

During audit presentations, the auditor should present all control weaknesses and specify in the report that appropriate management and governance has been informed of weaknesses [8].

13.3.4 Variations in Audit Types

This section has so far focused on an IS Audit. However other types of audits exist [2]:

- *IS Audit*: Evaluates Information Systems safeguards for data in efficiently providing confidentiality, integrity, and availability
- *Financial Audit*: Assures integrity of financial statements
- *Operational Audit*: Evaluates internal controls for a given process or area
- *Integrated Audit*: Includes a combination of Financial, IS and/or Operational audits
- *Forensic Audit*: Investigates a fraud or crime
- *Administrative Audit*: Assesses the efficiency of a process or organization

The Integrated Audit combines financial, operational and/or IS audit to focus on business risk [2]. A team of specialists work together to produce one integrated audit report. The integrated report helps management to better understand and relate to aspects they have less expertise with.

Control Self-Assessment is a form of internal audit that involves many people in the organization. Functional areas become the first line of defense, when teams attend workshops to learn to design and assess controls locally [2]. This technique is beneficial in that employees are trained and get involved in the security design process, thereby helping them to own the process and detect risks quickly. It enhances external audit.

13.4 Questions and Problems

1. *Vocabulary*. Match each meaning with the correct word.

Inherent risk	Audit risk	Audit subject	Audit engagement plan
Control risk	Detection risk	Audit scope	Compliance test
Constraint	Audit objective	Audit plan	Substantive test

   a) A business or industry is prone to specific risks.
   b) A strategic schedule to audit parts of the organization during different years.
   c) A test that ensures that proper processing of business transactions occurs.
   d) A statement of the coverage of the audit, specifying geography, time and/or business unit.
   e) A statement of the purpose of the audit, as defined in an audit plan.

f) A risk that a security control does not operate as expected.
g) A risk that an audit does not discover an existing problem.

2. *Audit Plan for a Specific Regulation*. Consider an industry you currently work in or would like to work in, and a regulation that applies to this industry. Assume the company is in your geographical region. You may use the Security Workbook Audit Chapter to complete the tables.

   a) Create an 'Audit Plan Schedule' Table, similar to Table 13.1. In this plan, consider how you might schedule testing of the entire regulation (related to information security) over time. Specify the objective of each audit being scheduled.
   b) Create an 'Audit Engagement Plan' Table, similar to Table 13.2. Develop one audit engagement plan, including a detailed checklist of tests, of the audits you planned in part (a) of this question. Hint: You may include reviewing documentation, interviewing or observing work, executing tests on data, or any other test functions shown or described in the section entitled: "Perform Compliance and Substantive Tests".

3. *Control Matrix for Specific Regulation*. Consider an industry you currently work in or would like to work in, and a regulation that applies to this industry. Assume the company is in your geographical region. You may use the Security Workbook Audit Chapter to complete the table.

   a) Create a 'Control Matrix' Table, similar to Table 13.3. Select six risks that you think are the highest priority for your industry. Then include as rows appropriate controls that you think will safeguard your organization. You have a blank check, and you may and should add controls as appropriate. Be sure to complete the table, showing whether controls are strong, medium or weak, and whether they are preventive, detective or corrective in nature. Add text explaining why you chose your controls, and why they warrant the rating you gave them.

   Note: Consider these sites:

a) HIPAA/HITECH: Chap. 14 of this text or www.hhs.gov (Health and Human Services) and search for HIPAA.
b) Gramm–Leach–Bliley and Red Flags Rule: Federal Trade Commission: http://www.business.ftc.gov/privacy-and-security
c) Sarbanes–Oxley: www.isaca.org (Organizations for standards/security) Your instructor may provide '*Information Security Student Book*: *Using COBIT®5 for Information Security*', available at www.isaca.org. Additional information is at www.sans.org, search for 'COBIT'.
d) PCI DSS: Access information from https://www.pcisecuritystandards.org/security_standards/. Select the PCI DSS link. Register and download 'PCI DSS v3.0'. Skim the Requirements, starting on page 19.
e) FISMA: Access www.nist.gov (National Institute for Standards and Technology) and search for FISMA. Specific link: http://www.nist.gov/itl/csd/soi/fisma.cfm. Access FIPS Publication 200 first.

13.4.1 Health First Case Study Problems

For each case study problem, refer to the Health First Case Study. The Health First Case Study and Security Workbook should be provided by your instructor or can be found at http://extras.springer.com.

Case study	Health first case study	Other resources
Developing a partial audit plan	√	Security workbook HIPAA slides or notes

References

1. Ludlow P (2013) OPINIONATOR; Hactivists as gadflies. New York Times, 14 April 2013
2. ISACA (2010) CISA review manual 2011. ISACA, Arlington Heights, IL, pp 33–72, 223–226
3. ISACA (2013) ITAF™: a professional practices framework for IS audit/assurance, 2nd edn. ISACA, Arlington Heights, IL, pp 9–40
4. SANS (2005) 507.1 auditing principles and concepts. SANS Institute. www.sans.org, Bethesda, MD
5. Harris S (2013) All-in-one CISSP® exam guide, 6th edn. McGraw-Hill Co., New York, NY, pp 121–125
6. ISACA (2013) IS audit and assurance guideline 2202 risk assessment in planning exposure, EXPOSURE DRAFT. ISACA, Arlington Heights, IL, pp 2–10
7. ISACA (2013) IS audit and assurance guideline 2201 engagement planning, EXPOSURE DRAFT. ISACA, Arlington Heights, IL, pp 2–8
8. ISACA (2013) IS audit and assurance guideline 2401 reporting, EXPOSURE DRAFT. ISACA, Arlington Heights, IL, pp 2–10
9. Walker M (2012) All-in-one CEH™ certified ethical hacker exam guide. McGraw-Hill Co., New York, NY
10. Verizon (2013) Verizon 2013 data breach investigations report. http://www.verizonenterprise.com/DBIR/2013. Accessed 20 Oct 2013
11. Payment Card Industry (2013) Payment card industry, requirements and security assessment procedures, ver 3.0, November 2013. www.pcisecuritystandards.org
12. ISACA (2013) IS audit and assurance guideline 2208 sampling, EXPOSURE DRAFT. ISACA, Arlington Heights, IL, pp 2–9

Chapter 14
Complying with HIPAA and HITECH

> According to our data, the healthcare sector contained the largest number of disclosed data breaches in 2013 at 37 % of those disclosed.—p. 42, Internet Security Threat Report 2014 [1]

The *Health Insurance Portability & Accountability Act* (*HIPAA*) of 1996 was a bipartisan bill introduced by Senators Edward Kennedy and Nancy Kassebaum, and implemented as part of United States law. HIPAA addressed group health insurance, tax/financial aspects, transaction standardization and security. Its Title II regulated the protection of personal health information, in addition to initiating standardization to achieve medical transaction uniformity. Later in 2009, the *Health Information Technology for Economic and Clinical Health* (*HITECH*) Act fixed implementation problems with HIPAA. Important security related sections of these U.S. and related laws include:

- *HIPAA Privacy Rule*: protects health information whether or not it is computerized.
- *HIPAA Security Rule*: applies to computerized health information.
- *HITECH Act*: updates HIPAA to strengthen penalties, protect patients who had been harmed, require breach notification, and ensure compliance by both health care providers and contractors performing healthcare-related work for them [2].
- *Genetic Information Nondiscrimination Act* (*2008*): Protects against genetic testing discrimination, including limiting use by insurance companies in determining eligibility or pricing patient premiums, and preventing employers from using genetic testing in hiring, promotion or firing.

HIPAA and HITECH were implemented because:

1. Employers and other organizations were regularly using health information in hiring, promoting, and laying off employees. Example abuses include [3]:
   - A woman was fired from job after a positive review but expensive illness
   - Thirty-five percent of Fortune 500 companies admitted checking medical records before hiring or promoting

S. Lincke, *Security Planning*, DOI 10.1007/978-3-319-16027-6_14

- A Midwest banker and county health board member matched customer accounts with patient information. He called due to the mortgages of anyone suffering from cancer.

2. Health organizations and their contractors were inappropriately accessing health information, for advertising and other purposes.

   - A patient at Brigham and Women's Hospital in Boston learned that employees had accessed her medical record more than 200 times [3].
   - The 13-year-old daughter of a hospital employee took a list of patients' names and phone numbers from the hospital when visiting her mother at work. As a joke, she contacted patients and told them they were diagnosed with HIV.

3. Health organizations and their contractors were negligent in safeguarding patient privacy, resulting in massive breaches. For example:

   - In 2006, a desk clerk at a Florida clinic stole the health info of over 1,000 patients. The clerk sold the data to a thief, who used the information to submit $2.8 million in fraudulent Medicare claims to the U.S. government.
   - Eli Lilly and Co. accidentally revealed over 600 patient e-mail addresses, when it sent a message without blind copy, to every person registered to receive reminders about taking Prozac [3].
   - In 2006, CVS pharmacies were caught throwing away unredacted pill bottles, medical instruction sheets, and pharmacy receipts. These contained patient names, addresses, prescriptions names, physician names, health insurance numbers and credit card numbers [4].
   - In 2009, Blue Cross Blue Shield in Tennessee had 57 hard disks stolen, releasing medical information and social security numbers for over one million people [5].

4. People avoid using health insurance when they fear their illness may adversely affect their career or health insurance availability.

   - Diseases such as cancer, AIDS, sexually transmitted disease, substance abuse and mental illness have not been reported by some patients [3].

A current problem with health care is *Medical Identity Theft*. In this form of identity theft, a person's name and parts of their medical identity (often, insurance) are stolen by persons without medical insurance to obtain medical services, prescriptions, and other medical supplies. This identity theft may be for prescriptions or operations—or to sell or use addictive prescription drugs—or for faked charges to Medicare for financial reimbursement. For the victim whose ID is stolen, this can lead to inaccurate medical records, since recent treatment notes relate to the thief, not the victim [1, 6, 7]. This incorrect information can become life-threatening when a doctor misdiagnoses or treats the victim using the thief's medical history. In addition, the thief may leave unpaid medical charges, forwarded to a different address, and leaving the victim with a degraded credit report. Alternatively, the thief may claim the victim's health as their own when submitting health information to third parties. Finally, there are few protections for consumers. Doctors' identifications are stolen to submit fake Medicare transactions [7]. There is demand for medical health records: a medical identity on the black market is worth $50, compared to $1 for credit card numbers in bulk [6].

An incentive for health organizations to take HIPAA seriously is a Health and Human Services (HHS) website that lists organizations that have suffered health information breaches. The website is known as "The Wall of Shame". Bitglass has analyzed these breaches and concludes that 68 % of breaches occurred due to device and data loss and theft—not hacking [6]. Again, protecting the human (with portable devices) is as important as protecting technology.

14.1 Introduction and Vocabulary

The typical medical transactions are shown in Fig. 14.1. Employers *enroll* or *disenroll* employees into a health plan, and make *premium payments* for those employees. A health care provider submits a *Health Plan Eligibility Inquiry* to a patient's health plan, to determine what the patient qualifies for and who to bill to. The nurse sends a *health care claim* to the insurance provider for bills to be paid, and may send a *referral* if the patient should see a specialist, undergo surgery or be admitted to a hospital. The *referral* is also sent to any specialist doctor or hospital, if appropriate.

The personal health information that is protected under the HIPAA Privacy Rule is called Protected Health Information (*PHI*). Under the HIPAA Security Rule, PHI is stored in computers in electronic form and thus renamed Electronic Protected

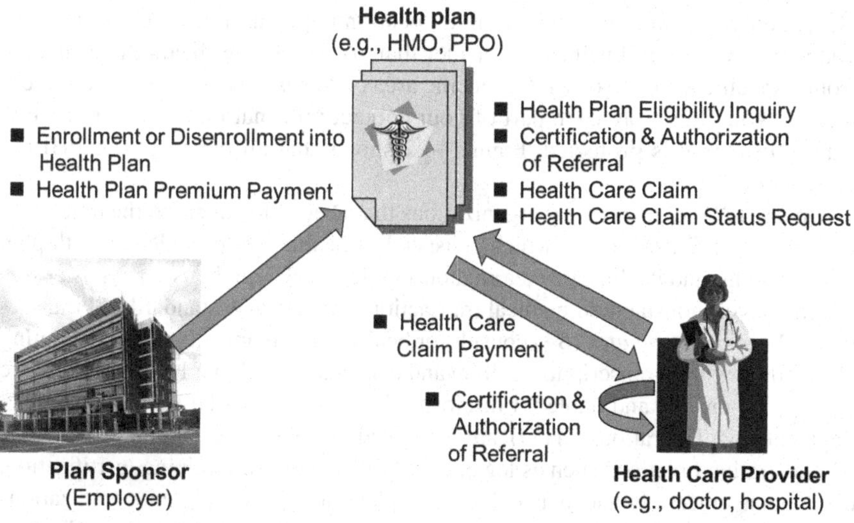

Fig. 14.1 Typical medical transactions

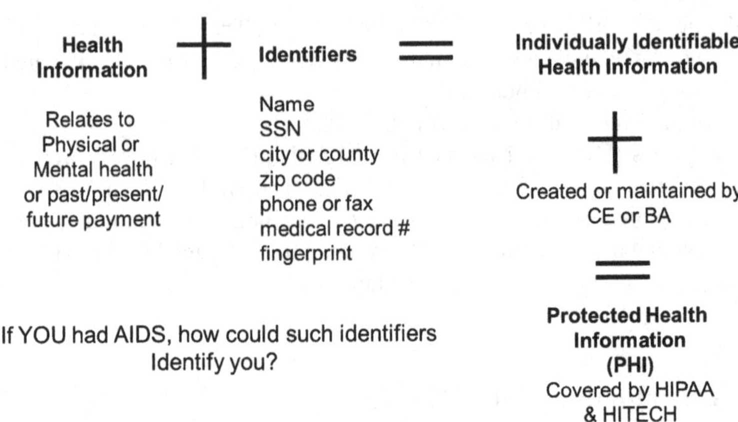

Fig. 14.2 Factors composing PHI

Health Information (*EPHI*). Note that the abbreviation is what is normally used; if you want to think of the first letter as Protected, Patient, Personal or Private, it does not really matter, since this data is all of those things!

All parts of your health information are protected. Let's consider a hypothetical case where you visit multiple times a doctor who specializes in cancer or a cancer center. That information alone could change your brilliant career or even your ability to gain health insurance (depending on current health laws). Therefore, every part of your medical treatment and medical bills are protected by HIPAA.

Let us consider next that you obtain medical insurance through your work place, and you commute from a remote location (e.g., rural or long distance), or you work for a small business. Consider that your employer hears that someone from a specific zip code or with a specific area code has cancer. That can uniquely identify you. Therefore each part of your contact information and any other private information is protected. Figure 14.2 shows that all parts of your PHI are protected.

Under HIPAA, the primary organizations that needed to adhere to the regulation were *Covered Entities* (*CE*), which consisted of health care providers, health plan organizations, and health care clearinghouses. Health clearinghouses are businesses which convert nonstandard medical transactions into HIPAA-standardized transactions. *Business Associates* (*BA*) consult for health care organizations by performing claims processing, transcription, billing and data analysis. Under HITECH, BAs are equally responsible and liable for disclosure [2]. All uses of PHI within Treatment, Payment and Operations (TPO) are protected. Health care Operations include administrative functions such as legal, quality improvement, training, certification, case management, financial and business planning aspects. Even organizations which maintain nurses' offices need to be concerned. Thus, HIPAA/HITECH now applies widely.

14.2 HITECH Breach Notification

The HITECH Breach Notification Rule specifies how a CE/BA should notify individuals and agencies if a breach of information occurs. To prevent breaches, PHI shall be shredded or destroyed and disposed of properly and EPHI shall always be encrypted in a way that is approved by HHS.

If a breach does occur, each affected patient needs to be notified within 60 days, although a documented, ongoing law enforcement investigation may delay the notification [8]. BAs must inform CEs of any breaches right away and shall provide details about the breach. Patient notification shall include a description of what happened, the date of the breach and its discovery, the type of information that was breached, steps the clients should take to protect themselves, and actions the CE is taking to investigate the breach, mitigate existing problems, and prevent new ones. The notification letter shall also provide contact information, for any questions. If more than ten affected people cannot be notified, e.g., due to change of address, then the CE must post the breach on their website for 90 days.

If more than 500 people were affected, the CE must also notify HHS as soon as possible, and inform local media. If fewer than 500 people were affected, the CE must notify HHS by 60 days after the end of the year.

HIPAA established penalties and jail time for violators of the law. The imposed jail time was up to 1 year for "wrongful disclosure" of PHI/EPHI, up to 5 years if this wrongful disclosure was "committed under false pretenses," and up to 10 years if the breach was performed "with intent to sell, achieve personal gain, or cause malicious harm." HITECH increased the penalties to what is shown in Table 14.1. The jail time still applies mainly for cases of fraud and criminal intent.

Breaches are seriously enforced! Concerning the CVS pharmacy breach, the FTC and Health and Human Services (HHS) each developed separate remediation plans with CVS that included the development of a security plan, security policies, and an employee training program. The remediation plans also required independent audits and HHS monitoring. CVS paid $2.25 million in fines [4]. Blue Cross Blue Shield, which lost 57 disks of PHI, paid $1.5 million to Office of Civil Rights, incurred a 3-year remediation plan, and spent $17 million in investigation, notification, and protection expenses [5].

Table 14.1 Penalties for HIPAA/HITECH violations

HITECH category	Each violation	Max $ per year
CE/BA exercised reasonable diligence but did not learn about violation	$100–50,000	$1.5 million
Violation is due to reasonable cause	$1,000–50,000	$1.5 million
CE/BA demonstrated willful neglect but corrected violation	$10,000–50,000	$1.5 million
CE/BA demonstrated willful neglect and took no corrective action	$50,000	$1.5 million

14.3 HIPAA Privacy Rule

The Privacy Rule addresses patient security regardless of whether or not the office uses computers or not. The Privacy Rule is meant to be reasonable, and not cause major expenses such as architectural changes. Hard copy patient information shall be maintained in locked cabinets or destroyed via paper shredders. Doctors and nurses should maintain patient privacy by shutting doors and keeping their voices down. Providers should maintain a clear desk policy so that patient information other than the patient being served is not visible. Computers should be protected by passwords and auto screen savers, to ensure that no patient information is divulged when a CE walks away from their terminal. Hospital patients are entitled to privacy curtains, but not necessarily private rooms or soundproof walls. It is also OK for doctors to talk to nurses at nurse stations about patient care. In summary, precautions shall be taken, but should not prevent regular patient care business.

The Privacy Rule ensures that health care providers maintain policies and procedures regarding patient privacy. Providers must regularly review these policies and procedures, and update policies when new requirements emerge. Providers shall validate that these policies/procedures are consistently implemented throughout the organization.

Some of those policies shall mandate that health information is not used for non-health purposes, including marketing [2, 3]. Workers shall have need-to-know and minimum necessary access to patient information, which is sufficient only to do their primary job. A data classification scheme, such as is defined in the Information Security chapter, documents permissions. Each CE organization shall name one person who is accountable for Privacy Rule compliance, and each full and part-time employee, volunteer, and contractor needs to be trained in privacy, sufficient to adhere to the law.

14.3.1 Patient Rights

Patients should know how their provider handles privacy, via a *Notice of Privacy Practices* (*NPP*). Health plans and health providers must provide their NPP to clients upon enrollment or on first service delivery, and both must request signed acknowledgment of receipt of the NPP. The NPP must be displayed prominently in the office, on any website, and copies should be available upon request. If privacy practices change, a revised NPP must be issued to clients within 60 days.

Patients have a right to obtain their own patient information (except psychotherapy notes) and request corrections to those health records. Patients can request a specific method of contact (e.g., specific phone or email) for privacy reasons. They have a right to learn who has accessed their health information. Patients can request restrictions as to who can see their PHI and allow and withdraw authorizations for use and disclosure, such as if they become involved in medical research.

Therefore, CEs must keep records of PHI disclosures for 3 years. Health providers must respond to patient requests for any information within 30 days, but can extend this delay for another 30 days if they notify the patient. Finally, patients may file a complaint to HHS if their rights are violated.

14.3.2 Disclosures

CEs and BAs must track both allowed and unintended disclosures of patient information. CEs shall obtain contracts from BAs, which indicate that BAs are responsible for HIPAA/HITECH, will use the PHI information only for the required and permitted purposes stated in the agreement, and that BAs will notify CEs of any breaches [8]. If the BA outsources any of the contracted work, similar contract agreements must be signed between BA and BA. Allowed disclosures include:

Required Disclosure Each patient shall be able to access their PHI, as noted above. In some cases, a parent, guardian or personal representative, such as next of kin, may require PHI. The Office of Civil Rights Enforcement, which is tasked with investigating violations of the Privacy Rule, may access PHI for suspected wrongdoing.

Permitted Disclosure PHI may be disclosed without patient authorization for judicial proceedings, coroner/funerals, organ donation, approved research, military-related situations, government-provided benefits, worker's compensation, domestic violence or abuse, and some law enforcement activities. The amount of disclosure should be the minimum necessary: for example for domestic violence, only treatments related to the violence are shared, and not the full medical history. Before PHI is provided, identity must be verified, for example by proof of identity/badge and documentation.

Routine Disclosure These PHI disclosures happen routinely, such as a referral to another health provider, as part of medical transcriptions, or to report births, deaths, communicable diseases and other vital statistics, or inform schools of immunization(s). These disclosures should be addressed in policies, procedures and forms to ensure that minimal information is provided in acceptable ways and the disclosure is documented.

Non-routine Disclosure These are non-routine disclosures for which no clear policy exists. An example might be health care used in research. Research does have special requirements, such as approval from an IRB/privacy review board and statements of privacy to protect patients. CEs shall have reasonable criteria to review requests for these non-routine PHI disclosures, so that they may occur following a standardized review process.

Incidental Disclosure Some disclosures may be unavoidable in performing regular health functions. For example, a patient may overhear advice given to another patient in a hospital room or by a nurse's desk. However, CEs shall take reasonable care that this is minimized but does not need to track such disclosures.

Disclosure Authorization Form

Description of Information:____________________________________

Patient making authorized disclosure____________________________

Person receiving information:__________________________________

Purpose of the disclosure:

Authorization Expiration Date:________________

Patient Signature________________________ Date:____________
A form to revoke authorization must be completed to terminate authorization.

Fig. 14.3 Disclosure authorization form

Finally, some disclosures are not permitted, such as *Inadvertent Disclosures* and *Breaches*. Inadvertent disclosures include a PHI disclosed by mistake without authorization. These disclosures must be tracked, and may require notification. Examples of breaches include when a computer or backup tape/disks are stolen or a hacker breaks into a PHI database. Breaches always require Notification as described in a previous section.

Any person who falls outside of the list of permitted disclosures may obtain the PHI if the patient agrees and signs a release form, such as Fig. 14.3, indicating his or her approval. This includes the patient's employer, a lawyer, another insurance company, another health care provider not involved in the patient's health care, or any person outside of the health care system. If the patient agrees, the patient should get a copy of the authorization and the CE or BA must maintain the authorization for 6 years. Note that the one case where an employer is entitled to specific drug-related PHI is for a mandated drug test.

14.4 HIPAA Security Rule

The Security Rule is required when computers are used in a CE/BA environment. To achieve that, the Security Rule recognizes that confidentiality, integrity and availability are each required to protect health information [2, 3]. With computerization, PHI becomes Electronic PHI (EPHI), the Minimum Necessary requirement translates into authentication and access control, and the tracking of disclosures is implemented using unique login credentials and transaction logging. Logs of medical transactions record who accessed or modified medical records, at what time and for what reason. This logging ensures nonrepudiation, making employees accountable for what they access and do to medical data. The goal of the regulation is that security is scalable, technology independent, and comprehensive. The regulation avoids specifying detailed technologies that are likely to change with time. However, the HIPAA Security Rule is also comprehensive in its security coverage.

The HIPAA/HITECH Security Rule requirements are listed in Table 14.2 [8]. Each requirement is defined as *Required* (*R*) or *Addressable* (*A*). Required standards specify the precise implementation that is expected—there is no leeway in implementation. Addressable options allow for documented, alternative implementations that are effective in achieving the intent of the standard.

The Security Rule is divided into three sections: administrative, physical and technical security requirements. As you shall see, virtually everything this book covers is required by HIPAA/HITECH.

14.4.1 Administrative Requirements

Administrative requirements include risk management, alarm/log monitoring, periodic policy review/audit, and personnel management. Risk management ensures that security costs correspond with risk: a hospital should spend more than a doctor's office. Risk assessment should be accurate, thorough and implemented. The implementation requirement includes monitoring of computer and network logs, performing vulnerability assessments, and performing audits to ensure worker adherence to procedures and control effectiveness.

A security official shall be allocated to be responsible for security policy and implementation. Workers should sign confidentiality agreements and be trained in policies and procedures; these workers must implement them or be disciplined. Workers must be periodically reminded of policies and security training, including creating good passwords and reporting malware and other potential concerns. Contractors must also sign confidentiality/HIPAA adherence agreements. Policies and procedures must be updated regularly to accommodate changes in the health care environment and operations, and shall be retained for 6 years after their creation or modification.

Realizing 'Minimum Necessary' in a computer environment translates into documenting procedures to allocate permissions (access control) to EPHI, ensuring that permissions remain appropriately minimal as job functions change, supervising EPHI access, and terminating access when employment ends. Typically, a data owner (or staff manager) allocates permissions.

A disaster will likely occur sometime, and can be caused by computer equipment failure or security breaches. Guidelines must be prepared to help employees deal with both inadvertent data loss and security incidents. These incidents must be handled appropriately and fully tracked. A contingency plan should indicate how data is normally backed up, how it can be restored following system (disk) failure, and how the organization will survive with minimal or no computer availability. Testing for such an eventuality is required.

While this chapter is an overview of HIPAA requirements, an appropriate implementation of Administrative Security is more fully defined in Chap. 4 on risk, Chap. 5 on business continuity, Chap. 6 regarding policy, Chap. 7 describing information security, Chap. 10 on personnel, and Chap. 11 on incident response.

14.4.2 Physical Security

Physical security is concerned with appropriate access to the health facility, to worker workstations and to organizational media. A facility security plan protects the facility from inappropriate access and theft, and considers when and where workers and patients may be present. Facility security shall also plan for emergency/continuity access and document equipment maintenance.

To protect EPHI, appropriate access and acceptable use of workstations can be documented within an acceptable use plan. Since EPHI will often be viewable on terminal screens, shoulder surfing can be minimized through positioning of workstations and/or use of computer terminal hoods. Workers will occasionally leave their stations; the loss of EPHI through the viewing or theft of documents, laptops, and memory must be prevented. Protections, such as walls or locked rooms, can minimize exposure.

EPHI may be exposed via sensitive paper documents, computers, terminals, backup copies, copy machines, and any other storage media used. Physical memory containing EPHI will eventually leave the facility, via disk backup, repair, reuse or disposal. Sensitive situations to consider include the handling of patients/visitors, the removal of equipment's sensitive memories before repair, and erasure or damage of memories before equipment reuse or disposal. Finally, any hardware/media movement must be tracked and documented.

Chapter 9 explores a more in-depth view of physical security.

14.4.3 Technical Controls

Technical controls ensure that computer equipment is accessed only by authorized individuals, and that EPHI is protected for confidentiality and integrity. Authentication controls include that each user has a unique login, that the user is identified accurately (through multi-factor or secure passwords), and that terminals timeout after a duration of no access, requiring relogin. Users are also accountable for their access to EPHI through transaction logging. Any emergency access methods should be well controlled.

Computers containing EPHI must meet confidentiality and integrity goals for EPHI storage, archival and transmission. This is achieved using encryption and integrity (message digest) controls on the EPHI. Potential attacks must also be logged. Regular maintenance includes software patching and review of logs. Issues include determining for which devices logs should be monitored, which logs may indicate potential attack and how such attacks should be handled, and which logs should be archived for security purposes. Technical controls are further explained in Chap. 7 on data security and Chap. 8 on network security.

Table 14.2 provides the actual HIPAA text for the Security Rule. The table has been slightly modified for readability: full legal paragraph numbers have been removed and replaced with a general paragraph name. In addition, the term electronic protected health information (EPHI) has been abbreviated.

Table 14.2 Security rule requirements

HIPAA administrative simplification text (slightly modified for simpler reading)	Required/addressable (& notes)
§ 164.308 Administrative safeguards	
(1) Standard: Security management process. Implement policies and procedures to prevent, detect, contain, and correct security violations	
(A) Risk analysis (required). Conduct an accurate and thorough assessment of the potential risks and vulnerabilities to the confidentiality, integrity, and availability of EPHI held by the covered entity or business associate	R
(B) Risk management (required). Implement security measures sufficient to reduce risks and vulnerabilities to a reasonable and appropriate level	R
(C) Sanction policy (required). Apply appropriate sanctions against workforce members who fail to comply with the security policies and procedures of the covered entity or business associate	R
(D) Information system activity review (required). Implement procedures to regularly review records of information system activity, such as audit logs, access reports, and security incident tracking reports	R
(2) Standard: Assigned security responsibility. Identify the security official who is responsible for the development and implementation of the policies and procedures required by this subpart for the covered entity or business associate	
(3) Standard: Workforce security. Implement policies and procedures to ensure that all members of its workforce have appropriate access to EPHI, as provided under paragraph (4) of this section, and to prevent those workforce members who do not have access under paragraph (4) of this section from obtaining access to EPHI	
(A) Authorization and/or supervision (addressable). Implement procedures for the authorization and/or supervision of workforce members who work with EPHI or in locations where it might be accessed	A
(B) Workforce clearance procedure (addressable). Implement procedures to determine that the access of a workforce member to EPHI is appropriate	A

(continued)

Table 14.2 (continued)

HIPAA administrative simplification text (slightly modified for simpler reading)	Required/addressable (& notes)
(C) Termination procedures (addressable). Implement procedures for terminating access to EPHI when the employment of, or other arrangement with, a workforce member ends or as required by determinations made as specified in paragraph (3)(B) of this section	A
(4) Standard: Information access management. Implement policies and procedures for authorizing access to EPHI that are consistent with the applicable requirements of subpart E of this part	
(A) Isolating health care clearinghouse functions (required). If a health care clearinghouse is part of a larger organization, the clearinghouse must implement policies and procedures that protect the EPHI of the clearinghouse from unauthorized access by the larger organization	R
(B) Access authorization (addressable). Implement policies and procedures for granting access to EPHI, for example, through access to a workstation, transaction, program, process, or other mechanism	A
(C) Access establishment and modification (addressable). Implement policies and procedures that, based upon the covered entity's or the business associate's access authorization policies, establish, document, review, and modify a user's right of access to a workstation, transaction, program, or process	A
(5) Standard: Security awareness and training. Implement a security awareness and training program for all members of its workforce (including management)	
(A) Security reminders (addressable). Periodic security updates	A
(B) Protection from malicious software (addressable). Procedures for guarding against, detecting, and reporting malicious software	A
(C) Log-in monitoring (addressable). Procedures for monitoring log-in attempts and reporting discrepancies	A
(D) Password management (addressable). Procedures for creating, changing, and safeguarding passwords	A
(6) Standard: Security incident procedures. Implement policies and procedures to address security incidents	
Response and reporting (required). Identify and respond to suspected or known security incidents; mitigate, to the extent practicable, harmful effects of security incidents that are known to the covered entity or business associate; and document security incidents and their outcomes	R
(7) Standard: Contingency plan. Establish (and implement as needed) policies and procedures for responding to an emergency or other occurrence (for example, fire, vandalism, system failure, and natural disaster) that damages systems that contain EPHI	

(continued)

Table 14.2 (continued)

HIPAA administrative simplification text (slightly modified for simpler reading)	Required/addressable (& notes)
(A) Data backup plan (required). Establish and implement procedures to create and maintain retrievable exact copies of EPHI	R
(B) Disaster recovery plan (required). Establish (and implement as needed) procedures to restore any loss of data	R
(C) Emergency mode operation plan (required). Establish (and implement as needed) procedures to enable continuation of critical business processes for protection of the security of EPHI while operating in emergency mode	R
(D) Testing and revision procedures (addressable). Implement procedures for periodic testing and revision of contingency plans	A
(E) Applications and data criticality analysis (addressable). Assess the relative criticality of specific applications and data in support of other contingency plan components	A
(8) Standard: Evaluation. Perform a periodic technical and nontechnical evaluation, based initially upon the standards implemented under this rule and, subsequently, in response to environmental or operational changes affecting the security of EPHI, that establishes the extent to which a covered entity's or business associate's security policies and procedures meet the requirements of this subpart	R
(9) (A) Business associate contracts and other arrangements. A covered entity may permit a business associate to create, receive, maintain, or transmit EPHI on the covered entity's behalf only if the covered entity obtains satisfactory assurances, in accordance with Organizational Requirements (§ 164.314), that the business associate will appropriately safeguard the information. A covered entity is not required to obtain such satisfactory assurances from a business associate that is a subcontractor	
(B) A business associate may permit a business associate that is a subcontractor to create, receive, maintain, or transmit EPHI on its behalf only if the business associate obtains satisfactory assurances, in accordance with § 164.314, that the subcontractor will appropriately safeguard the information	
(C) Written contract or other arrangement (required). Document the satisfactory assurances required by paragraph (9)(A) or (9)(B) of this section through a written contract or other arrangement with the business associate that meets the applicable requirements of § 164.314 [amended 1/25/13]	R
§ 164.310 physical safeguards	
(a) Standard: Facility access controls. Implement policies and procedures to limit physical access to its electronic information systems and the facility or facilities in which they are housed, while ensuring that properly authorized access is allowed	

(continued)

Table 14.2 (continued)

HIPAA administrative simplification text (slightly modified for simpler reading)	Required/addressable (& notes)
(i) Contingency operations (addressable). Establish (and implement as needed) procedures that allow facility access in support of restoration of lost data under the disaster recovery plan and emergency mode operations plan in the event of an emergency	A
(ii) Facility security plan (addressable). Implement policies and procedures to safeguard the facility and the equipment therein from unauthorized physical access, tampering, and theft	A
(iii) Access control and validation procedures (addressable). Implement procedures to control and validate a person's access to facilities based on their role or function, including visitor control, and control of access to software programs for testing and revision	A
(iv) Maintenance records (addressable). Implement policies and procedures to document repairs and modifications to the physical components of a facility which are related to security (for example, hardware, walls, doors, and locks)	A
(b) Standard: Workstation use. Implement policies and procedures that specify the proper functions to be performed, the manner in which those functions are to be performed, and the physical attributes of the surroundings of a specific workstation or class of workstation that can access EPHI	R
(c) Standard: Workstation security. Implement physical safeguards for all workstations that access EPHI, to restrict access to authorized users	R
(d) Standard: Device and media controls. Implement policies and procedures that govern the receipt and removal of hardware and electronic media that contain EPHI into and out of a facility, and the movement of these items within the facility	
(i) Disposal (required). Implement policies and procedures to address the final disposition of EPHI, and/or the hardware or electronic media on which it is stored	R
(ii) Media re-use (required). Implement procedures for removal of EPHI from electronic media before the media are made available for re-use	R
(iii) Accountability (addressable). Maintain a record of the movements of hardware and electronic media and any person responsible therefore	A
(iv) Data backup and storage (addressable). Create a retrievable, exact copy of EPHI, when needed, before movement of equipment [amended 1/25/13]	A

(continued)

Table 14.2 (continued)

HIPAA administrative simplification text (slightly modified for simpler reading)	Required/addressable (& notes)
§ 164.312 Technical safeguards	
(a) Standard: Access control. Implement technical policies and procedures for electronic information systems that maintain EPHI to allow access only to those persons or software programs that have been granted access rights as specified in Administrative Safeguards (§ 164.308(4))	
(i) Unique user identification (required). Assign a unique name and/or number for identifying and tracking user identity	R
(ii) Emergency access procedure (required). Establish (and implement as needed) procedures for obtaining necessary EPHI during an emergency	R
(iii) Automatic logoff (addressable). Implement electronic procedures that terminate an electronic session after a predetermined time of inactivity	A
(iv) Encryption and decryption (addressable). Implement a mechanism to encrypt and decrypt EPHI	A
(b) Standard: Audit controls. Implement hardware, software, and/or procedural mechanisms that record and examine activity in information systems that contain or use EPHI	R
(c) Standard: Integrity. Implement policies and procedures to protect EPHI from improper alteration or destruction	
Mechanism to authenticate EPHI (addressable). Implement electronic mechanisms to corroborate that EPHI has not been altered or destroyed in an unauthorized manner	A
(d) Standard: Person or entity authentication. Implement procedures to verify that a person or entity seeking access to EPHI is the one claimed	R
(e) Standard: Transmission security. Implement technical security measures to guard against unauthorized access to EPHI that is being transmitted over an electronic communications network	
(i) Integrity controls (addressable). Implement security measures to ensure that electronically transmitted EPHI is not improperly modified without detection until disposed of	A
(ii) Encryption (addressable). Implement a mechanism to encrypt EPHI whenever deemed appropriate [68 FR 8376, February 20, 2003, as amended at 78 FR 5694, January 25, 2013]	A
§ 164.314 organizational requirements	
(a) Standard: Business associate contracts or other arrangements. The contract or other arrangement required by Administrative Safeguards (§ 164.308(9)(3)) must meet the requirements of paragraph (i), (ii), or (iii) of this section, as applicable	

(continued)

Table 14.2 (continued)

HIPAA administrative simplification text (slightly modified for simpler reading)	Required/addressable (& notes)
(i) Business associate contracts. The contract must provide that the business associate will—(A) Comply with the applicable requirements of this subpart; (B) In accordance with § 164.308(9)(2), ensure that any subcontractors that create, receive, maintain, or transmit EPHI on behalf of the business associate agree to comply with the applicable requirements of this subpart by entering into a contract or other arrangement that complies with this section; and (C) Report to the covered entity any security incident of which it becomes aware, including breaches of unsecured protected health information as required by Notification Requirement § 164.410	
(ii) Other arrangements. The covered entity is in compliance with paragraph (a)(i) of this section if it has another arrangement in place that meets the requirements of Uses and Disclosures § 164.504	
(iii) Business associate contracts with subcontractors. The requirements of paragraphs (a)(i) and (a)(ii) of this section apply to the contract or other arrangement between a business associate and a subcontractor required by Administrative Safeguards (§ 164.308(9)(4)) in the same manner as such requirements apply to contracts or other arrangements between a covered entity and business associate	
(b) Standard: Requirements for group health plans. Except when the only EPHI disclosed to a plan sponsor is disclosed pursuant to Uses and Disclosures (§ 164.504 or § 164.508), a group health plan must ensure that its plan documents provide that the plan sponsor will reasonably and appropriately safeguard EPHI created, received, maintained, or transmitted to or by the plan sponsor on behalf of the group health plan	
Implementation specifications (required). The plan documents of the group health plan must be amended to incorporate provisions to require the plan sponsor to—(i) Implement administrative, physical, and technical safeguards that reasonably and appropriately protect the confidentiality, integrity, and availability of the EPHI that it creates, receives, maintains, or transmits on behalf of the group health plan; (ii) ensure that the adequate separation required by Uses and Disclosures (§ 164.504) is supported by reasonable and appropriate security measures; (iii) ensure that any agent to whom it provides this information agrees to implement reasonable and appropriate security measures to protect the information; and (iv) report to the group health plan any security incident of which it becomes aware [amended 1/25/13]	R

(continued)

Table 14.2 (continued)

HIPAA administrative simplification text (slightly modified for simpler reading)	Required/addressable (& notes)
§ 164.316 Policies and procedures and documentation requirements	
(a) Standard: Policies and procedures. Implement reasonable and appropriate policies and procedures to comply with the standards, implementation specifications, or other requirements of this subpart, taking into account those factors specified in Security standards: General rules (§ 164.306). A covered entity or business associate may change its policies and procedures at any time, provided that the changes are documented and are implemented in accordance with this subpart	
(b) (1) Standard: Documentation. (i) Maintain the policies and procedures implemented to comply with this subpart in written (which may be electronic) form; and (ii) If an action, activity or assessment is required by this subpart to be documented, maintain a written (which may be electronic) record of the action, activity, or assessment. (2) Implementation specifications:	
(i) Time limit (required). Retain the documentation required by paragraph (b)(1) of this section for 6 years from the date of its creation or the date when it last was in effect, whichever is later	R
(ii) Availability (required). Make documentation available to those persons responsible for implementing the procedures to which the documentation pertains	R
(iii) Updates (required). Review documentation periodically, and update as needed, in response to environmental or operational changes affecting the security of the EPHI [amended 1/25/13]	R

14.5 Questions and Problems

1. *Vocabulary*. Match each meaning with the correct word.

Security rule	Covered entity	Notice of privacy practices
Privacy rule	Business associate	Required disclosure
EPHI	Medical identity theft	Permitted disclosure
Required	HITECH	Routine disclosure
Addressable	HIPAA	Protected health information

a) Information relating to any part of a person's name, address, phone, medical condition, treatment and bills.

b) The aspect of HIPAA providing privacy/security requirements for all organizations working with health care, regardless of whether the health information is computerized or not.
c) The aspect of HIPAA listing privacy/security requirements for computerized systems containing health information.
d) Health providers must provide a statement to their patients indicating patient rights.
e) Patients are entitled to see their own medical records; in certain cases, legal guardians, parents and next of kin have access to this medical information.
f) Patient information may be communicated to other health care providers when referred; to report births, deaths, communicable diseases and other vital statistics; and to inform schools of immunizations.
g) An indication that a security rule requirement may be modified, if the rule's intention is met.
h) Regulation requiring organizations to notify patients and HHS if a breach occurs.
i) The HIPAA name for a health care provider, health plan organization or health care clearinghouse.
j) The HIPAA name for consultant organizations, which may (e.g.,) process claims, transcribe records or analyze data and bills.

2. *What is part of HIPAA/HITECH*? Consider the following security practices, and determine whether or not they are part of HIPAA/HITECH. If they are, what rule (Security, Privacy, Notification) applies? If the Security Rule applies, which aspect: Administrative, Physical, or Technical security?

   a) A doctor should have a clear desk policy.
   b) Computerized transactions which access patient records must be logged.
   c) Patients are entitled to private rooms in a hospital.
   d) If a breach of PHI/EPHI does occur, each affected patient should be notified.
   e) PHI must be locked either in a locked room or in a locked cabinet.
   f) Employees who divulge PHI are susceptible to dismissal.
   g) A person should be designated as a chief of security to ensure the safety of EPHI.
   h) Logs must be monitored on a regular basis.
   i) An organization may be required to pay a maximum penalty of $1 million dollars for a breach.
   j) There should be an incident response plan on how to handle a hacker attack.

3. *Notice of Privacy Practice*. Find a Notice of Privacy Practice for one of your doctors or a hospital near you. You may find it on-line or obtain a paper copy onsite. Summarize what the NPP says and how it protects you.

14.5.1 Health First Case Study Problems

For each case study problem, refer to the Health First Case Study. The Health First Case Study, Security Workbook and Requirements Document should be provided by your instructor or can be found at http://extras.springer.com.

Case study	Health first case study	Other resources
Fraud: Combating social engineering	√	HIPAA slides or notes
Security program development: Editing a policy manual for HIPAA	√	HIPAA slides or notes Security workbook
HIPAA: Including privacy rule adherence to requirements document	√	HIPAA slides or notes Requirements document
Application controls: Extending requirements preparation by planning for HIPAA security rule	√	HIPAA slides or notes Requirements document

References

1. Internet security threat report 2014, vol 19. Symantec Corporation, www.symantec.com, p 42
2. Kempfert AE, Reed BD (2011) Health care reform in the United States: HITECH act and HIPAA privacy, security, and enforcement issues. FDCC Q 61(3):240–273
3. Dalgleish C (2009) Course: HIPAA compliance. Triton College, River Grove, IL
4. Grama JL (2015) Legal issues in information security, 2nd edn. Jones & Bartlett Learning, Burlington, MA, pp 148–187
5. Dowell MA (2012) HIPAA privacy and security HITECH act enforcement actions begin. Employee Benefit Plan Rev 66:9–11, June 2012
6. Bitglass (2014) The 2014 Bitglass healthcare breach report. http://pages.bitglass.com/pr-2014-healthcare-breach-report.html. Accessed 8 Nov 2014
7. Schmitt R (2014) Inside the medicare strike force. AARP Bull 55(9):10–12
8. HHS (2013) HIPAA administrative simplification regulation text. U.S. Department of Health and Human Services Office for Civil Rights, March 2013, pp 59–115

Chapter 15
Developing Secure Software

> Computers have a strange habit of doing what you say, not what you mean. (CWE/SANS Top 25 Monster Mitigations [1])

Some organizations take the view that features are the most important delivery and with limited time and resources, this becomes the focus. At the end, security is added in. The problem with this approach is that deployment may occur with little to no security features. This ensures that the software is defenseless or near defenseless against attackers and data breaches are the inevitable result.

Consider instead that designers and developers know standard security practices, since they were trained in security before their projects began. Security requirements are decided based on risk analysis and regulatory compliance to ensure that high priority risks are mitigated and included in the schedule. Secure designs ensure that the architecture is effective and efficient. When code is written, secure utilities are familiar to the coders and correctly used the first time. Knowledgeable testers perform competent penetration testing and use automated test tools for faster, more accurate testing. The code may still be released before all bugs are fixed, but the organization knows and approves of any security flaws that remain.

This chapter introduces secure software engineering. These techniques are described within the software development lifecycle of Requirements, Design, Coding and Test. It is assumed that the reader has done some programming and testing before reading this chapter. This chapter builds on the Unified Modeling Language (UML), commonly used in design. However, in case the reader has not yet developed expertise in UML, an introduction to each UML diagram is discussed before describing the security enhancements to UML. However, every security-minded software developer should also be aware of common attacks to software.

S. Lincke, *Security Planning*, DOI 10.1007/978-3-319-16027-6_15

15.1 Important Concepts: Attacks to Software

This book has addressed a slew of attacks to computer systems and network, but there are vulnerabilities that are peculiar to software development. General software attacks include buffer overflow, integer/floating point overflows, SQL injection and OS command injection, directory traversal, race conditions, abusing direct object references, and network sniffing or otherwise causing a breach of confidential data.

Most of these attacks are further described elsewhere or will be addressed in specific sections in this chapter, but some attacks need to be further described here. Previously we defined an SQL injection as appending database commands to form input, causing an additional SQL command to occur in addition to the program's intended command. An *OS command injection* is similar, except that an OS command is appended to form input, and is possible if the software enables OS access through the database interface.

A *race condition* enables attackers to see data from other users or to cause a denial of service attack. A race condition is caused when multiple threads simultaneously access shared data within the same process. Critical sections, implemented with semaphores or monitors, ensure safe access when shared data is required.

15.1.1 Service Oriented Architectures and the Web

Most applications today use a client-server, distributed architecture, such as Service-Oriented Architecture (SOA). SOA uses platform neutral messaging, such as HTTP or Extensible Markup Language (XML). Components of the distributed architecture are interoperable, modular and reusable [2]. Services are discoverable, with contract-based interfaces. Service discovery may be implemented via a server yellow page (e.g. Universal Discover Description and Integration Server or UDDI). The discovery service employs an interface description language to describe the calling and return parameters for a web service (e.g., Web Services Description Language, or WSDL) [2]. We will evaluate web services as an example SOA architecture.

The World Wide Web enables hackers from around the world to attack your software from the convenience of wherever the attacker happens to be. In general, client software can easily be modified, rewritten or spoofed to attack. In addition to the attacks listed previously, web attacks may include reading and modifying cookies and causing a victim server to store or execute attacks [3, 4]. Web session IDs may be easily spoofed and cookies modified. Other web attacks are listed in Table 15.1 [5].

Because of the distributed nature of web services, security must be implemented on both client and server sides. Controls for both sides (and transmissions in between) include authentication, authorization, confidentiality, integrity, availability, and non-repudiation [5]. In addition, business rules and regulations must be in effect.

Table 15.1 Web form and web service attacks

Attack name	Attack description
Directory traversal	A URL is coded to access unexpected files or commands on the web server, such as www.company.com/../../cmd. In each of these cases, characters may be encoded to hide their contents: %2e%2e%2 f
WSDL enumeration	The discovery of web services via UDDI or a search for WSDL files for attack purposes
Replay	Transmitted packets may be copied and resent. Packets may also be modified before transmission
URL jumping	To attempt to avoid authentication, web references are accessed out-of-order
XPath injection	Modifies XML format or contents to create unintended data. Attacks are similar to SQL Injection except that XML is attacked instead of SQL
XML overflow	This Denial of Service attack constructs invalid or repeats XML structures in an attempt to confuse the server or overflow memory

Packet replay must be countered. If web sessions are maintained by the server, session IDs should time-out and not be easily guessable [3].

Cross-site scripting (*XSS*) is a common web attack that requires an extended explanation. In an XSS attack, a malicious user provides data that will be executed in other users' browsers. This can occur when an attacker injects data with embedded executable scripts into forms with prebuilt scripts which will be executed [6]. This can occur in three ways [4]:

- Local XSS: Webpage code is modified, often by modifying a Document Object Model (DOM) that is executed using JavaScript.
- Stored XSS: The attacker uses form input to modify a database. The input includes infected links or files.
- Reflective XSS: The victim server returns infected client data, submitted as part of the client input.

Cross Site Scripting can be defended against using a *same-origin policy*. This policy ensures that all components of a web page must use the same protocol and port number, and be derived from the same host. If we compare two URLs: http://www.organization.com/directory1 and https://organization.sales.com:85/directory3, we can see they differ in protocol (http versus https), in port number (default 80 versus specified 85) and in host (www.organization.com and organization.sales.com). Any single difference would violate the same-origin policy.

Cross-site request forgery occurs when a server provides an authentication token to a user, which an attacker copies and uses for similar or other purposes [3]. The root cause of this problem is the pre-approved nature of the authentication token, which instead should be validated on a per input basis. Complete *mediation* ensures that every request to an operating system or server is verified for authorization, regardless of the number of repeated accesses [2].

Attacks may also be application-specific. Therefore, being aware of secure practices at each development stage is important.

15.2 Requirements

The purpose of the Requirements Stage is to determine what the product to be developed will do, who will be using it, and why it is being developed. This stage involves interviewing the customer to find out how the software should look, act and perform; developing a prototype; and may include developing a requirements document, which serves as a contract between the software developers and the customer. A well-designed human–machine interface can minimize user errors and wasted time and thus assure data accuracy and integrity.

Contracts may require that products operate according to security regulation or industry standards, such as Common Criteria, Open Group, or American government standards: NIST or STIGs. ISO 15408 Common Criteria (www.commoncriteriaportal.org) offers a standard for product development and testing, with a rating system between one and seven [2]. Open Group (www.opengroup.org) requires that products specify a list of detailed security features pertaining to authentication, passwords, event notifications, failure handling, access control, object reuse, malware control, and the recognition of tampering [7]. U.S. Defense standards are called Security Technical Information Guides (STIGs): http://iase.disa.mil/stigs. These and NIST sources include a series of documents for security implementation.

The Health First Requirements Document, included at http://extras.springer.com, is an example of a professional requirements document that uses UML Use Cases. The current version of the Requirements Document lacks in privacy and security features and HIPAA adherence. Therefore, there are a number of exercises that the reader can perform to enhance this document for security, privacy and compliance.

The Health First Requirements Document includes a *Use Case Diagram*, which is a single diagram that shows the basic features of the software from a user's perspective—in this case, a doctors' office database. This document also includes *Use Case Descriptions*, which describes how each feature appears to work from a users' perspective. The Use Case Descriptions are described in text by listing the sequential steps of user-does-this and then system-does-this, etc. In the document, each use case is shown with its database form(s) to help the reader understand what the user will see. The reader is encouraged to look through the Requirements Document to get a better feel for these concepts, if the user has little or no experienced with UML requirements and design.

The example demonstrated in this chapter will be a simpler application of a registration system, which distributes documentation or source code to any person who registers for it. Figure 15.1 shows a simple Use Case Diagram for the registration system. In this figure, a Client actor Registers for documentation by entering their name, email and job function, and can Send Feedback after they receive the documentation. The Provider actor may Send Email to the Clients, notifying them of any updates to the documentation. In a Use Case Diagram, *actors*, who are shown as stick figures with labels, are the planned users of the system [8]. The diagram also shows ovals, called *Use Cases*, which each list one basic user feature. Now that you

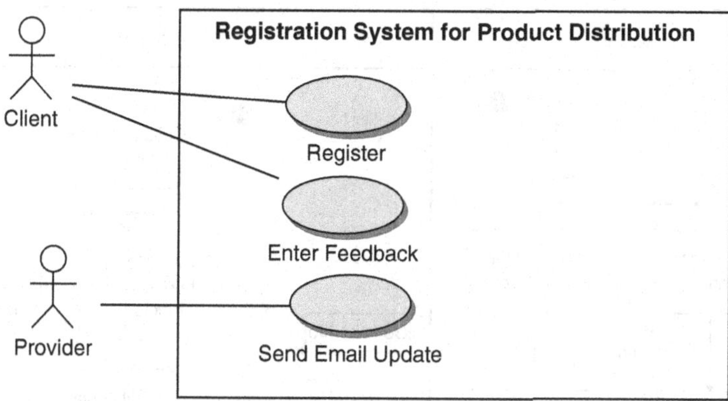

Fig. 15.1 Registration use case diagram

understand the basic demo application, we will proceed with designing requirements for it. The first step is risk analysis.

The *OCTAVE Security Requirements Process* defines how risk analysis (also known as threat modeling) can be performed for software. (OCTAVE is an abbreviation for Operationally Critical Threat, Asset and Vulnerability Evaluation.) OCTAVE steps include [9]:

1. Identify critical assets
2. Define security goals
3. Identify threats
4. Analyze risks
5. Define security requirements

The first step, *Identify Critical Assets*, is concerned with describing the assets (e.g., data) that the software will be working with. Figure 15.2 shows a Business Process Model (or Activity Diagram) for the Registration System, split into two parts to demonstrate a flow chart for each of the two actors, Client and Administrator. The solid bullet is where each user starts, and each actor performs the activities (shown as rounded-corner rectangles) in order as the arrows indicate. Notice that the data, shown as squared-off rectangles, are either created or accessed by both the actors. When the dotted arrow points to the data, the data is created or modified, whereas if the dotted arrow points to the activity, the activity is reading the data. In any case, the data (or assets) to protect in this diagram include Contact Information, Materials and Comments. This represents the registration information (name, email, job function), documentation to be distributed, and feedback, respectively.

The second OCTAVE step, *Define security goals*, considers how the three security goals: confidentiality, integrity and availability each relate to the three data assets of the Registration System. In Table 15.2, each data is rated from 1 to 3 to represent low (*), moderate (**) and high (***) for each security goal. For this example, we want to distribute the materials to the public (preferably with their

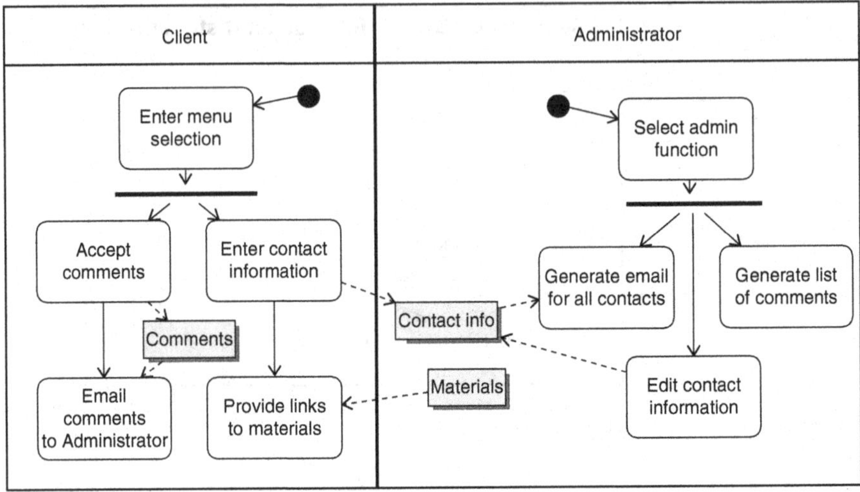

Fig. 15.2 Business process model for registration system

Table 15.2 Define security goals

Assets	Confidentiality	Integrity	Availability
Contact Info	** No PII maintained	*** Require accurate list of interested persons	* Weekly backup
Materials	* Public with login	*** Accurate – tamper-proof	** 24/7 preferred
Comments	** Confidential pref.	*** Accurate – tamper-proof	* Weekly backup, email

registration), so the requirement for Confidentiality of Materials is rated low = 1. However, we would like the materials to be accurate, so the requirement for Integrity of Materials is rated high = 3. Availability for the materials is important, but if the registration system is down for a couple days, since the materials are free, there is no financial loss. Therefore the requirement for Availability of Materials is rated moderate = 2.

The third OCTAVE step, *Identify threats*, considers what threats the software may be vulnerable to. Consider who your adversaries are, and what they are interested in. Figure 15.3 shows the *STRIDE threat model*, where each letter in STRIDE represents a threat to consider (S = Spoof, T = Tamper, etc.) In this diagram, the left column describes what the threat is, then the two right describes example software enhancements, in increasing sophistication, to combat that threat.

A much more extensive threat model is provided by The *Common Attack Pattern Enumeration and Classification* (*CAPEC*™) initiative (https://capec.mitre.org).

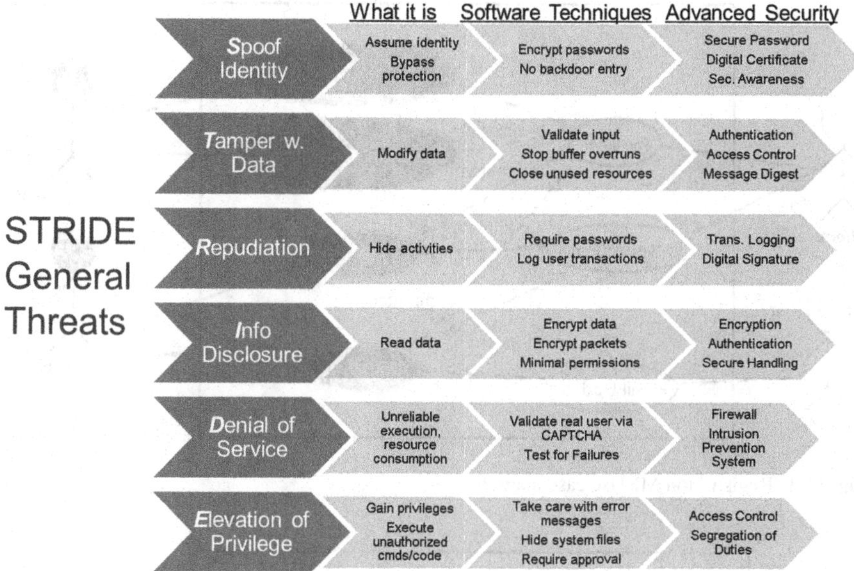

STRIDE General Threats
What it is
Software Techniques
Advanced Security
Spoof Identity
Assume identity
Bypass protection
Encrypt passwords
No backdoor entry
Secure Password
Digital Certificate
Sec. Awareness
Tamper w. Data
Modify data
Validate input
Stop buffer overruns
Close unused resources
Authentication
Access Control
Message Digest
Repudiation
Hide activities
Require passwords
Log user transactions
Trans. Logging
Digital Signature
Info Disclosure
Read data
Encrypt data
Encrypt packets
Minimal permissions
Encryption
Authentication
Secure Handling
Denial of Service
Unreliable execution, resource consumption
Validate real user via CAPTCHA
Test for Failures
Firewall
Intrusion Prevention System
Elevation of Privilege
Gain privileges
Execute unauthorized cmds/code
Take care with error messages
Hide system files
Require approval
Access Control
Segregation of Duties

Fig. 15.3 Identify threats with STRIDE

The "What it is" column in Fig. 15.3 is a summary of their weaknesses. Their Common Weakness Risk Analysis Framework recommends prioritizing weaknesses specifically for your software, from their accumulated weakness list. Your implementation would address your highest priority weaknesses.

After gaining an understanding of threats, we need to apply them to the Registration System. For that we can use a *MisUse Case Diagram*—a kind of Use Case Diagram that also shows the 'features' or attacks a hacker or fraudster may use to threaten our system (Fig. 15.4). The MisUse Case Diagram adds attackers or MisUsers as black-headed stick persons, and MisUse Cases as black ovals, naming attacks [10]. (This is of course, independent of the skin color of the actual actor and MisUser!) The dotted arrows point from the MisUse Cases to the Use Cases they "threaten". MisUse Cases are labeled similar to Use Cases in 'Verb Noun' or 'Verb Adjective Noun' form, such as 'Launch DOS' or 'Change Valid Data'. Most of these diagrams are drawn with SeaMonster [11], but in many cases other commercial tools or Suraksha can also color use cases and/or actors with some finagling.

With further consideration, we can think of more attacks, which causes the diagram to become a bit unruly. Inheritance can compress our threats, by having specific threats point to generalized threats. This is shown in Fig. 15.5. An alternative solution is to generate a MisUse Case Diagram per Use Case.

A *Threat Tree* may also document likely attacks [13], such as in Fig. 15.6. An advantage of developing such a Threat Tree is that they are portable to other similar products/environments. A good one can be reused from one similar product to another, and need only be maintained as new threats, products, and/or environments arise.

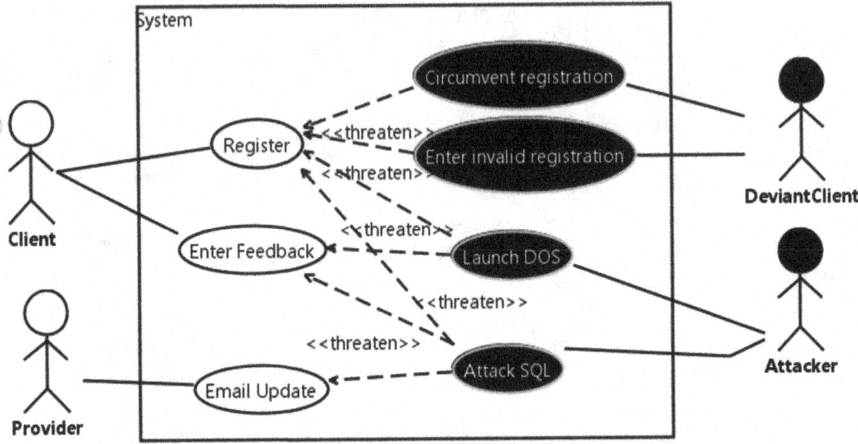

Fig. 15.4 Registration MisUse case diagram

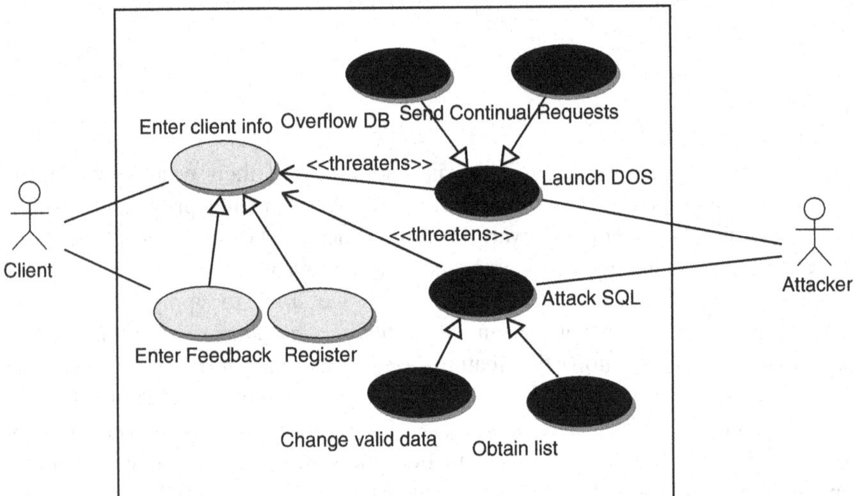

Fig. 15.5 MisUse case diagram with inheritance [12]

There are three main attacks we will discuss here in depth. One attack is that someone might obtain materials without registering, for example by searching the Internet for them. Another attack may be a Denial of Service, where an automated system registers random garbage to quickly fill up our database with garbage registrants. A third problem might be an SQL attack, where an attacker adds SQL commands to our form input, to perform unintended database commands.

We have an idea of the possible threats, but now let us consider the details. For each MisUse Case oval, we create one *MisUse Case Description*. The MisUse Case

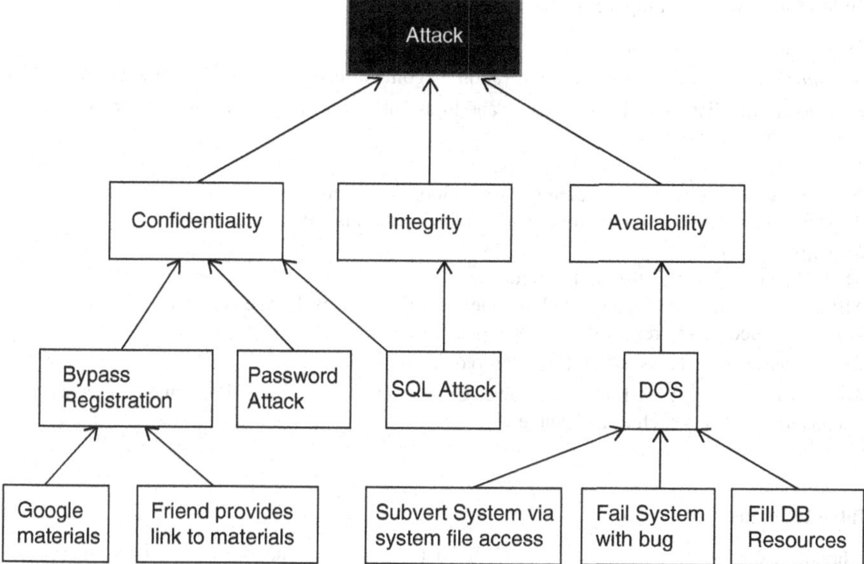

Fig. 15.6 Threat tree for registration system

Table 15.3 Launch denial of service MisUse case

MisUse Case: Launch denial of service
Summary: An attacker issues repeated Registrations, resulting in filling the database with fake data, and depleting system and file resources
Basic path: 1. Do forever 2. The attacker requests a Registration form 3. The attacker sends random fake data in the form 4. Enddo
Alternative paths: AP1. Repeat data is entered
Mitigation points: MP1. At BP Step 2–3 use CAPTCHA in Registration form to avoid bot attack MP2. At BP Step 3 validate data: no duplicates, data type matching

Description describes the steps of an attack [14], similar to how a Use Case Description describes the steps of a normally executing process. Table 15.3 shows the detailed Launch Denial of Service MisUse Case attack. The Basic Path is a numbered outline of the steps of the attack. The Alternate Paths section describes slightly variant attack methods. The Mitigation Points section describes how we intend to defend against this attack type. Our Mitigation Point 1 (MP1) says that at Basic Path (BP) steps 2–3 we will use CAPTCHA to avoid a Distributed Denial of Service (DDOS) attack. A CAPTCHA requests that users enter the letters/numbers shown in an image on the form. CAPTCHA is used to maximize the possibility that the user is a real person, and not an automated program.

Table 15.4 Circumvent input MisUse case

Misuse case: Circumvent input
Summary: Deviant client bypasses registration by going directly to the download web page
PreCondition: Client does Google search and finds link to download web page OR obtains link reference from a colleague
Basic path: 1. DeviantClient obtains web reference from Google or friend 2. DeviantClient uses web reference to download materials without registering
Mitigation points: MP1: Web page has no other web references MP2: Create dynamic web page with unique reference. This web page is accessible only if a key is provided during registration. Key expires in 1 week
Related business rule: Users must register to obtain materials
Mitigation guarantee: MP1 and MP2 solves Google search problems. MP2 could be used by friends for 1 week, which is acceptable

Table 15.5 Risk analysis

Threat	Impact	Likelihood	Priority = I*L
DOS	***	***	9
SQL Attack (affects integrity, confidentiality)	***	***	9
Invalid Input	*	***	3
Circumvent input	**	***	6

Heavyweight Misuse Case Descriptions include additional information, such as: Extension points, Triggers, Preconditions, Assumptions, Mitigation guarantee, Related business rules, Stakeholders and threats, Terminology and explanations, Scope, Abstraction level and Precision level [14]. An example MisUse Case Description with more options is shown in Table 15.4, which describes how a user could bypass registration. This description includes a Precondition, Related Business Rule and Mitigation Guarantee.

The fourth OCTAVE step is *Analyze risks*. In this step, SANS recommends considering the damage that may arise from loss of reputation and user productivity, and legal issues. Consider also the ease of attack and attack repetition, and the ease of detecting a successful penetration [15]. Similar to calculating organizational risk, the risk priority is calculated as Impact multiplied by Likelihood. In Table 15.5, both Impact and Likelihoods are rated on a 1–10 scale (here 1–3, with three stars being serious.) Any threat which negatively affects the database is considered serious (***). Invalid Input affects only one user's registration, and so has a low impact rating. The final priority scores are high (9) for Launch DOS and SQL Attack, moderate (6) for Circumvent Input, and low (3) for Invalid Input.

The fifth and last OCTAVE step is *Define security requirements*. In this step we document the security functions or features in detail using a Security Use Case Diagram and Security Use Case Descriptions.

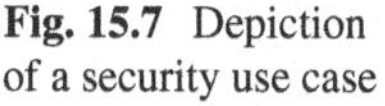

Fig. 15.7 Depiction of a security use case

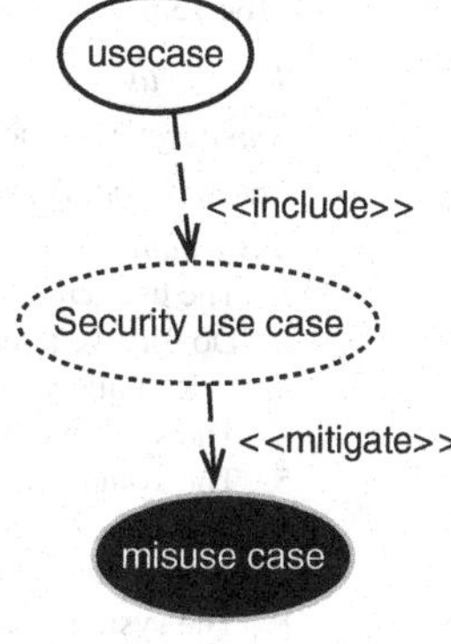

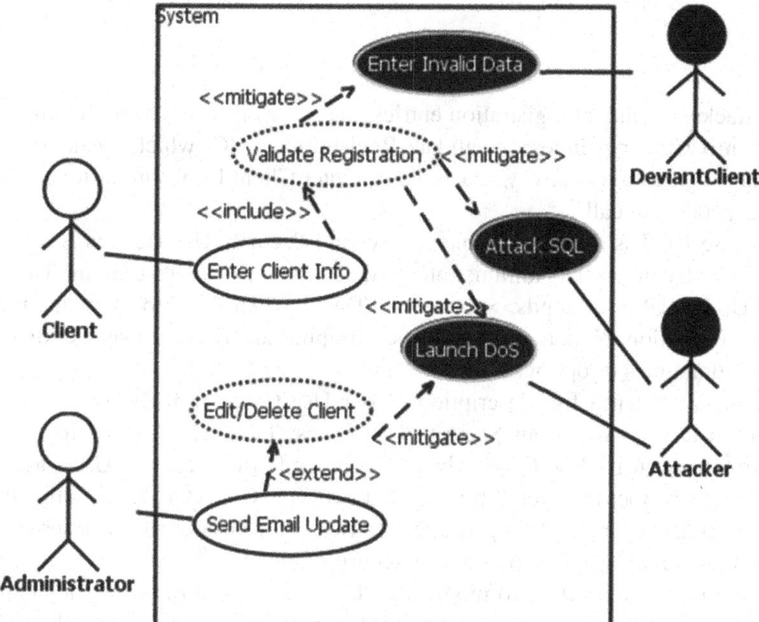

Fig. 15.8 Security use case diagram for three threats

We can modify our MisUse Case Diagram to include *Security Use Cases*, which are white ovals describing a security feature. (Retain a copy of the original MisUse Case Diagram, before modifying it!) A Security Use Case (SUC) is shown in Fig. 15.7. Basically, our original user feature, shown as a use case (UC), <<includes>> a SUC which <<mitigates>> one or more misuse cases (MUC).

Figure 15.8 is an applied Security Use Case Diagram mitigating three of our threats: Launch DOS, Attack SQL, and Enter Invalid Data MUCs. The Validate Registration SUC will include a CAPTCHA check and will validate input to prevent

Table 15.6 Validate registration security use case

Security use case: Validate registration
Summary: This include validates a registration
Precondition: A name, email, job function, and Captcha are provided
Basic path: 1. The user enters a name, email, and job function in Step 3 of Register 2. Do for five attempts or until valid CAPTCHA: 3. Rerequest form with new CAPTCHA 4. The system checks for valid characters, to prevent SQL injection 5. The system checks for valid name, email and job function 6. If email is unique in database 7. Save record to database 8. The system returns success
Postconditions: The input has been checked for bot attempt, SQL injection, and validity

SQL attacks, redundant registration entries and other mistakes. Note that the Enter Client Info UC <<includes>> Validate Registration SUC, which means that that Validate Registration is *always* executed by Enter Client Info, similar to an unconditional procedure call.

Because DOS is a severe problem, a second Security Use Case is Edit/Delete Client, which enables the Administrator to delete suspicious registrations. The Send Email Update UC <<extends>> to the Edit/Delete Client SUC to show that it is an optional execution. Note that <<includes>> implies always, whereas <<extends>> implies sometimes or optional.

We have written a full description of our Use Cases and MisUse Cases, and we should also do so of our Security Use Cases. Table 15.6 shows the Validate Registration Security Use Case, which is patterned after a regular Use Case. The Basic Path describes the overall functions of verifying CAPTCHA, validating input, and checking for duplicate registration entries. The Postcondition describes the attacks that are mitigated as part of this security function.

Certainly it is important to modify the Use Cases to show when they call the SUCs. An example is shown in Table 15.7, which shows the Register Use Case. An Include statement is shown in bold and italic for emphasis. The Include calls the Validate Registration SUC.

While the full requirements cannot be fully shown in this chapter, we summarize the Security Requirements with the following Business Rules [12]:

1. Users cannot access the web pages without registering their emails into the system;
2. Email registrations shall be accurate;
3. The database with user emails shall not be easily broken into;
4. It is not easy to circumvent the registration process;
5. The registration system is near-immune to DDOS attacks; and
6. Obvious attacks would be logged and emailed to the administrator.

Table 15.7 Use case includes security use case

Use case: Register
Summary: Client registers to obtain access to download materials
Preconditions: Client is at welcome web page
Basic path: 1. The client selects the Obtain Materials link 2. The system asks the client for name, email address, job function, and CAPTCHA 3. The client enters all three required information 4. ***Include (validate registration)*** 5. The system displays the URL for the download materials
Alternative path: AP1. If an attack is detected, no URL is displayed
Postcondition: The client has access to the download materials The database contains the client contact information

This example has given an overview of the different steps and activities that make up the OCTAVE risk analysis through using MisUse Cases. To complete the full requirements would mean documenting all the UCs, MUCs and SUCs. A Requirements Inspection provides feedback from the customer, experienced security/design staff and/or auditors, to avoid future problems. Errors found and fixed at this stage save re-development time and the high costs of security breaches, following deployment.

15.2.1 Specify Reliability

The availability requirements are not severe for this registration system. However, for mission critical systems, such as air transportation or defense software, reliability may be a life or death concern. Reliability can be defined as software operating as expected, for a defined duration of time and within defined conditions [16]. Reliability engineers calculate the failure rate of all mission critical components of a system, to determine the allowable tolerance (or intolerance) for failure. Reliability requirement statistics are defined in the contract and requirements, and then must be implemented in later development stages. Metrics that may be specified in a contract, project plan, reliability plan and/or the non-functional requirements section of a Requirements document include [16]:

- Number of defects in software: failure rate data, measured during test and deployment; or defect density, measured as the number of defects per thousand lines of code.
- Total test time/performance: Considers the failure count relative to total test time or total CPU time during testing; mean time between failures.

- Defect elimination metrics: defects found per development stage: A mature organization can predict, for a given size of code, how many defects should be found per development stage inspection and testing. If expected defects are not found, quality control is probably lacking and the project is at risk of a high defect rate.

These metrics may be required to be simply provided and/or to achieve a specified level of reliability.

15.3 Analysis/Design

The purpose of the Analysis/Design Stage is to determine how the software will be built to fulfill the features specified during the Requirements Stage. During design, the eventual product is taking shape and details in the implementation are becoming known. If we consider that a suit of armor protects a knight's attack surface (by covering nearly his entire body), how can our program also be completely protected? An *attack surface analysis* considers where newly arising vulnerabilities may lie that have not already been considered. An *attack surface minimization* considers how features may be turned off, wherever possible, as part of a least privilege implementation [2]. Error or exception handling is also carefully designed. Considering our Registration System case, new concerns will naturally arise during Design related to a web service implementation.

Within UML, two aspects of design include [8]:

1. Static Model: These diagrams show the structure of the software, including classes, components and subsystems.
2. Dynamic Model: These diagrams describe the system behavior, including how each Use Case is executed.

15.3.1 Static Model

In large standardized systems, such as Open Group's Common Data Security Architecture (CDSA), security may be layered as shown in Fig. 15.9 [17]. The application issues requests through an Application Programming Interface to the Common Security Services Manager. Within the security manager, the upper layer includes security services, such as digital certificate and key management, while the lowest layers are library utilities for specific functions. All interfaces are specified. This implementation takes advantage of software reuse and reliability.

Regardless of the actual architecture used, during Static Modeling a blueprint of the new service is developed. Subsystems are shown as folders in UML. Figure 15.10 shows how a CAPTCHA and Sanitizer security packages <<protects>> the Registration Subsystem. The purpose of the Sanitizer package is to validate

Application					
Common Security Services Manager Application Programming Interface					
System Security Services (Digital Certificate, key management, integrity services, security contexts)					
Cryptographic Services Mgr.	Trust Policy Services Mgr.	Authorization Computation Mgr.	Certificate Library Mgr.	Data Storage Library Mgr.	Elective Module Mgr.
CS Library	Trust Library	AC Library	Cert. Library	DS Library	New Services Lib.

Fig. 15.9 Open group's common data security architecture

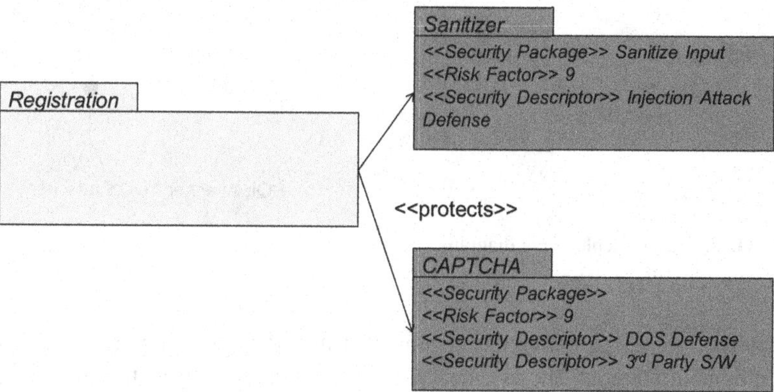

Fig. 15.10 Documenting security packages

(or sanitize) user input. Security packages can be labelled with a <<Security Package>> label and name, a <<Risk Factor>> showing the priority calculated during Requirements, and one or more <<Security Descriptor>>, which describe the threat(s) that the package defends against [18].

At a more detailed (drill-down) level, each subsystem could be diagramed using a class diagram. Of course some classes and even patterns of classes will have security functions, but security does not change how Class Diagrams work.

Components are reusable software modules that could be classes or subsystems. For example, CAPTCHA, VPN, database server, and Sanitizer modules are plug-in utility software, which certainly qualify as components. Figure 15.9 is an example of a MisUse Deployment Diagram showing components as pink (or gray) rectangles. Components have standardized input and output to serve as an explicit interface that the utility component advertises to the outside world.

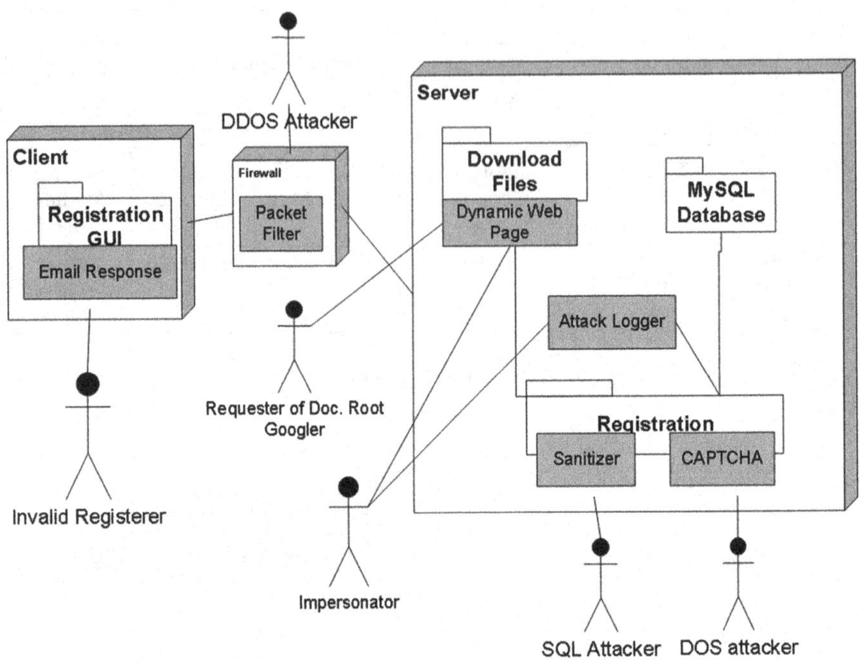

Fig. 15.11 A MisUse deployment diagram

With the Internet, software has become distributed in its deployment and/or use. A Deployment Diagram shows where the various components of the software will reside (e.g., on client or server) [8]. A *MisUse Deployment Diagram* or *MDD* (Fig. 15.11) in addition shows where security components reside, and the attacks that those security components mitigate. This single diagram is useful in that it easily shows the concrete security deployment, including how attacks can be mitigated across systems [12]. For example, input validation must occur to combat SQL attacks. But if this validation occurs only on the client side, security is inadequate. Therefore, the location of security code is as important as its existence. In Fig. 15.11, the Sanitizer is on the Server side, protecting against an SQL Attack there.

In a MDD, Misusers represent general attack types. Packages are shown in white to represent application subsystems, and in pink to represent security components or packages. The attack name is assigned to the misuser. Figure 15.10 was drawn with Microsoft Visio [12].

Security components for the Register System are described as follows [12]:

- Dynamic web pages: Ensures documents are available only at download time. Server-side programs enforce registration, by requiring users to register their email address.
- Downloads provided by email: Users obtain the Dynamic web page via email following registration.

- CAPTCHA: CAPTCHA helps to mitigate automated Distributed Denial of Service attacks.
- Input sanitization and validation: A server-side program allows all user input from the registration form to be sanitized of input attacks such as cross-site scripts or SQL injections. The program also validates all incoming data.
- Event logging: A server-side program logs any event needing to be tracked, thus providing a record of activity at the web site. Each system module has the ability to write information to the system log. The amount of logging is configurable.

15.3.2 Dynamic Model

The purpose of this model is to design the behavior of the classes, components and subsystems defined in the Static Model. Sequence Diagrams show how objects (or class instances) interact in order to fulfill a use case [8]. Figure 15.12 is an example Sequence Diagram for the Register Use Case. At the top of the diagram are objects, shown as actor instances or as rectangles listing object names. Theoretically, objects send messages to other objects, which are shown as labelled arrows between the objects. In practice, messages are method calls or packet transmissions, and the labels represent the method or packet name. Figure 15.12 shows packet transmissions between the actors on the client side, and the Register and Download software on the Server side [12]; each arrow represents one packet transmission, where dotted arrows show responses to solid arrows.

In Fig. 15.12, a Legal:Client requests the materials using the Request_Info message sent to the Register program. The Register program replies with the

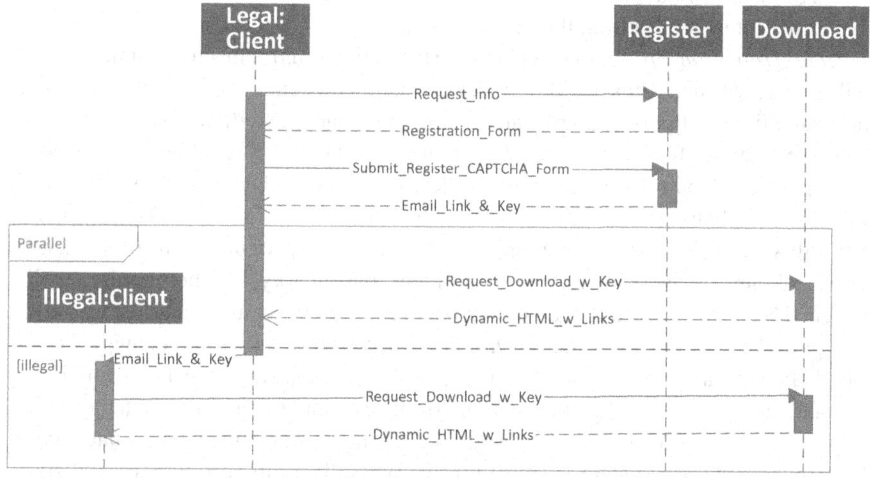

Fig. 15.12 MisSequence diagram for the register use case model [12]

Registration_Form, which the Legal:Client completes and sends in as a completed Submit_Register_CAPTCHA_Form. The form data is received by Register, which sanitizes and validates the form data including verifying the CAPTCHA input. Once the input is validated, Register inserts Legal:Client's registration data into the database, together with a newly generated unique key. Register then sends an email to Legal:Client's email address, shown in Fig. 15.11 as the message Email_Link_&_Key. This email contains a link back to the dissemination web site. The link includes an appended unique access key.

When the link is clicked by the user, an HTTP Request_Download_with_Key message is sent to the Download program. The key contained in the packet identifies the user as having previously registered with the web site and serves as a type of password for temporary access to the downloadable files. Thus, without a valid email, no download occurs.

When the Download program receives the key or temporary password, it generates a Dynamic_HTML_with_Links for Legal:Client. The downloadable files are provided temporarily during the web access and deleted soon after. This minimizes the possibility of non-registrants obtaining the downloadable files. The dynamic web page ensures that search engines will not ordinarily provide access to this page.

While Sequence Diagrams generally shows normally executing logic, *Mis-Sequence Diagrams* also show attack handling logic [19]. Attacks are shown as conditional logic, which demonstrate how attacks are received and handled. The Parallel box at the bottom of the diagram shows the normal occurrence on top half of the Parallel box, and the attack in the bottom half, below the dashed line. The Parallel label indicates that the two activities can occur together. In this attack, Legal:Client passes the email with link and key to their friend, Illegal:Client, during the one week duration the key is valid. This is shown as the Email_Link_&_Key message sent from Legal:Client to Illegal:Client, and Illegal:Client's subsequent access to the downloadable data. We have no easy fix to this, but some risk is acceptable in the interest of getting the system up quickly.

State Transition Diagrams (STDs or State Diagrams) can ensure integrity of real-time processing, thus avoiding incorrect actions when receiving a right input at the wrong time [20]. For example, an ATM money machine will not give you money whenever you ask for it; you must slide your card and enter your PIN first, then you can input the amount of money you would like. Thus, STDs show how one class/object should behave, depending on what state that object is in. STDs can ensure that software retains the proper order of processing, recognizes out-of-sequence steps, and can change behavior based on time or past history. In other words, a well-designed STD can ensure that an object behaves properly in all scenarios.

Figure 15.13 is an example STD. STDs have states, shown as rectangles with rounded edges, and transitions, shown as labelled arrows. Any object can only be in one state at a time. The object transitions from one state to another when any of its outgoing transitions is received or becomes true; then it transitions to the state where the arrow points. Each state is split into two parts. The top part contains the state name. The bottom part shows the processing that occurs in the state, and which does not cause a transition to a different state. This bottom part describes Events that may

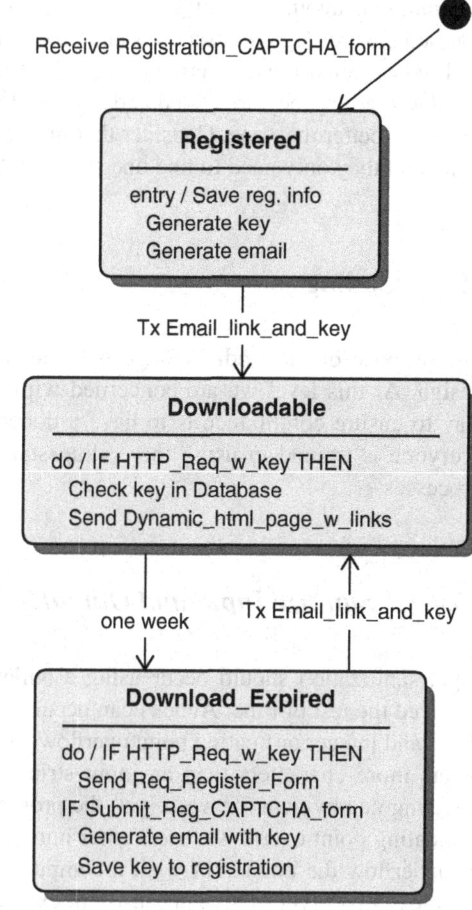

Fig. 15.13 State transition diagram for client

be received, and how they are handled. In Fig. 15.13, events include entry/ and do/. The entry/ event indicates that this processing should occur once, on entry to the state. The do/ text indicates that this processing should occur whenever the described event occurs: in Fig. 15.13, when a HTTP_Request_with_Key is received. In other words, with do/ the described processing can occur multiple times; once per event.

Figure 15.13 is a state diagram for the state of a Client. The first state, Registered, is entered upon receipt of a validated Submit_Register_CAPTCHA_form. On entry/ to the Registered state, the Register program saves the registration information, and generates the email with associated key for LegalClient. This is transmitted to LegalClient in the Email_Link_and_Key message, which then sets the new state of LegalClient to Downloadable. In the Downloadable state, the Download program validates the key in the database before sending the Dynamic_HTML_page_with_links. LegalClient stays in the Downloadable state until 1 week expires. Then LegalClient transitions to the Download_Expired state. The single remaining transition that can get LegalClient back to the Downloadable state, is if the Register program gets another Email_Link_and_Key message from LegalClient. This state diagram ensures legal transactions and processing for any Client object.

The last step is the inspection for the Design. Security experts can help find security flaws before they are coded and deployed. When evaluating a design, multiple heads are better than one. Consider that multiple heads will be attacking your software, and they only need to find one strong vulnerability.

15.4 Coding

The purpose of the Coding Stage is to develop the programs to implement the design. At this level we are concerned with secure coding techniques. The best way to ensure compliance is to have a documented coding standard and ensure everyone is trained in using the coding standard as well as secure utilities and processes.

15.4.1 Sanitize Input and Output!

Input sanitization should occur using a bullet-proof standardized utility that has survived the test of time. Attacks can occur at raw input stage, such as buffer overflows and integer or floating point overflows. In the case of buffer overflow, the user enters more characters than an input string buffer allows for, spilling over and affecting nearby data (or worse yet, the program stack) [21]. In the case of integer or floating point overflows, users enter numbers large or small enough to overflow or underflow the bounds of what a computer can store in a normal integer, float, double or other type. This can cause (for example) large numbers to appear small or become negative, and cause negative numbers to become positive [21]. Calculated totals are also subject to underflow and overflow. Therefore, verify length before reading in data and use an input utility where you specify the maximum buffer size.

Data should also be correctly typed and the syntax should be checked. Java and other type-safe languages are safer than C/C++, which allow more flexibility in type conversions. Any input from an external source should be suspect, including: parameters or arguments, cookies, network packets, environment variables, client request headers/data, query/server results, URL components, e-mail, files and databases [1].

A second type of input error is data that may appear correct in length, type and syntax, but is not correct. One example is the SQL or OS Injection attack, where SQL or OS statements are appended to form input to attack a database [21]. Standard utilities can help to prevent attacks. OWASP is an organization dedicated to free, open source, secure application code. Their ESAPI (Enterprise Security Applications Programmer Interface) includes a Validation API that defends against masterfully coded attacks.

Fig. 15.14 A car purchase form

Car Sale

Model: Chevrolet XR2 Price $: 25.45
VIN: 12K4FG436DDE842 Status: New

Sale to: Rubber Ducky
2222 Atlantic Ocean
Antarctica, NY, 00000

Phone: 911 VISA: RUAFOOL444

Figure 15.14 shows a second example, where most data is typed reasonably and does not overflow, but is horribly fraudulent. Useful input validation techniques include *whitelisting*, which checks against a list of acceptable input, or *blacklisting*, which rejects suspect input [1]. Regardless, input should be consistent across the form and adhere to business rules. Simple business rules specify required and optional input data. The Audit chapter describes other input validation checks that can prevent this type of fraud.

Let us assume that you (or another programmer) validate all input, but missed one spot. Now your application is spreading an attack to other internal systems and possibly to anyone unfortunate enough to click on your website. These dangerous attacks include cross-site scripting and cross-site request forgery, discussed previously. You can counteract these attacks by separating your database commands from data streams [1], carefully validating input, and by specifying strong character encoding on output such as UTF-8 or ISO-8859. (These are standardized character sets: UTF-8 is an abbreviation for Unicode Transformation Format using 8 bits.)

Finally, it is important to sanitize input at the server, since client input validation can easily be circumvented [1]. Also, when coding reusable modules, it is important to ensure that all data is cleared between different entities [7]. Input from any source shall not be trusted, whether it is from the keyboard, a data transmission, a file, an internal or external process, or an attached device. Any source may become hacked, affecting your code.

15.4.2 Never Expose Internal Data Structures

Web programmers may send information within forms or encoded URLs to help servers process them once these transactions are submitted back. This information may consist of database keys, object references or IDs, or file references. An attacker can manipulate this information within forms to directly access other records or resources [3]. To prevent attacks on integrity, perform all transaction translations at the server, and/or use strong encryption to cipher internal information.

15.4.3 Minimize Access

If an attacker successfully attacks your code, restrain what they can do and have access to. Therefore, limit access to privileges, resources and the operating system. When privileges are needed raise them; but lower them as soon as possible thereafter. Here are some important considerations [1]:

- Permissions: Use authorization levels and access control to minimize permissions at all times: anonymous, normal, privileged, administrative. Only provide higher level access when you need it.
- Resources: Keep resources such as files, devices, and communications open for the smallest period possible. If you are done using a resource, close it! Not closing resources leaves file open to attack and keeps unnecessary resources busy.
- *Jail*: The operating system can impose resource limits on programs, including I/O bandwidth, disk quotas, network access restrictions and a restricted file system namespace.
- Caching: Sensitive pages are never cached and must have an active authorization token.
- Credentials: Never hardcode a login/password credential, in case the login/password is discovered.

15.4.4 Use Tried-and-True Security Algorithms

An *Open Design* builds on algorithms created and shared by multiple users to withstand the test of time. In addition to input sanitization algorithms, other algorithms critical to security include: encryption, integrity, authentication, authorization, session management, logging, and good random number generators [1]. Rather than designing your own security algorithms and software, public software survives based on the strength of the security algorithm and correctness of implementation [2]. Investigate development frameworks to find one that provides solid and standard utilities for security operations. However, even with apparently tried-and-true open source software, you are responsible for your code. Use due care and due diligence to evaluate, properly implement, and test these tools well. After all, public authentication algorithms may exist with no or poor password encryption.

Developing secure software requires using secure software methods. Encryption and integrity (hashing) tools or protocols must be of standardized high-security algorithms, used for both storage and transmissions of sensitive data. Integrity hashes protect file transfers of code and data files from DNS spoofing or cache poisoning attacks [21]. Session key generation must rely upon a good random number generator to create random session keys. If keys are not random, attackers will figure out the next key sequence. Encryption should be used end-to-end, such that wherever the data is transmitted or stored, the data is safely encrypted.

When implementing encryption, consider that an attacker may replay a known good packet. A defense against replay is the *nonce*, which is an active authorization ticket. The nonce is a security passcode or permission tag that limits the maximum time the user has to respond. CAPTCHA is an example of a nonce used for session authentication.

Logs used for audit purposes (as opposed to debug) should include [6]: identity (e.g., username or email and IP address); UTC time and date; event code, description and outcome; and important events such as user authentication/authorization, changes to configuration for security or logging, and logging maintenance activities.

15.4.5 Validate and Control the Configuration

Programs often require additional files to run properly, such as configuration or environmental files. If these files are accessible to an attacker, they can be changed, which can cause your program to operate in a way you did not intend. These files should be stored in a location that prevents access to users. Consider two scenarios:

- Your program is on a client computer, accessing files on the client computer;
- Your program is a web program, accessing files that are unintentionally publicly accessible (via URL).

To ensure that the files you depend on are properly stored in a secure location, use the full pathname to access the file, then validate that the file does indeed have the required minimal access permissions. These are good defenses to ensure an administrator has installed the files properly. If instead you specify "security.dat" as a pathname, indicating the file is in the current directory, this file can be replaced when the executable is run from another location.

If your program is on a website, there must be an agreement that certain paths where files are stored have restricted outside access [21].

It may be tempting to avoid a configuration file and hardcode all necessary configurations in your code. First, assume that the attacker can and will reverse engineer your code and can easily learn your hard-coded secrets [1]. Second, this is a particularly bad idea if specifying a password—if an attacker finds it, every system can be broken into before software is changed on all computers [21]. Instead, passwords should be stored in an encrypted file.

15.4.6 Managing Exceptions

Reliable code does not fail easily. Problems may occur due to operational failures of hardware, software components or networks, or due to permission failures or revocations, policy failures, and context invalidations, among other causes [22].

When an exception occurs, the programmer can abort, continue or commit (complete) the operation. From the user perspective, recovery is preferable and may be required for a mission critical function. Exceptions should be recovered from at lower action-oriented levels where the specific condition is known, when possible. If not, exceptions can be handled at a higher operational level. While automatic exception handling is preferred, a means of manual intervention may be required for mission critical code. Deciding the proper functionality during failure is best decided during the Requirements and Analysis stages.

15.4.7 Use Safe Coding Practices

Static analysis inspects the code without execution [23]. This can occur via code inspections and/or automated testing. Automated static analysis tools provide warnings beyond what a compiler normally provides. Alternatively, some compilers have security-related options that can notify you of security vulnerabilities [1]. It is recommended to fix all warnings. These analysis tools, for example, point out variable or environment contents that may not be initialized, thereby potentially leaking previous data to unrelated users. An example tool is HP Fortify Software [23]. Fortify tests for SQL injection, overflows and HTTP response validation, which can catch cross-site scripting vulnerabilities, cache poisoning and hijacking attacks [4, 23]. NIST offers a Source Code Security Analyzers evaluation sheet at: http://samate.nist.gov/index.php/Source_Code_Security_Analyzers.html.

Error messages should be helpful to the user, but some messages can be too explicit. Chatty error messages tell an attacker about your configuration and internal software operations: e.g., "Cannot find file: C:/users/Lincke/validation.txt" or "Invalid password for login ID", or "Lab.cs.uwp.edu error: divide by zero". Error messages should avoid file, network configuration and personal information [1]. Be sure to remove debug information before release.

15.5 Testing

The purpose of the Test Stage is to *verify* that the code fulfills the requirements and *validate* that the code works as expected. The first step before testing occurs is to determine the attack surface [6]. OCTAVE Risk Analysis results can be used as input for test development. A minimum standard of acceptance (Bug Bar) is determined and also used in developing test plans for certification. Testing plans and results should be documented as part of quality assurance. After the product is certified, an accreditation authority then approves the product for production and use.

Automated testing is cheap to perform and is likely to be performed by crackers. It is better to know the results first! Automated tools include vulnerability or penetration tests, for example for web security in testing SQL injection. Other dynamic tools include fuzz testing, robustness testing, and vulnerability scanners. In some cases, test code may need to be developed since the available tools will not work with your configuration.

Fuzz and robustness testing generate a large number of inputs or interactions that can find subtle flaws that may be missed by static analysis, such as environmental problems. *Fuzz testing* generates random input to test handling of exceptions and incorrect input [6].

Reliability testing ensures that the software can survive unusual conditions, such as faults or unusual operating conditions. Some software failures can impact human life; thus it is important to determine the failure rate particularly of mission critical functions, whose functions shall not fail. Some tools (e.g., Holodeck) can simulate faults to debug error handling [23]. Some tools perform load testing, with multiple simultaneous users, to evaluate performance and bottlenecks (e.g., Load Runner). It is also helpful to run the program under low memory conditions or insufficient privileges, and to break a connection before a transaction is completed [6]. Software may slow down but should not crash or generate incorrect results.

Third party code is the quick way to coding—but it can be risky. It is recommended to avoid third party code unless that software is highly trusted [21]. If you do use this code, the software should be well tested. This program should be first evaluated within a *sandbox*, which quarantines an untrusted program as it runs. Monitoring tools that examine processes as they interact with the OS include Truss (Solaris), Strace (Linux), FileMon, RegMon, Process Monitor, Sysinternals (Windows), sniffers and protocol analyzers.

At the end of the testing process, the software may be certified [24]. A *Bug Bar* is a security threshold for release that ensures that software is not released with high risk security defects. The threshold is defined preferably at the requirements stage, and software is not released until the defined security threshold is achieved. Microsoft uses the Bug Bar standard to evaluate the effects of security defects, which they consider the most important and reliable attribute in measuring a security fault. The Bug Bar defines defect levels for each STRIDE threat category as high, moderate or low. A simplified sample for the Tampering and Repudiation threat categories, related to servers, is shown in Table 15.8 [25].

Table 15.8 Bug bar example for tampering/repudiation

Bug bar standard for tampering and repudiation	Severity
Permanent modification of any user data in a common scenario that persists after restarting the OS/application	High
Permanent modification of any user data in a specific scenario, or temporary modification of user data in a common scenario	Moderate
Temporary modification of data in a specific scenario that does not persist after restarting the OS/application	Low

15.5.1 *Testing Websites*

Websites require special testing for web-type attacks. Even PCI DSS mandates testing for specific attacks [3]. Special testing tools are available for websites.

Vulnerability scanners can test for web attacks, such as integer, float or string overflows, SQL injection and cross-site scripting [4]. In addition, insecure configuration options can cause problems, such as autocomplete enabled for forms.

Web spiders are automated tools that parse website(s) to find embedded links [4]. The web spider follows all links recursively to determine and display the full connectivity of a website. This is useful to fight cross-site scripting, when websites unknowingly are infected with unexpected links.

Manual tests can be tailored for the specific application according to the threat model. Manual penetration testing is essential, and requires knowledgeable penetration testers [6]. Tools that can help in manual testing include proxies and vulnerability scanners, which allow dynamic packet creation. A *Proxy* intercepts commands and responses between the browser and the server, enabling the user to view and modify the packet before transmission [4].

Free tools which support these many of these web-testing features include Paros and OWASP's Zed Attack Proxy (ZAP). Both Paros and ZAP support automated and dynamic manual testing [4]. Commercial products include Fortify and Acunetix web vulnerability scanners. Fortify supports static analysis and automated vulnerability scanning of traditional web and mobile interfaces, while Acunetix' feature set includes HTTP, SOAP, AJAX and flash content.

15.6 Deployment, Operations, Maintenance and Disposal

Following an evaluation, governments and larger organizations may require a *certification* and *accreditation* (C&A) process to approve the product for general deployment and use. A product may be certified after evaluation by an independent (non-development) group, which ensures all required standards have been met. Accreditation is an administrative process to ensure that complete products, including all IT and non-IT parts, operate properly in their full operational environment [26]. Such accreditation ensures that the supply chain for a secure product is vetted.

Configuration Management ensures a stable development and release process. Quality control shall test software built via a formal release process, using configuration management. Software that is released to production should be built similarly, independent of the development environment.

During software release and deployment, care shall include that the software is properly configured, patched and monitored [24]. The configuration must be locked down, with configuration, environment, and data files not accessible to the user. The client and server applications must be hardened as described in the Information Security and Network Security chapters. Highly secure server applications can be placed on their own physical or virtual machines.

Even if the developed software does not need to be patched, software that the application relies on, such as operating system and database, will need to be. Logs will need to be monitored.

When the software product is retired, security considerations include archiving the data and program, sanitizing remaining media, and disposing of the software [24].

15.7 Secure Development Life Cycle

This chapter has described techniques to build security into the product, instead of adding it after the fact. This chapter has described techniques for requirements and design, and guidelines for coding and testing to ensure security. These tools and techniques become a tool chest that you can choose from to best fit your application and organizational needs. However, these techniques and guidelines can be enhanced by building quality into each stage of the Waterfall pipeline (potentially within a multiple-iteration lifecycle). Consider that each development stage has input criteria, process and output/deliverable criteria. If the deliverable of each stage has been verified to be of good quality, then defects will not snowball into later stages and there will be less rework after release. This will save project time, improve product quality, and prevent nasty security problems at release.

There are groups that develop standards for secure development, including the Building Security In Maturity Model (26; www.26.com) and Software Assurance Maturity Model (SAMM). The 26 software security framework includes four domains of three practices each, giving 12 total practices as displayed in Table 15.9 [27]. The SAMM model is nearly identical [28]. Notice that SAMM's Business Function categories align closely with development stages. The Operational Enablement practice ensures the operator can configure, deploy and operate the software in a secure way. SAMM also defines a maturity model with four levels (0–3 Comprehensive Mastery), enabling an organization to assess and advance its maturity level.

You will recognize many of these security touchpoints from this chapter's previous description. For more detailed information, NIST provides a special publication: Security Considerations in the System Development Life Cycle, available at http://csrc.nist.gov/publications/nistpubs/800-64-Rev2/SP800-64-Revision2.pdf. An alternative recommended reference is Gary McGraw's text: *Software Security: Building Security In*.

Mature organizations not only train all their software engineers for secure development, but also train users in security awareness. They also have certified security developers on staff. For those interested in becoming certified, two certs to choose from include:

- CSSLP®: ISC2's Certified Secure Software Lifecycle Professional with knowledge areas in Secure Software Concepts, Software Requirements, Software Designing, Software Implementation/Coding, Software Testing, Software Acceptance,

Table 15.9 Twelve practices: SAMM vs. 26

Software assurance maturity model (SAMM)		Building security in maturity model (26)	
Governance	Strategy and metrics	Governance	Strategy and metrics
	Policy and compliance		Compliance and policy
	Education and guidance		Training
Construction	Threat assessment	Intelligence	Attack models
	Security requirements		Security features and design
	Secure architecture		Standards and requirements
Verification	Design review	Secure software development life cycle touchpoints	Architectural analysis
	Code review		Code review
	Security testing		Security testing
Deployment	Vulnerability management	Deployment	Penetration testing
	Environment hardening		Software environment
	Operational enablement		Configuration management and vulnerability management

Software Deployment, Operations, Maintenance and Disposal, and Supply Chain and Software Acquisition. Further information is available at: https://www.isc2.org/csslpdomains.

- ITIL (IT Infrastructure Library): This independent organization offers a more general certification, with knowledge units in Basics, Service Strategy, Service Design, Service Transition, Service Operation, and Continual Service Improvement. Find more at http://itilexam.net.

15.8 Secure Agile Development

Agile development is becoming popular, but uses less structure than traditional software engineering. Here are some techniques to ensure security is integrated into the development environment [29, 30]:

1. Security training is even more important in this less structured environment. Define security roles.
2. Include Evil User Stories in every sprint, such as "As a hacker, I can send bad data in HTTP forms, so I can access and modify the database in unauthorized ways."
3. Include risk analysis at the start of every sprint and whenever the product backlog changes.

4. Address Evil User Stories for every sprint feature/check-in, every sprint, every epic and every product release. Security features shall include authentication, access control, input validation, output encoding, error/exception handling, encryption, data integrity, logging and alarms, and data communication security for all applications.
5. Include security-minded code reviews, code analyzers, fuzz testing and automated and manual penetration tests.

15.9 Questions and Problems

1. *Vocabulary*. Match each meaning with the correct word.

Bug bar	Reliability test	Fuzz test	Misuse case description
Sandbox	Static Analysis	Certification	Misuse deployment diagram
Nonce	Threat tree	OCTAVE	Attack surface analysis
Jail	Misuse case	Security use case	Misuse case diagram
STRIDE	Accreditation	State diagram	Missequence diagram

a) An operating system imposes resource limits on a program, to limit I/O, disk and network resource consumption.
b) This security requirements process analyzes assets, goals, threats and risks.
c) A tool which inspects code for flaws without executing the code.
d) This threat model includes categories of attacks, such as information disclosure, spoof identity, tamper with data, denial of service, elevate privilege, repudiation.
e) A UML diagram that shows the implementation of attacks and attack handling logic, by diagramming messages (calls or packets) between objects or subsystems.
f) A threshold level of security flaws is defined. Before release, software must meet this threshold.
g) This tool develops random input to test handling of exceptions and incorrect input.
h) An authorization ticket that defends against replay.
i) A UML diagram that shows where security components reside and the attacks that the security components mitigate.
j) This requirements diagram displays attackers as stick figures and attacks as black ovals.
k) In a use case diagram, this use case oval is the security action that mitigates the attack.
l) This table and text describes an attack in a numbered step-by-step description.
m) This test technique ensures that software can survive unusual conditions, such as faults, errors, loading and low resources.
n) A test for untrusted programs, which quarantines the software to observe actions.
o) An analysis technique that considers all aspects of software exposure to determine potential vulnerabilities.

2. *Development Framework Evaluation*. Evaluate your programming framework to determine which utilities are available to implement security features such as: input sanitization, encryption, integrity (hashing), authentication/authorization and logging. Indicate which security-related classes exist and document the key methods that may be useful in using these utilities.
3. *Find Process Flaws*. A customer reports that the customer website is vulnerable to SQL attacks. What went wrong during the development stages, as well as the development process, that allowed this flaw to be released?
4. *Web Programming Protections*. What security practices would you recommend for a web programmer? Consider each development stage: requirements, analysis/design, coding, testing and deployment.
5. *Web Research*. The Open Web Application Security Project (OWASP) organization provides some important help for web developers. What information does this website provide for secure coding? http://www.owasp.org
6. *Fuzz Testing*. Some fuzz testers are specified below. Often they need to be modified to get them to work properly for an application [6]. Look at all available fuzz testers, and compare two of them for their capabilities and uses.

   a) Zzuf: http://caca.zoy.org/wiki/zzuf
   b) Peach: http://peachfuzzer.com/
   c) Radamsa: https://code.google.com/p/ouspg/wiki/Radamsa
   d) Untidy: http://untidy.sourceforge.net/

7. *Security Lifecycles*. What recommendations do the following organizations make relative to secure software development? Select one source to evaluate. What additional or different recommendations does it include compared to what is recommended in this text?

   a) 26: Building Security In Maturity Model: Software Security Framework: http://www.bsi-mm.com or http://26.com/online/
   b) SAFEcode: Secure Software Development http://www.safecode.org
   c) CERT: https://www.securecoding.cert.org/confluence/display/seccode/Top+10+Secure+Coding+Practices

8. *Find Security Bugs*. Evaluate the following set of pseudo-code for security problems. What problems do you see, and what fixes would you recommend?

```
Security() {
      String contents, environment;
      String spath = "config.dat";
      File config = new File();
      if (config.open(spath) >0)
            contents = config.read();
            environment = config.read();
      else
            print("Error: config.dat not found");
}
```

```
purchaseProduct() {
    password = "Pass123phrase";
    count = form.quantity;
    total = count * product.cost();
    Message m = new Message(name,password,product,total);
    m.myEncrypt();
    server.send(m);
}
```

15.9.1 Health First Case Study Problems

For each case study problem, refer to the Health First Case Study. The Health First Case Study, Security Workbook and Health First Requirements Document should be provided by your instructor or can be found at http://extras.springer.com.

Note that the Optional Extensions listed as case studies below are extensions to the named case study. It is recommended that you perform the original case study, or at least read the case study all the way through, before designing the Extension.

Case study	Health first case study	Other resources
Update requirements document to include segregation of duties	√	Health first Requirements document
Fraud: Combatting social engineering Optional extension: Computerizing the disclosure forms	√	Health first Requirements document HIPAA slides or notes
Planning for incident response Optional: Software design for incident detection	√	Health first Requirements document
Defining security metrics Optional: Designing metrics for the requirements doc	√	Health first Requirements document
Software requirements: Extending UML with MisUse cases	√	HIPAA slides or notes
HIPAA: Including privacy rule adherence to requirements document	√	HIPAA slides or notes Requirements document
Application controls: Extending requirements preparation by planning for HIPAA security rule	√	HIPAA slides or notes Requirements document

References

1. 2011 CWE/SANS top 25: monster mitigations. http://cwe.mitre.org/19/mitigations.html. Accessed 15 Nov 2014
2. Conklin WA, Shoemaker D (2014) CSSLP® certification all-in-one exam guide. McGraw-Hill Education, New York, NY
3. PCI Security Standards Council (2013) Requirements and security assessment procedures, v 3.0, November 2013. www.pcisecuritystandards.org
4. Dukes L, Yuan X, Akowuah F (2013) A case study on web application security testing with tools and manual testing. In: Proceedings of IEEE Southeastcon. Inst. Electrical & Electronics Eng. (IEEE), http://ieeexplore.ieee.org, pp 1–6
5. Larson D, Liu J (2013) A new security metric for SOA implementation. In: Seventh international conference on software security and reliability companion. IEEE Computer Society, http://ieeexplore.ieee.org, pp 102–108
6. SAFECode (2011) Fundamental practices for secure software development, 2nd edn. Software Assurance Forum for Excellence in Code. 8 February 2011, www.safecode.org, pp 1–56
7. Open Group. COE Security Software Requirements Specification (SSRS) Technical Standard Doc. Number C035
8. Arlow J, Neustadt I (2005) UML2 and the unified process, 2nd edn. Pearson Education Inc., Upper Saddle River, NJ
9. Woody C, Alberts C (2007) Considering operational security risk during system development. IEEE Secur Priv 5(1):30–35
10. Sindre G, Opdahl AL (2005) Eliciting security requirements by misuse cases. Requir Eng 10(1):120–131, Springer, New York, NY
11. SeaMonster. http://sourceforge.net/projects/seamonster/ Accessed 7 June 2014
12. Lincke S, Knautz T, Lowery M (2012) Designing system security with UML misuse deployment diagrams. In: IEEE international workshop on information assurance (IA2012). IEEE
13. Tondel IA, Jensen J, Rostad L (2010) Combining misuse cases with attack trees and security activity models. In: International conference on availability, reliability and security, 15–18 February 2010, pp 438–445
14. Sindre G, Opdahl AL (2008) Misuse cases for identifying system dependability threats. J Inf Priv Secur 4(2):3–22, Taylor & Francis Online, http://www.tandfonline.com
15. SANS (2009) Practical risk analysis and threat modeling spreadsheet. http://cyber-defense.sans.org/blog/2009/07/11/practical-risk-analysis-spreadsheet. Accessed 6 Dec 2014
16. Payne RS (2013) A practical approach to software reliability for army systems. In: 2013 Proceedings of the annual reliability and maintainability symposium (RAMS). IEEE, pp 1–5
17. Open Group. CDSA and CSSM, Vers 2.3 (with Corrigenda) Technical Standard. Doc. # C914
18. Peterson MJ, Bowles JB, Eastman CM (2006) UMLpac: an approach for integrating security into UML class design. In: Proc. IEEE SoutheastCon, IEEE. pp 267–272
19. Whittle J, Wijesekera D, Hartong M (2008) Executable misuse cases for modeling security concerns. In: ACM/IEEE 30th international conference on software engineering (ICSE 08), pp 121–130
20. Kong J, Xu D (2008) A UML-based framework for design and analysis of dependable software. In: 32nd IEEE international computer software and applications (COMPSAC '08). IEEE, pp 28–31
21. Christey S (2011) 2011 CWE/SANS top 25 most dangerous software errors. 13 September 2011. http://cwe.mitre.org/19
22. Kulkarni D, Tripathi A (2010) A framework for programming robust context-aware applications. IEEE Trans Softw Eng 36(2):184–197, MARCH/APRIL 2010
23. Simpson S (ed) (2011) Fundamental practices for secure software development, 2nd edn. SAFECode. 8 February 2011. http://www.safecode.org/publication/SAFECode_Dev_Practices0211.pdf. Accessed 15 Nov 2014

24. Harris S (2013) All-in-one CISSP® exam guide, 6th edn. McGraw-Hill Co., New York, pp 1094–1111
25. Sullivan (2014) Security brief: add a security bug bar to Microsoft team foundation server 2010. MSDN Magazine. http://msdn.microsoft.com/en-us/magazine/ee336031.aspx, Accessed 7 Jan 2014
26. Common Criteria (2012) Common criteria for information technology security evaluation: part 1: introduction and general model. vers 3.1, rev. 4. September 2012
27. Chess B, Arkin B (2011) Software security in practice. IEEE Secur Priv 9(2):89–92
28. Open Web Application Security Project (OWASP) (2014) Software assurance maturity model, ver 1.0. http://www.opensamm.org/downloads/SAMM-1.0.pdf. Accessed 22 Aug 2014
29. OWASP (2014) Agile software development: don't forget EVIL user stories. https://www.owasp.org/index.php/Agile_Software_Development:_Don%27t_Forget_EVIL_User_Stories. Accessed 28 Nov 2014
30. Puhakainen A, Sääskilaht J (2012) Mastering security in agile/scrum, case study. http://www.rsaconference.com/writable/presentations/file_upload/asec-107.pdf. Accessed 28 Nov 2014

Printed in the United States
By Bookmasters